INDIANS FROM NEW YORK:

A GENEALOGY REFERENCE
VOLUME THREE

TONI JOLLAY PREVOST

HERITAGE BOOKS
2007

HERITAGE BOOKS
AN IMPRINT OF HERITAGE BOOKS, INC.

Books, CDs, and more—Worldwide

For our listing of thousands of titles see our website
at
www.HeritageBooks.com

Published 2007 by
HERITAGE BOOKS, INC.
Publishing Division
65 East Main Street
Westminster, Maryland 21157-5026

Other books by the author:

Indians from New York in Wisconsin and Elsewhere: A Genealogy Reference, Volume One
Indians from New York in Ontario and Quebec, Canada: A Genealogy Reference, Volume Two
The Delaware and Shawnee Admitted to Cherokee Citizenship and the Related Wyandotte and Moravian Delaware

International Standard Book Number: 978-0-7884-0306-0

DEDICATION

The author dedicates this book to my husband Ronald Prevost and Christopher and Nicholas Innis direct descendants of Martin Prevost from France and Marie Silvestre-Olivier Manitobewich an Algonquin or Huron native, who married on the 3rd of November 1644 in Quebec, Canada. This marriage is reported to have been the first sanctioned union between a Frenchman and a Native Canadian. Sources: "The Jesuit Relations and Allied Documents," The Travels of French Jesuit Missionaries Among the Indians of Canada and the Northern and Northwestern States of the United States, By Reuben Gold Thwaites, 1610-1791, Ed., 73 Volumes in French, Latin and Italian, with a Page by Page Complete English Translation, Published 1895, Reprint Published 1959, New York, Published 1960 by Microcord Foundations, Washington, D.C., Volume V (5), Pg. 288.

INTRODUCTION

This book is the last of three volumes intended to be genealogical reference guides for those seeking to identify a name or family relationship among the Indians who live in the state of New York. Volume III provides information about the Cayuga, Munsee (Delaware) Mohawk Onondaga, Oneida, Seneca and Shinnecock/Montauk/Poosapatuck. Secondary alphabetical surname lists are included for related Indian groups in Canada, Indian Territory (Oklahoma) and Wisconsin. Topics in this volume include: 1. Basic Native American Research Sources. 2. Reservation and Museum information. 3. Bibliography References. 4. Biographical References. 5. Using the Persi File. 6. Using the Accelerated Indexing System. 7. The New England Society 8. Using the Family History Library. 9. Using the International Genealogy Index. 10. Emigration/Immigration. 11. Seneca Treaties. 12. Alphabetical 1886 abstracts of B.I.A. Censuses for all of the Six Nations Indian Reserves in New York. 13. Alphabetical 1900 U. S. Census Abstracts for all of the residents of the Alleghany/Cattaraugus, St. Regis, Tuscarora and the Shinnecock/ Montauk Reserves in New York. 14. The U. S. 1900 Census abstract for the Quaker School For Indian Children in New York.

DISCLAIMER

The term "Indian," is used in this book only to represent how it was used in original records and references. Accordingly a researcher should be aware that this term was created by a white colonial society. It may not be in favor with some native groups. Material abstracted from the United States Census for this book should be used with caution. Some errors may exist. The original records used to compile this book often contained poor handwriting, faded ink and faded pages. This book is intended to be only a name reference source. It should not replace the research of any original government or tribal records. For more information write the tribal offices. No attempt was made to alter the original name spellings for this book. All of the names were abstracted exactly as they appeared in the original records.

Table Of Contents

Table Of Contents-Continued

Table Of Contents-Continued

Table Of Contents-Continued

THE IROQUOIS CONFEDERACY

The League of Five Nations was created about 1560-70. The purpose of this confederation was to end feuding among neighboring tribes in what is now the state of New York. The Cayuga, Mohawk, Oneida, Onondaga and Seneca made up the five nations. The Tuscarora had originally lived in North Carolina. They became the sixth nation to be adopted into the league about 1720. Today most of the people from the Six Nations live in New York, Oklahoma, Wisconsin in the United States and Ontario and Quebec in Canada.

In 1621, the Dutch granted a charter to the Dutch West Indies Company for 24 years to trade in the Americas. In 1624, some settlers were sent as part of a colonization plan. New Amsterdam on Manhattan Island became the headquarters of the New Netherlands colony. Fur trading was a major source of commerce. In 1664 New Amsterdam became an English Colony. The colony of New Amsterdam became the colony of New York. The two major religions in the colony were the Dutch Reformed and the Anglican of Episcopalian Church of England. Land in western New York was claimed by both New York and Massachusetts. The Land in dispute included three large tracts known as the Holland Land Purchase, the Morris Reserve, and the Phelps and Gorham Purchase. The Holland Land Purchase included the present Niagara, Erie, Chautauqua, and Cattaraugus Counties plus western portions of Allegany County.

Following the American Revolution, Canada became a refuge for Mohawk's and other native groups from the United States who had sided with the English. About 1780 Mohawk Chief Joseph Brant was given land on the Grand River in Ontario, Canada by the British government. Other native groups besides the Mohawk's who lived at or near the Six Nations Reserve (In Canada) included the Cayuga, Delaware, Mississauga Chippewa (Ojibway), Munsie (Delaware), Oneida, Ottawa, Seneca and Tuscarora. Some Cayuga moved to Canada at the start of the Revolution. Others joined the Seneca in Ohio or lived among tribes in New York. Delaware mixed with Mahican and Munsie lived among the Cayuga on the Grand River in Canada. Another group of Moravian Delaware (From settlements in Ohio & Michigan) settled on the Thames River in Ontario. Some Seneca from western New York who joined the British settled on the Six Nations Reserve. Some Tuscarora lived on the Six Nations Reserve while others lived on a reserve in Niagara County, New York.

The Seneca from western New York who joined the British settled on the Six Nation Reserve (In Canada) after the American Revolution. Others settled in the Sandusky area of Ohio and eventually removed to Indian Territory (Oklahoma). The Cayuga-Seneca have communities in Oklahoma, the Six Nations Reserve in Canada, and the Cattaraugus Reservation in New York. The Cayuga moved to Canada at the start of the revolution while others joined the Seneca in Ohio. Between 1828 and 1832 the Senecas of Sandusky, Ohio negotiated and received a tract of land at the bend of the Grand River, near the southwestern corner of Missouri. A mixed band of Seneca and Shawnee from Ohio obtained land just north of the Seneca tract. In 1867 the Sandusky Senecas ceded part of their land for the Wyandottes (Hurons) to settle on. The Seneca-Shawnee band separated. The Seneca from that group then joined the Seneca from Sandusky who had settled in Northeastern Indian Territory (Oklahoma).

The Oneida of Brown County, Wisconsin formerly occupied the country south of Oneida Lake in Oneida County, New York. In the 1830's many joined the Stockbridge/Brotherton Indians in Wisconsin.

THE GEOGRAPHICAL RESEARCH AREA

The Six Nations Indians reside today in Canada, New York, Oklahoma and Wisconsin. Among other things this extended geographical range has significant research advantages. You will find this especially true after you have exhausted information sources in one area.

INTER-TRIBAL RELATIONSHIPS

Over time Inter-marriage and inter-family relations have developed between the Cayuga, Mohawks, Oneida, Onondaga, Seneca and Tuscarora. Meanwhile, some intermarriage has also taken place with the Chippewa (Ojibway) Delaware, Huron, Munsee, Shawnee and lesser known Indian groups. Few will object that the complexities of such knowledge can be confusing. To summarize, only a thorough study of tribal history can help to traverse these additional problems to successful conclusions.

MATRILINEAL DESCENT

Matrilineal descent can have an effect on researching tribal rolls. Most, but not all of the Iroquois, Zuni and Hopi Indians had or now have matrilineal societies. In such a society usually the children of a marriage belong to the tribe of the mother. An example would be the children of a Mohawk father with an Onondaga mother would belong to the Onondaga. If a son of this marriage married an Oneida woman, his children would be members of the Oneida. Do not overlook the effect this information can have on your research. Consider that a mother and her children will appear on one B.I.A. Census Roll while the father may be enrolled on another.

BIBLIOGRAPHY AND REFERENCES

ABRAMS, GEORGE H. J., "The Seneca People," Published by Indian Tribal Series, Phoenix, Copyright 1976, page 32.

ADAMS, WILLIAM, "Historical Gazetteer and Biographical Memorial of Cattaraugus County," W. C. Cox Company, 1974, Tucson, Arizona, 1,164 pages, original published 1893.

ADKINS, EDWIN P., "Setauket, the First Three Hundred Years," 1655-1955, by David Mc Kay Company, 1955, 108 pages (Indians of Long Island).

ALL, STEVE, AND HARVEY ARDEN, "Wisdomkeepers: Meetings with Native American Spiritual Elders," (Seneca) Hillsboro, Oregon, Published by Beyond Words Publishing, 1990, 128, pages.

AMERICAN SOCIETY OF GENEALOGISTS, "Genealogical Research: Method and Sources," volume I, Polyanthos, Inc., New Orleans, Louisiana, Copyright 1980, Chapter 11, New York, pages 168-220.

ANNUAL REPORT OF THE BUREAU OF AMERICAN ETHNOLOGY TO THE SECRETARY OF THE SMITHSONIAN INSTITUTION, (1879-80) (1930/31), Gelen Rock, New Jersey, Microfilming Corporation of America, 1974, 2 microfilm reels, includes maps, periodicals by and about the North American Indians: Package No. 2., micro-reproduction of original publications of the Government Printing Office 1881-1938. The reports for 1879/80-1893-94 have been entitled: "Annual Report of the Bureau of Ethnology." A microfilm copy is also available on inter-library loan through The Church of Jesus Christ of Latter-day Saints (Mormon) Family History Library Centers. The 4th-7th reports 1882-1886 is on film number 1025191 and the 11th report 1892-93 is on film number 0244162.

BAYLES, THOMAS R., "The Long Island Indians," four (4) pages. A microfilm copy is available on inter-library loan through the Church of Jesus Christ of Latter-day Saints (Mormon) Family History Library Centers on film number 1036082, item 11.

BEAUCHAMP, WILLIAM, "History of New York Iroquois," 1905. Reprint of the 1905 edition was published by the New York State Education Department, Albany, issued as Bulletin 329 of the University of the State of New York, Bulletin 78 of the New York Museum's Bulletin.

BECHARD, HENRI, S. J., "The Original Caughnawaga Indians," International Publishers, Montreal, Canada, 1976, preface vii-x. This book includes historical notes about the Iroquois before 1700 in Canada in connection with the present-day Iroquois of St. Regis (Franklin County, New York), Oka (Quebec), and Brantford in Ontario.

BIEN, J. R., "Atlas of the State of New York," Bien & Company, New York, New York, 1895, Map 3.

BILLINGTON, R. A., "Fort Stanwix Treaty of 1768," with map, in proceedings of New York Historical Association, 1944, XLII, pages 182-194.

BRUMBLE, DAVID H., "An Annotated Bibliography of American Indian and Eskimo Autobiographies," Lincoln, Nebraska, University of Nebraska Press, 177 pages, 1981.

CAMPBELL, WILLIAM W., "Annals of Tryon County," (New York) 78 pages, J. & J. Harper, 1831.

CAMPISI, JACK, E. D., "The Oneida Indian Experience," 1988.

CATLIN, GEORGE, "Letters and Notes on the Manners, Customs, and Conditions of North American Indians," by George Catlin, Volume II, pages 103-107.

CAYUGA INDIANS ENUMERATIONS OF PAYMENT OF ANNUITIES, June 1969, Cayuga Tribes- 1971, on one microfilm reel. This reel lists names and birth dates. A microfilm copy is available on inter-library loan through the Church of Church of Jesus Christ of Latter-day Saints (Mormon) Family History Centers.

CENSUS TAKEN AT THE QUAPAW AGENCY IN OKLAHOMA, 1 January 1940, by the Department of the Interior, Office of Indian Affairs, microfilmed by the National Archives. This census includes birth dates, place of birth, present address and degree of Indian blood for members of the New York Indians who had removed from New York and resided in Oklahoma. Included is the addresses of the New York Indians who had once lived in Oklahoma and had moved elsewhere.

CERNEY, JOHNI & WENDY ELLIOTT, "The Library: A Guide to the LDS Family History Library," Edited by Johni Cerney & Wendy Elliott, New York Section, pages 106-111, Ancestry Publishing, 1988.

CHALMERS, HARVEY, "West to the Setting Sun," The Career of Joseph Brant Mohawk Indian and the Trials of his People, Macmillan, Toronto, 362 pages, 1944, includes maps.

CHRONOGRAPHICAL MAP OF THE PROVINCE OF NEW YORK IN NORTH AMERICA 1779, A reprint Paramus, New Jersey, Highway Printing, 1970. This map shows counties, manors, and patents compiled from surveys deposited at the Patent Office in New York.

CLARK, JOSHUA V., "Onondaga Indians," 1803-1869, Millwood, New York, Kraus reprint, 1973, original published at Syracuse, New York, Stoddard and Babcock. A copy is available on inter-library loan through the Church of Jesus Christ of Latter-day Saints (Mormon) Family History Centers on film number 0962458, Item 1-2.

COMMISSIONERS ON THE ONONDAGA INDIANS, Report to the legislature of the state of New York concerning the condition of the Onondaga Indians from the commissioners appointed by Chapter 345 of the laws of 1882. Ann Arbor, Michigan, University Microfilms International, 1905. A copy is available through the Church of Jesus Christ of Latter-day Saints (Mormon) Family History Library Center in Salt Lake City, Utah, on microfiche number 6061639, 48 pages. No circulation to branch libraries is permitted.

CONNORS, DENNIS, "Onondaga a Portrait of a Native People," Onondaga County, Department of Parks and Recreation, Syracuse University Press, 1986, 110 pages.

CONOVER, GEORGE S., (George Stillwell 1824-?) Kanadesaga and Geneva, Waterloo, New York, filmed by Brigham Young University, 1970 on microfilm number 0812868, item 1, 1970, 821 pages including an index.

CONOVER, GEORGE S., "The Genesee Tract Cessions between New York and Massachusetts," The Philips and Gorham Purchase, 16 pages, 1889. A copy is available on inter-library loan through the Church of Jesus Christ of Latter-day Saints (Mormon) Family History Library Centers on film number 1036528, Item 8.

COOLEY, L. C., "Name Index to O. Turner's Pioneer History of the Holland Purchase of Western New York," published by L. C. Colley in 1946.

DANKERS, JASPER & PETER SLUYTER, "Journal of a Voyage to New York," and a Tour in Several of the American Colonies in 1679-80. This journal has been translated from the original in Dutch for the Long

Island Historical Society, by Henry C. Murphy in 1867, reprint by University Microfilm Inc., 1966.

DENTON, DANIEL, "A Brief Description of New York," Formerly called New-Netherlands, London, England, published by Daniel Denton in 1670, reprinted by University Microfilms, Inc., 1966, pages 6-12.

DISTURNELL, JOHN A., "A Gazetteer of the State of New York," Albany, 1842. A copy is available on inter-library loan through the Church of Jesus Christ of Latter-day Saints (Mormon) Family History Library Centers on film Number 982372, item 4.

DOTY, LOCKWOOD RICHARD, "History of Livingston County, New York," 1876, Chapter II, page 21. This books includes an account of the Seneca Nation of Indians, an biographical sketches of early settlers, originally published in 1876, by Edward E. Doty, 685 pages. A copy is available on inter-library loan through the Church of Jesus Christ of Latter-day Saints (Mormon) Family History Library Centers on film number 0844650.

DOTY, L. R. "History of the Genesee Country," Clarke Publishing Co., Chicago, 1925 (reprint?) four (4) volumes, Allegany, Cattaraugus, Chautauqua, Cheming, Erie, Genesee, Livingston, Monroe, Niagara, Ontario, Orleans, Schuyler, Steuben, Wayne, Wyoming and Yates Counties.

DRAPER, LYMAN COPELAND: "Lyman Copeland Draper Manuscripts," Wisconsin Historical Society.

DUKE UNIVERSITY LIBRARY, "Duke Indian Oral History Collection and Index," Cambridge, Mass: filmed by the General Microfilm Company, 1981, on 310 microfiche, representing fifty five (55) volumes. These are typescripts of interviews with Indians from many native groups. Some interviews include information about New York Indians in Indian Territory (Oklahoma).

DUTCH TRADERS OF THE MOHAWK, 18th Century., Detroit (Article) NYGB, 116-2, April 1985, Persi File Index, Allen County Genealogical Library, Allen County, Indiana.

FARB, E.P., "Man's Rise to Civilization," As Shown by the Indians of North America, Dutton & Company Inc., New York, 1968, pages 82, 97, 99. (This book includes a reference to the Matrilineal Society among the Iroquois).

FLICK, A. C., EDITOR, "History of the State of New York," Columbia University Press, New York, New York, 1933, ten (10) volumes.

FRENCH, J. H., "Gazetteer of the State of New York," Albany, New York, 1860.

FROTHINGHAM, WASHINGTON, "History of Montgomery County, New York," 1892, Syracuse, New York, D. Mason, 349 pages. A copy is available on inter-library loan through the Church of Jesus Christ of Latter-day Saints (Mormon) Family History Library Centers on film number 0934839, Item 2.

GALPIN, W. F., "Central New York," An Inland Empire, Comprising Oneida, Madison, Onondaga, Cayuga, Tompkins, Cortland and Chenango Counties and Their People, Lewis Historical Publishing Co., New York, New York, 1941, 4 Volumes.

GRAYMONT, BARBARA, "The Iroquois," 1989.

GRAYMONT, BARBARA, "The Fighting Tuscarora," 1973.

GREENE, N., "History of the Mohawk Valley," four (4) volumes, Chicago, 1925.

HAGAN, WILLIAM, "Longhouse Diplomacy and Frontier Warfare," No date.

HAMILTON, HILTON, "Sir William Johnson & The Indians of New York," 1975.

HENRY, THOMAS R., "Wilderness Messiah," The Story of Hiawatha and the Iroquois.

HOLLAND LAND COMPANY RECORDS, Original records at the Buffalo and Erie County Historical Society. The Holland Land Company Records have been microfilmed for the State University College at Fredonia by Biels, 1986 on 23 microfilm reels. Maps are included. BUF 22-44 includes records for the counties of Genesee, Orleans, Erie & Niagara and a schedule of settler's names and their land holdings. BUF 59-66 includes Printed Supreme Court Cases involving Indian Land Claims 1851-1858.

HOLLAND LAND COMPANY PAPERS COLLECTION 1792-1850, in the Buffalo Historical Society Collection.

HOUGH, F. B., "A Map of the State of New York with its Counties," defined by statute 7, March 1788, frontispiece to Proceedings of the Commissioners of Indian Affairs appointed by law for the Extinguishment of Indian titles in the state of New York, an original manuscript in the library of the Albany Institute with an introduction by F. B. Hough, Albany, 1861.

HOUGH, F. B., "History of St. Lawrence and Franklin Counties, New York, Albany, 1853.

JENNINGS, FRANCIS, "The Ambiquous Iroquois Empire," 1984.

JENNINGS, FRANCIS, E. D., "The History and Culture of Iroquois Diplomacy," 1985, Syracuse, New York, Syracuse University Press, 278 pages, includes maps.

JEWETT, F. G., "A Catalogue of Records in the Secretary of State Office on 1 January 1820," New York, Sen. Doc. 2, 1820, (Compiled by F. G. Jewett in Albany in 1898). The Land Office of the Secretary of State of New York recorded all Indian Land purchases.

JONES, GERTRUDE H., "Vital Statistics (About 1883-1940) Kept in Old Ledgers and Miscellaneous Papers by the Indians on Cattaraugus Reservation, New York," copied by Gertrude H. Jones, Buffalo, New

York, 1956. A microfilm copy is available on inter-library loan through the Church of Jesus Christ of Latter-day Saints (Mormon) Family History Library Centers on film number 0962208, Item 7.

JOSEPHY, ALVIN, M., JR., "Cornplanter Can You Swim," American Heritage Magazine & Book, Volume XXX, Number 1, December 1968 Issue, Berne and Pan-American copyright Conventions, page 4. This article contains a detailed reference of the conception of the Alleghany Reserve and the history of the reserve past and present.

IROQUOIS LAND CLAIMS, edited by Christopher Vecsey and William A. Starna, Syracuse, New York, University Press, 1988, 186 pages, includes maps.

JUDKINS, RUSSELL ED., "Iroquois Studies: Guide to Documents & Ethnological Resources," 1987.

KELSEY, ISABEL, "Joseph Brant, 1743-1807: Man of Two Worlds," Syracuse, New York, Syracuse University Press, 1984.

KIMM, SILAS CONRAD, "The Iroquois: A History of the Six Nations of New York," Middleburg, New York, Press of Pierce, W. Danforth, 1900.

LANKES, FRANK J., "Reservation Supplement," A Collection of Memorabilia Related to the Buffalo Creek Reservation," West Seneca, New York, Historical Society, 1966, 55 pages.

LOOKUP, GEORGE E., "Index to the History of the Pioneer Settlement of Phelps and Gorham's Purchase," compiled by George E. Lookup, published by the Wayne County, Historical Society, Lyons, New York, 1973.

MAC KENZIE, J. B., "The Six Nations Indians," In Canada, Toronto, The Hunter Rose Company, 1896, page 45.

MAC LEAN, JOHN, "Canadian Savage Folk," The Native Tribes of Canada, published by W. Briggs, Toronto, Canada, 1896, 641 pages.

MORGAN, LEWIS, "League of the Iroquois," 1962.

MORRIS, JOHN W., CHARLES R. GOINS AND EDWIN C. MC REYNOLDS, "Historical Atlas of Oklahoma," University of Oklahoma Press, Second Edition, 1976, page 45, Small Indian Groups in Northeast Oklahoma (The Seneca Cayuga and Wyandotte Reserve).

NEW YORK DEPARTMENT OF SOCIAL SERVICES ENUMERATION OF INDIANS FOR PAYMENT OF ANNUITIES 1969, Cayuga Tribe, 15 pages. A microfilm copy is available on inter-library loan through the Church of Jesus Christ of Latter-day Saints (Mormon) Family History Library Centers on film number 0824184, item 3.

NEWELL, W. B., "Crime and Justice Among the Iroquois Nations" (No further information).

NICHOLLS, RICHARD, "Treaty between Governor Richard Nicholls and the Sachems of the Esopus Indians," 7 October 1665. A copy is available on inter-library loan through the Church of Jesus Christ of Latter-day

Saints (Mormon) Family History Library Centers on film number 0497536.

O'CALLAGHAN, E. B., ED., "Proceedings of Albany Congress of 1754, 1980.

OSGOOD, PROF. H. L., "Inventory of State Archives," Report of the Archives of New York State, (67-250) issued as volume two (2) of the American Historical Association for 1900, Washington, 1901.

PARKER, ARTHUR C., "The Life of General Ely S. Parker Last Grand Sachem of the Iroquois and General Grant's Military Secretary," published by AMS Press Inc., New York, New York, 1985, 346 pages, original published in Buffalo, New York by the Buffalo Historical Society, 1919.

PARKER, ARTHUR CASELL, 1881-1955 "Red Jacket-Last of the Seneca," Washington D. C., Library of Congress-197? original published in New York, by Mc Graw-Hill, 228 pages.

PLACE, FRANK, "Index of Personal Names in J. H. French's Gazetteer of the State of New York," (1860) compiled by Frank Place, Courtland County, Historical Society, Cortland, New York.

PREVOST, TONI JOLLAY, "The Delaware and Shawnee Admitted to Cherokee Citizenship and the Related Wyandotte and Moravian Delaware," 1992, Heritage Press, contains census abstracts of the Delaware, Munsee, Oneida and Wyandotte (Huron) in Essex, Kent and Middlesex County, Ontario Canada.

PREVOST, TONI JOLLAY, "New York Indians in Wisconsin and Elsewhere," Heritage Press, 1995. This books provides U. S. Census, B.I.A. Census and Civil War Veteran Census abstracts. Included is members of the Six Nations attending school in Kansas, Pennslyvania and Virginia in 1900. Included is information about the Oneida and Stockbridge Brotherton (Mohegan and remnants of New England Indians) who migrated from New York to Wisconsin. Additional cross reference information about the related Oneida/Delaware in Ontario, Canada and Cayuga/Wyandotte/Seneca in Indian Territory (Oklahoma) is included.

PREVOST, TONI JOLLAY, "New York Indians in Ontario and Quebec, Canada," Heritage Press, 1995. This books provides census abstracts from 1851 and 1881Canadian Census. These abstracts include information about the Cayuga, Chippewa (Ojibway) Delaware (Munsee) Mohawk, Onondaga, Oneida, Ottawa, Seneca, Shawnee Tuscarora and lesser known Indian groups. Many were born in the United States.

PRUCHA, FRANCIS PAUL, "Atlas of American Indian Affairs," University of Nebraska Press, Lincoln & London, Copyright 1984, 191 pages.

RICHARDS, CARA F., "The Oneida People," published by Indian Tribal Series, Phoenix, 1974. Included is a small Map entitled "The Oneida Country," showing the location of places where events important in Oneida history occurred from the earliest European contacts to removal from New York. Another map shows former Oneida Reservation area and lands in current Oneida tribal ownership.

ROCHESTER HISTORICAL SOCIETY, "Old Northampton and Northampton Records," 1922.

RUTTENBER, EDWARD MANNING, "History of the Indian Tribes of Hudson's River," published by J. Munsell, Albany, New York, 1872.

SAUTHIER, CLAUDE JOSEPH, "A Map of the Provinces of New York and New Jersey," with a part of Pennsylvania and the Province of Quebec, 1777.

SCHOOLCRAFT, HENRY ROWE, 1793-1864, "Notes on the Iroquois: or, Contributions to the Statistics, Aboriginal History, Antiquities and General Ethnology of Western New York," Published in New York, Bartlett & Wilford, 1846, 285 pages.

SKINNER, ALANSON BUCK, 1886-1925, "Indians of Greater New York," Cedar Rapids, Iowa, Torch Press, 1915, 150 pages.

SMITH, JAMES H., "History of Livingston County," New York, published by D. Mason & Company, 1881.

STATE ARCHIVES (NEW YORK), Volume XV, "Documents Relating to the Colonial History of the state of New York."

STONE, WILLIAM LEETE, 1792-1844 "The Life and Times of "Sa-Go-Ye-Wat-Ha," or Red Jacket, originally published in Albany, New York, 1866, by J. Munsell, 509 pages. This history includes four parts. 1. The Early History of the Iroquois 2. The Life of Sir William Jonson 3. The Life of Brant (Joseph Brant Mohawk Chief). 4. The Life of Red Jacket (Seneca Chief).

SULLIVAN, JAMES, "History of New York State," 1523-1927: five (5) volumes, Lewis Historical Publishing Company, New York, 1929.

THE COMORAH MISSION RECORDS, (New York Stake) Church of Jesus Christ of Latter-Day Saints (Mormon) Records. These records contain Seneca family pedigree charts and includes some information about relationships between the Senecas in New York and Canada. A copy of these records is available on inter-library loan through the Church of Jesus Christ of Latter-day Saints (Mormon) Family History Library Centers on film number 0924575.

THUNDERBIRD, MARGO, "Native Nations," (Magazine) Volume 1, Number 4, June/July 1991, page 10, article entitled "Judgement Day at Salamanca (New York)." This article presented a look at the Seneca-Salamanca land dispute.

TRIGGER, BRUCE ED., "Handbook of North American Indian," Volume 15 (The Northeast), 1978.

TRUAIR, MRS. L. M., "The History of Madison County," State of New York, Smith & Company 1872, pages 120-122.

TURNER, O., "History of the Pioneer Settlement of Phelp's and Gorham's Purchase and Morris Reserve, " Heart of Lakes Publishers, Interlaken, New York, 1854, reprint 1976.

UNIVERSITY OF THE STATE OF NEW YORK, "The Papers of Sir William Johnson," fourteen (14) volumes, Albany, New York, 1921-62.

VAN DEN BOGAERT, HARMEN, "Journey into Mohawk & Oneida Country," 1634-1633, 1988.

VAN SICKLE, JOHN: "The Cayuga Reservation and Colonel John Harris," Ann Arbor, Michigan University Microfilms International, published in Ithaca, New York, by Dewitt Historical Society of Tompkins County, 1965, 19 pages.

WALLACE, ANTHONY F. C., "The Death and Rebirth of the Seneca," published by Alfred A. Knopf, New York, 1970.

WALLACE, PAUL W. W., "Indians in Pennsylvania," Pennsylvania Historical and Museum Commission, Harrisburg, Copyright 1989.

WILSON, J. G., Editor, "Memorial History of the City of New York from its earliest settlement to 1892, " New York, History Company, New York, New York, 1892-3, four (4) volumes.

WISE, JENNINGS C., "The Red Man in the New World Drama," A Politico-Legal Study with a Pageantry of American Indian History, The Macmillan Company, New York, New York, 1871, 418 pages, Chapter 6, pages 52-59, "Dekanawida, Hiawatha and the Hodenosaunnee," Chapter 8, Page 77-87, "New England-the Iroquois and New Netherlands," Chapter 10, page 96, "Sir William Jonson and the French War."

WITMER, T., "Deed Tables in the County of Erie," as sold by the Holland Land Company, Clapp, Mathews and Company, Buffalo, New York, 1859.

WOLCOTT, FRED RYTHER, 1862-1946, "Onondaga: Portrait of a Native People," preface by Dennis J. Connors: foreword by Laurence M. Hauptman, introduction by Ray Conyea, Onondaga Parks and Recreation, Syracuse University Press in association with Everson Museum of Art, 1986, 110 pages.

WYANDOTTE COUNTY AND CITY, KANSAS, Historical and Biographical, the Goodspeed Publishing Company, Chicago 1890, pages 149-152.

MEETING TRIBAL MEMBERSHIP REQUIREMENTS

Most people become interested in Native American genealogy research for two reasons: 1. To find a Native American ancestor. 2. To become a certified member of a Native American tribe. Two major requirements are necessary for tribal memberships: 1. Finding an ancestor on agency records, treaties or tribal rolls. 2. Meeting acceptable Native American blood quantum requirements. If you know the tribe and want to find out more about current tribal membership requirements two options are available: 1. You can write directly to the tribe. 2. You can write to the Bureau of Indian Affairs. To become a certified member of a Native American tribe, a researcher should understand from the start, that the Bureau of Indian Affairs holds that if your ancestor does not appear on the Bureau of Indian Affairs Rolls or is recognized by the tribe, the burden of proof is on you. Verification of your ancestors Indian heritage may require specific information. Problems may occur if you have failed to gather as much available family information as possible.

Be aware that registration forms for applications for a certificate of degree of Indian blood usually asks that you: 1. Submit copies of yours, your parents and grandparents certified birth certificates. A question is asked if there has been any probate proceedings for a parent or grandparent? You are asked to provide: 1. Your name, home address, date of birth, place of birth. 2. Your father's name, date of birth, place of birth, tribe, Bureau of Indian Affairs Roll Number if any. 3. Your mother's name, date of birth, place of birth, tribe, Bureau of Indian Affairs Roll Number if any. Similar questions are asked for your grandparents and great grandparents. One important aspect to remember is that most applications will state that additional information such as probate, affidavits, and supplemental documentary evidence will be required. A knowledge of basic genealogy research may be helpful in finding supplemental documentary evidence.

A basic genealogy approach begins with recording your personal family history information in a easy to read format on a pedigree chart. Standard pedigree charts can be obtained from some public libraries with genealogy collections, Family History Library Centers (Mormon) and historical or genealogy groups. Start with yourself. Record the names of your parents, grandparents and great grandparents. Continue as far back as you can go. If it is known, provide birth, marriage and death information for each ancestor on your chart. This chart will not only confirm what you already know, but will provide a detailed analysis of your individual research problem areas. The next step is to consult a good basic genealogy research guide. Then extend your search to include records outlined in the research guide such as census records, cemetery records, church records, county histories, family histories, land records, military records, probate records, school records and vital records. Once you've created a family history you can identify the names of your ancestors, the time periods they lived and the locality where they resided. In addition you will be able to cite documentary evidence based on original records.

GENERAL NATIVE AMERICAN BIBLIOGRAPHY

ADAIR, JAMES, "The History of the American Indian," 1775, reprint ed., 1930, Johnson City, Tennessee.

AMERICAN ANTHROPOLOGIST, Volume 56, 1954, pages 973-1,002.

AUTOMATED RESEARCH, INC., CD ROM. This CD includes all of the treaties the United States made with Indian tribes, government documents, a Indian source guide to the National Archives and maps included on approximately 10,000 pages. However, it does not include names of the individuals on B.I.A. Census Rolls.

COLLIER, JOHN, "The Assault on Assimilation," and the Origins of Indian Policy Reform, 1983.

COOKE, DAVID COX, "Fighting Indians of America," Dodd Mead & Company, 1966.

CURTIS, EDWARD S., "The North American Indian," Twenty (20) volumes, Johnson Reprint Corporation, New York, 1970.

DEBO, ANGIE, "A History of the Indians of the United States," Norman, Oklahoma, 1970.

DEBO, ANGIE, "The Road to Disappearance," Norman, University of Oklahoma Press, 1941.

DOWNEY, FAIRFAX DAVIS, "Indian Wars of the U.S. Army," 1776-1865, by Doubleday & Company, 1963.

FEDERAL MAPS IN THE NATIONAL ARCHIVES: AN ANNOTATED LIST: (A Catalogue to the Collection) Copies of 17th and 18th Century maps are on file at the National Archives.

FRAZIER, GREGORY W., "The American Indian Index," A Directory of Indian Country, USA, Denver, Colorado, Arrowstar Publishing, 1985, 320 pages.

HAGAN, William T., "American Indians," (Chicago: University of Chicago Press 1961).

HILL, Edward E, (comp.) Preliminary Inventory No. 163. "Records of the Bureau of Indian Affairs," Washington: GPO, 1965, Volume 1 & 2.

HODGE, FREDERICK WEBB, "Handbook of American Indians," North of Mexico, Washington D. C., Smithsonian, Bulletin 30, 1912.

INIDAN AFFAIRS, LAWS AND TREATIES," Two (2) volumes, Washington, D. C., 1904.

INDIAN-WHITE RELATIONS IN THE UNITED STATES: A Bibliography of Works Published 1975-1980, published 1982.

JEANNETTE, HENRY, "Two Centuries of Dishonor," (Indian Treaties) 243 pages, 1972-1977, Indian Historian Press, Volume 5.

KAPPLER, CHARLES J., "Indian Affairs: Laws, Treaties," 1904, seven (7) volumes.

KIRKHAM, E. K., "Our Native Americans and Their Records of Genealogical Value," Everton Publishers, Logan, Utah 1980-4, two (2) volumes.

LEITCH, BARBARA A., "A Concise Dictionary of Indian Tribes of North American," Algonac, Michigan, Reference Publications, 1979, 646 pages, includes maps.

LINCOLN UNIVERSITY, OF NEBRASKA PRESS, "American Indian Policy in the Jacksonian Era, " 1975.

LIST OF CARTOGRAPHIC RECORDS IN THE BUREAU OF INDIAN AFFAIRS, Maps pertaining to Indian treaties, removal policy, land use, reservations, and settlements are on file with CBNA. (SL 13), which is available in the CBNA Research Room at the National Archives in Washington D. C.

LITTLEFIELD, DANIEL F. JR., AND JAMES W. PARINS, "Biobibliography of Native Writers," 1772-1924, 1981, supplement 1985.

MC EVERS, J., "Indian Genealogy," Polyanthos, New Orleans, Louisiana, 1980.

PARKER, JIMMY B., "American Indian Genealogical Research," National Genealogical Society Quarterly, Volume 63, No. 1 (March 1975) pages 15-21.

PRUCHA, FRANCIS PAUL, "Atlas of American Indian Affairs," University of Nebraska Press: Lincoln & London, 1990. This book Includes old and new maps showing Indian reserves, schools, treaty land cessions, tribal land sales and old forts for the entire United States.

PRUCHA, FRANCIS PAUL, "Documents of United States Indian Policy," University of Nebraska Press, 1975, 1990.

ROYCE, CHARLES C., "Indian Land Cessions in the United States," 1899.

SCHMECKBIER, FREDERICK LAURENCE, "The Office of Indian Affairs," 1877-1959, AMS Press, 1972, 591 pages (Includes a history of the organization).

SOUTHWESTERN JOURNAL of ANTHROPOLOGY, "Toward a Theory of Acculturation," Volume XVIII, app. 30-39.

STUART, PAUL, "Nations within a Nation," Historical Statistics of American Indians, Greenwood Press, New York, 1987, 251 pages.

STURTEVANT, WILLIAM C. AND SAMUEL STANLEY, "Indian Communities in the Eastern States," 1968, Indian Historian, I (3) 15-19.

SURVIVING INDIAN GROUPS OF THE EASTERN UNITED STATES, United States Government Printing Office 1949, pages 407-438 (From a Smithsonian report in 1948).

UNIVERSITY MICROFILMING, "Tribal Migrations East of the Mississippi," 1974, Smithsonian Collection, Volume 89, No. 12 (Includes Maps), Ann Arbor Michigan.

VAN EVERY, DALE, "Disinherited: The Lost Birthright of the American Indian," New York, 1966.

WALDMAN, CARL, "Atlas of the North American Indians," Maps and Illustrations by Molly Braun, Facts on File Publications, 1985.

WALKER, DEWARD E. JR., "The Emergent Native American," University of Colorado, Little Brown and Company, Boston, copyright 1972, page 6, "The Distinctive Aspects of Acculturation," by Ralph Linton.

WAR DEPARTMENT, "The War of the Rebellion: A Compilation of the Official Records of the Union and Confederate Armies," Series I, Volumes 1, 3, 8 and 13.

WISE, JENNINGS C., "The Red Man in the New World Drama," A Politica-Legal Study with a Pageantry of American Indian History, The Macmillan Company, New York, New York, 1871, 418 pages.

YOUNKIN, C. GEORGE, "Researching American Indian Ancestry," Regional Archives Branches," Recueil du 11th Congres International des Sciences Genealogique et Heraldique, 1972.

DETERMINING A GROUP'S NATIVE IDENTITY?

What evidence must be present to learn a group's Indian identity according to the federal government? The answer to this question is outlined in "Documents of United States Indian Policy," By Francis Paul Prucha, Second Edition, University of Nebraska Press, Lincoln, London, 1990 and in Federal Register 43:39362-64 (September 5, 1978) Code of Federal Regulations 54: 1. Repeated identification by federal authorities. 2. Longstanding relationships with state governments based on identification of the group as Indian. 3. Repeated dealings with a county, or local governments as an Indian group. 4. Identification as an Indian group by records in courthouses, churches, or schools. 5. Identification as Indians by anthropologists, historians, or other scholars. 6. Repeated identification as an Indian Group in newspapers and books. 7. Repeated identification and dealings as an Indian Group with other Indian tribes or organizations.

RECORDS THAT MAY PROVIDE NATIVE AMERICAN GENEALOGY INFORMATION?

One of the first requisites for a beginner is to become aware of the range of records that may provide Indian genealogy information. Records of special interest include: 1. Allotment Records 2. American State Papers 3. Bureau of Indian Affairs (B.I.A.) Tribal Census Rolls. 4. College and Boarding School Records 5. Colonial Records in England, Spain and France 6. County Histories 7. County Land Records 8. County Vital Records 9. Continental Congress Records 10. Denominational Archives: Pamphlets, Newspapers, Indian Missionary Diaries and Progress Reports 11. Emigration/Immigration Records between the United States, Canada and Mexico 12. Factory or Government sponsored Trading Post Records (B.I.A.) 13. Family Histories 14. Freedmen Bureau Records (Former Slaves) 15. Fur Trading Company Records. 15. Government Sponsored Indian School Records 16. Heirship & Probate Records 17. Indian Agents Records (B.I.A.) 18. Indian Missionary Records 19. Indian Removal Records 20. Land Company Records 21. Local Cemetery Records 22. Local Church Records 23. Local Newspapers 24. Local Tax Lists 25. Local School Records 26. Manuscript Collections in Colleges and Genealogy Libraries 27. Military Records (Forts, Histories, and Soldiers Pension Applications) 28. Mission School Records 29. National Indian Ethnic Periodicals & Newspaper Obituaries 30. Old County and State Maps. 31. Old Tribal Photographs. 32. Passports through Indian Nations (Mostly southern Indians) 33. Per Capita Payments 34. Slave Census Records. 35. Social Security Applications 36. State Census Records 37. State Vital Records 38. Supreme Court Records 39. Territorial Census Records 40. Tribal Enrollment Applications 41. Tribal Council Records 42. Tribal Court Records 43. Tribal Histories 44. Tribal Museum Records 45. Tribal Vital Records 46. United States Federal Census Records. These types of records and other reference information can be found in original Records, published books, microfiche collections, microfilms and CD ROM disks.

BASIC GENEALOGY RESEARCH GUIDES

Important to a beginning researcher is finding and reading a good basic genealogy research guide. Three such guides are: 1. "The Researchers Guide to American Genealogy," by Val D. Greenwood,

Genealogical Publishing Company, Inc., Baltimore, Maryland 1988. 2. "The Source," by Arlene Eakle and Johni Cerny, Salt Lake City, Ancestry Publishing, 1984. 3. "Genealogical Research," Methods and Sources, Volume 1 & 11, American Society of Genealogists, Copyright 1980. Some guides were written with a particular area or state in mind. The guide "New York (State) Genealogical Research," by George K. Schweitzer, Ph. D., Sc. D., Knoxville, Tennessee, 1988, lists available state wide records and a county by county inventory of available court records, local libraries and genealogy societies in the state of New York.

BOOKS THAT PROVIDE UNITED STATES LOCALITY INFORMATION

Books that provide locality information for genealogy research include: "The Handy Book for Genealogists," Everton Publishers, Inc., Logan, Utah 1986. This book provides information about counties created from Indian Land. "Map Guide to the U. S. Federal Censuses 1790-1920," by William Thorndale and William Dollarhide, Baltimore, Maryland, Genealogy Publishing Company, 1987. This book provides information about counties and states created from Indian Land.

BOOKS THAT PROVIDE TRIBAL LOCALITY INFORMATION

Significant to your research is to locate the geographical area where Indians reside in the Untied States. Consult the following publications: 1. "The Native American Directory," Alaska, Canada and United States, Published by National Native American Cooperative, San Carlos, Arizona, 1994. This comprehensive directory provides the addresses of native associations, colleges, museums, reservations and much more. 2. "Indian America, A Traveler's Companion," by Eagle/Walking Turtle, John Muir Publications, Santa Fe, New Mexico, 1989. This book provides addresses of reservations in the United States. 3. "Atlas of Indian Affairs," by Francis Paul Prucha, University of Nebraska Press: Lincoln & London, 1990. This book provides old and new maps showing the locality of Indian reserves, schools, tribal land sales and old forts. 4. "Atlas of the North American Indian," by Carl Waldman, Facts on File publications, 1985. This book Includes addresses of Indian reserves and tribal Museums in the United States and Canada.

WHERE TO FIND BOOKS AND MAGAZINE ARTICLES ABOUT NATIVE AMERICANS

A wealth of published books, magazines and articles about Indians can be found at the following facilities: 1. Local Libraries. 2. Local Book Stores 3. Tribal Museums 4. Local Urban Indian Associations. 5. Indian Pow Wows 6. Municipal Museums 7. College and University Bookstores. 8. Resale Book Shops. 9. Library Resale Shops. 10. Write the Bureau of Indian Affairs. A few copies of Native American magazines and newspapers may be found in large public libraries. Most large book outlets have Native American sections. Look for magazines with references to American History, American Indian Art, Anthropology, Ecology, Ethnohistory, Historical Military Wars, even Shamanism. One of the best sources of published material is Tribal Museums. The easiest solution here is to write for a list of publications for sale. Some surviving back issues of tribal and Native

American magazines and periodicals have been microfilmed. An example would be the "Indian Voice, 1971-1973," Glen Rock, New Jersey which has been filmed by Microfilming Corporation of American on two reels. Several types of Native American magazines, periodicals and newsletters deposited in the Family History Library (Mormon) Salt Lake City, Utah includes: "The Journal of American Indian Family Research," Volume I, No. 1, 1980, Lawton, Oklahoma, quarterly premier issue, "The Journal of American Indian Family Research Monthly Newsletters," Volume I, March 1988, Laguna Hills, California, a monthly issue, premier issue and "Indians at Work," A News Sheet for Indians and the Indian Service, Volume 1, August 1933 through May/June 1945, Washington, D.C., Office of Indian Affairs, issued monthly and later six issues yearly. The library has volume 2, 14, 19, and volume 12, No. 1-5, volume 13, No. 1.

USING YOUR PUBLIC LIBRARY INTER-LIBRARY LOAN SYSTEM

Exceptionally useful to a researcher is the ability to obtain books and microfilmed records on inter-library loan. Records of genealogical value that can be ordered through participating public libraries include: 1. State and County Records from State Archives. 2. Records from the National Archives (B.I.A.). 3. Special Collections on loan from other libraries. 3. Records from the Canadian Archives.

NEW YORK STATE LIBRARIES

Consult the following Local libraries in New York State for Indian material: 1. The Allegany County Historical Society, Belmont, Allegany County. 2. The Cattaraugus County Memorial and Historical Museum Library, Little Valley, Cattaraugus County. 3. The Wead Library, Malone, Franklin County. 4. The Franklin County Historical and Museum Society, Malone, New York. 5. The Niagara County Historical Society Library, Lockport. 6. The New York, Public Library, New York, New York 7. The Buffalo and Erie County Public Library, Buffalo, New York. 8. The Montgomery County Department of History and Archives, Fonda, New York. 9. The Onondaga County, Public Library, Syracuse, New York. 10. The Olin Library, Cornell University, Ithaca, New York. 11. Columbia University, New York, New York. 12. Fordham University, The Bronx, New York. 13. Long Island University, Greenvale, New York. 14. State University of New York, Albany, New York. 15. University of Rochester, Rochester, New York. 16. Syracuse University, Syracuse, New York. 17. The New York State Archive, Albany, New York. 2. The New York Genealogical and Biographical Society Library. 3. New York, Historical Society, New York, New York. The addresses of many state, county and city libraries within the state of New York can be found in the following sources: "New York Genealogical Research," by George K. Schweitzer, Ph.D., Sc.D., 1988. "The Handy Book for Genealogists," Published by The Everton Publishers, Inc., Logan, Utah.

THE PERSI FILE

The Persi File is an especially important source for finding articles published in genealogical newsletters, magazines and periodicals. The Persi File has been developed by the Allen County Genealogy Library in Fort Wayne, Indiana. This extensive index lists thousands genealogy articles that have been published in the United States. The file is arranged by surname, subject and locality in alphabetical order. Many articles that have been written about Native Americans can be located by using the Persi File. One example reads: Locality Section, State of New York, Niagara County, History, Article Entitled: "Native Am/Indians of Niagara County," NYNI, Volume 2, Number 6, November 1980. For a small fee per page the Library will mail you a copy of the article. The Index to the holdings of the Persi File is available on microfiche. Copies of the index to the Persi File can be found in some Family History Library Centers (Mormon) and public libraries.

TRIBAL NEWSPAPERS

Tribal sponsored newspapers have been in existence for many years. The "Cherokee Phoenix and Indian Advocate," was published as early as 1828 in Georgia. Modern tribal newspapers offer the researcher an opportunity to advertise their genealogy problem. In current tribal newspapers expect to find articles concerning: 1. Birth Announcements 2. Marriages 3. Obituaries 4. Dates of Pow Wows. 5. Local and National Native American News Items. Occasionally articles about tribal history, old treaty rolls and current membership rolls will appear. Most of these publications are members of the Native American Journalist Association. Subscription and circulation of some tribal newspapers may be limited to tribal members only. Write to the tribal offices for further information.

LOCAL NEWSPAPERS

A popular but sometimes not a widely used research source is local old newspapers. A rule of thumb is that newspapers that were published in county seat towns, large cities and state capitals offer the most information. Consider the genealogical information found in the following article that appeared on the 29th of July 1920 in the Green Bay Press-Gazette. Mary-Rain-In-The-Face who lived in Tomah, Wisconsin, had recently died. She was survived by her father Spoon Decorah, a Winnebago Indian and Civil War veteran. Spoon Decorah's white name was given as "John Sherman." He enlisted in the Third Wisconsin Regimental Infantry and was with (General) Sherman on the march to the sea. Further information mentions that Mary-Rain-in-the-Face could trace her ancestry through her father to the queen of the Decorah family, "Glory-of-the-Morning." The Decorah family was one of the most prominent of the Nebraska and Wisconsin tribes of the Winnebago Nation. Although old newspapers remain a valuable research source, difficulties exist. Most surviving old newspapers are limited in quantity. Regrettably, some have been indexed only by article titles. A page by page search may have to be made to find individual names. Expect to find microfilmed copies of old newspapers to be deposited in the following facilities: 1. Public Libraries 2. Colleges and Universities 3. Historical Societies 4. State Archives. A source for early New York newspapers is "Genealogical Data from Colonial New York Newspapers," by Kenneth R. Scott, Baltimore, Maryland, published by the Genealogical Publishing Co., 1977. One of the best-known newspaper indexes is the "Personal Name Index to the New York Times," 1851-1979, by Byron A. Falk, Roxbury Data Interface, 1979. Many colleges and universities have microfilm copies of the "Name Index to the New York Times."

GENEALOGY AND HISTORICAL SOCIETIES

Genealogy and Historical societies can present another research source. A simple letter can yield otherwise unknown data. Keep in mind that some Historical Societies are devoted only to the study of local history. As a rule, the best results can be obtained by keeping your letter short, and always provide a self addressed stamped envelope. Historical societies in the state of New York are numerous. Addresses for Genealogy and Historical Societies in New York can be found in "New York Genealogical Research," by George K. Schweitzer, Ph. D., Sc. D., Knoxville, Tennessee, 1988. Addresses of State, Regional and County Genealogy and Historical Societies in New York and the United States can be found in "The Handy Book For Genealogists," by George B. Everton, published by Everton, Publishers, Inc., Logan, Utah.

ON LINE SERVICES

So far the topics discussed in this book have dealt only with books, microfilms, microfiche and newspapers. Computer data bases can present another possible source for genealogy research. Some of the more popular and widely used data bases include: CompuServe, Genie, Prodigy and America On-line. Many offer genealogy forums.

RECORDS OF THE BRITISH COLONIAL OFFICE 1700-1783

"Records of the British Colonial Office," 1700-1783 exists in volumes housed in the Manuscript Room of the Library of Congress, Washington, D.C. These volumes have been microfilmed on 53 rolls. A guide has been compiled by Linda Womaski, Frederick, Md.: University Publications of America, Copyright 1972. Volume 225 contains "Out Letters: Indian Affairs, 1766-1768," volume 227 contains "In Letters: Indian Affairs," 1768-1771 & volume 284 contains "Indian Affairs," 1756. These records contain information on Indian Affairs before the American Revolution. They are available at the Library of Congress. The three volumes containing Indian Affairs information are also available on inter-library loan through the Church of Jesus Christ of Latter-day Saints (Mormon) Family History Library Centers on film number 1549671.

THE PAPERS OF CONTINENTAL CONGRESS 1774-1789

"The Papers of Continental Congress," 1774-1789 have been microfilmed on 69 rolls by the National Archives, Record Group M247. An Index was published in the "Papers of the Continental Congress," 1774-1789, Compiled by John P. Butler, 1978, National Archives. These Records contain Congress drafts of treaties 1775-1784. Also included is information about Indians who aided the Continental Army. These records are available on inter-library loan through: 1. The National Archives and its branches. 2. Your local participating library. 3. The Church of Jesus Christ of Latter-day Saints (Mormon) Family History Library Centers on film number 0199740. 4. Also check with the American Genealogy Lending Library.

THE AMERICAN STATE PAPERS, 1789-1827

"The American State Papers," include documents created by the Congress of the United States from 1789-1837. Class 2: Indian Affairs, 1st through 19th Congress, 25th of May 1789-March 1827, Volume II (2) contains information about Indian treaties, removals, military operations, hostilities and land sales. The American State Papers were originally published by Gales and Seaton, 1832-1861 in thirty-eight volumes. Indexes are included. These volumes are often found in large public libraries. They are also available on interlibrary loan through the Church of Jesus Christ of Latter-Day Saints (Mormon) Family History Library Centers. The film number is 0194334. "The House of Representatives Reports," contain information on Indian Affairs. Among these documents one can find records relating to fishing rights and tribal identity. The booklet "Government Depository Libraries," gives the locations of university and public libraries that receive government documents. The serial numbers are part of a system that began in 1817 called "Congressional Serial Set," 1817-1899, Published by Clearwater Publishing Company. Published 1978, National Archives.

THE OFFICE OF INDIAN AFFAIRS SINCE 1789

Any attempt to use the records of the United States Department of Bureau of Indian Affairs should include a study of the chronological history of that department. Since 1789, two government departments have been responsible for keeping government records on Indians. These departments are the War Department and the Department of Interior. The War Department was created on the 7th of August 1789. The Department of Indian Affairs was under its jurisdiction until 1849. The Office of Indian Affairs was established within the War Department on the 11th of March 1824. On the 3rd of March 1849 the Department of Interior was created. The Office of Indian Affairs was transferred to this department. In 1947 the Office of Indian Affairs was renamed The Bureau of Indian Affairs also known as the B. I. A. Sources: "Handbook of Federal Indian Law," 1982 Edition by Felix S. Cohen. "Documents of United States Indian Policy," By Francis Paul Prucha, University of Nebraska Press, Copyright 1984, Second Edition 1990. Some Indian Agent reports where published in Washington, D.C., under the title: "Report of the Secretary of Interior." For a list of Bureau of Indian Affairs Agencies and the location of their records see: "The Guide to Genealogical Research in the National Archives," Washington, D.C., U.S. Government Printing Office, 1991. Also, consult the New York State Department of Indian Services.

UNITED STATES SUPREME COURT RECORDS 1792-1909

The Supreme Court of the United States was established by the Act of September 24th 1789. Indexes are available to the appellate case files of the Supreme Court of the United States from 1792-1909. These indexes have been microfilmed by the National Archives on twenty microfilm rolls. They are part of Record Group Number M408. These indexes represent 59,000 cards arranged in alphabetical order by name. The index provides the name of the individual in the case, the file number, the case title, the date of docket, the date of decisions. References may also be made to case files in lower courts. The features and benefits of these records is that they contain a variety of Indian land disputes, hunting and fishing rights violations and tribal memberships. Minutes to the Supreme Court Records 1790-1950 have been microfilmed by the National Archives on Record Group Number M215 on 41 microfilm rolls. The minutes are arranged chronologically by court dates. The indexes to the records are available on interlibrary loan through: 1. The National Archives and its branches 1. Your local public library. 2. The Church of Jesus Christ of Latter-day Saints (Mormon) Family History Library Centers on film numbers 1452154-1452173.

THE NATIONAL ARCHIVES

The National Archives is located between Pennsylvania and Constitution Avenues and 7th and 9th Streets, NW, Washington, D.C. A branch is located in New York (Bayonne, New Jersey). A published guide is available under the title "The Guide to Genealogical Research in the National Archives," Washington, D.C. Also available is "The Guide to Records in the National Archives of the United States Relating to the American Indian," By Edward E. Hill, Washington, D.C., U. S. Government Printing Office, 1991. Publications address: Publications Sales Branch (NEPS) National Archives & Records Administration, 8th & Pennsylvania, Avenue, NW Washington, D.C. 20408.

NEW YORK STATE CENSUS 1825-1925

The New York State census provides an additional research feature. New York State Censuses exist for 1825, 1835, 1845, 1855, 1865, 1875, 1892, 1905, 1915 and 1925. Reference: "New York State Census Records 1790-1925," Douglas and M. Yates, New York State Library, Albany, New York, 1981. Electoral Censuses were taken 1795, 1801, 1807, 1814, and 1821. Source Information: "State Censuses," An annotated bibliography of censuses of population taken after the year 1790, by States and Territories of the United States, Prepared by Henry J. Durester, Chief, Census Library Project, Library of Congress, Washington, D.C. 1948, reprinted in 1983, pages 45-50. The 1855 New York State Census includes an appendix report on data taken for the census of Indians and comments.

THE BUREAU OF INDIAN AFFAIRS CENSUS RECORDS 1885-1940

Literally thousands of Native Americans are listed in the records of the Bureau of Indian Affairs. The Bureau of Indian Affairs began taking annual census records of individuals residing on reservations in 1885. The Bureau of Indian Affairs Census for 1885-1940 has been microfilmed on 692 rolls by the National Archives. They are available for interlibrary loan through: 1. The National Archives and its Branches. 2. Local Public Libraries 3. The Church of Jesus Church of Latter-day Saints (Mormon) Family History Library Centers. 4. The American Genealogy Lending Library. Although these records represent major Native American research, limitations exist. Consider: 1. Some early rolls are faded and unreadable. 2. Some list only the names of heads of households. 3. Some provide only a population count. 4. Some are not arranged in alphabetical order. 5. The spelling of the names were dependant on the interpretation of the government agent. 6. Family relationships were not always provided. 7. Only a tribal name was given. Keep in mind the Bureau of Indian Affairs Census Rolls did not extend to all Indians. Only those living on reservations or who maintained their tribal membership through the U.S. government are listed.

THE UNITED STATES FEDERAL CENSUS, 1790-1920

The 1900 census included special inquiries relating to Indians. A special census was created for the enumeration of Indians living on reservations. Whites or blacks living in Indian families were enumerated as members of the Indian Family. If an Indian lived with either a white or black family outside the reservations they were enumerated into the general population schedule. The United States Federal Census provides unique Native American information that many early B.I.A. Census Rolls do not. The United States Federal Census 1790-1920 is available for research on interlibrary loan through: 1. The National Archives and its branches. 2. Your local participating public library. 3. The Church of Jesus Christ of Latter-day Saints (Mormon) Family History Library Centers. 4. The American Genealogy Lending Library. Reference Source: "Bureau of the Census, 13th Census, 1910," Special instructions to enumerators relating to the enumeration of the Indians, Washington, Library of Congress Photo-duplication Service, 1975, seven pages, entitled: "Department of Commerce and Labor, Bureau of the Census, Thirteenth Census of the United States, April 15, 1910."

RESEARCHING TRIBAL NAMES

At the best, researching tribal names present problems. A novice should use caution with Indian names found in treaties, census records or computerized indexes. In the past the spelling or interpretation of an Indian name may have depended on how that name sounded phonetically. For example, the surname Papeno appears on the 1886 B.I.A. Roll for the St. Regis Mohawk in New York. The same family name appears as Papineau in the 1900 U. S. Census of the St. Regis Mohawk Reserve in New York. The name John George may appear on a B.I.A. Roll when further investigation proves that the surname was actually John. George was the given name. Cornplanter mentioned in this book was the son of a white trader named Abeel often referred to as O'Bail and a Seneca woman. Descendants of Cornplanter used both the name Cornplanter and O'Bail as surnames. The printed or written name may not reflect the actual tribal language and may vary from record to record. Consider the following actual case studies. Sophronia Wolf Finger applied in 1906 for the Cherokee (Eastern) Miller Roll. She claimed through her father and grandmother who were enrolled as Roll Numbers 1222 and 1219 on the 1851 Eastern Cherokee Chapman Roll. She gave her father's name as Joseph Wolf. She included the information that he had a brother named David. She listed that her father's parents were Wilson and Nicey Wolf. The name Jo-wuh, a male age five, appears for Roll Number 1222 on the original Chapman Roll. The name Nicey (Listed as a wife) age twenty-six appears for Roll Number 1219. The name of the head of this household was Wah-Yuh-Ah-Til-Lih, a male, whose Roll Number was 1218. Based on Sophronia Finger's information you might conclude that Jo-wuh was her father Joseph and Nicey was her grandmother. However, who was Wah-Yuh-Ah-Til-Lih? Did any other members of the Wolf family apply for the Miller Roll in 1906? Yes, her uncle David Wolfe did. He applied through his father Wilson Trotting-Wolfe or Wahliya-Atley and his mother Nicey or Nahyesa, who maiden name was Tsulexsi or Welch. He gave his father's Chapman Roll Number as 1218. His mother's Chapman Roll Number was 1219. His father's father was Thundstel? or Panther. You conclude that Joseph Wolf or Jo-

22

wuh Wolfe was the son of Wilson Trotting-Wolfe or Wah-Yuh-Ah-Ti-Lih? or Wahliya-Atley? who was the son of Thundstel? or Panther. The easiest solution here is to make a search comparison of other types of records.

THE ACCELERATED INDEXING SYSTEM

The Accelerated Indexing System, commonly called the A.I.S., is produced by A.I.S. Database Corrections. This is a private company based in Salt Lake City, Utah. They produce and publish census indexes in book and microfiche form for United States researchers. The microfiche indexes are divided into individual searches. Each search is divided into time periods and then geographical localities. Each search is arranged in alphabetical order by surnames. The greatest value in using the A.I.S is: Any specific surname which appeared on a United States Census Record from about 1790 to 1850 is grouped together in one index for the entire United States. Some entries exist as early as 1607 and extend to 1906. However, the period for most entries exists from 1800 to 1850. There is one important fact that applies. Care must be taken to search all possible spellings of a surname. It's important to know that individual surname entries are spelled as they appeared in the original United States Census. An example would be the following entries found in the index: Abram Doxtader, Herkimer County, New York, page 300, 1850 and Mary Doxtater, Oneida County, New York, page 60, 1850. Additional information may follow an entry. Race or ethnic origin is not listed on the A.I.S. However, of particular interest to Native American researchers is the locality abbreviation "REV" or "RSVN," which follows an entry indicating a residence on a reservation. The locality abbreviation "IY" suggests a residence in Indian Territory (Oklahoma). The locality abbreviation "CN" indicates Cherokee Nation. The locality abbreviation "AN" indicates Arapaho Nation. The locality abbreviation "CW" indicates Choctaw Nation. Look under the term "Indian," which is arranged alphabetically between surnames and you will find many singular Indian names. Wolf Shotter is listed as follows: Indian, Wolf Shotter, Indian Reservation, DT (Dakota Territory) 1880. A researcher should also look under the spelling of a tribe. Here's an example: Navajo, Ma Dolores, Rio Arriba County, NM (New Mexico) Page 539, Santa Clara Ind RSVN, 1870. The next option is the Mortality Search. This search was made up from U.S. Census Mortality Schedules 1850-1880. Individuals who had died in the previous twelve months before the census was taken were listed. Clearly we can see the value of this search in the following entries: Indian, Towning Choctaw, Attala County, Mississippi, age 2, died in June 1880 and Indian, Settin Bull, Choteau County, Montana, age 24, Male, died in July 1880. Other original records such as census records, old tax lists, militia rolls and petitions were also used to compile entries in the A.I.S. Two of the contributing libraries included the New York State Library at Albany, New York and the Oklahoma Historical Society Library, Oklahoma City, Oklahoma. Expect to find copies of the A.I.S. microfiche collection to be available at most Family History Library Centers (Mormon) and some large public libraries.

NEW YORK NATIVE AMERICAN ASSOCIATIONS

Native American Associations in western New York state include: 1. The Native American Center for the Living Arts, Inc., Niagara, Falls, New York. 2. The North American Indian Club, Syracuse. 3. American Indian Club of Rochester, Inc., Rochester, New York. "The Native American Directory," published by the Native American Co-op in San Carlos, Arizona, provides Native American Associations addresses in the United States.

THE FAMILY HISTORY LIBRARY CENTER

The Family History Library of the Church of Jesus Christ of Latter-day Saints (Mormon) is the largest genealogy library in the world. The main library is located in Salt Lake City, Utah. The library has branch libraries called Family History Library Centers in the United States and throughout the world. Over ninety percent of the holdings of the main library is available on loan to branch libraries on microfilm and microfiche. A small nominal cost for the loan of the microfilms and microfiche is involved. The FHLC Catalog (Family History Library Center Catalog) is available on microfiche or computer. The catalog is the guide to the Library's entire holdings. It is divided into four major sections, author/title, locality, subject and surname. The key to effectively using the library lies in the knowledge that everything within the four major catalog sections is arranged in alphabetical order. Finding out what Native American material is available in the catalog is just a matter of good research procedures. Start by searching the locality section. The easy-to-use locality section is arranged from the largest to the smallest geographical area in alphabetical order. Look for the largest geographical division to be listed under the title United States/Native Races. Review the types of records available in this section. To learn more about the availability of specific records, extend your search in the locality section to include geographical subdivisions within the United States such as a state, county, city or town. The example would be, New York/Native Races, New York/Niagra County/Native Races or New York/Niagra County/Town of Lewiston/Native Races. When using the subject section consider the name of the tribe as your subject. Look for records in the subject section on native tribes in North and South America to be listed in alphabetical order such as Abenaki, Cayuga, Oneida then Seneca. The surname section is arranged in alphabetical order by individual or family surname. Search this section for family histories. Researchers use the author/title section to find out if a book or manuscript has been deposited in the main library. In order to use this section, you need to know the author's name or the title of the book. If you know the author's name, search in alphabetical order first by the author's surname then the given name such as Prevost, Toni Jollay. If you do not know the author's name but know the book title, search in alphabetical order by title such as "Delaware and Shawnee Adopted by the Cherokee." Two computerized indexes, the International Genealogical Index (I.G.I.) & Ancestral File also contains Native American information. For published references consult the following: "The Library," A Guide to the LDS Family History Library, Edited by Johni Cerny & Wendy Elliott, Ancestry Publishing, Salt Lake City, Utah, 1988. "Our Native Americans and Their Records of Genealogical Value," Volume I, By Kay Kirkham.

(Includes a brief discussion about the Family History Library and record call numbers.) Compiled and arranged from the Computer Catalog of the Family History Library is the "Register of Native American Indians," United States and Canada. This register is available on microfiche number 6049508. It is arranged in alphabetical order by state. It lists the library's film call numbers for Native American material. "The Native American Directory, Alaska, Canada, United States," published by the National Native American Cooperative, San Carlos, Arizona is a comprehensive directory that provides the addresses for reserves from Alaska to the Mexican border. Also, included are the addresses of native newspapers, colleges and many other related facilities. The library has the July 1982 copy available on microfiche number 6048680 (A printed copy has since been updated). For further information write to the library at 35 North West Temple, Street, Salt Lake City, Utah, 84150.

FINDING INDIANS IN THE INTERNATIONAL GENEALOGICAL INDEX

The International Genealogical Index or the I.G.I., has been developed by the Church of Jesus Christ of Latter-day Saints (Mormon) Family History Library Center. It is available on microfiche or CD ROM. This comprehensive index represents the data for millions of individual births, christenings and marriages. The time periods covered range from about 1500 to 1900. The index encompasses the United States and over ninety countries of the world. Death records are not listed on the I.G.I. The information compiled for this index came from family genealogist and original census, church and county records. The I.G.I. is basically used by researchers for three reasons: 1. It provides beginning genealogists a means to determine if any information has been compiled on their direct family lines. 2. It can confirm existing genealogy information. 3. It provides advanced genealogists a means of locating additional information to extend their family lines. The I.G.I. is arranged strictly in alphabetical order by country, then by state or province, then by surname, and finally by given name. A researcher will find genealogy entries for many Indian people of the United States, Canada and South America. However, in most cases a prior search of United States Census and Bureau of Indian Affairs Census Rolls may be helpful. Some names clearly show Native American information. Depicted here is the type of obvious Indian entries: New York State, Susanah Cornelius, born in 1837 to Thomas O. or Ti-O-Ga-Wah or The Paddle Cornelius and his wife Elizabeth in Madison County, New York. Another example is: Mary Jemison married Sheninjee in 1760, North American, Seneca Tribe, New York State. Also present in the index is a microfiche entitled "Native Americans." which is filed before the state of Alabama. It contains many kinship entries for four of the five civilized tribes which include the Cherokees, Chickasaw, Choctaws and Creeks. Other ways of finding Indians in the I.G.I. are: 1. Choose the first microfiche of a given state. Look for singular Indian names such as Kak-ush-ka to be listed alphabetically before the surnames that start with the letter "A." 2. Look for names such as Buffalo Tamer to be listed under the surnames beginning with the letter "B." 3. Look for names such as Henry Osceola to be listed under the surname Osceola. 4. Look for names such as Glory In The Morning Dorian to be listed under the surname Dorian. The I.G.I. does not chronicle an individual's race. The entry for Jarett Smith is a good example. Jarett Smith is listed in the I.G.I. as a child living in the household of his father Henry Smith in 1850 in North Carolina. The source of this entry is the 1850 United States Census. In no way does the index suggest that either Jarett Smith or his father were Indians. However, Jarett Smith was a Cherokee. He later became a Chief of the Eastern Band. Consider tribal locations and the regional area where the event took place as a clue. Another exampe in the index would be John Marsh or Mursh who was born in 1786 at the Pamunkey Indian Reservation, King William County, Virginia. In conclusion, there are hundreds of Indians listed on the I.G.I.

THE ANCESTRAL FILE

The Ancestral File is a computerized data base on CD ROM. The data base has been developed by the Church of Jesus Christ of Latter-day Saints (Mormon) Family History Library Center. Millions of names have been compiled for this database. It differs from the International Genealogical Index in that most of the genealogy was submitted by individuals on computer disks. The concept behind the Ancestral File is that it is designed to make searching very simple. A knowledge of the surnames found among the Indians from New York is helpful. Consider the following entry listed in the file: Hannah Doxtator born in 1856, Oneida, Brown County, Wisconsin, Parents: William Doxtator/Elizabeth Poudry. The Ancestral File is available for use at Family History Library Centers and large public libraries. It must be remembered that although that the Ancestral File is very helpful to genealogists. However, caution should be used. Researchers with various degrees of genealogy experience have submitted their information. A researcher should always follow up entries found in computerized indexes with further documentation.

THE AMERICAN GENEALOGY LENDING LIBRARY

The American Genealogy Lending Library loans and sells microfilms and microfiche to public libraries, genealogy groups and individual members. Their holdings include United States Bureau of Indian Affairs Census Rolls and the Draper Manuscripts. Write to: P.O. Box 329, Bountiful, Utah, 84011-0329.

MUSEUMS IN THE STATE OF NEW YORK

Museums that display collections and provide information about New York Indians includes: 1. The Akwesasne Museum, St. Regis Mohawk, Reservation, Hogansburg. 2. Fort Edward Historical Association, Fort Edward, New York. 3. Fort Johnson, Amsterdam, New York. 4. Fort William Henry Restoration and Museum, Lake George, New York. 5. The Kateri Galleries, The National Shrine of North American Martyrs, Auriesville, New York. 6. The Seneca-Iroquois National Museum, Salamanca. 7. The Six Nations Indian Museum, Onchiota. 8. The Suffolk County Indian and Archaeological Museum, Huntington. 9. The Tonawanda-Seneca Museum, Basom. 10. The Mohawk-Caughnawaga Museum, Fonda, New York. 11. The Iroquois Indian Museum, Schoharie, New York. 12. The Cayuga Museum of History and Art. 13. The Archaeological Society of Central New York, Auburn. 14. The Shenandoah Trading Post, Oneida, New York. 15. The Museum of the American Indian, Heye Foundation, New York, New York. 16. The Franklin County Historical and Museum Society. 17. The Schoharie Museum of the Iroquois, Schoharie, New York. 18. The

Brooklyn Museum, Brooklyn, New York. Addresses for Native American Museums in the United States and Canada can be found in "Atlas of North American Indian," By Carl Waldman, Facts on File Publications, 1985.

CHURCHES, MISSIONARIES AND SCHOOLS

From the earliest days of European settlement in North America religious missionaries have established missions among the Indians. In time records began to be kept. The type of records created included baptism, christenings, marriages, and progress reports. Those who are seeking to find a Native America ancestor before the Revolutionary War should consider missionary records a major research source. The challenge for a researcher is to find old missionary records. Existing old missionary records were often deposited in denominational sponsored archives, colleges and libraries. Furthermore, some missionary records have been published. These can be divided into classifications such as missionary pamphlets, magazines, and newspapers. A good example of a missionary periodical is the "American Baptist Missionary Magazine," 1817-1835, which has been made available on microfilm by the Historical Commission of the Southern Baptist Convention, Nashville, Tennessee. Missionaries were the first to establish schools among Native Americans. This example was illustrated in "The American State Papers," which disclosed that a Mr. Kirkland a missionary had obtained a charter for the "Hamilton Oneida Academy," a seminary for the education of Indians in New York. According to the same source education was the responsibility of the following religious societies among the Six Nations in New York: 1. The Seneca Nation, on the Buffalo Reserve by the Missionary Society of New York (1820). 2. The Oneida in New York, by the Hamilton Baptist Missionary Society 3. The Tuscarora Nation, New York, by the United Foreign Missionary Society. 4. The Seneca Nation, by the United Foreign Missionary Society (1824). Look for a directory for denominational archives at your local public library reference department.

DENOMINATIONAL BIBLIOGRAPHY

BEAUCHAMP, WM. M., "Moravian Journals Relating to Central New York," 1745-1766, for the Onondaga Historical Association, 1916, Syracuse, New York, Dehler Press, 1916.

BECHARD, HENRI S. J., "The Original Caughnawaga Indians," International Publishers, Montreal 1976, 258 pages (Catholic Missions).

COX, JOHN JR., "Quaker Records in New York," in the New York Genealogical and Biographical Records, 1914, XLV, pages 263-269, 366-373.

FLIEGEL, JOHN CARL, "Index to the Records of the Moravian Mission Among the Indians of North America," New Haven, Research Publications, 1970, 1,408 pages, four (4) volumes.

HISTORICAL RECORDS SURVEY, "Guide to the Vital Statistics of Churches in New York State, " two (2) volumes, 1942.

HOUGHTON LIBRARY, HARVARD UNIVERSITY, "Records of The American Board of Commissioners for Foreign Missions," Cambridge, Massachusetts.

PIERCE, BEAVER R., "Church, State, and the American Indians-Two and a Half Centuries of Partnership in Missions between Protestant Churches and Government," 1966.

RECORDS OF THE MORAVIAN MISSION AMONG THE INDIANS OF NORTH AMERICA, New Haven, Connecticut, Research Publications, 1969, 40 microfilm reels. The original records in the Archives of the Moravian Church, Bethlehem, Pennsylvania. Text in English and German, indexed by Carl John Fliegel, Box 111-113, The Shekomeko, New York Missions 1739-1746 on three rolls of film.

SHEA, JOHN DAWSON GILMARY: 1824-1892 "History of the Catholic Missions Among the Indian Tribes of the United States," 1529-1854, AMS Press, New York, 1973, 514 pages (Originally printed by Edward Dunigan & Brothers, New York, 1855).

SOCIETY OF FRIENDS (HICKSITE) Executive Committee of the Four Yearly Meetings. The case of the Seneca Indians in the state of New York: illustrated by facts/ printed by direction of the joint committees on Indian affairs, of the four yearly meetings of Friends of Genesee, New York, Philadelphia, and Baltimore: Merrihew and Thompson, 1840, 256 pages. A microfilm copy is available through the Church of Jesus Christ of Latter-day Saints, Family History Library Centers on film number 1697422, item 5.

CUMORAH MISSION RECORDS

The Cumorah Mission Records (Mormon Church) were compiled at Versailles, New York, in 1974. The transcripts include Seneca Indian Rolls- Cattaraugus & Allegany Indian Reservation and genealogy records and pedigree charts. These records have been microfilmed by the Church of Jesus Christ of Latter-day Saints Family History Library on film number 0924575, Item 1. This film contains the original records collected by Mr. and Mrs. Hyrum K. Mortensen. Included is: 1. A transcription of part of the Seneca Rolls and census records from the Cattaraugus and Allegany Indian Reservations. 2. Genealogical records and pedigree charts from members of the Cattaraugus Branch, Cumorah Mission, Versailles, New York. 3. A census of Senecas living at Buffalo Creek in 1789 arranged by clan and the name of the head of household. The number of men, women, boys and girls in each household is represented. 4. The names of Delaware living at Buffalo and Kadvragyerac in 1789 an Onondaga and Cayugas at Buffalo Creek. 5. Tuscaroras at the landing and Tuscaroras at Genessee, by Reverend Sam'l Kirkland in 1789. 6. An article entitled: "The Seneca Chiefs," A bill of Morality, from the Friend's (Quaker?) Intelligencer of 1860 to the editor of the Chester County, Times. 7. A list of Seneca Chiefs who were involved in the Ogden Land Company, with the Seneca Nations residing in the state of New York. 8. Names of some of the Chiefs who had died and some places of death. 9. Some birth and death records for the Cattaraugus Reserve from the 1880's to the 1930's. 10. Pedigree information about Peter Crouse the captive. 11. An 1880 Census of Indians living at Cattaraugus Old Town, Cold Spring, Red House, Cattaraugus Reservation and Jimersontown. 12. Some 1879 and 1881 census entries. 13. Allegany 1882 Census of the Seneca at Horse Shoe, Jimerson Town, Red House, Cold Spring and Old Town. 14. Census entries from the Thomas Orphan Asylum, Allegany Indian Reservation 1885 and Cattaraugus 1888. 15. A few random entries from the 1895, 1915, 1925, 1935 Allegany and Cattaraugus Census entries. 16. Family pedigree charts and family bible information for some Seneca Families.

THE NEW ENGLAND SOCIETY RECORDS

The New England Society was established in 1649 as a trading company. It was established by members of the Church of England and Protestant Dissenters. Missionaries were sent from England by the society as early as 1712 to New England and adjacent colonies. After the end of the American Revolution the New England Society still had influence in Upper Canada, (Ontario) particularly among the Mohawk. The original New England Society records are housed at the Guildhall Library in London, England. The New England Company Records 1660-1906 have been microfilmed on 11 reels. Included in the New England Society Records is the following: 1. Minute books: Commissioners of Indian Affairs at Boston, Massachusetts 1699-1784. 2. Minute Books, Commissioners of Indian Affairs in New Brunswick 1787-1818. 3. Correspondence, from Boston to London. 4. Indian Affairs 1677-1761. 5. "Papers Relating to Indians 1669-1727." Microfilm copies of the New England Society Records have been made available in England. Copies of these films are available on interlibrary loan through the Church of Jesus Christ of Latter-day Saints (Mormon) Family History Library Centers.

FORT HUNTER AND QUEEN ANNE'S CHAPEL

In 1708 five Iroquois were taken to England and were given an audience by the Queen of England and Governor Hunter. In time Governor Hunter built a chapel for the Mohawks at Ticonderoga about 1712. The chapel was enclosed by a stockade named Fort Hunter. The Reverend Dr. Henry Barlcay became one of the custodians of funds arising from the sale of the lands belonging to the Queen's Chapel Parish. The original records have been microfilmed under the title "County of Montgomery," Register of Queen Anne Chapel, Fort Hunter, New York State Library, Albany, Register of Baptisms, Marriages & Communicates & Funerals begun by Henry Barclay, Fort Hunter January 26, 1734." Just a few of the surnames mentioned in the records of Queen Anne's Chapel in the 1730's and 1740's includes Brant, Johnson, Montour and Wysenbergh. These records have been made available on microfilm. Consult: 1. Your Local Public Library. 2. The New York State Library and the New York State Archives. 3. A microfilm copy is available on interlibrary loan through the Church of Jesus Christ of Latter-day Saints (Mormon) Family History Library Centers.

ST. JOHN'S ANGLICAN CHURCH

Very important to Six Nations Research in New York, Wisconsin and Canada is the Church Records of St. John's Anglican Church of Canada located in Onondaga, Brant County, Ontario. The Registers of St. John's Church from 1829 include baptisms, confirmations, deaths, marriages and burial registrations for local natives. A search of these records may yield genealogy information for those Indian families residing in the state of New York today. Just to name a few, some of the surnames among these records include: Alvis, Anderson, Anthony, Bearfoot, Big-Deer, Burham, Carrier, Cayuga, Crawford, Cusac, Denny, David, Doctor, Dolson, Doxtater, Fish, Fishcarrier, Fowler, George, Green, Henrick, Harris, Hill, Huff, Jacobs, Jack, Jackson, Jemison, John, Keys, Kick, Longbourd, Longfish, Moses, Mt. Pleasant, Obediah, Patterson, Pembleton, Peters, Printup, Silver, Smith, Smoke, Spring, Thomas, Thompson, Wilson and Williams. Also death or burial records for several Cayuga, Delaware and Tuscarora Chiefs is included. The original St. John's Church Records have been made available in Canada. 1. Contact the Canadian Archives. 2. A film copy is available on interlibrary loan through the Church of Jesus Christ of Latter-day Saints (Mormon) Family History Library Centers on film number 1015812.

BRANT COUNTY, ONTARIO, CANADA CEMETERY RECORDS

A useful tool to genealogist is cemtery records.The Brant County, Ontario, Canada, Genealogy Society has compiled the following Indian Cemetery Records located in Brant County: Bethany Mission Cemetery, Christ Church Anglican Cemetery, Delaware Mission Cemetery of the Delaware United Church Cemetery, First Line Cemetery, Jamison Cemetery, St. John's Mission, New Credit Reserve Cemeteries of the Six Nations Indian Reserve, Salvation Army Cemetery and the Grand River Mission United Church Cemetery. Also the records of the "Mohawk Chapel Cemetery," on six pages and "Indian Burial Sites," which includes sites in Tuscarora, Onondaga and Oneida Township have been compiled on four pages, including a map. Abundant among these early cemetery records are surnames found among the Six Nations Indians in the state of New York. 1. Contact the Canadian Archives. 2. Write to the Brant County Genealogy Society. 3. Microfiche copies are available on interlibrary loan through the Church of Jesus Christ of Latter-day Saints (Mormon) Family History Library Centers.

THE DRAPER MANUSCRIPT COLLECTION

Frequent mention has been made about "The Lyman Copeland Draper Manuscript Collection." A wealth of Six Nations Indian family and genealogy relationships can be found in these Manuscripts. The Collection is in the State Historical Society of Wisconsin. The volumes that contain information about the Indians of New York include: Series F, Volume 1-3 "Joseph Brant's Papers," 1740-1807 (New York), Series F, Volume 4-5 "Brant Manuscripts," 1778 (New York), Series F, Volume 12 "Brant's Later Years and Death," (New York), Series F, Volume 13-15 "Brant's Relatives and Descendants," (New York), Series F, Volume 13-15, "Sir William Johnson Papers," Series F, Volume 16-18 "Brant Manuscripts," (New York), Series F, Volume 19, "Brant Notes and Letters," (New York), Series U, Volume 21-24 "Indian Treaties Relating to Frontier Wars," 1756-1834. Microfilm copies of the Draper Manuscripts are available at: 1. Many Universities and Colleges. 2. On interlibrary loan from Major Wisconsin Libraries. 2. The American Genealogy Lending Library. 2. The Church of Latter-day Saints (Mormon) Family History Library Centers.

HOLLAND LAND COMPANY RECORDS IN NEW YORK

A key to the survival of Indians in the United States remains the land. For this reason "The Holland Land Company Records," involving land in western New York are of particular interest. Included is: Indian Land Claims, 1851-1858, title papers 1794-1829 (Includes maps) and records relating to Indian Affairs. These records include: 1. lists of Indians and land owned in 1842. 2. Various treaties from 1797-1846. 3. Indian cases before the Supreme Court of New York, 1854-1856. 4. Intrusion dispute on the Tonawanda Reservation occupied by the Seneca Nation. The surnames or names of those who gave testimony in the 1850's included: Blacksmith, Cone, Cooper, Hot-Bread, Jemison, Johnson, Jonas, Logan, Seneca. Many listed their ages. Of particular interest was the testimony of George Jemsion age about fifty or sixty from Cattaraugus a grandson of Mary Jemsion the white captive. Other surnames or names of Indians mentioned included: Cornplanter, Destroy-Town, Farmers Brother, Gov. Blacksnake, Hudson, Jones, Little-Bread,

O'Beal, Pierce, Pollard, Rielly, Shongo, Snow, Tall-Chief, Tiffany, Tall-Chief, Warrior and Young-King. Most were deceased by 1850. For more details consult the "Name Index to Turner's Pioneer History of the Holland Purchase of Western New York," published by L. C. Colley in 1946. The Holland Land Company Records have been made available on microfilm. Copies are available on interlibrary loan through the Church of Jesus Christ of Latter-day Saints (Mormon) Family History Library Center. Film numbers (FHLC) 1550000-1550001 includes BUF 59-66 & BUF 69-100 Indian Land Claims. Besides the Family History Library consult: 1. The AGLL Lending Libary. 2. Your public library.

MILITARY RECORDS

In the colonial period, Indians of the Six Nations were involved in the following wars: 1. The French and Indian War 1754-63. 2. The Anglo French Conflict 1755-58 in Canada. 3. The American Revolution 1775-83. Beginning in the post-colonial period conflicts occurred on the Michigan, Canadian border in Ontario, which extended to the Niagara area. Most Oneidas and Tuscaroras fought on the American Side during the Revolution. Some remained neutral. The Mohawk supported the English. Other members of the Six Nations were divided in their loyalties. For the researcher the historical and genealogy data found in military related records can be invaluable.

MILITARY BIBLIOGRAPHY

BURLEIGH, H. C., "Confiscations," Albany, Charlotte and Tryon Counties, New York, 1970, Toronto, Canada, Ontario, United Empire Loyalists, Association, eleven pages. The original is in the New York State Library. A copy is available on inter-library loan through the Church of Jesus Christ of Latter-day Saints (Mormon) Family History Library of microfilm number 1321358. Item 3.

DIVISION OF ARCHIVES AND HISTORY, ALBANY, "The American Revolution in New York: Its Political and Social and Economic Significance," 1926.

DRAPER, LYMAN COPELAND, Volume 17, Loyalist of the American Revolution 1780-1782, Wisconsin Historical Society.

FITZGERALD, E. KEITH, Loyalist Lists: Over 2,000 Loyalist names and families from the "Haldimand Papers," including a roll of King's Rangers and Returns of the 1st Battalion of the King's Royal Regiment of New York." Copyright 1984, Toronto, Ontario Genealogical Society. A copy is available on inter-library loan through the Church of Jesus Christ of Latter-day Saints (Mormon) Family History Library Centers on microfiche number 6010886.

GRAYMONT, BARBARA, "The Iroquois in the American Revolution," Syracuse University Press, Copyright 1972, page 146.

HAGAN, EDWARD, "War in Schohary 1777-1783," 1989.

HILL, WILLIAM H., "Old Fort Edward before 1800," privately printed, Fort Edward, New York, 1929.

MOHAWK, JOHN, "War Against the Seneca-French Expedition of 1687," No date.

NEW YORK STATE, SECRETARY OF STATE, "List of Names of Persons to whom Military Patents have been issued from the Secretaries Office and to whom delivered." Printed by Francis Child and John Swaine, printers to the state 1793, a copy is in the Library of Congress.

OFFICE OF GENERAL SERVICES, B.S.R.P., Albany New York, Card Index to Patents 1784 Dryden to Pompey Land Patents and Deeds. This record is in the New York State Library. A microfilm copy is available on inter-library loan at the Church of Jesus Christ of Latter-day Saints (Mormon) Family History Library Centers on film numbers 945293 and 945295.

ONEIDA AND TUSCARORA OFFICERS IN THE REVOLUTION FROM NEW YORK, Battalion Book- deposition of Lands, Albany, New York, 1825 (Lands in Onondaga County).

PENROSE, MARILY B., "The Mohawk Valley in the Revolution," Franklin Park, N.J.: Liberty Bell Associates, 1978.

REID, W. MAX, "The Story of Old Fort Johnson," G. P. Putnam & Sons, New York and London, The Knickerbocker Press, Copyright 1906.

ROBERTS, JAMES A., "New York in the Revolution," as Colony and State, two (2) volumes, Albany, Comptroller's Office, 1898, 1904, compiled by James A. Roberts. This records contains names of American soldiers, British prisoners, British Loyalist, estates confiscated and refugees. A microfilm copy is available on inter-library loan from the Church Jesus Christ of Latter-day Saints (Mormon) Family History Library Center libraries on microfilm number 040048, item 2.

THE QUEEN'S RANGERS IN AMERICA AND CANADA 1781-1783 (Office of Public Record, London, England). Made available in England. A microfilm copy is available on inter-library loan at The Church of Jesus Christ of Latter-day Saints (Mormon) Family History Centers on microfilm number 098977 item 3.

THE UNITED EMPIRE LOYALIST ASSOCIATION OF CANADA, "Loyalist Lineages of Canada," 1783-1983, Generation Press, Ontario, 1984.

WALDMAN, CARL, "Atlas of the North American Indian," Facts on File Publications, 1985, pages 109-114, article entitled "Indians in the American Revolution," page 159, article entitled, "Canadian Indian Wars."

EMIGRATION/IMMIGRATION, THE ST. ALBANS DISTRICT MANIFEST RECORDS

Material abstracted from Canadian and United States Census before 1900 shows that many natives living on reserves in Ontario and Quebec Canada were born in the United States. Relatives often lived in New York, Michigan, Wisconsin or Oklahoma. The United States 1900, 1910 and 1920 Census provides information about the year an individual immigrated to the United States. The St. Albans (Vermont) District

Manifest Records exist from January 1895-1950's. These records provide information about individuals who crossed the Canadian border into the United States from the east to west coast regardless of where they crossed the border. The names, age, place of birth, ethnic origins are listed. A unique advantage is that often the names of the person or relation the immigrant was visiting in the United States was given. The records are part of the National Archives Record Group Numbers M1461, M1463 and M1465 on 937 microfilm rolls. An abstract card index is arranged in alphabetical order by the individual's surname who crossed the border into the United States. The cards represent indexes to the original manifests. These records are available on interlibrary loan through: 1. The National Archives and its Branches. 2. Check with your local public library. 3. The Church of Jesus Christ of Latter-Day Saints (Mormon) Family History Library Centers. (See the FHLC Catalog, Locality Section, Canada/Emigration/Immigration.)

SURNAMES FOUND AMONG THE SIX NATIONS RESERVES
IN NEW YORK, OKLAHOMA, WISCONSIN, CANADA AND SCHOOLS IN CANADA,
KANSAS, PENNSYLVANIA AND VIRGINIA.

Today the locations of the Indian Reserves or tribal offices in the state of New are located at: 1. The Cayuga Nation at Versailles, New York. 2. The Oneida Nation of New York at Oneida, New York. 3. The Onondaga Nation at Nedrow, New York. 4. The Seneca Nation at Irving, New York. 4. The Tuscarora nation at Lewiston, New York. 5. The Tonawanda Band of Senecas Council of Chiefs at Basom, New York. The St. Regis Mohawk Council Chiefs, St. Regis Reservation at Hogansburg, New York. 6. The Shinnecock Reservation, Southampton, New York.

Surnames found among the Indian students who attended the Mt. Elgin Industrial Institution, Brant County, Ontario, Canada, 1851: Bird, Buckwheat, Cheehook, Cutt, Finger, Fisher, Herkimer, Jackson, Jim, Johnson, King, Secord, Wesly and Wilson. Source: The 1851 Canadian Census.

Surnames found among the Indian students of Six Nations ancestry who attended Hampton Normal Institute in Elizabeth City County, Virginia, 1900: Abrams, Archiquette, Bailey, Cornelius, Doctor, Doxtator, Elm, George, Ground, Johnson, Jones, Jordon, Metoxin, Patterson, Pemberton, Peters, Poodry, Printup, Seneca, Silverheels, Skenandore, Quinney, Webster, Wheelock and Williams. Source: The 1900 United States Census.

Surnames found among the Indian students of Six Nations ancestry who attended Carlisle Institute, in Carlisle, Pennsylvania, 1900: Archiquette, Armstrong, Baird, Bigtree, Billings, Billy, Bishop, Blackchief, Bowen, Bruce, Brushel, Charles, Christjohn, Chubb, Clute, Coates, Conners, Cook, Cornelius, Cusick, Dennis, Denny, Doxtator, Elm, Gansworth, Garlow, George, Good, Gordon, Green, Halftown, Hammer, Hare, Harris, Henry, Herring, Hill, Homer, Honiyost, Island, Jackson, Jacobs, Jamison, Jimison, Joe, John, Johnny-John, Johnson, Jonas, Jones, Jordon, Kenjockety, Kennedy, Killbuck, King, La France, Laughing, Lay, Lee, Lewey? Lewis, Loren, Maybee, Miller, Mitten, Mohawk, Moore? Morris, Moses, Mr. Pleasant, Nephew, Niles, Palmer, Parker, Patterson, Peters, Pierce, Powlas, Printup, Rickard, Schenandore, Scott, Schuyler, Scrogg, Seneca, Shanks, Sickles, Silverheels, Skye, Smith, Snyder, Spring, Sylvester, Tallchief,

Tarbell, Taylor, Terance, Thomas, Thompson, Turkey, Washburne, Waterman, Webster, Welch, Wheeler, Wheelock, White, Williams and Woodman. Source: The 1900 United States Census.

Surnames found among the Indian students of Six Nations ancestry attending Haskell Institute in Douglas County, Kansas, 1900: Archiquette, Bearskin, Butler, Doxtator, Evans, Hill, Hunt, Huron, Jones, Shiffenour, Skenandoah, Smith, Spitlog, Swamp and Webster. Source: The 1900 United States Census.

Surnames found among the Indian students of Oneida and Stockbridge/Brotherton ancestry who attended the United States Indian School in the village of Wittenberg, Shawano County, Wisconsin, 1900: Antone, Baird, Bothan, Butler, Chrisjohn, Cornelius, Coulon, Danforth, Denny, Doxtater, Henderson, Hill, House, Huff, John, Kick, Martin, Metoxen, Paulus? or Powless? Powless, Roulet, Roulette, Smith, Stevens, Webster and Welch. Source: The 1900 United States Census.

Surnames found among Indians of Six Nations ancestry who temporarily resided in Bucks County, Pennsylvania, 1900: Beaupary? Billy, Cornelius, Doxtator, Garlow, George, Good, Green, Harris, Hare, Herring, Hill, Jamieson, John, Johnson, Kennedy, La France, Lay, Lee, Miller, Pierce, Scanandoah, Scott, Scrogg, Silverheels, Sky, Smith, Tarbell, Taylor, Thomas, Walker, Webster, Williams and Woodman. Source: The 1900 United States Census.

Surnames found among the Cayuga, Seneca and Wyandotte (Huron) who resided on the Seneca/Cayuga Reserve in Northeastern Indian Territory (Oklahoma) 1900. The Wyandottes or Hurons originally migrated from Canada to Ohio and then to Kansas before settling in Indian Territory. Allen, Armstrong, Basset, Boofing? Captain, Carihoo, Cayuga, Charles, Hubard, Jamison, Janes? Jneau, Johnson, Kingfisher, Lewis, Logan, Mingo, Nichols, Schripoter, Smith, Spicer, Splitlog, Standbone, Tsour, Turkey? or Tinkey? Whitecrow, Whitetree, Winnie and Young. Source: The 1900 United States Federal Census.

Surnames among the Oneida in Wisconsin in 1900: Aaron, Abrams, Adams, Anthony, Anton, Antone, Archiquett, Archquitte, Aron, Baird, Beechtree, Beaulieu, Beecher, Benet, Bennette, Bowman, Bread, Butler, Button, Charles, Cheats, Christ-John, Church, Clench, Coolong, Cooper, Cornelius, Coulon, Coy? Cusick, Danforth, Davids, Davidson, Denny, Dick, Docstator, Doxtator, Elm, Frost, Fowler, Gardner, Gardiner, George, Green, Haas, Hammer, Hart, Hayes, Henricks, Hill, House, Howe, Huff, Huntingdon, Jacobs, John, Johns, Johnson, Jones, Jordon, Jourdon, Kanandy, Kelly, Kennedy, Kick, King, Konkapot, La Framboise, Laws, Le Roy, Ludowick, Mc Allister, Mohawk, Malone, Miller, Minor, Moon, Morgan, Nynham, Palmer, Parker, Parkhurst, Patterson, Peters, Powels? Powless, Pyawano, Pye, Reed, Reid, Rhodes, Robinson, Rowlette, Schmidt, Sears, Sheriff, Sickles, Silas, Skanendore, Skeene? Skenandore, Scanadoah, Smith, Sprague, Somers, Stafford, Stephens, Stevens, Summers, Swamp, Thomas, Tousey, Turkey, Quiney, Webster, Welch, Wheelock, White, Wilber, Williams, Wilson, Woodman and Yocum. Sources: The 1886 Bureau of Indian Affairs Census. The 1900 United States Federal Census. The Oneida Reserve is in Oneida, Wisconson. Some Oneida in Wisconsin have inter-married with Stockbridge/Brothertons, Menominee and Winnebago. The

Stockbridge/Brotherton Indians originally came from areas in New England by way of New York. The Stockbridge-Munsee Tribal Council is located in Bowler, Wisconsin.

Surnames among the Indians of the Oneidao among the United States Civil War 1890 Census of Soldiers and Widows in Wisconsin: Antone, Archiquette, Baird, Bread, Chrisjohn, Colon, Danforth, Doxtator, Hill, House, King, Metoxin, Ninham, Parker, Peters, Powless, Schuyler, Silas, Shenandoah, Smith, Stevens, Swamp, Thompson, Webster, Wheelock, Woodman and Williams.

Surnames among the Indians of the Six Nations Reserve who resided in Brant County, Ontario, Canada in 1851 and 1881: Aco, Adams, Agetonce, Alvis, Anderson, Anthony, Aron, Babcock, Batist or Baptist, Battese, Beachtree, Bearfoot, Beaver, Bennett, Bill? Blacknose, Bluejay, Bombary or Bompary, Bomberry, Bomby, Booty, Brant, Brestin? Brown, Buck, Bull, Burnham, Burke, Burning, Butlor, Buzzar, Camp, Canada, Cannon, Carpenter, Carrie, Carrier, Case, Charles, Clause, Clinch, Canada, Captain, Cero, Chubb, Ckeek? or Cheek? Ciskum, Coffee, Cook, Copeland, Cornelius, Crain, Crawford, Cristeen, Culp, Curley, Cusic, Dangerfield, David, Davis, Delaware, Denny, Dickson, Dixon, Dee, Doctor, Dodge, Douglas, Doxtator, Dredge, Duncan, Elliot, English, Everett, Farmer, Fielden, Finger, Fish, Fishcarryer, Forsyth, Foster, Fowler, Froman, Fraser, Frasier, Funn, Garlough, Garlow, General, George, Gevens, Gibson, Goose, Green, Groat, Halfaday, Harris, Henhawk, Henry, Herkimer, Heren, Herrin, Hess, Hill, Hobkins, Hottenburg, Hope, House, Husk, Isaac, Jack, Jackson, Jacob, Jamieson, Jemison, John, Johnathan, Johnson, Jones, Jordon, Joseph, Key, Kerr, Keshego, Kick, King, La Form, Lewis, Lickers, Lock, Loft, Longboat or Longbord, Longfish, Lothridge, Maple-Sugar, Maracle, Mericle, Martin, Matock, Mc Collum, Mc Donald, Mc Dougal, Mc Gee? Mike, Miller, Mitten, Monture, Moses, Moray, Murdock, Noah, Nash, Nendikook, Newhouse, Niles or Nelles, Notten, Oats, Obe, Obediah, Olds, Otter, Owen, Patterson, Peter, Philip, Powles, Rachett, Rancier, Rankin, Rap? or Raft? Roundsky, Russell, Ryan, Sage, Sampson, Sawat, Sawyer, Secord, Seneca, Schuyler, Scott, Scunady, Seneca, Sero, Shaw, Sherry, Sky, Silver, Silversmith, Simon, Sit-Down, Six-Does, Skiler, Smith, Snake, Snow, Spencer, Springs, Sterling, Stoats, Stump, Sugar, Summerfield, Thomas, Thompson, Tobeco, Tobico, Tom, Towah, Turkey, Twofish, Van Every? or Venery? Walker, Wampun, Washington, Webster, Wesley, Whitby, White, Whitecoat, Wickley, Williams, Wilson, Wing, Winn, Wood, Woodruff, Wright, Yellow and Young. Source: The 1851 and 1881 Canadian Census. Surnames among the Indians of the Six Nations who resided in Haldimand County, Ontario, Canada in 1851 and 1881: Abraham, Alvis, Anthony, Bill, Baron, Barnes, Beaver, Bill, Bull, Burnam, Cayuga, Chebock, Cook, Conston? Cornelius, Crawford, Curley, Davie, Dixon, Doxtator, Dockstader, Drake, Everyday, Fish, Fishcarrick? or Fishcarrier, Garlow, Groat, Hardy, Haris, Herkimer, Hess, Highflyer, Hill, Hoag, Horn, Huff, Jacob, Jackson, Jamison, John, Johnson, Key, Kick, Latham, Lock, Longsboat? Martin, Muartson? Noab or Noah, Montore, Moses, Peters, Ritcherd? Russell, Salt, Sandy, Sawyer, Scott, Seittis, Silversmith, Simon, Sixpence, Smith, Smoke, Snake, Stere, Styers, Thomas, Van Every, Warner, Wampun and Williams, Source: The 1851 and 1881 Canadian Census.

Surnames among the Indians of the Six Nations (Mohawks) who resided in Hastings County, Ontario, Canada in 1881: Bardy, Barnhart, Battece, Brant, Brown, Buck, Burdy, Cero, Chaundeau, Clause, Cosby? of Cosly, Crawford, Culbertson, Frizzone, Funn, Green, Hill, Hollowday, Jack, Jacob, John, Johnson, Kerby, King, Lewis, Loft, Lorien or Dorin, Louis, Maracle, Martin, Mericle, Mitchell, Penn, Picard, Pierce, Powles, Thompson, Reid, Smith, Smart, Snider, Thompson and Williams. Source: The 1881 Canadian Census.

Surnames among the Indians of the Moravian Delaware (Including some Munsee) who resided in Kent County, Ontario, Canada in 1881: Anthony, Clingersmith, Cornelius, Fish, Henricks, Hill, Hopkins, Jacobs, Lacell, Lastnight, Lewis, Logan, Mac Donald, Noah, Peters, Pheasant, Snake, Stonefish, Timothy, Tobias, Tomice, Wampun and Whiteye. Source: The 1881 Canadian Census.

Surnames among the Indians of the Six Nations who resided in Middlesex County, Ontario, Canada in 1881: Abraham, Ahnyot, Alway, Anderson, Antone, Armstrong? Askin, Athill? Autinger? Beeswax, Beaver, Bear, Beeswax, Bench, Birch, Bird, Bob, Braid, Brant, Brigham, Brown, Bunn? Buckwheat, Caleb, Carey, Case, Casey, Charles, Cheehook, Chicken, Chrisjohn, Cloud, Cooper, Cornelius, Craig, Cucutt, David, Davis, Delary, Delaware, Dixon, Dolson, Douglas? Doxtator, Danford? or Dunford? Egg, Elm, Farmer, Finger, Fisher, Fox, Franklin, French, Frenchman, George, Grausebeck, Green, Groat, Halfaday, Halfmoon, Hall, Hank, Hawk, Henrick, Henry, Hess, Herkimer, Hill, Hoin, Homer, Hophins? Huff, Isaac, Ireland, Jack, Jackson, Jacobs, James, Jim, John, Johnson, Jones, Kennedy, Kewa, Kick, King, Kushig, Leaves, Lewis, Logan, Luck, Maddin, Madison, Manass, Mac Donald, Moses, Mudhead, Nail, Nicalas, Nicholas, Ninham, Noah, Oneida, Peters, Pollock, Powles, Powlis, Racoon, Riley, Roddy, Rogers, Secord, Seneca, Scanado, Shank, Sickles, Skinido, Silver, Simon, Skanado, Skyler, Smith, Snake, Sunday, Taylor, Thomas, Thompson, Timothy, Tom, Tomico, Turkey, Turner, Waddinglow, Waldron, Webster? Wesly, White, Whiteloon, Whitney, Wiick, Wilcox, Williams, Wilson, Woolfe and Young. Source: The 1851 and 1881 Canadian Census. The Indians who reside in Middlesex County, Ontario included Oneida, Delaware and Munsee.

Surnames among the Indians of the Six Nations (Mohawks) who resided in La Prarie County, Quebec, Canada in 1881: Asennase, Barnes, Beauvais, Bruce, Canadien, Capitaine, Charles, Curotte, Dailleboat, De Lorimer, Deliles, Diome, Dominique, Fraser, Jacko, Jacob, Jaques, Jeandron, Johnson, Lahache La Ronde, La Ronte, La Tour, Le Claire, Le Febre, Le Flore, Maillou, Maris, Mc Comb, Mc Comber, Michel, Monette, Monique, Montour, Moons, Murray, Rayment, Rice, Roland, Stacey, Stump, Thomas, Viau, Vigneau, Vincent, Williams and Wingo. Source: The 1881 Canadian Census.

Surnames among the Indians of the Six Nations (Mohawks) who resided in Huntingdon or Huntington County, Quebec in 1881: Adams, Allick, Broken-Leg, Buchshott, Charron? Cook, Curley, Daye, Foote, Fox, Friday, Garrow, George, Isaac, Jack, Jacob, John, Joseph, La France, Loran, Lozoire, Marcoux, Mc Donald, Mitchell, Oake, Papineau, Paul, Philips, Pique, Ranaro, Sawatas, Sawyer, Sheepe, Skin, Skine, Smoke, Solomon, Stogna, Street, Sucksilia, Sugar-Bush, Thompson, Wood and Woodman. Source: The 1881 Canadian Census.

FRINGE GROUPS

Some Native American groups are not recognized by the federal government but their existence is known at the state and county level. As white men steadily moved westward the Indians that remained became isolated. They banded together in sparsely populated areas. The types of records that may provide local Indian information on the county level include: 1. A County History 2. Local Land Records. 2. Church Records. 3. Old Newspapers 4. Old School Records. 5. Local Public Library. 6. Local College and University Libaries. 7. Local Historical and Genealogy Societies. To find out if a county history has been published for the county where your ancestor resided consult: "A Bibliography of American County History," compiled by P. William Filby, Genealogical Publishing Company, Inc., Baltimore, Maryland, 1987. Certain fringe groups in New Jersey regard themselves as remnants of the Tuscarora. Another group lived in the northeast corner of Pennsylvania near Tonawanda. Source: "Handbook of North American Indians," Northeast, by William C. Sturtevant, Smithsonian Institution, Washington 1978 and 1988, "Marginal Groups," by Brewton Berry, pages 291-293, volume XV (15) and volume lV (4), "The Pool Tribe."

BIOGRAPHICAL REFERENCES

ABEEL/O'BALE/CORNPLANTER FAMILY: John Abeel a white trader and a Seneca woman were the parents of Cornplanter. Sources: "The Story of Old Fort Johnson," by W. Reid, G. P. Putnam & Sons, New York and London, The Knickerbocker Press, Copyright 1906, page 175. A Henry O'Bale a son of Cornplanter graduated from Dartmouth College. "History of Livingston County," New York, by Lockwood Richard Doty, Chapter V, page 108. The original was published in 1876, 685 pages.

ADAMS FAMILY: Daniel Adams was a Mohawk Indian Methodist missionary to the Oneida. His wife Electa Quinney Adams was a Stockbridge Indian. They moved west where Daniel died and she later she married John Walker Candy a Cherokee Indian. Sources: "Stockbridge Past and Present," by Miss Electa F. Jones (A History of Stockbridge, Massachusetts), published by Springfield, Samuel Bowles and Company, 1854, pages 118, 119. "The History of the Cherokee Indians," by Emmet Starr, Hoffman Press, Hoffman Printing Company, 1984, Oklahoma, page 350.

ALLEN, EBENEZER/OR INDIAN ALLEN: Ebenezer Allen was an early settler in Livingston County, New York. Later he became a trader in Ontario, Canada. He had several Indian children. Sources: "History of Livingston County," New York, by Lockwood Richard Doty, page 69. "The Lyman Copeland Draper Manuscripts," Series U/193/194, Wisconsin Historical Society.

ANTHONY FAMILY: The surname Anthony is found among the Delaware. Sources: "Wilderness Christians," The Moravian Mission to the Delaware Indians, Toronto, Canada, Macmillan Company, Copyright 1956, page 320. "History of the Mission of the United Brethren Among the Indians in North American," London 1794, Pt. 1, pages 125, 126.

BENNETT FAMILY: Lewis (Deerfoot) Bennet a Seneca whose father was a white captive died at the Cattaraugus Reservation in New York. Source: The Comorah Mission Records (Pedigree Chart) of the Mormon Church.

BIG-TREE FAMILY: Big-Tree fought in the Revolutionary War. Source: "History of Livingston County," New York, by Lockwood Richard Doty, 1876, pages 112-115.

BLACKSNAKE OR HANDSOME LAKE: Blacksnake or Handsome Lake was mentioned as a half brother of Cornplanter. Sources: "History of Livingston County," New York, by Lockwood Richard Doty, Chapter III, pages 57, 58, published in 1876. "The Iroquois in the American Revolution," by Barbara Graymont, Syracuse University Press, Copyright 1972.

BLUE-SKY FAMILY: Blue Sky was mentioned in "The Life & Times of Sa-Go-Ye-Wat-Ha or Red Jacket," by William L. Stone, Albany, New York, J. Munsell, publisher, 1866, page 391.

BREAD: A portrait of "Bread," the Oneida Chief painted by George Catlin is shown in "Letters and Notes on the Manners, Customs, and Conditions of the North American Indians," (1832-1839) by George Catlin, Volume II, Dover Publications, Inc., New York, plate No. 201, page 103.

BREWER, FAMILY: A James Brewer a native is mentioned in "History of Livingston County, New York," by Lockwood Richard Doty, 1876, page 126.

COOK, JOHN: John Cook a Seneca Chief supposedly married a descendent of Madam Montour. Source: "The Story of Old Fort Johnson," by W. Max Reid, published by G. P. Putnam & Sons, New York and London, the Knickerbocker Press, Copyright 1906, page 110.

COOK, LOUIS: Louis Cook a St. Regis Mohawk served on the American side during the Revolutionary War. Supposedly he was born about 1740 and was of African and Indian descent. Sources: "Historical and Statistical, Gazetteer of New York States," 1860, J. H. French, Franklin County, New York, pages 307-313. "Genealogical Index to Historical Sketches of Franklin County (New York)," by Frederick J. Seaver, pages 580, 581, 582.

COOPER FAMILY: The Cooper family surname is found among the Oneida of New York and Canada. Source: "National Geographic Magazine," September 1987 issue, Volume 172, No. 3, page 393.

CORNPLANTER, Cornplanter was a leading Chief in the Mohawk Valley in 1780's. He was the son of a white trader named John Abeel (sometimes called O'Bail) and a Seneca woman. After the Revolution, he moved to the Allegheny River area along the New York-Pennsylvania border. Sources: "The Story of Old Fort Johnson," by W. Max Reid, Published by Putnam & Sons, New York and London, The Knickerbocker Press, copyright 1906, page 111. "Cornplanter, Can You Swim?" article by Alvin M. Josephy, Jr., "American Heritage Magazine," December 1968 issue, Volume XX, Number 1, under Berne and Pan-American Copyright Conventions, 1968, page 4. "The Seneca People," by George J. J. Abrams, published by Indian Tribal Series, Phoenix, Arizona, copyright 1976, page 61. "Sesqui-Centennial Celebration of Huntingdon County, Pennsylvania," by the Huntingdon County, Historical Society 1787-1937, article entitled "Last Days of Cornplanter," pages 470-472.

CUSICK, JOSEPH: Joseph Cusick a Tuscarora served for the state of New York in the War of 1812. His widow received what may have been the only pension granted to an Indian for services in the War of 1812. Sources: "Chicago Times Newspapers," 1888, article entitled: "A Brave Indian's Service," "Lyman Copeland Draper Manuscripts," Series U, Volume 11 & Xll, Wisconsin Historical Society. "Letters and Notes on the Manners, Customs, and Conditions of the North American Indians," (1832-1839) by George Catlin, Volume II, Dover Publications, Inc., New York, New York, 1973, plate 202, page 103-104, shows a portrait of Cu-sick, son of Cu-sick of the same name, a Tuscarora Chief and Baptist minister.

CUSICK, LIEUTENANT NICHOLAS: Nicholas Cusick a Tuscarora served during the American Revolution as body guard for General La Fayette. Sources: "Lyman Copeland Draper Manuscripts," Wisconsin Historical Society, "Indians in Pennsylvania," by Paul A. W. Wallace, page 160, published by Pennsylvania Historical and Museum Commission, "Stockbridge Past and Present," by Miss Electa F. Jones, Springfield, Samuel Bowles and Company, 1854, page 98.

DE LORIMIER/DELORIMER FAMILY: George De Lorimer was a Mohawk Chief at Caughnawaga in the 1830's. Source: "The History of the County of Huntingdon or Huntington and the Seigniories of Chateaugay and Beauharnois," Huntingdon, Quebec, The Canadian Gleaner, 1888, Chapter XVIII, page 513.

DENNY/ SUNDOWN FAMILY: A Dr. John Denny or Sundown was mentioned in: "History of Madison County, State of New York," by Mrs. L. M. Hammond Truair, Smith & Company, 1872. page 117. The Denny family is said to have descended from a French captive. Source: "Lyman Copeland Draper Manuscripts," Series U, Volume 11-12, Wisconsin Historical Society.

DESERONTYON FAMILY: A John Desrontyon a Mohawk fought in the Revolutionary War. Source: "The Iroquois in the American Revolution," by Barbara Graymont, Syracuse University Press, Copyright 1972, page 92.

DOLSON FAMILY: The surname Dolson can be found among the Delaware. Sources: "Wilderness Christians," The Moravian Mission to the Delaware Indians, by Elma E. Gray, Toronto, Canada, Macmillan Company, 1956, page 320. "The Delaware Indians," A History: by C. A., Weslager, Rutgers University Press, New Brunswick, New Jersey, Copyright 1909, pages 22-24, 320, 352.

DOXTATOR/DOCKSTEDER FAMILY: The Doxtator family is mentioned in the following sources: "Lyman Copeland Draper Manuscripts," Series U, Volume 11-12, Wisconsin Historical Society. At the Battle of Fort Stanwyck (Revolutionary War) Oneidas from the Oriska settlement, was commanded by Thawengarakwen, or Honyeny Doxtator. "The Green Bay Associates," newspaper article entitled: "A Notable Death," December 21, 1882. "The Kings Rangers," by John Brick, published by Doubleday & Company, Inc., Copyright 1954, page 49.

FISH-CARRIER FAMILY: Fish Carrier a famous Cayuga fought in the Revolutionary War. Source: "The Iroquois in the American Revolution," by Barbara Graymont, Syracuse, University Press, Copyright 1972, page 225.

FOWLER, DAVID: David Fowler was a Montauk Indian missionary who worked with the Oneida of New York and removed with them to Wisconsin. Source: "The Oneida People," by Cara E. Richards, published by: Indian Tribal Series, Phoenix, Arizona, 1974, pages 42.

GRAY, JOHN: A John Gray was an Iroquois scout in the 1840's. He guided wagon trains to California. Souce: "The Scouts," Time Life Books, published in Alexandria, Virginia, pages 52--54, article by Keith Wheeler.

GRAY, WILLIAM: William Gray was a Revolutionary soldier from New York. He later lived with the Indians at St. Regis. Source: "Historical Sketches of Franklin County," by Frederick J. Seaver, and its Several Towns, published by J. B. Lyon Company, Albany, 1918, pages 311-312.

GREEN, THOMAS: A Thomas Green was a white man who acted as an interpreter at the Eastern Conference held January 27, 1777. He had a Mohawk wife. Source: "The Indian Chiefs of Pennsylvania," by C. Hale

Sipe, Arno Press & The New York Times reprinted edition 1971, from a copy in the Pennsylvania State Library, originally printed by the Ziegler Company, Incorporated, Butler, Pennsylvania, Copyright 1921, page 476.

HALF-KING: Half-King an Oneida Chief aided George Washington in 1754. Source: "The Indian Chiefs of Pennsylvania," by C. Hale Sipe, Arno Press & the New York Times reprint edition 1971, from a copy in the Pennsylvania State Library, originally printed by the Ziegler Company Incorporated, Butler, Pennsylvania, copyright 1927, pages 200-202, 528, article entitled: "Tanacharison (Half-King) Helps Washington Fight first Battle of His Career."

HALF-TOWN, Halftown fought in the American Revolution. Sources: "History of Livingston County, New York," By Lockwood Richard Doty, 1876, page 120. "The Iroquois in the American Revolution," By Barbara Graymont, Syracuse University Press, Copyright 1972, "American Heritage Magazine," article entitled: "Cornplanter Can You Swim?" by Alvin M. Josephy, Jr., December 1968, pages 8-9.

HENRY/KILLBUCK FAMILY: The surname Henry can be found among the Delaware. The name may have come from a famous Delaware known as Gelemend or Killbuck who was baptized with the surname of Henry. Source: "Dictionary of the American Indian," by John Stoutenburgh Jr., Reprint 1960, published by Philosophical Library, Inc., page 121.

HERKIMER FAMILY: William Herkimer a native toured northern Michigan for the Methodist Church in 1832. Source: "The First Century of Methodism in Canada, Volume I, Chapter 21, pages 286, 1775-1839, by J. E. Sanderson, M.A., published by William Briggs, Toronto, 1908.

HILL/BRANT FAMILY: A daughter of Mohawk Chief Joseph Brant was said to have married a Hill who was a Mohawk. Sources: "Lyman Copeland Draper Manuscripts, Volume 13/32/13/33, Volume 13/29, 13/38, Volume 14/F/62/63/63/1/63/2, 14/S/52. "The Loyalists In Ontario," The Sons and Daughters of the American Loyalists of Upper Canada, by William D. Reed, Hunterdon House, Lambertville, New Jersey, Copyright 1973.

JACOBS FAMILY: The Jacob family name is found among the Delaware. Sources: "The Moravian Mission to the Delaware Indians," by Elma E. Gray, Toronto, Canada, pages 406, 407, 422, 423.. "Wilderness Empire," A Narrative, by Allan W. Eckert, published 1969, Little, Brown and Company, Boston, Toronto, Canada, Macmillan, Publishing Co, "Journals of Major Robert Rogers," London Printed MDCCLXV, The account of the French and Indian War, published in London in 1765, pages 31, 109.

JEMIISON, MARY: Mary Jemison was a white captive. She was captured about 1758. She married first a Delaware named Sheninjee. After the death of her first husband she married a Seneca named Kiokatoo or Gardow. Sources: "The Indian Chiefs of Pennsylvania," by C. Hale Sipe, Arno Press & The New York Times, reprint edition 1971 from a copy in the Pennsylvania State Library, originally published by the Ziegler Company Incorporated, Butler, Pennsylvania, Copyright 1927, article entitled: "Mary Jemison, White Woman of Genesee," pages 357-358. "Mary Jemison 1743-1833," The Life of Mary Jemison, The White Woman of Genesee," New York, by James Everett Seaver, the American Scenic and

Historic Preservation Society, New York, 1942, 459 pages (Includes maps). Newspaper article "The Milwaukee Sentinel, "An Indian Pilgrimage," dated March 20th & April 2nd issue 1874. "Comorah Mission Records," Church of Jesus Christ of Latter-day Saints, available on interlibrary loan through the Family History Library Centers on film number 0924575 item 1. This film contains pedigree charts for the family of Mary Jemison.

JEMISON, THOMAS: Thomas Jemison a son of Mary Jemison was mentioned in the "Loyalist Lineages of Canada 1783-1983," Toronto Branch, The United Empire Loyalists Association of Canada, published by Generation Press, Toronto Branch, Ontario, Canada, copyright 1981, page 343.

JOHN/DESERONTYON FAMILY: Catherine Brant a daughter of Chief Joseph Brant married a Mr. John or Deserontyon. Sources: "Lyman Copeland Draper Manuscripts," Volume 12/38, Volume 13/38, Volume 14/S/53, Volume 15/F/14/14/1/14/2/14/3, Wisconsin Historical Society. "The Loyalists In Ontario," The Sons and Daughters of the American Loyalists of Upper Canada," by William D. Reed, Hunterdon House, Lambertville, New Jersey, Copyright 1973.

JOHNSON, HENRY (CATTARAUGUS HANK): Henry Johnson was a white man who was made a prisoner as a child. Source: "The Life & Times of Sa-Go-Ye-Wat-Ha or Red Jacket," by William L. Stone, Albany, New York, Munsell publishing, 1866, page 334.

JONES, FAMILY: Augustus Jones a white man had a two Indian wives. One wife was a Chippewa (Ojibway) the other a Mohawk. His daughter Mary or Polly his daughter Jacob Brant a son of Mohawk Chief Joseph Brant. A son Peter Jones was a Methodist missionary among the Indians in Ontario. He traveled to England and was presented to the King and Queen. He became a Deacon of the Methodist Church. His brother John also worked at Methodist Missions in Ontario. Sources: "Lyman Copeland Draper Manuscripts," Volume 13/14/14/1/14/2/14/3, Wisconsin Historical Society. "The First Century of Methodism in Canada," Volume I, 1775-1839, by J. E. Sanderson, M. A. Copyright in Canada, 1908, by William Briggs, Chapter Vl, page 131, Chapter II, page 154, page 169, Chapter 18, page 239. This book contains a portrait of Peter Jones.

KENJOCKETY FAMILY: the Kenjockety family is said to have been the last of and almost extinct tribe. Source: "History of Livingston County, New York," by Lockwood Richard Doty, Chapter IV, pages 91, 92 & Chapter VII, page 187, includes interview with Philip Kenjockety in 1865, published in 1876.

LA FORT, CAPTAIN: Captain La Fort was a chief among the Onondaga. Source: "The Life & Times of Red Jacket," by William L. Stone, Albany, New York, J. Munsell publisher 1866, page 344.

LE CLAIR, FAMILY: Isaac Le Clair was an Indian agent for the St. Regis in 1820. Sources: "The History of the County of Huntingdon (Or Huntington) and the Seigniories of Chateaugay," by Robert Seller. "Genealogical Index," to Historical Sketches of Franklin County, by Frederick J. Seaver, New York State, "Index to Seaver's History of Franklin County," by C. Walter Smallman, Franklin County, Historian, Fort Covington, New York.

LOGAN FAMILY: The name Logan can be found among the Shawnee and Delaware. A Captain James Logan a Shawnee, came from Piqua (Ohio) to Fort Wayne (Indiana) to escort women & children safely to Piqua during the siege of Fort Wayne in the War of 1812. Sources: "Indiana Historical Collections Volume XV." Fort Wayne Gateway of the West 1802-1813, page 54. "Indians in Pennsylvania," by Paul A. W. Wallace, Pennsylvania, Historical and Museum Commission, 1989, page 177.

MOHAWK/DESERONTO, FAMILY: Deseronto or Odiserundy often called John Mohawk was a Mohawk Chief during the Revolutionary War. Source: "Dictionary of the American Indians," by John Stoutenburgh, Jr., copyright 1960, published by Philosophical Library Inc., page 293.

MONTURE FAMILY: The Montour Family name can be found among the Delaware and Mohawk. A Andrew Montour represented the Six Nations in the 1750's Source: "The British Colonial Office Records," Class 5, Part I, 1700-1783, London, England. "Indians in Pennsylvania," by Paul A. W. Wallace, Pennsylvania Historical and Museum Commission, 1989, pages 174, 175, 178. Margaret Monture who lived at the time of the American Revolution was mentioned as a half Seneca in the following source: "Wilderness Messiah," The Story of Hiawatha and the Iroquois, by Thomas R. Henry, Bonanza Press, copyright MCMLV, pages 233-234. A Roland Monture was an Indian Captain on the British side. Source: "The Iroquois in the American Revolution, by Barbara Graymont, Syracuse University Press, copyright 1972, page 204. A John Monture and part of his family lived at Big-Tree village in New York. Source: "History of Livingston County New York," by Lockwood L. Doty, Chapter III, page 61, Chapter IV page 86.: "The King's Rangers," by John Brick, published by Doubleday and Company, Inc., copyright 1854, page 46. A Captain Montour's Company of Delaware Indians served for the United States during the American Revolution. Source: National Archives film number M-881-Roll 146, Service Card 391226999. His service commenced on the 15th of June 1780 & ended on the 31st of October 1781.

Mt. PLEASANT, FAMILY: The Mt. Pleasants were Tuscarora's supposedly descended from a British Officer by that name. Sources: "The Chicago Times Newspapers," article entitled "The Tuscaroras," dated August 13th 1885, "Lyman Copeland Draper Manuscripts," Volume 15/F/35, Wisconsin Historical Society.

PARKER, BERTHA (YEWAS): Bertha (Yewas) Parker Cody was the daughter of Seneca Indian Anthropologist Dr. Arthur C. Parker of New York. She was affiliated with the southwest Museum of Los Angeles and did archeological and ethnological research. She married Indian actor "Iron Eyes Cody," who was of Cherokee Indian descent. Sources: "How to Indian Sign Talk In Pictures," by Iron Eyes Cody, published by Homer H. Boelter, Hollywood, California, copyright 1952. "Indians of Today," published by the Indian Council Fire, Chicago, 1947. "Secret Medicine Societies of the Seneca," by A. C. Parker, 1909, reprinted in New York State Museum, Museum Bulletin 163, Albany, 1913, page 129. "Seneca Myths and Folk Tales," by Arthur C. Parker 1923, Buffalo Historical Society, Buffalo, New York.

PARKER, ELI S: (1828-1895) Eli S. Parker was a grandson of Chief Red Jacket. He served under General Grant during the Civil War. Eli S. Parker penned the surrender that was signed by General Robert E. Lee.

After the war he was appointed "Commissioner of Indian Affairs," by President Grant. Sources: "Bury My Heart at Wounded Knee," by Dee Brown, copyright 1970, published in Canada, by Holt, Rinehart and Wiston Limited, pages 175-190, "After Columbus," The Smithsonian Chronicle of the North American Indians," by Viola, Herman J. Crown publishers, 1990, page 152. "The Six Nations Indians," In Canada, by J. B. Mackenzie, Toronto, the Hunter Rose Company, 1896, page 45. "Handbook of North American Indians," by William C. Sturtevant, Smithsonian Institution, Washington, 1978, page 8.

PATTERSON/BLACKSNAKE FAMILY: A John Patterson born about 1820 was descended from Governor Blacksnake. Source "The Comorah Mission Records," (Pedigree Chart) Church of Jesus Christ of Latter-day Saints Family History Library Center on film number 924575.

PIERCE FAMILY: A member of the Pierce family is mentioned as a descendant of Cornplanter in "American Heritages," Magazine's & Books, December 1968 issue, Volume XX, Number 1, reserved under Berne and Pan-American Copyright Conventions, 1968 article entitled: "Cornplanter, Can You Swim," by Alvin M. Josephy, Jr., page 6.

POLLARD, CAPTAIN: Captain Pollard was the son of an English trader and a Seneca woman. A Edward Pollard was a post commissary at Fort Niagara who lived among the Senecas and Cayugas. Sources: "History of Livingston County, New York," by Lockwood Richard Doty, page 118. "The King's Ranger's," by John Brick, published by Doubleday & Company, Inc., copyright 1854, page 116.

RED-JACKET: Red Jacket was a famous Seneca Chief who died about 1832. Sources: "History of Livingston County, New York," by Lockwood Richard Doty, Chapter V, page 106. "Red Jacket-Last of the Seneca," by Arthur Caswell Parker 1881-1955, Washington D. C., Library of Congress 197? originally published in New York, by Mc Graw-Hill, 228 pages.

SILVERHEELS FAMILY: The name Silverheels can be found among the Six Nations Indians and Shawnee. Rachel Barnes Silverheels was born in January 1855 in Texas. Her father was born in Pennsylvania. Her mother was born in Ohio. She was listed as a white woman. Her son George Silverheels was born in October 1879 in Indian Territory (Oklahoma) in October 1879. He was listed as a Shawnee. His father was a Shawnee who was born in Kansas. "The 1900 Federal Census of the Cherokee Nation, Indian Territory, page 40, E.D., 5, Household 88. Moses Silverheels was enumerated as a Shawnee admitted to Cherokee Citizenship in Indian Territory in 1869, Roll Numbers 611-618. Federal Archives and Records Center, Fort Worth, Texas, 7RA-74, RG-75, Bureau of Indian Affairs, Muskogie area office. In the spring of 1774 while crossing Big Beaver (on the way to Pittsburgh) a Shawanese, named Silverheels a man of note in his nation was wounded. "Thomas Jefferson-Notes on the State of Virginia," by Thomas Perkins Abernethy, published by Harper Torchbooks, Harper & Row publishers, New York, 1964, originally published 1961, page 222. A pedigree chart for the family of Robert Silverheels is found in the "Comorah Mission Records," Church of Jesus Christ of Latter-day Saints, Family History Library Centers on film number 924575.

SKENANDOA, SKENANDOAH (SHENANDOAH) BRANT/PETERS FAMILY Skenandoa was a chief of the Oneida who favoured remaining neutral during the Revolutionary War. Sources: "Dictionary of the American Indian," by John Stoutenburgh Jr., Copyright 1921- reprint 1960, by Philosophical Library, Inc., page 387. "Lyman Copeland Draper Manuscripts," Series U, Volume 11-12, Wisconsin Historical Society.

TALL-CHIEF: Tall-Chief who met with George Washington is mentioned in the "History of Livingston County, New York," by Lockwood Richard Doty, Chapter III, page 51, Chapter V, pages 111, 112, published in 1876.

TARBELL FAMILY: The Tarbell brothers were captured in Massachusetts about 1723. They lived with the Mohawks at Caughnawaga and later at the St. Regis Reservation. Sources: "Seaver's History of Franklin County," pages 578, 580, 582. "Historical Sketches of Franklin County, and its Several Towns," published by J. B. Lyon Company, Albany, New York, 1918, page 3? A Sarah-Marguerite of Groton, Massachusetts was captured in 1693 and made a prisoner. Source: "Dictionnarie Genealogique des Familles du Quebec," by Rene Jette, 1983, University of Montreal Press, Montreal, Quebec, Canada.

TIMOTHY FAMILY: The surname Timothy is found among the Delaware. Source: "Wilderness Christians," The Moravian Mission to the Delaware Indians, by Elma Gray, Toronto, Canada, Macmillan Company, Copyright 1956, page 320.

WILLIAMS, ELEAZER: Eleazer Williams was the son of Thomas Williams a chief of the Mohawks of the St. Regis Indians. He was said to be a descendent of Reverend John Williams who was taken prisoner by the Indians at Deerfield, Massachusetts in 1704. Reverend Eleazer Williams was an Indian minister and teacher born at Caughnawaga before 1800. He was at the Oneida Settlement in Wisconsin and later at the St. Regis, New York Reservation. Supposedly he was descended from a Eunice Williams who was captured in the Indian raid at Deerfield, Massachusetts. Her Indian husband took her surname. Eleazer Williams attended school in New England. He fought on the American side during the War of 1812. After the war he was appointed to the northern Indian department. He became involved with the Episcopal Church at Oneida in New York. He later removed with the Oneida to Green Bay, Wisconsin. He remained as a missionary at Green Bay until about 1850. He relocated to the St. Regis Reservation. "Franklin County," And Its Several Towns, by Frederick J. Seaver, Malone, New York, Albany, J.B. Lyon Company, Printers, 1918, Chapter 1, page 4, Chapter XXX pages 583, 677-695. "Historical New Hampshire Index," to Volumes 1-25, 1944-1970, compiled by Virginia L. Close, Librarian, Dartmouth College Library, The New Hampshire Historical Society, article entitled "Eunice Williams," Deerfield, Massachusetts, captive married Indian, VII (2) October 52, 29. "The History of Madison County, New York. "Dictionnarie Genealogique des Familles du Quebec," by Rene Jette, 1983, University of Montreal Press, Montreal, Quebec, Canada, page 1,133.

THE ST. REGIS MOHAWK RESERVATION OF FRANKLIN COUNTY, NEW YORK

The St. Regis Reservation is located in the northernmost part of New York State along the St. Lawrence River. Part of the Reserve extends across the border into Huntington or Huntingdon County, Quebec. The earliest settlement in Franklin County was at St. Regis. This settlement was made up of a colony of Indians an a Jesuit priest from Caughnawaga (Quebec) in 1760. The inter-national boundary was surveyed after the treaty of 1795. It was supposed to run on the 45th degree of North Latitude. A few members of the tribe lived on Cornwall Island. A 1818 survey showed that the former line was to far to the north. By the treaty of 1842, the old line was restored. The St. Regis Mohawk's Mohawks have a matrilineal society. Tribal membership is inherited from mother to son. Most, but not all St. Regis Iroquois were Catholic. Consult the following records: "The Saint-Francois-Regis, Catholic Church Records," Registers Paroissiaux 1762-1876, in English, French, Latin and Indian. (Huntingdon County, Quebec). These church records contain baptisms, marriages and death records. They have been made available in Canada. A microfilm copy is available on inter-library loan through the Church of Jesus Christ Latter-day Saints (Mormon) Family History Library Centers. Franklin County was formed in 1808 from Clinton County, New York. Malone is the county seat of Franklin County. Clinton County was created in 1788 from Washington County, New York. Washington County (Called Charlotte County until 1784) New York was created in 1772 from Albany County, New York. Albany County was created in 1683 as an original county of New York. Montgomery County (Called Tryon until 1784) was taken from Albany County in 1772.

BIBLIOGRAPHY

COX, W.C., "History of Clinton and Franklin Counties, New York," Tucson, Arizona, Copyright 1974.

FEDERAL AND STATE INDIAN RESERVATION HANDBOOK, U.S. Department of Commerce 1971.

FRENCH, J., H., "Historical and Statistical, Gazetteer of New York State," 1960, Franklin County, New York, pages, 307, 313.

HOUGH, FRANKLIN B., "History of the St. Lawrence and Franklin County, New York," Albany, New York, 1855, Little (Publishing?).

O'RIELLY COLLECTION, New York, Historical Society.

SEAVER, FREDERICK J., "Genealogical Index to Historical Sketches of Franklin County," New York, State, "Seaver's History of Franklin County," pages 572, 574, 578, 579, 580, 581, 584, 585.

SELLAR, ROBERT, "The History of the County of Huntingdon or Huntington, (Quebec) and the Seigniories of Chateaugay and Beauharnois 1838." (The Canadian Gleaner 1888). District of Beauharnois, pages 1-4, Sault St. Louis at Caughnawaga pages 6, 48.

THE 1887 BUREAU OF INDIAN AFFAIRS CENSUS OF THE ST. REGIS MOHAWK RESIDING IN THE STATE OF NEW YORK.

Only the names of heads of household were listed in this original B.I.A. Census. The names in this abstract have been alphabetized for this book. The original census was alphabetized by first or given name, then by the surname. This abstract is arranged in alphabetical order by the surname, then the given name. The B. I. A. Roll Number follows the given name. This census abstract should be used only as a reference. It should not take the place of any original government records.

ABRAM, PETER, Roll Number 162. **ARQUET**, ANNA, Roll Number 28. **ARQUET**, JACOB Roll Number 243. **ARQUET**, JOHN, Roll Number 66. **ARQUET**, John Roll Number 76. **ARQUET**, Loran Roll Number 186. **ARQUET**, Mary Roll Number 139. **ARQUET**, Mathew Roll Number 127. **ARQUET**, Mitchel Roll Number 111. **ARQUET**, Peter Roll Number 143. **ARQUET**, Thomas Roll Number 221. **BACK**, Angus, Roll Number 16. **BACK**, John Roll Number 259. **BACK**, Lewey Roll Number 97. **BACK**, Peter Roll Number 149. **BANON**, Lewey Roll Number 108. **BENEDICT**, Mathew Roll Number 125. **BESO? OR BEVO? OR BOVA?** Joseph Roll Number 207. **BEVO? OR BESO?** Lozor, Roll Number 192. **BEVO**, Alexander Roll Number 12. **BEVO**, Charlotte Roll Number 246. **BEVO**, Lewey Roll Number 257. **BEVO**, Thomas Roll Number 223. **BIG-APPLE**, Joseph Roll Number 205. **BIG-APPLE**, Joseph Roll Number 215. **BIGTREE**, Phillip Roll Number 173. **BILLINGS**, Adolfus Roll Number 3. **BILLINGS**, Agat Roll Number 29. **BILLINGS**, Alexander Roll Number 11. **BILLINGS**, Jacob Roll Number 244. **BILLINGS**, James Roll Number 77. **BILLINGS**, John Roll Number 71. **BOOTS**, Frank Roll Number 47. **BOOTS**, Loran Roll Number 191. **BOVA**, Louisa Roll Number 198. **BRUCE**, David Roll Number 42. **BRUCE**, Sarah Roll Number 40. **BRUCE**, Thomas Roll Number 217. **BRUCE**, John Roll Number 253. **CAPTAIN**, Lewey Roll Number 104. **CHICKUCKE?**, Mitchel Roll Number 117. **CHICKUCKE**, Peter Roll Number 148. **CHUBB**, Alexander, Roll Number 5. **CHUBB**, Joseph Roll Number 214. **CHUBB**, Loran Roll Number 189. **CHUBB**, Margaret (Her Children) Roll Number 81. **CHUBB**, Martin Roll Number 128. **CHUBB**, Mitchel Roll Number 116. **CHUBB**, Peter Roll Number 165. **COLE**, Alexander, Roll Number 13. **COLE**, Lewey Roll Number 102. **COLE**, Peter Roll Number 153. **CONNER**, Loran Roll Number 184. **COOK**, Alexander Roll Number 10. **COOK**, Charles Roll Number 31. **COOK**, Charles Roll Number 34. **COOK**, Charles Roll Number 36. **COOK**, Jacob Roll Number 239. **COOK**, John Roll Number 3. **COOK**, John Roll Number 64. **COOK**, John Roll Number 72. **COOK**, Joseph Roll Number 211. **COOK**, Lewey Roll Number 93. **COOK**, Loran Roll Number 182. **COOK**, Mathew Roll Number 126. **COOK**, Mitchel Roll Number 115. **COOK**, Peter Roll Number 159. **COOK**, Thomas Roll Number 226. **ORNSTOCK**, Peter Roll Number 156. **CREE**, Jacob Roll Number 241. **CREE**, Mary Roll Number 133. **CREE**, Peter Roll Number 157. **CREE**, Thomas Roll Number 232. **CROOP**, Terace Roll Number 234. **CROSS**, Catherine Roll Number 78. **CROUND? OR GROUND?** Peter Roll Number 155. **CURLYHEAD**, Charles Roll Number 32. **CURLYHEAD**, Phillip Roll Number 171. **CURLYHEAD**, Thomas Roll Number 231. **DAVID**, Loran Roll Number 175. **DEOME**, Alexander Roll Number 255. **DEOME**, Betsey Roll Number 129. **DEOME**, Lewey Roll Number 98. **DEOME**, Loran Roll Number 179. **DAVID**, Sarah Roll Number 41. **GORROW**, Angus Roll Number 18. **GORROW**, Abram Roll Number 23. **GORROW**, Charles Roll Number 37. **GORROW**, Felix Roll Number 169. **GORROW**, Joseph Roll Number 206. **GORROW**, Joseph Roll Number 210. **GORROW**, Joseph Roll Number 216. **GORROW**, Lewey Roll Number 90. **GORROW**, Loran Roll Number 181. **GORROW**, Mary Roll Number 135. **GORROW**, Mitchel Roll Number 113.

GORROW, Mitchel Roll Number 122. **GORROW**, Peter Roll Number 158. **GORROW**, Peter Roll Number 164. **GRAY**, Caceta Roll Number 80. **GRAY**, Emma Roll Number 45. **GRAY**, Jacob Roll Number 245. **GRAY**, John Roll Number 68. **GRAY**, Joseph Roll Number 258. **GRAY**, Lewey Roll Number 2, **GRAY**, Lewey Roll Number 94, Mitchel Roll Number 124. **GRAY**, Paul Roll Number 142. **GRAY**, Peter Roll Number 152. **GRAY**, Peter Roll Number 152. **GRAY**, Silas Roll Number 237. **GRAY**, Thomas Roll Number 222. **GROUND OR CROUND**, Peter Roll Number 155. **HERRING OR HENNING?**, Abram Roll Number 22. **HERRING** Julius Roll Number 238. **HERRING**, John Roll Number 67. **HERRING**, Lewey Roll Number 103. **HERRING**, Peter Roll Number 144. **HERRING**, Richard Roll Number 195. **HERRING**, Silas Roll Number 235. **HILL**, George Roll Number 57. **HILL**, John Roll Number 70. **HILL**, Thomas Roll Number 220. **JACKSON**, Charles Roll Number 33. **JACKSON**, Francis Roll Number 50. **JACKSON**, Joseph Roll Number 204. **JACKSON**, Lewey Roll Number 87. **JACKSON**, Loran Roll Number 178. **JACKSON**, Loran Roll Number 183. **JACKSON**, Mary Roll Number 138. **JACKSON**, Mary Jose Roll Number 131. **JACKSON**, Mitchel Roll Number 110. **JACKSON**, Peter Roll Number 161. **JACOB**, Agness Roll Number 25. **JACOB**, Alexander Roll Number 9. **JACOB**, Domanic Roll Number 43. **JACOB**, Jacob Roll Number 240. **JACOB**, John Roll Number 75. **JACOB**, Levi Roll Number 256. **JACOB**, Lewey Roll Number 95. **JACOB**, Lewey Roll Number 107. **JACOB**, Moses Roll Number 140. **JACOB**, Peter Roll Number 146. **JORDON**, Louisa Roll Number 199. **LA FRANCE**, Charles Roll Number 252. **LA FRANCE**, Lewey Roll Number 84. **LA FRANCE**, Lewey Roll Number 92. **LA FRANCE**, Loran Roll Number 187. **LA FRANCE**, Mary Ann Roll Number 82. **LA FRANCE**, Peter Roll Number 166. **LAUGHING**, Angus Roll Number 15. **LAUGHING**, Angus Roll Number 19. **LAUGHING**, Lucy Roll Number 83. **LAUGHING**, Mary Roll Number 136. **LAUGHING**, Peter Roll Number 160. **LAUGHING**, Mitchel Roll Number 109. **LAUGHING**, Mitchel Roll Number 118. **LONG-TOM**, Joe Roll Number 201. **LOON**, Lozor Roll Number 193. **LORAN**, John Roll Number 74. **LORAN**, Loran Roll Number 176. **LORAN**, Peter Roll Number 150. **LOZOR**, John Roll Number 69. **LOZOR**, Lewey Roll Number 106. **LOZOR**, Mitchel Roll Number 119. **PEPENO (OR PAPINEAU)** Francis Roll Number 51. **PEPENO**, Merick Roll Numer 250. **PEPENO**, Mitchel Roll Number 60. **RANSOM**, Alexander Roll Number 7. **RANSOM**, Angus Roll Number 17. **RANSOM**, John Roll Number 1. **RANSOM**, John Roll, Number 63. **RANSOM**, Lewey Roll Number 88. **RANSOM**, Loran Roll Number 188. **RANSOM**, Sloss? Roll Number 55. **RANSOM**, Terance Roll Number 233. **RANSOM**, Thomas Roll Number 4. **SAWYER**, Lewey Roll Number 105. **SAWYER**, Sarah Roll Number 247. **SAWYER**, Serick Roll Number 248. **SMOKE**, Agness, Roll Number 24. **SMOKE**, John Roll Number 73, **SMOKE**, Joseph Roll Number 203. **SMOKE**, Lewey Roll Number 91. **SMOKE**, Lewey Roll Number 96. **SMOKE**, Lewey Roll Number 101. **SMOKE**, Mitchel Roll Number 123. **SMOKE**, Thomas Roll Number 218. **SNOW**, Nancy Roll Number 79. **SOLOMON**, Alexander Roll Number 8. **SOLOMON**, Mitchel Roll Number 112. **STOCO**, Lewey Roll Number 99. **STOCO**, Noah Roll Number 61. **SQUARE**, George Roll Number 54. **SQUARE**, Mary Roll Number 134. **SWAMP**, Agat, Roll Number 30. **SWAMP**, Charlotte Roll Number 137. **SWAMP**, Loran Roll Number 190. **SWAMP**, Paul Roll Number 141. **TARBEL**, John Roll Number 65. **TARBEL**, Joseph Roll Number 202. **TARBEL**, Lewey Roll Number 254. **TARBEL**, Peter Roll Number 168. **TARBEL**, Terance Roll Number 209. **TARBEL**, Thomas Roll Number 224. **TERANCE OR TERENCE**, Mitchel Roll Number 114. **TERANCE**, Francis Roll Number 46. **TERANCE**, Francis Roll Number 48. **TERANCE**, Francis Roll Number 49. **TERANCE**, Francis Roll Number 52. **TERANCE**, Francis Roll Number 53. **TERANCE**, George Roll Number 58. **TERANCE**, Joseph Roll Number 212. **TERANCE**, Mitchel Roll Number 121. **TERANCE**, Peter Roll Number 147. **TERANCE**, Peter Roll Number 154. **TERANCE**, Richard Roll Number 194. **TERANCE**,

Silas Roll Number 236. **TERANCE**, Thomas Roll Number 219. **TERENCE**, Thomas Roll Number 228. **TERANCE**, Thomas Roll Number 229. **TERANCE**, Thomas Roll Number 230. **THOMAS**, Mary Jose? or Jane? Roll Number 132. **THOMAS**, Richard Roll Number 197. THOMAS, Terance Roll Number 228. **THOMAS**, Terance Roll Number 229. **THOMAS**, Terance Roll Number 230. **THOMPSON**, Agnes Roll Number 249. **THOMPSON**, Charles Roll Number 38. **THOMPSON**, Lewey Roll Number 89. **THOMPSON**, Loran Roll Number 177. **QUART**, Abram Roll Number 21. **QUART**, Peter Roll Number 167. **QUART**, Richard Roll Number 196. **QUART**, Thomas Roll Number 227. **VILNAVE OR VILANEAUVE**, John Roll Number 260. **VILNAVE**, Louisa Roll Number 200. **WEBSTER**, Merrick? Roll Number 130. **WHITE**, Anna Roll Number 26. **WHITE**, Anna Roll Number 29. **WHITE**, Angus Roll Number 6. **WHITE**, Angus Roll Number 14. **WHITE**, Charles Roll Number 35. **WHITE**, Felix Roll Number 170. **WHITE**, Lewey Roll Number 85. **WHITE**, Loran Roll Number 180. **WHITE**, Loran Roll Number 185. **WHITE**, Isaac Roll Number 59. **WHITE**, John Roll Number 62. **WHITE**, Joseph Roll Number 213. **WHITE**, Mitchel Roll Number 120. **WHITE**, Peter Roll Number 145. **WHITE**, Phillip Roll Number 174. **WILLIAMS**, Jacob Roll Number 242. **WOOD**, Thomas Roll Number 225. **WOOD**, George Roll Number 56. **WOOD**, Joseph Roll Number 208. **WOOD**, Lewey Roll Number 251. **WOOD**, Peter Roll Number 163. **WOOD**, Phillip Roll Number 172.

THE ST. REGIS MOHAWK

1900 UNITED STATES CENSUS ABSTRACT OF THE ST. REGIS MOHAWK'S WHO RESIDED IN FRANKLIN COUNTY, NEW YORK

This census abstract was taken from the original 1900 United States Census of Franklin County, New York. The following abstract is not in its original order. It has been alphabetized for this book. All of the people in each of the following households were enumerated as Iroquois. Exceptions were noted where individuals were members of another tribe, or race. Everyone in each household was born in the state of New York unless otherwise stated. Everyone in each household has the same surname as the head of that household. If an individual had a different surname than the head of that household that surname was highlighted by capital letters. A cross reference for these surnames can be found at the end of this abstract. The following names were recorded as they were spelled in the original records. The accuracy of the genealogy information represented in this abstract depends on how that information was recorded for the creation of the original census. A question mark was placed after the names, ages and dates where the spelling or information was in doubt. Use caution with the relationship term "adoption." The term used to indicate adoption was "ad," in the cesus appeared similar to the term "gd," used to indicate a grand child. This abstract begins with enumeration district number 62, page 90A.

ABRAMS, PETER: (Iroquois) Age 41 was born in November 1858 in New York. Both of his parents were born in Canada. Sarah, his wife age 39, was born in July 1860 in New York. Both of her parents were born in New York. Mary A., a daughter age 17 was born in 1882. Maggie a daughter age 14 was born in May 1886. Christie a daughter age 11 was born in July 1888. Annie a daughter age 5 was born in July 1894. Kate a daughter age 3 was born in July 1896. St. Regis, Mohawk Reserve, E. D. 62, Page 98A, Household 63/65? or 62/63.

ARMSTRONG? OR STOVEPIPE? MITCHELL: (Iroquois) Age 74 was born in February in 1826 in Canada. Both of his parents were born in Canada. He immigrated in 1865. Loran son age 43 was born in March 1857. Joseph a son age 35 was born in March 1865. John a son age 23 was born in September 1876. Mitchell a grand son age 12 was born in April 1888. Peter JACKSON, a nephew age 52, was born in January in 1848 in New York. Both of his parents were born in New York. St. Regis, Mohawk Reserve. E.D. 62, Page 113A, Household 164/166. Note: See second census page giving tribal origins. Mitchell Armstrong was also listed as Mitchell Stovepipe.

ARQUETTE, JACOB: (Iroquois) Age 66 was born in February in 1834 in Canada. Both of his parents were born in Canada. He immigrated in 1849. Susan, his wife age 62 was born in November in 1837 in Canada. Both of her parents were born in Canada. She immigrated in 1848. John a son age 33 was born in August 1866. Minnie a daughter-in-law age 30 was born in September 1869 in New York. Both of her parents were born in New York. Teresia a grand daughter age 5 was born in February 1895. Peter a grand son age 18 was born in March 1882. St. Regis, Mohawk Reserve. E.D. 62, Page 118B, Household 202/204.

ARQUETTE, MICHAEL: (Iroquois) Age 46 was born in March in 1854 in New York. Both of his parents were born in Canada. Sarah, his wife, age 36, was born in February in 1864 in Canada. Both of her parents were born in Canada. She immigrated in 1876. Angus DEOME, a stepson age 19, was born in January in 1881 in New York. His father was born in New York. His mother was born in Canada. Mary A. DEOME a step daughter age 17. Frank DEOME a step son age 15. Maggie DEOME a step daughter age 8 was born in May 1892. a John CUROOD, the father-in-law (Of Michael Arquette) age 62 was born in July 1837 in Canada. Both of his parents were born in Canada. He immigrated in 1895. All of the Deome step children were born in New York. Their father was born in New York. St. Regis, Mohawk Reserve. E.D. 62, Page 119A, Household 207/209.

ARQUETTE, MITCHELL: (Iroquois) Age 34 was born in October in 1865 in New York. Both of his parents were born in Canada. Minnie, his wife age 25, was born in September in 1874 in New York. Her father was born in Canada. Her mother was born in New York. Mary a daughter age 6 was born in May 1894. Peter a son age 4 was born in May 1896. Susan a daughter age 1 was born in July 1898. St. Regis, Mohawk Reserve. E.D. 62, Page 119A, Household 208/210.

ARQUETTE, SUSAN: (Iroquois) Age 60 was born in August 1839 in Canada. Both of her parents were born in Canada. She immigrated in 1862. Alexander a son age 18 was born in October 1881 in New York. His father was born in New York. His mother was born in Canada. St. Regis, Mohawk Reserve. E.D. 62, Page 118B, Household 204/206.

BACK, ABRAM: (Iroquois) Age 23 was born in January 1877 in New York. Both of his parents were born in New York. Sarah his wife age 26, was born in January 1874 in Canada. Her father was born in Canada. Her mother was born in New York. She immigrated in 1899. Annie FRIDAY, a sister-in-law age 20, was born in January 1880 in Canada. Her father was born in Canada. Her mother was born in New York. She immigrated in 1900. All of the people in this household were listed as Iroquois. All of the parents of the people in this household were listed as Iroquois. St. Regis, Mohawk Reserve. E.D. 62, Page 90B, Household 7/7.

BACK, LEWIS: (Iroquois) Age 44 was born in December 1855 in New York. Both of his parents were born in New York. Catharine, his wife age 42, was born in June 1857 in Canada. Both of her parents were born in Canada. She immigrated in 1876. Louisa a daughter age 23 born in January 1877, Angus a son age 15 born in October 1884, peter a son age 14 born in January 1886, David a son age 11 born in November 1888. St. Regis, Mohawk Reserve. E.D. 62, Page 120A, Household 214/216.

BACK, PAUL: (Iroquois) Age 27 was born in January 1873 in New York. Both of his parents were born in New York. Sarah, his wife age 29, was born in March 1871 in Canada. Both of her parents were born in Canada. She immigrated in 1900. Mary A., a daughter age 3 was born in May 1897. St. Regis, Mohawk Reserve. E.D. 62, Page 96A, Household 44/45.

BEAUBIEN, CHARLOTTE: (Iroquois) Age 70 was born in November in 1829 in New York. Both of her parents were born in Canada. Sarah WHITE, age 9 a niece, was born in March 1891 in New York. Both of her parents were born in New York. St. Regis, Mohawk Reserve. E.D. 62, Page 116B, Household 191/193.

BEAUBIEN, WILLIAM: (Iroquois) Age 38 was born in March 1862 in New York. His father was born in Canada. His mother was born in New York. Nelly, his wife age 38, was born in July 1861 in New York. Her father was born in Canada. Her mother was born in New York. Peter a son age 11 was born in June 1888. Joseph a son age 10 was born in November 1889. Addie a daughter age 6 was born in May 1894. John a son age 4 was born in November 1895. Teresia a daughter age 2 was born in January 1898. St. Regis, Mohawk Reserve. E.D. 62, Page 108B, Household 133/135.

BENEDICT, JOHN: (Iroquois) Age 41 was born in December 1858 in New York. Both of his parents were born in New York. Charlotte, his wife age 30, was born in January 1870 in New York. Her father was born in Canada. Her mother was born in New York. Polly a daughter age 11 was born in July 1888. Lizzie a daughter age 5 was born in March 1895. Lewis a son age 4 was born in May 1896. Annie a daughter age 1 was born in August? 1898. St. Regis, Mohawk Reserve. E.D. 62, Page 104A, Household 103/105.

BENEDICT, THOMAS: (Iroquois) Age 36 was born in May 1864 in Canada. His father was born in Canada. His mother was born in New York. He immigrated in 1889. Margaret a daughter age 5 was born in February 1895. David BENEDICT a brother age 26 was born in January 1874. Loran a brother age 22 was born in January 1874. Peter a brother age 20 was born in December 1871. St. Regis, Mohawk Reserve. E.D. 62, Page 119A, Household 209/211.

BEVO, DAVID: (Iroquois) Age 29 was born in February in 1871 in New York. Both of his parents were born in New York. Minnie, his wife age 24, was born in November 1875 in Canada. Both of her parents were born in Canada. She immigrated in 1893. Andrew a son age 3 was born in November 1896. Mitchell a son age 1 was born in December 1898. All of the people in this household were listed as Iroquois. All of the parents of the people in this household were listed as Iroquois. St. Regis, Mohawk Reserve. E.D. 62, Page 90B, Household 6/6.

BEVO, JOSEPH: (Iroquois) Age 67 was born in August in 1832 in Canada. Both of his parents were born in Canada. He immigrated in 1836. Annie, his wife age 64, was born in December 1835 in Canada. Both of her parents were born in Canada. She immigrated in 1840. St. Regis, Mohawk Reserve. E.D. 62, Page 97B, Household 58/60.

BEVO, LEWIS: (Iroquois) Age 23 was born in June 1876 in New York. Both of his parents were born in Canada. Louisa, his wife age 26, was born in July 1873 in New York. Both of her parents were born in New York. Joseph a son was born in May 1900. St. Regis, Mohawk Reserve. E.D. 62, Page 97B, Household 59/61.

BEVO, MICHAEL: (Iroquois) Age 31 was born in November 1868 in New York. Both of his parents were born in Canada. Charlotte, his wife age 28 was born in April 1872 in Canada. Both of her parents were born in Canada. She immigrated in 1899. Peter a son age 4 was born in August 1895. Lewis a son age 2 was born in March 1898. All of the people living in this household were listed as Iroquois. All of the parents of the people in this household were listed as Iroquois. St. Regis, Mohawk Reserve. E.D. 62, Page 91A, Household 10/10.

BEVO, SARAH: (Iroquois) Age 38 was born in January 1862 in New York. Her father was born in New York. Her mother was born in Canada. Lean a daughter age 5 was born in 1894. Loran a son age 3 was born in January 1897. Margaret HOPPS, a cousin age 25, was born in November 1874 in New York. Her father was born in Canada. Her mother was born In New York. St. Regis, Mohawk Reserve. E.D. 62, Page 92A, Household 19/20.

BEVO, THOMAS: (Iroquois) Age 28 was born in August in 1871 in New York. Both of his parents were born in New York. Maggie, his wife age 25, was born in March 1875 in Canada. Both of her parents were born in Canada. She immigrated in 1892. David a son age 4 born in August 1895, Lewis a son age four months born in January 1900. St. Regis, Mohawk Reserve. E.D. 62, Page 97A, Household 55/57.

BEVO, WILLIAM: (Iroquois) Age 66 was born in April 1834 in New York. Both of his parents were born in New York. Catherine, his wife age 56, was born in August 1843 in Canada. Both of her parents were born in Canada. She immigrated in 1859. Lewis a son age 36 was born in February 1864. John a son age 32 was born in March 1868. Jacob a son age 21 was born in May 1879. Paul a son age 15 was born in December 1884. Mary Ann a daughter-in-law age 33 was born in August 1866? Both of her parents were born in New York. Peter a grand son age 4 was born in March? 1895. All of the people in this household were listed as Iroquois. All of the parents of the people in this household were listed as Iroquois. St. Regis Mohawk Reserve, E.D. 62, Page 94B, Household 30/30.

BIGTREE, PHILLIP: (Iroquois) Age 52 was born in September 1847 in New York. Both of his parents were born in New York. Massie his wife age 48 was born in December 1851 in New York. Her father was born in New York. Her mother was born in Canada. Mary Ann a daughter age 26 was born in March 1874. Charlotte a daughter age 17 was born in May 1883. George a son age 12 was born in December 1887. Catherine TARBELL mother-in-Law (Of Phillip Bigtree) age 66 was born in May 1834 in Canada. Both of her parents were born in Canada. She immigrated in 1858. Sarah BILLINGS a sister-in-law age 28 was born in February 1872 in New York. Her father was born in New York. Her mother was born in Canada. John COOK a nephew age 16 was born in August 1883 in New York. Both of his parents were born in New York. All of the people in this household were listed as Iroquois. All of the parents of the people in this household were listed as Iroquois. St. Regis Reservation, E.D. 62, Page 94A, Household 31/31.

BILLINGS, CAROLINE: (White) Age 71 was born in July 1828 in New York. Her father was born in New York. Her mother was born in Canada. Louisa a daughter age 23 was born in August 1876 in New York. Both of her parents were born in New York. Charles a son age 22 was born in May 1878 in New York. Both of his parents were born in New York. Lizzie BENEDICT a daughter age 19 was born in July 1880 in New York. Both of her parents were born in New York. Mathew BENEDICT a son-in-law age 22 was born in April 1878 in Canada. Both of his parents were born in Canada. He immigrated in 1900. The children of Caroline BILLINGS were all listed as one fourth Iroquois. Mathew BENEDICT was listed as three fourth Iroquois. St. Regis Reserve, E.D. 62, Page 101B, Household 85/87.

BILLINGS, JACOB: (Iroquois) Age 62 was born in April 1838 in New York. Both of his parents were born in New York. Christie his wife age 53 was born in May 1847 in New York. Her father was born in New York. Her mother was born in Canada. Isiah a son age 25 was born in November 1874. Alex a son age 23 was born in November 1876. Margaret a daughter age 14 was born in July 1885. Joshua a son age 12 was born in March 1888. St. Regis, Mohawk Reserve, E.D. 62, Page 99B/100A, Household 73/76.

BILLINGS, JAMES: (Iroquois) Age 51 was born in August in 1848 in New York. Both of his parents were born in New York. Elizabeth, his wife age 39, was born in March 1861 in New York. Both of her parents were born in New York. Caroline a daughter age 18 was born in September 1881. Louisa a daughter age 16 was born in May 1884. Samuel a son age 12 was born in March 1888. Julia a daughter age 10 was born in November 1889. Hateenas a daughter age 5 was born in July 1894. Peter a son age 3 was born in October 1896. Alsie a son age ten months was born in September 1899. St. Regis, Mohawk Reserve. E.D. 62, Page 103A, Household 96/98.

BILLINGS, THOMAS: (Iroquois) Age 24 was born in August in 1875 in New York. Both of his parents were born in New York. Sarah his wife age 18, was born in November 1881 in Canada. Both of her parents were born in Canada. She immigrated in 1897. Dora a daughter age 2 was born in October 1897, Sarah a sister age 9 was born in February 1891. St. Regis, Mohawk Reserve. E.D. 62, Page 102A, Household 91/93 or 90/91.

BONAPART, CHRISTIAN: (Iroquois) Age 49 was born in May 1851 in New York. Both of her parents were born in New York. Agnes a daughter age 13 was born in January 1887. Both of her parents were born in New York. Both of her parents were Iroquois. St. Regis, Mohawk Reserve. E.D. 62, Page 91B, Household 15/15.

BONAPART, JOHN: (Iroquois) Age 25 was born in July 1874 in New York. Both of his parents were born in New York. Maggie his wife age 23 was born in February 1876 in New York. Both of her parents were born in New York. Both of her parents were Iroquois. Angus a son age 2 was born in June 1897. Ida a daughter age 1 was born in February 1899. St. Regis, Mohawk Reserve, E.D. 62, Page 91A? or B? Household 13/13.

BONSPIEL, GABRIEL: (Iroquois) Age 31 or 39 was born in April 1861 in Canada. Both of his parents were born in Canada. He immigrated in 1896. Elizabeth, his wife age 35, was born in July 1864 in Canada. Both of her parents were born in Canada. She immigrated in 1890. Daniel a son age 17 was born in June 1882. Mary J., a daughter age 11 was born in February 1889. Mercy a daughter age 9 was born in March 1891. Charles a son age 6 was born in November 1893. Margaret a daughter age 4 was born in March 1896. Lizzie a daughter age 1 was born in July 1898. All of the people in this household were listed as Iroquois. All of the parents of the people in this household were listed as Iroquois. St. Regis, Mohawk Reserve. E.D. 62, Page 90A, Household 4/4.

BOOTS, JOHN: (Iroquois) Age 77 was born in June 1822 in New York. Both of his parents were born in Canada. Nancy, his wife age 60, was born in February 1840 in New York. Her father was born in New York. Her mother was born in Canada. Dennis a son age 22 was born in March 1878. St. Regis, Mohawk Reserve. E.D. 62, Page 107A, Household 125/127 or 124/125.

CHUBB, ALEXANDER: (Iroquois) Age 54 was born in February in 1846 in New York. Both of his parents were born in New York. Sarah, his wife age 32, was born in December 1867 in New York. Her father was born in Canada. Her mother was born in New York. Agnes a daughter age 12 born in September 1887, Louise a daughter age 10 born in February 1890, Mary a daughter age 6 born in May 1894. St. Regis, Mohawk Reserve. E.D. 62, Page 111B, Household 155/157.

CHUBB, LORAN: (Iroquois) Age 96 was born in February in 1804 in New York. Both of his parents were born in New York. Loran CHUBB a grand son age 31 was born in September 1868 in New York. Both of his parents were born in New York. St. Regis, Mohawk Reserve. E.D. 62, Page 120B, Household 220/222.

CHUBB, MARTIN: (Iroquois) Age 42 was born in January 1858 in New York. His father was born in New York. His mother was born in Canada. Cecilia a daughter age 17 was born in August 1882. John a son age 15 was born in June 1884. Catharine a daughter age 8 was born in April 1892. St. Regis, Mohawk Reserve. E.D. 62, Page 120B, Household 218/220.

CHUBB, MARY: (Iroquois) Age 30 was born in April 1870 in New York. Both of her parents were born in New York. Lewis a son age 10 was born in November 1889. Thomas a son age 5 was born in August 1894. St. Regis, Mohawk Reserve. E.D. 62, Page 120B Household 217/219.

COLE, ALEXANDER: (Iroquois) Age 40 was born in July 1859 in Canada. His father was born in New York. His mother was born in Canada. He immigrated in 1882. Mary Ann, his wife age 33, was born in August 1866 in New York. Both of her parents were born in New York. Polly a daughter age 15 was born in November 1884. Peter a son age 11 was born in July 1888. Mary a daughter age 9 was born in August 1890. Charles a son age 6 was born in January 1894. Annie a daughter age 4 was born in May 1890. Sarah a daughter age 1 was born in August 1898. Celesia COLE, mother (Of Alexander Cole) age 64, was born in January 1836 in Canada. Both of her parents were born in Canada. She immigrated in 1882. All of the people in this household were listed as Iroquois. All of the parents of the people in this household were listed as Iroquois. St. Regis, Mohawk Reserve. E.D. 62, Page 94A, Household 26/26.

COLE, LEWIS: (Iroquois) Age 47 was born in December 1852 in New York. Both of his parents were born in New York. Adelia, his wife age 39, was born in November 1860 in New York. Both of her parents were born in Canada. Paul a son age 20 was born in December 1879. Louisa a daughter age 14 was born in January 1886. Thomas a son age 5 was born in July 1894. Mary a daughter age six months was born in November 1899. St. Regis, Mohawk Reserve. E.D. 62, Page 110A, Household 143/145.

COLE, PETER: (Indian) Age 65 was born in August 1831 in New York. Both of his parents were born in New York, E.D. 62, Page 99B, Household 73/75.

COLE, PETER: (Iroquois) Age 65 was born in August 1834 in New York. Both of his parents were born in New York. Mary, his wife age 44, was born in August 1855 in New York. Nellie a daughter age 15 was born in August 1884. John a son age 13 was born in November 1886. Joseph a son age 10 was born in November 1899. Abram a son age 5 was born in December 1894. St. Regis, Mohawk Reserve. E.D. 62, Page 93A, Household 27/27.

CONNORS, JOSEPH: (Iroquois) Age 54 was born in July 1855 in Canada. Both of his parents were born in Canada. He immigrated in 1860. Mary, his wife age 35, was born in March 1865 in Canada. Her father was born in Canada. Her mother was born in New York. Isaac a son age 20 was born in November 1879. Mary GORROW, mother (Of Joseph Connors) age 72, was born in May 1828 in Canada. Both of her parents were born in Canada. She immigrated in 1860. Betsey THOMPSON a step daughter age 4, was born in September 1895 in Canada. Both of her parents were born in Canada. She immigrated in 1899. St. Regis, Mohawk Reserve. E.D. 62, Page 100A, Household 75/77.

CONNORS, MITCHELL: (Iroquois) Age 30 was born in November 1861 in New York. Both of his parents were born in New York. Margaret, his wife age 24, was born in May 1876 in New York. Both of her parents were born in New York. Nancy a daughter age 8 was born in August 1891. Lewis a son age 4 was born in August 1895. Charles a son age 3 was born in April 1897. Emma a daughter age 1 was born in May 1899. St. Regis, Mohawk Reserve. E.D. 62, Page 100A, Household 74/76.

COOK, ABRAM: (Iroquois) Age 30 was born in February 1870 in New York. His father was born in New York. His mother was born in Canada. Rhoda, his wife age 26, was born in February in 1874 in New York. Both of his parents were born in New York. Jacob a son age 9 was born in December 1890. Thomas a son age 7 was born in July 1892. Lewis a son age 6 was born in April 1894. Mitchell a son age 4 was born in January 1896. Maggie a daughter age 1 was born in December 1898. St. Regis, Mohawk Reserve. E.D. 62, Page 114B, Household 177/179.

COOK, DAVID: (Iroquois) Age 25 was born in February 1875 in New York. His father was born in New York. His mother was born in Canada. Mary his wife age 24 was born in November 1875 in New York. Both of her parents were born in New York. Annie a daughter age 2 was born in August 1897. St. Regis Mohawk Reserve, E.D. 62, Page 114A, Household 173/175.

COOK, DAVID: (Iroquois) Age 31 was born in March 1869 in New York. Both of his parents were born in New York. Nancy, his wife age 27, was born in January in 1873 in Canada. Both of her parents were born in Canada. She immigrated in 1886. John a son age 6 was born in August 1893. Hattie a daughter age 2 was born in July 1897. Louise a mother age 65 was born in August 1834. Joseph a nephew age 13 was born in March 1887. John PAPPINEAU, brother-in-law (Of David Cook) age 40, was born in February in 1860 in Canada. Both of his parents were born in Canada. He immigrated in 1885. Andrew PAPPINEAU a nephew (Of David

Cook) age 5 was born in July 1894. Everyone in this household was listed as Iroquois. St. Regis, Mohawk Reserve. E.D. 62, Page 117A, Household 194/196.

COOK, JACOB: (Iroquois) Age 32 was born in November in 1867 New York. Her father was born in New York. His mother was born in Canada. Sarah, his wife age 29, was born in June in 1870 in New York. Both of his parents were born in New York. John a son age 11 was born in March 1899. Mary a daughter age 9 was born in November 1890. Maggie a daughter age 6 was born in June 1893. Peter a son age 3 was born in May 1897. Frank COOK a cousin age 18 was born in November 1881. St. Regis, Mohawk Reserve. E.D. 62, Page 116A, Household 186/188.

COOK, JAMES: (Iroquois) Age 34 was born in January in 1866 in New York. Both of his parents were born in New York. Alice, his wife age 24, was born in April 1876 in New York. Both of her parents were born in New York. Mary a daughter age 5 was born in April 1895. Isaac a son age 3 was born in March 1897. Sarah a daughter age eight months was born in September 1899. Louise BIGTREE, a servant age 19, was born in August 1880 in New York. Both of her parents were born in New York. Everyone in this household were listed as Iroquois. St. Regis, Mohawk Reserve. E.D. 62, Page 94A, Household 33/33.

COOK, JOHN: (Iroquois) Age 57 was born in May 1843 in New York. Both of his parents were born in New York. Margaret, his wife age 55, was born in October in 1844 in Canada. Both of her parents were born in Canada. She immigrated in 1860. Lewis a son age 18 was born in April 1882. Agatha a daughter-in-law age 21 was born in February 1879. Josephine COOK a grand daughter age 13 was born in April 1887. Lewis SMOKE, a servant age 67, was born in October in 1832 in New York. Both of his parents were born in New York. St. Regis, Mohawk Reserve. E.D. 62, Page 114B, Household 173/174.

COOK, JOHN: (Iroquois) Age 41 was born in October 1858 in New York. Both of his parents were born in New York. Mary, his wife age 42, was born in March 1858 in Canada. Her father was born in New York. Her mother was born in Canada. She immigrated in 1885. Joseph a son age 11 was born in April 1889. Mitchell a son age 8 was born in August 1891. St. Regis, Mohawk Reserve. E.D. 62, Page 94A, Household 34/34.

COOK, LEWIS: (Iroquois) Age 67 was born in January 1833 in New York. His father was born in New York. His mother was born in Canada. Susan LA FRANCE, a grand daughter age 22, was born in December 1877 in New York. Both of her parents were born in New York. Sarah JACKSON, a grand daughter age 16, was born in November 1883 in New York. Both of her parents were born in New York. Richard JACKSON a grand son age 26 born in September 1873. Everyone in this household was listed as Iroquois. St. Regis, Mohawk Reserve. E.D. 62, Page 101A, Household 81/83.

COOK, PETER: (Iroquois) Age 31 was born in August 1868 in New York. Both of his parents were born in New York. Both of his parents were Iroquois. Sarah, his wife age 29, was born in July 1870 in Canada. She immigrated in 1889. Both of her parents were born in Canada. Both of her parents were Iroquois. St. Regis, Mohawk Reserve. E.D. 62, Page 93B, Household 22/23.

COOK, PETER: (Iroquois) Age 24 was born in July 1875 in New York. Both of his parents were born in New York. Susan, his wife age 25, was born in June 1874 in New York. Both of her parents were born in New York. St. Regis, Mohawk Reserve. E.D. 62, Page 117A, Household 195/197.

COOK, PETER: (Iroquois) Age 44, was born in October? 1855 in New York. Both of his parents were born in New York. Maggie, his wife age 41, was born in April 1859 in Canada. Both of her parents were born in Canada. She immigrated in 1875. Jacob a son age 23 was born in July 1876. Mary a daughter age 20 was born in November 1879. Annie COOK a daughter-in-Law (She was listed as white) age 17 was born in October 1882 in Canada. Both of her parents were born in Canada. She immigrated in 1898. Lena a daughter age 9 was born in July 1890. Addie a daughter age 7 was born in December 1892. Peter a son age eight months was born in October 1899. Peter COOK father (Of Peter Cook) age 77 was born in April 1823 in New York. Both of his parents were born in New York. Nancy COOK, a step mother (Of Peter Cook) age 56, was born in October 1843 in New York. Both of her parents were born in New York. St. Regis, Mohawk Reserve. Everyone in this household except Annie COOK were listed as Iroquois. E.D. 62, Page 106A, Household 117/119.

COOK, SARAH: (Iroquois) Age 56 was born in February 1844 in Canada. Both of her parents were born in Canada. She immigrated in 1892. Rhoda COOK a daughter age 16 was born in May 1884, Mitchell A. WHITE, a brother age 32, was born in September 1867 in Canada. Both of his parents were born in Canada. He immigrated in 1892. Charles WHITE a brother age 38 was born in October 1861 in Canada. Mary WHITE a niece age 8 was born in November 1892 in Canada. Lewis WHITE a nephew age 3 was born in March 1897 in Canada. St. Regis, Mohawk Reserve. E.D. 62, Page 96B, Household 49/50.

COOK, WILLIAM: (Iroquois) Age 42 was born in September 1857 in New York. Both of his parents were born in New York. Sarah, his wife age 37, was born in May 1863 in New York. Both of her parents were born in New York. Lewis a son age 19 was born in April 1881. Mary a daughter age 17 was born in March 1883. Loran a son age 15 was born in May 1885. Sarah a daughter age 13 was born in January 1887. James a son age 8 was born in September 1891. Agnes a daughter age 6 was born in September 1893. Charlotte a daughter age 3 was born in June 1896. St. Regis, Mohawk Reserve. E.D. 62, Page 117A, Household 196/198.

CORNELIUS, THOMAS: (Iroquois) Age 56 was born in April 1844 in New York. Both of his parents were born in New York. Emily, his wife age 51, was born in September 1848 in New York. Both of her parents were born in New York. James a son age 24 was born in March 1876. Ida a daughter age 13 was born in November 1886. John MC DONELL, a nephew age 12, was born in May 1888 in New York. Both of his parents were born in New York. St. Regis, Mohawk Reserve. E.D. 62, Page 100B, Household 79/81.

CREE, JACOB: (Iroquois) Age 48 was born in February in 1852 in New York. Both of his parents were born in New York. Annie, his wife age 49, was born in January in 1851 in New York. Both of her parents were born in New York. Lewis a son age 17 was born in December 1882. Agnes a daughter age 11 was born in January 1889. St. Regis, Mohawk Reserve. E.D. 62, Page 120A, Household 216/218.

CREE, THOMAS: (Iroquois) Age 53 was born in December 1846 in New York. Both of his parents were born in New York. Annie, his wife age 48, was born in May 1852 in Canada. Her father was born in Canada. Her mother was born in New York. She immigrated in 1875. Mary A., a daughter age 18 was born in January 1882. Magdalen a daughter age 14 was born in May 1886. Paul CHUBB, a grand son age 11, was born in April 1889 in New York. Both of his parents were born in New York. Peter TARBELL, a grand son age 6, was born in January in 1894 in New York. Both of his parents were born in New York. St. Regis, Mohawk Reserve. E.D. 62, Page 119B, Household 210/212.

DAVID, ANDREW: (Iroquois) Age 33 was born in June 1866 in Canada. Both of his parents were born in Canada. He immigrated in 1887. St. Regis, Mohawk Reserve. E.D. 62, Page 118B, Household 203/205.

DELORMIER, PAUL: (Iroquois) Age 53 was born in March 1847 in Canada. Both of his parents were born in Canada. He immigrated in 1877. Agatha, his wife age 41, was born in May 1859 in New York. Both of his parents were born in New York. Abram a son age 19 was born in June 1880. Mary a daughter age 18 was born September 1881. Philip a son age 15 was born in June 1884. Nancy a daughter age 13 was born in July 1886. Margret a daughter age 11 was born in May 1889. Thomas a son age 4 was born in June 1895. Richard THOMPSON, a grandson age 2, was born in April 1898 in New York. Vernece? THOMPSON, a grand daughter age three months, was born in January 1900 in New York. Her father was born in Canada and her mother was born in New York. St. Regis, Mohawk Reserve.. E.D. 62, Page 90A, Household 2/2.

DEOME, BETSEY: (Iroquois) Age 80 was born in February 1820 in New York. Both of her parents were born in Canada. Francis GORROW, a brother age 67, was born in December 1832 in New York. Both of his parents were born in New York? Loran GORROW a nephew age 25 was born in October 1874. Mary GORROW a grand daughter age 2 was born in May 1898. St. Regis, Mohawk Reserve. E.D. 62, Page 105B, Household 114/116 or 113/114.

DEOME, PHILLIP: (Iroquois) Age 41 was born in May 1859 in New York. His father was born in Canada. His mother was born in New York. Mary, his wife age 30, was born in November in 1869 in New York. Both of her parents were born in New York. Monica a daughter age 13 was born in March 1887. Lewis a son age 10 was born in February 1890. Francis a son age 1 was born in July 1898. E.D. 62, Page 119B, Household 212/214.

DIXON, MITCHELL: (Iroquois) Age 32 was born in November 1867 in Canada. Both of his parents were born in Canada. He immigrated in 1885. Maggie, his wife age 29, was born in January 1871 in Canada. Both of her parents were born in Canada. She immigrated in 1885? Annie a daughter age 13 was born in June 1886. Loran a son age 12 was born in January 1888. Mary A., a daughter age 10 was born in March 1890. Peter a son age 7 was born in November 1892. Christie a daughter age 1, was born in March 1891. St. Regis, Mohawk Reserve. E.D. 62, Page 108A, Household 130/132.

FERGUSON, JOHN: (Iroquois) Age 54 was born in July 1845 in New York. Both of his parents were born in New York. Minnie, his wife age 55, was born in May 1845 in Canada. Both of her parents were born in Canada. She immigrated in 1865. St. Regis, Mohawk Reserve. E.D. 62, Page 102A, Household 89/91.

FRANCIS, AGNES: (Iroquois) Age 43 was born in June 1856 in New York. Her father was born in Canada. Her mother was born in New York. Mary FRANCIS a daughter age 14 born in June 1885, John ADAMS a son age 21, was born in March 1879 in New York. His father was born in Canada. His mother was born in New York. All of the people in this household were listed as Iroquois. All of the parents of the people in this household were listed as Iroquois. St. Regis, Mohawk Reserve. E.D. 62, Page 96B, Household 48/49 or 50.

FRANCIS, LEWIS: (Iroquois) Age 26 was born in October 1873 in Canada. Both of his parents were born in Canada. He immigrated in 1897. Both of his parents were listed as Iroquois. Nancy, his wife age 23, was born in November 1876 in Canada. Both of her parents were born in Canada. Both of her parents were listed as Iroquois. She immigrated in 1897. St. Regis, Mohawk Reserve. E.D. 62, Page 90A, Household 1/1.

FRIDAY, MITCHELL: (Iroquois) Age 58 was born in October in 1841 in Canada. Both of his parents were born in Canada. He immigrated in 1856. Mary Ann, his wife age 55, was born in August in 1844 in New York. Both of her parents were born in Canada. St. Regis, Mohawk Reserve. E.D. 62, Page 114A, Household 171/172.

GORROW, ABRAM: (Iroquois) Age 52 was born in February in 1848 in New York. His father was born in New York. His mother was born in Quebec Canada. Rose A., his wife (She was listed as a white woman.) age 32, was born in August in 1867 in French Canada (Quebec). Both of her parents were born in French Canada. She immigrated in 1892. John a son age 16 was born in December 1883. Georgia a daughter age 13 was born in August 1886. Laura a daughter age 7 was born in January 1893. Annie M., a daughter age 3 was born in September 1896. Gertrude a daughter age 1 was born in September 1898. St. Regis, Mohawk Reserve. E.D. 62, Page 111B, Household 153/155.

GORROW, ANGUS: (Iroquois) Age 49 was born in February in 1851 in New York. Both of his parents were born in Canada. Charlotte his wife age 42, was born in November 1857 in New York. Her father was born in Canada. Her mother was born in New York. Mary a daughter age 7 was born in June 1892. Mary Ann a daughter age 5 was born in September 1894. Joseph a son was age 1. David MITCHELL, a nephew age 8, was born in August in 1891 in New York. Both of his parents were born in New York. Margaret BARRON, grand mother (Of Angus Gorrow) age 74, was born in April 1826 in Canada. Both of her parents were born in Canada. Both of her parents were Iroquois. She immigrated in 1856. St. Regis, Mohawk Reserve. E.D. 62, Page 113B, Household 170/171.

GORROW, ANNIE: (Iroquois) Age 40 was born in April 1860 in New York. Both of her parents were born in New York. Angus a son age 20 was born in April 1880. Sarah a daughter age 15 was born in November 1884. Loran a son age 10 was born in October 1889. Louise PETERS, a daughter age 18, was born in July 1881 in New York. Both of her parents were born in New York. George PETERS, son-in-law age 27, was born in February in 1873 in New York. Both of his parents were born in New York. Mitchell PETERS a grand son age 2 was born in May 1898. St. Regis, Mohawk Reserve. E.D. 62, Page 116A, Household 188/190.

GORROW, CHARLES: (Iroquois) Age 40 was born in January 1860 in New York. Both of his parents were born in New York. Mary his wife age 36, was born in March 1864 in New York. Both of her parents were born in New York. Peter a son age 14 was born in February 1886. John a son age 12 was born in December 1887. Jacob a son age 12 was born in December 1887. Jacob a son age 8 was born in September 1891. Isaac a son age 6 was born in May 1894. Oliver a son age 4 was born in February 1896. Noah a son age 2 was born in March 1898. George a son age one month was born in April 1900. Mary WHITE, a step daughter age 17, was born in July 1882 in New York. Her father was born in Canada. Her mother was born in New York. St. Regis, Mohawk Reserve. E.D. 62, Page 98A, Household 65/67.

GORROW, JOSEPH JR.: (Iroquois) Age 35 was born in March 1865 in New York. His father was born in New York. His mother was born in France. Both of his parents were listed as Iroquois. Emily his wife (She was listed as a white woman) age 29, was born in May 1871 in England. Both of her parents were born in England. She immigrated in 1895. William a son age 4 was born in January 1896. St. Regis, Mohawk Reserve. E.D. 62, Page 95A, Household 40/42.

GORROW, JOSEPH: (Iroquois) Age 38 was born in January 1862 in New York. Both of his parents were born in New York. Sarah GORROW a sister age 20 was born in November 1879. Peter GORROW a brother age 22 was born in March 1878. St. Regis, Mohawk Reserve. E.D. 62, Page 99A, Household 68/70.

GORROW, JOSEPH: (Iroquois) Age 73 was born in July 1826 in New York. His father was born in Canada. His mother was born in New York. Lillie his wife (She was listed as a white woman) age 52, was born in December 1847 in France. Both of her parents were born in France. She immigrated in 1860. Moses a son age 32 was born in October 1867. John a son age 30 was born in November 1869. Sarah a daughter-in-law age 26 was born in September 1873 in New York. Both of her parents were born in New York. Emily a daughter-in-law (She was listed as a white woman) age 27 was born in August 1872 in England. Both of her parents were born in England. She immigrated in 1896. Lewis a grand son age 9 was born in December 1890. Elizabeth a grand daughter age 7 was born in July 1892. Emily a grand daughter age 5 was born in May 1895. Mary a grand daughter age 2 was born in December 1897. Solomon a grand son age one month was born in April 1900. St. Regis, Mohawk Reserve. E.D. 62, Page 95A, Household 39/41.

GORROW, LORAN: (Iroquois) Age 27 was born in May 1873 in New York. His father was born in New York. His mother was born in Canada. Sarah his wife age 25, was born in March 1875 in New York. Her parents were both were born in New York. Moses a son age 8 was born in August 1891. Eva a daughter age 2 was born in June 1897. Rosa a daughter age 1 was born in February 1899. St. Regis, Mohawk Reserve. E.D. 62, Page 102A, Household 90/92 or 89/90.

GORROW, MARY: (Iroquois) Age 66 was born in April 1834 in Canada. Both of her parents were born in Canada. She immigrated in 1849? Mitchell JACKSON, a son age 51, was born in February in 1849 in Canada. Both of his parents were born in Canada. He immigrated in 1849. Thomas MC DONALD, a grand son age 2, was born in May 1899 in New York. Both of his parents were born in New York. St. Regis, Mohawk Reserve. E.D. 62, Page 116A, Household 187/189.

GORROW, PETER: (Iroquois) Age 41 was born in May 1859 in New York. His father was born in New York. His mother was born in Canada. Phebe his wife (She was listed as a white woman) age 27, was born in September in 1872 in New York. Her father was born in French Canada (Quebec). Her mother was born in French Canada (Quebec). Maggie a daughter age 15 was born in August 1884. Eva a daughter age 6 was born in April 1894. Ethel a daughter age 4 was born in June 1895. Genevieve a daughter age 2 was born in March 1898. Albert H., a son age six months was born in November 1899. St. Regis, Mohawk Reserve. E.D. 62, Page 111B, Household 154/156.

GORROW, PHILLIP: (Iroquois) Age 48 was born in November 1851 in New York. His father was born in Canada. His mother was born in New York. Susan his wife age 38, was born in June 1861 in New York. Her father was born in Canada. Her mother was born in New York. St. Regis, Mohawk Reserve. E.D. 62, Page 92A, Household 17/18.

GORROW, SARAH: (Iroquois) Age 25 was born in September 1874 in Canada. Both of her parents were born in Canada. She immigrated in 1886. Catharine a daughter age 5 was born in August 1894. Louise a daughter age 1 was born in March 1899. St. Regis, Mohawk Reserve. E.D. 62, Page 96A, Household 45/46.

GRAY, JOHN: (Iroquois) Age 40 was born in February 1860 in New York. His father was born in New York. His mother was born in New York. Nancy his wife age 27, was born in December 1872 in New York. Both of her parents were born in New York. Agnes a daughter age 6 was born in June 1893. Mary a daughter age 4 was born in October 1895. Maggie a daughter age 3 was born in June 1896. Minnie a daughter age 2 was born in December 1897. Julia a daughter age 1 was born in March 1899. Louise a daughter age 14 was born in January 1886. St. Regis, Mohawk Reserve. E.D. 62, Page 94B, Household 37/38.

GRAY, LEWIS: (Iroquois) Age 70 was born in September 1829 in New York. Both of his parents were born in New York. Mary A., his wife age 70, was born in December 1829 in New York. Both of her parents were born in New York. St. Regis, Mohawk Reserve. E.D. 62, Page 121A, Household 222/224.

GRAY, MARY: (Iroquois) Age 67 was born in December 1832 in New York. Both of her parents were born in Canada. Susan a daughter age 34 was born in November 1865. Joseph a Grand son age 29 was born in March 1871. Annie a grand daughter age 20 was born in February 1880. Agnes GRAY a great grand daughter age 1 was born in August 1893. Loran GRAY a great grand son age six months was born in May 1900. St. Regis, Mohawk Reserve. E.D. 62, Page 90B, Household 8/8.

GRAY, MITCHELL: (Iroquois) Age 30 was born in March in 1870 in New York. His father was born in New York. His mother was born in Canada. Margaret his wife age 24, was born in May in 1876 in English Canada (Ontario). Her father was born in New York. Her mother was born in English Canada (Ontario). She immigrated in 1890. Mary a daughter age 5 was born in January 1895. Moses a son age one month was born in April 1900. St. Regis, Mohawk Reserve. E.D. 62, Page 118B, Household 206/208.

GRAY, PAUL: (Iroquois) Age 65 was born in August 1834 in Canada. Both of his parents were born in Canada. He immigrated in 1852. Margaret a daughter age 16 was born in August 1883. Mary A., a daughter age 12 was born in May 1888. Moses a son age 6 was born in September 1893. St. Regis, Mohawk Reserve. E.D. 62, Page 111A, Household 151/153.

GRAY, SILAS: (Iroquois) Age 48 was born in November 1851 in New York. His father was born in Canada. His mother was born in New York. Elizabeth his wife age 43, was born in February 1857 in New York. Her father was born in Canada. Her mother was born in New York. Abram a son age 19 was born in June 1880. Sarah a daughter age 17 was born in June 1882. Thomas a son age 5. Jonas a son age 3 was born in November 1896. St. Regis, Mohawk Reserve. E.D. 62, Page 94B, Household 36/37.

GRAY, THOMAS: (Iroquois) Age 46 was born in December 1853 in New York. Both of his parents were born in New York. Julia his wife age 54, was born in September 1845 in New York. Her father was born in Canada. Her mother was born in New York. Peter a son age 20 was born in August 1879. John WHITE, an adopted son age 11, was born in March 1889 in New York. His father was born in Canada. His mother was born in New York. Daisy CONNORS, a boarder age 18, was born in April 1882 in New York. Both of her parents were born in New York. Everyone in this household was listed as Iroquois. St. Regis, Mohawk Reserve. E.D. 62. Page 98B, Household 66/68.

GRAY, WILLIAM: (Iroquois) Age 53 was born in October 1846 in New York. Both of his parents were born in New York. Julia a daughter age 19 was born in January 1881. Polly a daughter age 17 was born in November 1882. St. Regis, Mohawk Reserve. E.D. 62, Page 99A, Household 69/71.

HART, FRANK: (Iroquois) Age 29 was born in November 1870 in Canada. Both of his parents were born in Canada. He immigrated in 1875. Agnes his wife age 26, was born in August 1873 in Canada. Both of her parents were born in Canada. She immigrated in 1899. John a son age 4 was born in October 1890. Mary LORAN, a step daughter age 9, was born in 1890 in Canada. Both of her parents were born in Canada. She immigrated in 1899. Annie LORAN a step daughter age 6 was born in December 1893 in Canada. Both of her parents were born in Canada. She immigrated in 1899. St. Regis, Mohawk Reserve. E.D. 62, Page 107A, Household 128/130.

HERRIN, ABRAM: (Iroquois) Age 53 was born in March 1847 in New York. Both of his parents were born in New York. Annie his wife age 57, was born in November in 1842 in New York. Both of her parents were born in Canada. Annie QUART, an adopted daughter age 22, was born in October 1877 in New York. Both of her parents were born in New York. Joseph QUART, a adopted son-in-law age 27, was born in January in 1873 in New

York. Both of his parents were born in New York. Teresia QUART a grand daughter age 1 was born in November 1898. Ida QUART a grand daughter age six months was born in April 1900. St. Regis, Mohawk Reserve. E.D. 62, Page 110A, Household 142/144.

HERRIN, JOHN P. (Iroquois) Age 34 was born in August 1865 in New York. Both of his parents were born in New York. Annie his wife age 30, was born in July 1869 in New York. Her father was born in New York. Her mother was born in Canada. Joseph a son age 13 was born in January 1887. Katie a daughter age 10 was born in May 1890. Thomas a son age 5 was born in September 1894. Arthur a son age 2 was born in February 1898. St. Regis, Mohawk Reserve. E.D. 62, Page 109A, Household 137/139.

HERRIN, JOHN: (Iroquois) Age 32 was born in July 1867 in New York. Both of his parents were born in New York. Mary his wife age 28, was born in January 1872 in New York. Both of her parents were born in New York. Alexander a son age 8 was born in May 1892. Julius a son age 6 was born in April 1894. Charles a son age 2 was born in February 1898. George a son age ? was born in May 1900. St. Regis, Mohawk Reserve. E.D. 62, Page 110B, Household 148/150.

HERRIN, JULIUS: (Iroquois) Age 47 was born in October in 1852 in New York. Both of his parents were born in New York. Millie his wife age 38 was born in August 1861 in New York. Her father was born in New York. Her mother was born in Canada. Philip a son age 17 was born in July 1882. Louis a son age 16 was born in March 1882? Lizzie a daughter age 14 was born in April 1886. Mary a daughter age 11 was born in June 1888. Andrew a son age 9 was born in January 1891. William a son age 7 was born in February 1893. Moses a son age 5 was born in January 1895. Peter a son age 3 was born in March 1897. Margaret a daughter age 1 was born in February 1899. St. Regis, Mohawk Reserve. E.D. 62, Page 110A, Household 145/147.

HERRIN, LEWIS: (Iroquois) Age 35 was born in October 1864 in New York. Both of his parents were born in New York. Delia his wife age 39 was born in June 1860 in Canada. Her father was born in Canada. Her mother was born in New York. She immigrated in 1882. Peter a son age 17 was born in December 1882. Joseph a son age 15 was born in April 1885. Mitchell a son age 11 was born in January 1889. Moses a son age 8 was born in August 1891. Maggie a daughter age 7 was born in September 1892. Louisa a daughter age 4 was born in October 1895. Nancy a daughter age 1 was born in October 1898. St. Regis, Mohawk Reserve. E.D. 62. Page 108B, Household 134/136.

HERRIN, PETER: (Iroquois) Age 56 was born in December 1843 in New York. Both of his parents were born in New York. Kate his wife age 36 was born in March 1864 in Canada. Both of her parents were born in Canada. She immigrated in 1882. Mary MC DONELL, a step daughter was 17, was born in March 1883 in New York. Both of her parents were born in Canada. Mitchell VILLENEAUVE, an adopted son age 3, was born in January in 1897 in New York. His father was born in New York. His mother was born in Canada. Everyone in this household was listed as Iroquois. St. Regis, Mohawk Reserve. E.D. 62, Page 109B, Household 141/143.

HERRIN, RICHARD: (Iroquois) Age 51 was born in January in 1849 in New York. Both of his parents were born in New York. Rhoda his wife age 38, was born in October 1861 in New York. Her father was born in New York. Her mother was born in Canada. Lewis a son age 16 was born in August 1883. Sarah a daughter age 11 was born in August 1888. Jacob a son age 4 was born in February 1896. St. Regis Mohawk Reserve, E.D. 62, Page 91A, Household 12/12.

HILL, FRANK: (Iroquois) Age 54 was born in March 1846 in Canada. Both of his parents were born in Canada. He immigrated in 1899. Hedwidge his wife age 40, was born in October in 1859 in Canada. Both of her parents were born in Canada. She immigrated in 1899. Mitchell HILL a nephew age 18 was born in September 1881 in Canada. Both of his parents were born in Canada. He immigrated in 1899. Cecile HILL a niece age 16 was born in April 1884 in Canada. Both of her parents were born in Canada. She immigrated in 1900. Loran MARTIN, a nephew age 27, was born in March 1873 in Canada. Both of his parents were born in Canada. He immigrated in 1900. Josephine MARTIN age 17 was born in March 1883 in Canada. Both of her parents were born in Canada. She immigrated in 1900. Nancy DEER, a boarder age 18, was born in July in 1881 in Canada. Both of her parents were born in Canada. She immigrated in 1900. The parents of everyone in this household were listed as Iroquois. St. Regis, Mohawk Reserve. E.D. 62, Page 104B, Household 108/110.

HILL, JAMES: (Iroquois) Age 47 was born in August in 1852 in New York. Both of his parents were born in New York. Mary his wife age 41, was born in February 1859 in New York. Both of her parents were born in New York. Lewis a son age 21 was born in July 1878. Mary A., a daughter age 6 was born in June 1893. Selesia a daughter-in-law age 20 was born in January 1880. George a grand son age 1 was born in January 1899. St. Regis, Mohawk Reserve. E.D. 62, Page 99A, Household 67/69.

HILL, NANCY: (Iroquois) Age 78 was born in April 1822 in New York. Both of her parents were born in New York. Both of her parents were listed as Iroquois. St. Regis, Mohawk Reserve. E.D. 62, Page 103B, Household 98/100.

HOOPS, CHRISTIE (Iroquois) Age 49 was born in December 1850 in New York. Her father was born in Canada. Her mother was born in New York. John BILLINGS, a nephew age 21, was born in December 1878 in New York. Both of his parents were born in New York. St. Regis, Mohawk Reserve. E.D. 62, Page 97A, Household 54/55.

HOOPS, JOHN: (Iroquois) Age 42 was born in January in 1858 in New York. Both of his parents were born in Canada. He immigrated in 1897. Mary his wife age 22, was born in January 1878 in Canada. Both of her parents were born in Canada. She immigrated in 1897. John a son age 2 was born in July 1897. Lizzie a daughter age 1 was born in February 1899. Annie a daughter age three months was born in February 1900. Ida BOVAH, grand mother (Of John Hoops?) age 63, was born in October 1836 in Canada. Both of her parents were born in Canada. She immigrated in 1898. Everyone in this household were listed as Iroquois. St. Regis, Mohawk Reserve. E.D. 62, Page 97A, Household 52/54.

HOPPS, PETER: (Iroquois) Age 59 was born in October 1840 in Canada. Both of his parents were born in Canada. He immigrated in 1863. Agnes his wife age 48, was born in January 1852 in New York. Both of her parents were born in New York. Peter a son age 22 was born in October 1877. Margaret a daughter age 17 was born in September 1882. Susan a daughter age 12 was born in March 1888. Mitchell a son age 8 was born in April 1892. St. Regis, Mohawk Reserve. E.D. 62, Page 106B, Household 123/125.

HOPPS, PETER: (Iroquois) Age 22 was born in October 1877 in New York. His father was born in Canada. His mother was born in New York. St. Regis, Mohawk Reserve. E.D. 62, Page 107A, Household 123/125.

JACK, THOMAS: (Iroquois) Age 49 was born in March 1851 in Canada. Both of his parents were born in Canada. He immigrated in 1877. Ettie his wife age 44 born in August 1855 in New York. Her father was born in Canada. Her mother was born in New York. Joseph a son age 16 was born in August 1883. Louise a daughter age 13 was born in December 1886. Rose a daughter age 11 was born in February 1881. Peter a son age 9 was born in March 1891. Agnes a daughter age 5 was born in July 1894. Francis a son age 3 was born in March 1897. Noah a son age 1 was born in May 1899. St. Regis, Mohawk Reserve, E.D. 62, Page 112A, Household 157/159.

JACKSON, JOSEPH: (Iroquois) Age 48 was born in September 1851 in New York. Both of his parents were born in New York. Julia his wife age 59, was born in February 1841 in New York. Both of her parents were born in New York. Frank a son age 27 was born in April 1873. Lewis a son age 19 was born in July 1880. Hattie a daughter age 17 was born in November 1882. Simon a son age 14 was born in July 1885. Christie a cousin age 13 was born in February 1887. St. Regis, Mohawk Reserve. E.D. 62, Page 99B, Household 71/73.

JACKSON, LORAN: (Iroquois) Age 51 was born in August 1849 in New York. His father was born in New York. His mother was born in Canada. Christenia his wife age 53 was born in August in 1846 in Canada. Both of her parents were born in Canada. She immigrated in 1874. Louisa a daughter age 23 was born in June 1876. Susan a daughter age 22 was born in October 1877. Lewis a son age 20 was born in September 1879. Thomas a son age 5 was born in March 1885. John a son age 12 was born in March 1888. St. Regis, Mohawk Reserve. E.D. 62, Page 109B, Household 139/141.

JACKSON, LORAN: (Iroquois) Age 51 was born in August 1849 in New York. Both of his parents were born in New York. Charlotte his wife age 33 was born in August 1866 in New York. Both of her parents were born in New York. Daniel a son age 4 was born in November 1895. Peter a son age 3 was born in January 1897. Charles a son age two months was born in March 1900, Mata? a son age 18 was born in November 1881. St. Regis, Mohawk Reserve. E.D. 62, Page 96A, Household 47/48.

JACOBS, ABRAM: (Iroquois) Age 26 was born in June 1873 in New York. Both of his parents were born in New York. Lizzie his wife age 19, was born in November 1880 in New York. Both of her parents were born in New York. St. Regis, Mohawk Reserve. E.D. 62, Page 106A, Household 116/118.

68

JACOBS, ALEXANDER: (Iroquois) Age 52 was born in June 1847 in New York. Both of his parents were born in Canada. Catharine JACOBS mother (Of Alexander Jacobs) age 94, was born in June 1805 in Canada. Both of her parents were born in Canada. She immigrated in 1827. David a son age 23 was born in December 1876. Mary A., a daughter age 21 was born in April 1879. St. Regis, Mohawk Reserve. E.D. 62, Page 102A, Household 88/90.

JACOBS, DOMINICK: (Iroquois) Age 62 was born in October in 1837 in Canada. Both of his parents were born in Canada. He immigrated in 1850. Philoena? his wife (She was listed as a white woman) age 63 was born in December 1836 in French Canada (Quebec). Both of her parents were born in French Canada (Quebec). She immigrated in 1845. Dominick a son age 22 was born in February 1878. Levi a son age 19 was born in December 1880. St. Regis, Mohawk Reserve. E.D. 62, Page 111A, Household 150/152.

JACOBS, JACOB: (Iroquois) Age 59 was born in April 1841 in New York. His father was born in New York. His mother was born in Canada. St. Regis, Mohawk Reserve. E.D. 62, Page 111A, Household 149/151.

JACOBS, LEVI: (Iroquois) Age 40 was born in July in 1859 in New York. Both of his parents were born in New York. Christie a sister age 35 was born in April 1865. Catharine a sister age 30 was born in August 1869. William a brother age 26 was born in October 1873. Mitchell a brother age 23 was born in March 1877. St. Regis, Mohawk Reserve. E.D. 62, Page 112B, Household 161/163.

JACOBS, LEWIS: (Iroquois) Age 43 was born in September in 1856 in New York. Both of his parents were born in New York. Mary his wife age 33, was born in April in 1867 in New York. Both of her parents were born in New York. James a son age 12 was born in June 1887. Louisa a daughter age 10 was born in June 1889. Angus a son age 8 was born in July 1891. David a son age 3 was born in August 1896. Andrew a son age 1 was born in August 1898. St. Regis, Mohawk Reserve. E.D. 62, Page 121A, Household 221/223.

JACOBS, LEWIS: (Iroquois) Age 62 was born in November 1837 in New York. Both of his parents were born in New York. Margaret his wife age 57, was born in September 1842 in New York. Both of her parents were born in Canada. John a son age 36 was born in August 1863. Mary A. LA FRANCE, a daughter age 26, was born in April 1874 in New York. Both of her parents were born in New York. Christina JACOBS, a daughter age 20, was born in April 1880 in New York. Both of her parents were born in New York. Sankey JACOBS a son age 22 was born in April 1878. David JACOBS a grand son age 9 was born in March 1891. Thomas LA FRANCE, a grand son age 5, was born in January 1895 in New York. Both of his parents were born in New York. St. Regis, Mohawk Reserve. E.D. 62, Page 100A, Household 76/78.

JACOBS, LEWIS: (Iroquois) Age 30 was born in October 1869 in New York. His father was born in New York. His mother was born in Canada. Jennie his wife age 22, was born in July 1877 in New York. Her father was born in Canada. Her mother was born in New York. Libbie a daughter age 1 was born in August 1898. St. Regis, Mohawk Reserve. E.D. 62, Page 110B, Household 147/149.

JACOBS, MOSES: (Iroquois) Age 38 was born in February 1862 in New York. His father was born in Canada. His mother was born in French Canada. Agnes his wife age 32, was born in May 1868 in New York. Her father was born in New York. Her mother was born in Canada. Philoma? a daughter age 14 was born in February 1886. Paul a son age 9 was born in February 1891. Paul SMOKE, a servant age 18, was born in June 1881 in Canada. Both of his parents were born in Canada. He immigrated in 1888. St. Regis, Mohawk Reserve. E.D. 62, Page 111A, Household 152/154.

JACOBS, PETER: (Iroquois) Age 74 was born in August 1825 in New York. Both of his parents were born in Canada. Both of his parents were Iroquois. Susan his wife age 68, was born in January? 1832 in Canada. Both of her parents were born in Canada. She immigrated in 1833. Both of her parents were Iroquois. St. Regis, Mohawk Reserve. E.D. 62, Page 92B, Household 25/26.

JOCK, THOMAS: (Iroquois) Age 49 was born in March 1851 in Canada. Both of his parents were born in Canada. He immigrated in 1878. Ettie his wife age 44, was born in August 1855 in New York. Her father was born in New York. Her mother was born in Canada. St. Regis, Mohawk Reserve. E.D. 62, Page 112A, Household 157/159.

JOHNDROW, SARAH: (Iroquois) Age 36 was born in July in 1873 in New York. Her father was born in Canada. Her mother was born in New York. Julia a daughter age 11 was born in August 1888. Mitchell OAKS a boarder age 34 was born in January 1864 in New York. His father was born in Canada. His mother was born in New York. Mary PHILLIPS a boarder age 34 was born in March 1878 in Canada. Both of her parents were born in Canada. She immigrated in 1900. Annie WILLIAMS a boarder age 19 was born in September 1880 in Canada. Both of his parents were born in Canada. She immigrated in 1900. Everyone in this household was listed as Iroquois. St. Regis, Mohawk Reserve. E.D. 62, Page 105A, Household 109/111.

JOHNS, MITCHELL: (Iroquois) Age 32 was born in August 1867 in New York. His father was born in Canada. His mother was born in New York. Susan his wife age 28, was born in April 1872 in New York. Her father was born in New York. Her mother was born in Canada. Margaret a daughter age 10 was born in April 1890. Addie a daughter age 8 was born in August 1891. Mary a daughter age 6 was born in September 1893. John a son age 3 was born in September 1896. Susan a daughter age 1 was born in August 1898. Mohawk Reserve. E.D. 62, Page 108B, Household 132/134 or 131/132.

JOHNSON, MITCHELL: (Iroquois) Age 44 was born in November in 1855 in Canada. Both of his parents were born in Canada. He immigrated in 1870. Agnes a daughter age 12 was born in December 1887. Andrew a son age 8 was born in January 1892. John a son age 16 was born in March 1884. Margaret ISAAC, a daughter age 22, was born in September 1877 in New York. Both of her parents were born in Canada. John ISAAC, a son-in-law age 27, was born in September 1872 in New York. Both of his parents were born in Canada, Louise a grand daughter age three months born in February 1900. Everyone in this household were listed as Iroquois. St. Regis, Mohawk Reserve. E.D. 62, Page 91A, Household 11/11.

LA FRANCE, LEWIS: (Iroquois) Age 70 was born in March 1830 in Canada. Both of his parents were born in Canada. He immigrated in 1831. Lewis Jr., a son age 46 was born in August 1853 in New York. His father was born in Canada. His mother was born in New York. Margaret a daughter-in-law age 26 was born in July 1873 in New York. Both of her parents were born in New York, Mary A., a grand daughter age 10 was born in April 1890. Sarah a grand daughter age 1 was born in August 1898. Margaret JACOB, a servant age 22, was born in December 1877 in New York. Both her parents were born in New York. Everyone in this household were listed as Iroquois.. St. Regis, Mohawk Reserve. E.D. 62, Page 91B, Household 16/16.

LA FRENCE? or LA FRANCE?, PETER: (Iroquois) Age 46 was born in November 1853 in New York. Both of his parents were born in Canada. Catherine his wife age 44, was born in December 1855 in New York. Both of her parents were born in New York. Susan a daughter age 22 was born in January 1878. Minnie a daughter age 20 was born in March 1880. Loran a son age 17 was born in December 1882. Richard a son age 4 was born in September 1895. Annie a daughter age 1 was born in September 1898. Sarah GARROW a daughter age 26, was born in July 1873 in New York. Both of her parents were born in New York. Lewis GARROW, a son-in-law age 28, was born in December 1871 in New York. Both of his parents were born in New York. John GARROW a grand son age 1 was born in December 1898. Everyone in this household were listed as Iroquois. St. Regis, Mohawk Reserve. E.D. 62, Page 98A, Household 64/66. or 63/64?

LA FRENCE? OR LA FRANCE? PETER: (Iroquois) Age 39 was born in December 1860 in New York. Both of his parents were born in New York. Mary his wife age 36, was born in August 1863 in Canada. Both of her parents were born in Canada. She immigrated in 1880. Phillip a son age 17 born in January 1883, Mitchell a son age 15 was born in March 1885. Thomas a son age 13 was born in December 1886. Charlotte a daughter age 9 was born in August 1890. Sarah BOVAH?, a sister-in-law age 40, was born in March 1860 in Canada. Both of her parents were born in Canada. John BENEDICT, a nephew age 14, was born in March 1886 in New York. Both of his parents were born in New York. All of the people in this household were listed as Iroquois. St. Regis, Mohawk Reserve. E.D. 62, Page 95A, Household 39/40.

LAUGHING, AGNES: (Iroquois) Age 48 was born in August in 1851 in Canada. Both of her parents were born in Canada. She immigrated in 1886. Loran a son age 14 born in March 1886, Mitchell a son age 7 was born in August 1892. Alexander Francis, a son age 23, was born in November 1876 in New York. Both of his parents were born in Canada. St. Regis, Mohawk Reserve. E.D. 62, Page 116B, Household 189/191.

LAUGHING, ANGUS: (Iroquois) Age 35 was born in October in 1864 in New York. Both of his parents were born in New York. Annie his wife age 30, was born in January in 1870 in Canada. Both of her parents were born in Canada. She immigrated in 1878. St. Regis, Mohawk Reserve. E.D. 62, Page 113B, Household 168/170.

LAUGHING, BAZILE: (Iroquois) Age 24 was born in February 1876 in New York. Both of his parents were born in New York. Josephine his wife age 19, was born in February 1881 in New York. Both of her parents were born in New York. Mary TARBELL, mother (Of Bazile Laughing) age 50, was born in October 1849 in New York. Both of her parents were born in Canada. Antoine LAUGHING a brother age 12 was born in January 1889 in New York. All of the people in this household were listed as Iroquois. St. Regis, Mohawk Reserve. E.D. 62, Page 96B, Household 50/51.

LAUGHING, MITCHELL: (Iroquois) Age 31 was born in June 1868 in New York. Both of his parents were born in New York. Agatha his wife age 32, was born in July 1867 in New York. Both of her parents were born in New York. Mary a daughter age 12 was born in August 1887. Angus a son age 9 was born in May 1891. Mary Ann a daughter age 7 was born in January 1893. Sarah a daughter age 3 was born in February 1897. Richard a son age eight months was born in September 1899. Julia CHUBB, mother-in-law (Of Mitchell Laughing) age 73, was born in July 1826 in New York. Both of her parents were born in New York. All of the people in this household were listed as Iroquois. St. Regis, Mohawk Reserve. E.D. 62, Page 95A, Household 41/43.

LAUGHING, PETER: (Iroquois) Age 48 was born in August 1851 in New York. His father was born in New York. His mother was born in Canada. Nancy his wife age 39, was born in November 1860 in New York. Her father was born in Canada. Her mother was born in New York. Noah a son age 3 was born in August 1896. St. Regis, Mohawk Reserve. E.D. 62, Page 97B, Household 57/59.

LAUGHING, RICHARD: (Iroquois) Age 25 was born in June 1874 in New York. Both of his parents were born in New York. Susan his wife age 24, was born in November 1875 in Canada. Both of her parents were born in Canada. She immigrated in 1893. Joseph a son age 6 was born in April 1894. John a son age 3 was born in September 1896. Maggie a daughter age eight months was born in September 1899. St. Regis, Mohawk Reserve. E.D. 62, Page 96B, Household 51/52.

LAZOR, JOHN: (Iroquois) Age 42 was born in September 1857 in New York. His father was born in Canada. His mother was born in New York. Mary his wife age 36 was born in October 1863 in Canada. Both of her parents were born in Canada. She immigrated in 1878. Charles a son age 19 was born in February 1881. Daniel a son age 16 was born in January 1884. Frank a son age 13 was born in March 1887. Mary A., a daughter age 8 was born in August 1891. Elizabeth a daughter age 2 was born in April 1898. Joseph a son age 6 was born in March 1894. St. Regis, Mohawk Reserve, E.D. 62, Page 102B, Household 93/95.

LAZOR, LEWEY: (Iroquois) Age 42 was born in October 1857 in New York. Both of his parents were born in New York. Phebe his wife age 40, was born in December 1859 in New York. Both of her parents were born in New York. Phiillip a son age 17 was born in August 1882. Andrew a son age 14 was born in January 1886. Lewis a son age 12 was born in May 1888. Levi a son age 9 was born in January 1891. Thomas a son age 5 was born in September 1894. Catharine LA FRENCE? OR LA FRANCE?, a servant age 23, was born in November 1876 in Canada. Both of her parents were born in Canada. She immigrated in 1894. Everyone in this household was listed as Iroquois. St. Regis, Mohawk Reserve. E.D. 62, Page 105B, Household 113/115.

LAZOR OR LOZOR? MITCHELL: (Iroquois) Age 34 was born in December 1865 in New York. His father was born in Canada. His mother was born in New York. Mary his wife age 32, was born in June 1867 in New York. Her father was born in New York. Her mother was born in Canada. Abram a son age 15 was born in October 1884. John a son age 13 was born in January 1897. Mary a daughter age 11 was born in September 1888. Julia daughter age 9 was born in September 1890. Frank a son age 7 was born in August 1892. Frederick a son age 5 was born in January 1895. Peter a son age 3 was born in May 1897. Loran a son age 1 was born in August 1898. St. Regis, Mohawk Reserve. E.D. 62, Page 93B, Household 24/25.

LEAF, MITCHELL: (Iroquois) Age 45 was born in October 1854 in Canada. Both of his parents were born in Canada. He immigrated in 1875. Joseph a son age 33 was born in November 1866. Lewis a son age 9 was born in May 1891. Mary SEARS, a daughter age 28, was born in November 1871 in New York. Her father was born in Canada. Her mother was born in New York. John SEARS, a son-in-law age 30, was born in January 1870 in Canada. Both of his parents were born in Canada. He immigrated in 1894. Minnie SEARS a grand daughter age 4 was born in November 1895. Terisia? SEARS a grand daughter age 1 was born in July 1898. Everyone in this household were listed as Iroquois. St. Regis, Mohawk Reserve. E.D. 62, Page 106B, Household 121/123.

LORAN, ALEXANDER: (Iroquois) Age 29 was born in December 1870 in New York. Both of his parents were born in New York. Teresia his wife age 23, was born in May 1877 in New York. Both of her parents were born in New York. St. Regis, Mohawk Reserve. E.D. 62, Page 113B, Household 167/169.

LORAN, DAVID: (Iroquois) Age 36 was born in August 1863 in New York. His father was born in New York. His mother was born in Canada. Christinia his wife age 35, was born in October 1864 in New York. Both of her parents were born in New York. Mary A., a daughter age 10 was born in January 1890. James a son age 5 was born in December 1894. Sarah Loran, mother (Of David Loran) age 60, was born in September 1839 in Canada. Both of her parents were born in Canada. She immigrated in 1860. Everyone in this household were listed as Iroquois. St. Regis, Mohawk Reserve. E.D. 62, Page 97A, Household 55/57.

LORAN, JOHN: (Iroquois) Age 36 was born in November 1863 in New York. Both of his parents were born in New York. Christine his wife age 35, was born in April 1865 in New York. Both of her parents were born in New York. Elizabeth a daughter age 8 was born in December 1891. David a son age 7 was born in August 1892. Abram a son age 4 was born in July 1895. Mary a daughter age 2 was born in August 1897. Annie WHITE, a boarder age 67, was born in November 1832 in New York. Both of her parents were born in New York. Mary COOK a servant age 20, was born in November 1879 in New York. Both of her parents were born in New York. All of the people in this household were listed as Iroquois. St. Regis, Mohawk Reserve. E.D. 62, Page 102A, Household 92/94.

LOTHRIDGE, MITCHELL: (Iroquois) Age 43 was born in October 1856 in Canada. Both of his parents were born in Canada. He immigrated in 1862. Christina his wife age 48, was born in November 1851 in New

York. Both of his parents were born in Canada. St. Regis, Mohawk Reserve. E.D. 62, Page 101A, Household 83/85.

LOZOR, PETER: (Iroquois) Age 35 was born in May 1865 in New York. His father was born in Canada. His mother was born in New York. Elizabeth his wife age 29, was born in April 1871 in New York. Both of her parents were born in New York. St. Regis, Mohawk Reserve. Louise a daughter age 8 was born in November 1891. George a son age 11 was born in November 1888. Emma a daughter age 7 was born in March 1893. Ida a daughter age 3 was born in February 1897. Michael a son age 1 was born in January 1899. E.D. 62, Page 101A, Household 80/82.

LOZOR, WILLIAM: (Iroquois) Age 67 was born in September 1833 in New York. Both of his parents were born in New York. Mary A. his wife age 66, was born in September 1833 in New York. Both of her parents were born in New York. Paul LOZOR, a nephew age 20, was born in January 1880 in Canada. Both of his parents were born in Canada. He immigrated in 1896. Julia GRAY a grand daughter age 18 was born in June 1881 in New York. Both of her parents were born in New York. Maria CHUBB a sister-in-law age 52, was born in March 1848 in New York. Both of her parents were born in New York. Margaret JACOBS, a niece age 29, was born in March 1871 in New York. Both of her parents were born in New York. Peter BOOTS, a nephew age 8, was born in March 1892 in New York. Both of his parents were born in New York. All of the parents of the people in this household were listed as Iroquois. St. Regis, Mohawk Reserve. E.D. 62, Page 103B, Household 101/103.

MC DONALD, DAVID: (Iroquois) Age 33 was born in September 1866 in New York. His father was born in Canada. His mother was born in New York. His wife, Elmira? or Elmina? (She was listed as a white woman) age 25, was born in January 1875 in New York. Both of her parents were born in New York. Wilbur L., a son age 4 was born in June 1895. Bertha L., a daughter age 3 was born in February 1897. James C., a son age 2 was born in April 1898. Eliza a daughter age two months was born in March 1900. St. Regis, Mohawk Reserve. E.D. 62, Page 104B, Household 107/109.

MC DONALD, ISAAC: (Iroquois) Age 28 was born in October 1871 in New York. Both of his parents were born in Canada. Mary A. his wife age 25, was born in May 1875 in New York. Her father was born in New York. Her mother was born in Canada. Clyde a son age 8 was born in May 1892. Eva a daughter age 3 was born in April 1897. St. Regis, Mohawk Reserve. E.D. 62, Page 105A, Household 112/114.

MC DONALD, JOHN: (Iroquois) Age 43 was born in June 1856 in New York. Both of his parents were born in New York. Christenia his wife age 42, was born in May 1858 in Canada. Both of her parents were born in Canada. She immigrated in 1878. Peter a son age 19 was born in April 1881. Mary a daughter age 17 was born in March 1883. Mary Ann a daughter age 13 was born in August 1880. Nancy a daughter age 11 was born in July 1888. Catharine a daughter age 9 was born in February 1891. Lewis a son age 6 was born in March 1894. Louisa a daughter age 4 was born in November 1895. Catharine Mc Donald, mother (Of John Mc Donald) age 81, was born in April 1819 in New York. Both of her parents were born in New York. Paul LAZOR an adopted son age 18, was born in June 1881 in Canada. Both of his parents were born in Canada.

He immigrated in 1896. Everyone in this household was listed as Iroquois. St. Regis, Mohawk Reserve. E.D. 62, Page 118A, Household 201/203.

MC DONALD, LEWEY: (Iroquois) Age 66 was born in March 1834 in Canada. Both of his parents were born in Canada. He immigrated in 1841. Louisa his wife age 55, was born in March 1845 in New York. Both of her parents were born in New York. Eliza a daughter age 22 was born in March 1878. Phillip a son age 20 was born in December 1879. Lizzie a daughter age 18 was born in April 1882. Susie a daughter age 16 was born in May 1884. St. Regis, Mohawk Reserve. E.D. 62, Page 104A, Household 106/108.

MC DONELL, ELIZA: (Iroquois) Age 44 was born in January 1855 in New York. Both of her parents were born in New York. Sarah a daughter age 17 was born in July 1880. Richard a son age 17? was born in July 1882? Nancy a daughter age 14 was born in December 1885. John a son age 12 was born in March 1888. Mary A., a daughter age 8 was born in September 1891. Peter a son age 4 was born in April 1896. Mitchell a son age 1 was born in September 1898. St. Regis, Mohawk Reserve. E.D. 62, Page 99B, Household 72/74.

OAKS, JOHN: (Iroquois) Age 40 was born in November 1859 in Canada. Both of his parents were born in Canada. He immigrated in 1878. Minnie his wife age 30, was born in January 1870 in New York. Her father was born in New York. Her mother was born in Canada. Richard a son age 18 was born in July 1881. Regis a son age 18 was born in July 1881. Annie a daughter age 16 was born in November 1883. Mary a daughter age 14 was born in October 1885. Charlotte a daughter age 11 was born in June 1888. Louisa a daughter age 5 was born in June 1894. Lewis a son age 3 was born in December 1896. Mitchell a son age 9 was born in August 1890. Annie a daughter-in-law age 18 was born in October 1881. Mary a grand daughter age 1 was born in August 1898. St. Regis, Mohawk Reserve. E.D. 62, Page 107A, Household 127/129.

OAKS, MITCHELL: (Iroquois) Age 61 was born in May 1839 in Canada. Both of his parents were born in Canada. He immigrated in 1860. Catharine his wife age 54, was born in May 1846 in New York. Both of her parents were born in New York. Richard a son age 20 was born in June 1879. Mitchell a son age 14 was born in January 1886. Mary LORAN a daughter age 18 was born in March 1882 in New York. Her father was born in Canada. Her mother was born in New York. Susan BOOTS a boarder age 23, was born in February in 1876 in New York. Both of her parents were born in New York. Everyone in this household was listed as Iroquois. St. Regis, Mohawk Reserve. E.D. 62, Page 108A, Household 131/133 or 130/131.

OAKS, PETER: (Iroquois) Age 48 was born in May 1852 in Canada. Both of his parents were born in Canada. He immigrated in 1887. Maggie his wife age 42, was born in July 1857 in Canada. Both of her parents were born in Canada. She immigrated in 1885. Annie a daughter age 12 was born in April 1888, John a son age 7 was born in January 1893. St. Regis, Mohawk Reserve. E.D. 62, Page 121A, Household 223/225.

OAKS, RICHARD: (Iroquois) Age 27 was born in October 1872 in New York. His father was born in Canada. His mother was born in New York. His wife, Susan age 21, was born in April 1899 in New York. both of her parents were born in New York. St. Regis, Mohawk Reserve. E.D. 62. Page 106B, Household 120/122.

PAPPENEAU, MITCHELL: (Iroquois) Age 52 was born in March in 1848 in Canada. His father was born in Canada. His mother was born in New York. He immigrated in 1878. Christinia his wife age 40, was born in October in 1859 in New York. Her father was born in New York. Her mother was born in Canada. Annie a daughter age 19 was born in March 1881. Joseph a son age 12 was born in April 1889. Paul a son age 10 was born in May 1890. Lena a daughter age 5 was born in June 1894. Jacob a son age 3 was born in September 1896. John a son age eleven month was born in June 1899. St. Regis, Mohawk Reserve. E.D. 62, Page 115A, Household 181/183.

PAUL, SARAH: (Iroquois) Age 36 was born in May in 1864 in New York. Her father was born in New York. Her mother was born in Canada. Annie a daughter age 15 was born in March 1885. Agnes a daughter age 5 was born in May 1895. Jacob a son age 3 was born in January 1897. Susan EDWARDS, a daughter age 18, was born in October 1881 in New York. Her father was born in Canada. Her mother was born in New York. Lewis EDWARDS, a son-in-law, was born in September in 1876 in New York. His father was born in New York. His mother was born in Canada. Everyone in this household was listed as Iroquois. St. Regis, Mohawk Reserve. E.D. 62, Page 118B, Household 205/207.

PETERS, GEORGE: (Iroquois) Age 51 was born in November in 1848 in Canada. Both of his parents were born in Canada. He immigrated in 1878. Philomene his wife age 47, was born in January 1853 in New York. Both of her parents were born in Canada. David a son age 22 was born in April 1878. Christinia a daughter age 20 was born in September 1879. Mary Ann a daughter age 19 was born in March 1881. Mary a daughter age 17 was born in December 1882. Abram a son age 15 was born in January 1885. Lewis a son age 11 was born in January 1889. Charlotte a daughter age 9 was born in April 1891. Margaret a daughter age 6 was born in September 1893. Agnes a daughter age 3 was born in October 1890. St. Regis, Mohawk Reserve. E.D. 62, Page 118A, Household 200/202.

PHILIPS, LEWIS: (Iroquois) Age 63 was born in November 1836 in New York. Both of his parents were born in Canada. Mary his wife age 56, was born in January 1844 in Canada. Both of her parents were born in Canada. She immigrated in 1888. John age son age 27 was born in May 1873. Mary A., a daughter age 22 was born in May 1878. Teresa SQUIRES, a daughter age 23, was born in June 1876 in Canada. Her father was born in New York. Her mother was born in Canada. She immigrated in 1888. Lewis SQUIRES, a son-in-law age 33, was born in January 1867 in New York. Both of his parents were born in New York. George SQUIRES a grand son age 1 born in July 1898. Everyone in this household was listed as Iroquois. St. Regis, Mohawk Reserve. E.D. 62, Page 107A, Household 126/128 or 127/129.

PRICE, SARAH: (Iroquois) Age 40 was born in March 1860 in Canada. Both of her parents were born in Canada. She immigrated in 1899. Mary Ann a daughter age 17 was born in June 1882. Angus a son age 15 was born in August 1884. Mary a daughter age 12 was born in April 1888. Peter a son age 6 was born in July 1893. Kate a daughter age 3 was born in February 1897. NOTE: Sarah PRICE was listed as the head of this household. She was not given a household number by the census taker. She was either a member of the Christian Bonapart household number 15/15 or she was not given a number for head of household by the census taker. St. Regis, Mohawk Reserve. E.D. 62, after Household 15/15 and before the Household of Lewis La France number 16/16 on page 91B.

QUART, ABRAM: (Iroquois) Age 47 was born in November 1852 in New York. Both of his parents were born in New York. Lodia his wife age 54, was born in December 1845 in New York. Both of her parents were born in New York. Thomas a son age 30 was born in November 1869. Mary a daughter age 15 was born in February 1885. Margaret a daughter age 11 was born in July 1888. Louise a daughter age 3 was born in February 1897. St. Regis, Mohawk Reserve. E.D. 62, Page 111B, Household 156/158.

QUART, ABRAM: (Iroquois) Age 28 was born in December 1871 in New York. Both of his parents were born in New York. Mary his wife age 24 was born in February 1876 in Canada. Both of her parents were born in Canada. She immigrated in 1895. Mary Ann GORROW a step daughter age 6, was born in February in 1894 in Canada. Both of her parents were born in Canada. She immigrated in 1895. Agnes COLE, a boarder age 23, was born in February in 1877 in New York. Both of her parents were born in New York. Annie COLE a boarder age 6 was born in April 1894. Peter Cole a boarder age 1 was born in February 1899. Everyone in this household was listed as Iroquois. St. Regis, Mohawk Reserve. E.D. 62, Page 112B, Household 162/164.

QUART, LEWIS: (Iroquois) Age 28 was born in September 1871 in New York. Both of his parents were born in New York. Annie his wife age 26, was born in February in 1874 in New York. Both of her parents were born in New York. Sarah a daughter age 2 was born in February 1898. Annie QUART a sister age 20 was born in December 1879. Sarah MC DONALD, a boarder age 19, was born in July 1880 in New York. Both of her parents were born in New York. Mary GRAY, a boarder age 19, was born in November 1880 in New York. Both of her parents were born in New York. Everyone in this household was listed as Iroquois. St. Regis, Mohawk Reserve. E.D. 62, Page 99A, Household 70/72.

QUART, PETER: (Iroquois) Age 39 was born in October 1868 in New York. His parents were born in New York. Mary his wife age 30, was born in December 1869 in New York. Her parents were both born in New York. Thomas a son age 12 was born in December 1887. Christie a daughter age 9 was born in February 1891. Mary a daughter age 7 was born in November 1892. Annie a daughter age 1 was born in November 1898. Lewis QUART father (Of Peter Quart) age 81 was born in March 1819 in New York. Both of his parents were born in New York. Both of his parents were Iroquois. St. Regis Mohawk Reserve, E.D. 62, Page 113A, Household 162/165.

QUART, RICHARD: (Iroquois) Age 40 was born in January in 1860 in New York. Both of his parents were born in New York. Teresia his wife age 39, was born in December 1860 in New York. Both of her parents were born in New York. Charles a son age 19 was born in January 1881. Peter a son age 17 was born in August 1882. Agnes a daughter age 14 was born in July 1885. St. Regis, Mohawk Reserve. E.D. 62, Page 112B, Household 159/161.

RANSOM, ALEXANDER: (Iroquois) Age 53 was born in May 1847 in New York. Both of his parents were born in New York. Margaret his wife age 49, was born in March 1851 in New York. Both of her parents were born in New York. Louisa a daughter age 20 was born in November 1879. Kate a daughter age 15 was born in June 1884. Annie a daughter age 11 was born in November 1888. Christenia a daughter age 6 was born in November 1888. St. Regis, Mohawk Reserve. E.D. 62, Page 114A, Household 172/173.

RAMSOM, ANGUS: (Iroquois) Age 35 was born in November 1864 in New York. Both of his parents were born in New York. Agnes his wife age 32, was born in March in 1868 in New York. Both of her parents were born in New York. Andrew COOK a nephew age 12, was born in October 1887 in New York. Both of his parents were born in New York. Both of his parents were Iroquois. St. Regis, Mohawk Reserve. E.D. 62, Page 115A, Household 179/181.

RANSOM, JOHN: (Iroquois) Age 67 was born in September 1832 in New York. Both of his parents were born in New York. Annie his wife age 66 was born in November 1833 in Canada. Both of her parents were born in Canada. She immigrated in 1868. Louisa a daughter age 29 was born in June 1870. Moses a grand son was born in May 1900. St. Regis, Mohawk Reserve. E.D. 62, Page 115A, Household 178/180.

RANSOM, JOHN: (Iroquois) Age 39 was born in November 1860 in New York. Both of his parents were born in New York. Polly his wife age 39, was born in December 1860 in New York. Both of her parents were born in New York. Susan a daughter age 18 was born in October 1881. Jacob a son age 16 was born in June 1883. Peter a son age 12 was born in March 1888. George a son age 11 was born in May 1889. Sarah a daughter age 6 was born in August 1893. St. Regis, Mohawk Reserve, E.D. 62, Page 117B, Household 199/201.

RANSOM, LORAN: (Iroquois) Age 48 was born in ? 1851 in New York. Both of his parents were born in New York. Sarah his wife age 47, was born in May 1853 in New York. Both of her parents were born in New York. Mary a daughter age 16 was born in September 1883. Moses a son age 12 was born in December 1887. Kate a daughter age 7 was born in July 1890. Christie a daughter age 3 was born in November 1896. Margaret GRAY, a servant age 16, was born in October 1883 in New York. Everyone in this household was listed as Iroquois. St. Regis, Mohawk Reserve. E.D. 62, Page 116B, Household 192/194.

RANSOM, MARGARET: (Iroquois) Age 70 was born in November in 1829 in New York. Both of her parents were born in New York. Annie COOK, a grand daughter age 22, was born in August in 1877 in New York. Both of her parents were born in New York. Francis COOK a grand son age 19 was born in September 1880. Charles COOK a grand son age 17 was born in July 1882. The parents of everyone in this household were Iroquois. St. Regis, Mohawk Reserve. E.D. 62, Page 119B, Household 211/213.

RANSOM, PHILMENA: (Iroquois) Age 47 was born in March 1853 in New York. Her father was born in Canada. Her mother was born in Canada. Lewis a son age 23 was born in November 1876. Abram a son age 21 was born in May 1879. Peter a son age 15 was born in April 1885. Thomas a son age 13 was born in February 1887. Margaret a daughter age 9 was born in July 1890. St. Regis, Mohawk Reserve. E.D. 62, Page 108B, Household 135/137.

RANSOM, TERANCE: (Iroquois) Age 67 was born in October 1832 in New York. Both of his parents were born in Canada. Lewis a son age 27 was born in August 1872. Frank LEAFE, a grand son age 9, was born in November 1890 in New York. His father was born in Canada. His mother was born in New York. Both of his parents were Iroquois. St. Regis, Mohawk Reserve. E.D. 62 Page 92A, Household 18/19.

RANSOM, THOMAS: (Iroquois) Age 64 was born in August in 1835 in New York. Both of his parents were born in New York. Louise his wife age 54, was born in August in 1845 in New York. Her father was born in Canada. Her mother was born in New York. Mary GORROW, mother-in-law (Of Thomas Ransom) age 96, was born in January 1804 in New York. Both of her parents were born in Canada. Both of her parents were Iroquois. St. Regis, Mohawk Reserve. E.D. 62, Page 113B, Household 169/171.

RUBADO, JOHN: (White) Age 22 was born in April 1878 in New York. His father was born in French Canada (Quebec). His mother was born in New York. Louisa his wife age 31, was born in March 1869 in New York. She was listed as an Iroquois. Both of her parents were born in New York. Margaret a daughter age 1 was born in June 1898. Peter CHUBB, father-in-law (Of John Rubado) age 58, was born in November 1841 in New York. Both of his parents were born in New York. Both of his parents were Iroquois. St. Regis, Mohawk Reserve. E.D. 62, Page 97A, Household 53/55.

SAUM?, JOSEPH: (Iroquois) Age 53 was born in October in 1846 in Canada. Both of his parents were born in Canada. He immigrated in 1884. Catharine his wife age 57, was born in May 1843 in Canada. Both of her parents were born in Canada. She immigrated in 1884. Mitchell a son age 33 was born in November 1866. Thomas a son age 27 was born in August 1872. Peter a son age 20 was born in January 1880. St. Regis, Mohawk Reserve. E.D. 62, Page 119B, Household 213/215.

SAWYER, FRANK: (Iroquois) Age 26 was born in June 1873 in New York. Both of her parents were born in New York. Margaret SAWYER mother (Of Frank Sawyer. She was listed as a white woman) age 73, was born in August 1826 in New York. Both of her parents were born in New York. Peter SAWYER a brother age 35 was born in March 1865. Maggie SAWYER a sister age 30 was born in March 1870. James H. COREY a boarder (He was listed as a white man) age 54 was born in August 1845 in New York. Both of his parents were born in New York. Ella COREY (She was listed as a white woman) a boarder age 29 was born in July 1870 in New York. Both of her parents were born in New York. John SAWYER an uncle (Of Frank Sawyer) age 69, was born in March 1831 in New York. Both of his parents were born in New York. Both of his parents were Iroquois. St. Regis, Mohawk Reserve. E.D. 62, Page 101B, Household 86/88 or 85/86.

SAWYER, JOHN: (Iroquois) Age 47 was born in March 1853 in New York. Both of his parents were born in New York. Sarah his wife age 42, was born in August 1857 in New York. Both of her parents were born in New York. Henry a son age 22 was born in February 1878. Emma a daughter age 20 was born in May 1880 in New York. George age 18 was born in November 1881. Alexander a son age 13 was born in June 1887. Edward a son age 11 was born in May 1889.. St. Regis, Mohawk Reserve. E.D. 62, Page 101B, Household 86/87?

SAWYER, LEWIS: (Iroquois) Age 45 was born in January 1855 New York. Both of his parents were born in New York. Julia his wife age 35, was born in September 1864 in New York. Her father was born in New York. Her mother was born in Canada. Frederick a son age 15 born in October 1884, Frank a son age 13 born in December 1886, Edith a daughter age 5 born in April 1895, Samuel a son age 2 born in November 1897, Nellie a daughter age one month born in April 1900. St. Regis, Mohawk Reserve. E.D. 62, Page 101A, Household 84/86.

SEYMOUR, JOSEPH: (Iroquois) Age 34 was born in July? 1865 in Canada. Both of his parents were born in Canada. He immigrated in 1886. Mary SEYMOUR a daughter age 13 was born in May 1887. Annie SEYMOUR a daughter age 7 was born in March 1893. John MITCHELL, his step son age 5, was born in June 1894 in New York. Both of his parents were born in Canada. St. Regis, Mohawk Reserve. E.D. 62, Page 105B, Household 115/117.

SEYMOUR, PETER: (Iroquois) Age 22 was born in December 1877 in Canada. Both of his parents were born in Canada. Charlotte his wife age 20, was born in April 1880 in New York. Both of her parents were born in New York. Francis a son age 2 was born in February 1898. St. Regis, Mohawk Reserve. E.D. 62, Page 90B, Household 5/5.

SIMMONS, MITCHELL: (Iroquois) Age 45 was born in January in 1855 in New York. His father was born in Canada. His mother was born in New York. Betsey his wife age 44, was born in August 1855 in New York. Her father was born in Canada. Her mother was born in New York. Abram a son age 16 was born in February 1884. Maggie a daughter age 13 was born in August 1886. Jacob a son age 9 was born in March 1891. Christie SIMMONS a sister age 14 was born in December 1885. All of the parents of the people in this household were listed as Iroquois. St. Regis, Mohawk Reserve. E.D. 62, Page 102A, Household 94/96.

SIMONS, JACOB: (Iroquois) Age 33 was born in November in 1866 in New York. Both of her parents were born in New York. Lucinda? or Lucina? his wife age 21, was born in May 1871 in Canada. Both of her parents were born in Canada. She immigrated in 1900. John a son age 2 was born in July 1897. Elizabeth SIMONS mother (Of Jacob Simons) age 50 was born in October 1849 in New York. Both of her parents were born in New York. Annie ABARE?, a sister age 36, was born in February in 1864 in New York. Both of her parents were born in New York. Peter SIMONS a brother age 20 born in January 1880. The parents of everyone in this household was listed as Iroquois. St. Regis, Mohawk Reserve. E.D. 62, Page 115B, Household 182/184.

SMITH, ANGUS: (Iroquois) Age 48 was born in May 1852 in Canada. Both of his parents were born in Canada. He immigrated in 1880. Philomene a daughter age 17 born in December 1882, Francis a son age 15 born in October 1894, Christenia a daughter age 10 was born in May 1890. Minnie a daughter age 8 was born in June 1891. Teresia a daughter age 6 was born October 1893. Margaret ANGUS, mother (Of Angus Smith) age 81, was born in April 1819 in New York. Both of her parents were born in Canada. All of the people in this household were listed as Iroquois. All of the parents of the people in this household were listed as Iroquois. St. Regis, Mohawk Reserve. E.D. 62, Page 115B, Household 183/185.

SMOKE, JOSEPH: (Iroquois) Age 40 was born in May 1860 in New York. Both of his parents were born in New York. Mary his wife age 34, was born in March? in 1866 in New York. Both of her parents were born in New York. Christie a daughter age 9 was born in March 1891. Minnie a daughter age eight months born in September 1899. St. Regis, Mohawk Reserve. E.D. 62, Page 91B, Household 14/14.

SMOKE, LOUISE: (Iroquois) Age 68 was born in March 1832 in Canada. Her father was born in New York. Her mother was born in Canada. She immigrated in 1860. Thomas BEVO, a son age 28, was born in June 1871 in New York. His father was born in New York. His mother was born in Canada. Sarah ISAAC, a grand daughter age 17, was born in August 1882 in Canada. Her father was born in Canada. Her mother was born in New York. She immigrated in 1885. St. Regis, Mohawk Reserve. E.D. 62, Page 94B, Household 35/36.

SMOKE, MITCHELL: (Iroquois) Age 37 was born in February in 1862 in New York. Both of his parents were born in New York. Mary his wife age 39, was born in December in 1860 in New York. Both of her parents were born in New York. Joseph a son age 12 was born in February 1888. Alexander a son age 11 was born in April 1889. Susan a daughter age 7 was born in October 1892. John a son age 5 was born in August 1892. Peter a son age 4 was born in January 1896. Thomas a son age 2 was born in March 1898. St. Regis, Mohawk Reserve. E.D. 62, Page 117B, Household 198/200.

SMOKE, THOMAS: (Iroquois) Age 49 was born in February in 1851 in New York. Both of his parents were born in New York. Christenia his wife age 46, was born in December 1853 in New York. Both of her parents were born in New York. Mary a daughter age 6 was born at July 1893. John a son age 4 was born in October 1895. Abram a son age 2 was born in July 1879. Margaret SIMONS, a step daughter age 13, was born in May 1887 in New York. Her father was born in Canada. Her mother was born in New York. Thomas WOOD, a step son age 9, was born in May 1891 in New York. Both of his parents were born in New York. All of the people in this household were listed as Iroquois. St. Regis, Mohawk Reserve. E.D. 62, Page 110B, Household 146/148.

SNOW, NANCY: (Iroquois) Age 50 was born in January 1850 in Canada. Both of her parents were born in Canada. She immigrated in 1855. Charles a son age 33 was born in October 1866 in New York. Both of his parents were born in Canada. Margaret GRAY a grand daughter age 3, was born in July 1896 in New York. Both of her parents were born in New York. Mary GRAY a grand daughter age 1 was born in June 1898 in New York. Both of her parents were born in New York. St. Regis, Mohawk Reserve. E.D. 62, Page 109B, Household 140/142.

SOLOMON, ALEXANDER: (Iroquois) Age 66 was born in August 1833 in New York. Both of his parents were born in New York. Sarah his wife age 45, was born in February 1855 in New York. Both of her parents were born in Canada. Alexander a son age 24 was born in October 1875. Lewis a son age 20 was born in December 1879. Michael a son age 16 was born in August 1883. Kate a daughter age 14 was born in February 1886. Mitchell a son age 12 was born in April 1888. David a son age 9 was born in April 1891. St. Regis, Mohawk Reserve. E.D. 62, Page 97B, Household 60/62.

SWAMP, CHARLOTTE: (Iroquois) Age 69 was born in November 1830 in New York. Both of her parents were born in Canada. David a son age 27 was born in January 1872. John a son age 25 was born in October? in 1874. Margaret SWAMP a daughter-in-law age 28 was born in October 1871 in Canada. Both of her parents were born in Canada. She immigrated in 1899. Everyone in this household was listed as Iroquois. St. Regis, Mohawk Reserve. E.D. 62, Page 105A, Household 111/113.

SWAMP, FRANK: (Iroquois) Age 30 was born in November 1869 in New York. Both of his parents were born in New York. Both of his parents were Iroquois. Margaret his wife age 23, was born in July 1876 in Canada. Both of her parents were born in Canada. Both of her parents were Iroquois. She immigrated in 1889. St. Regis, Mohawk Reserve. E.D. 62, Page 94A, Household 32/32.

SWAMP, LEWIS: (Iroquois) Age 25 was born in May 1875 in New York. Both of his parents were born in New York. Mary his wife age 22, was born in September 1877 in New York. Both of her parents were born in New York. St. Regis, Mohawk Reserve. E.D. 62. Page 116A, Household 185/187.

SWAMP, LORAN: (Iroquois) Age 38 was born in May 1862 in New York. Both of his parents were born in New York. Nancy his wife age 35, was born in April 1865 in New York. Both of her parents were born in New York. Thomas a son age 14 was born in December 1885. Peter a son age 8 was born in July 1891. Frank a son age 8 was born in July 1891. Susan a daughter age 6 was born in November 1893. Rosa a daughter age 6 was born in November 1893. St. Regis, Mohawk Reserve. E.D. 62, Page 116B, Household 190/192.

SWAMP, MAGDALENE: (Iroquois) Age 46 was born in August 1853 in New York. Both of her parents were born in New York. St. Regis, Mohawk Reserve. Peter a son age 26 was born in November 1873. Mary Ann a daughter age 21 was born in May 1879. Agnes a daughter age 17 was born in July 1882. Loran a son age 12 was born in August 1887. David a son age 8 was born in April 1892. Margaret a daughter age 5 was born in June 1894. St. Regis, Mohawk Reserve, E.D. 62, Page 115A, Household 180/182.

SWAMP, PHILLIP: (Iroquois) Age 26 was born in November 1873 in New York. Both of his parents were born in New York. Mary his wife age 22, was born in May 1878 in New York. Both of her parents were born in New York. Agnes a daughter age 5 was born in June 1894. Peter a son age 3 was born in July 1896. Lazor a son age 2 was born in May 1898. St. Regis, Mohawk Reserve. E.D. 62, Page 96A, Household 46/47.

TARBELL, CHARLES: (Iroquois) Age 56 was born in April 1844 in New York. Both of his parents were born in New York. Annie his wife age 51, was born in January 1849 in Canada. Both of her parents were born in Canada. She immigrated in 1865. Sarah a daughter age 26 was born in November 1873. Joseph a son age 19 was born in February 1881. Julia DAVID, a grand daughter age 11, was born in February 1889 in New York. Both of her parents were born in New York. Mitchell ARQUETTE an adopted son age 10, was born in March 1890 in New York. Both of his parents were born in New York. All of the people in this household were listed as Iroquois. St. Regis, Mohawk Reserve. E.D. 62, Page 114B, Household 176/178.

TARBELL, FRANK: (Iroquois) Age 49 was born in November 1850 in New York. His father was born in New York. His mother was born in Canada. Mary his wife age 45, was born in April 1855 in Canada. Both of her parents were born in Canada. She immigrated in 1841. St. Regis, Mohawk Reserve. E.D. 62, Page 104A, Household 105, 107.

TARBELL, JOHN L.: (Iroquois) Age 38 was born in February 1862 in New York. His father was born in New York. His mother was born in Canada. Nancy his wife age 31, was born in November 1868 in New York. Both of her parents were born in New York. Peter a son age 13 was born in November 1886. Annie a daughter age 12 was born in May 1888. Lewis a son age 9 was born in January 1891. Thomas a son age 7 was born in April 1893. Mitchell a son age 3 was born in August 1896. Jacob a son age 1 was born in May 1899. St. Regis, Mohawk Reserve. E.D. 62, Page 104A, Household 104/106 or 103/104.

TARBELL, JOHN: (Iroquois) Age 63 was born in June 1836 in Canada. Both of his parents were born in Canada. Her immigrated in 1845. Minnie his wife age 61, was born in January 1839 in New York. Her father was born in Canada. Her mother was born in New York. Lewis CHUBB age 16, was born in February 1884 in New York. Both of his parents were born in New York. Catharine CHUBB a niece age 13 was born in May 1887 in New York. Both of her parents were born in New York. St. Regis, Mohawk Reserve. E.D. 62, Page 109A, Household 136/138.

TARBELL, JOHN: (Iroquois) Age 40 was born in March 1860 in New York. Both parents were born in New York. Agnes his wife age 35, was born in August in 1864 in New York. Both of her parents were born in New York. Walter a son age 12 was born in October 1887. Johnathan a son age 10 was born in August 1889. Thomas a son age 8 was born in May 1892. Nancy a daughter age 4 was born in July 1895. Libbie a daughter age 2 was born in August 1897. Lucy a daughter age 1 was born in February 1899. St. Regis, Mohawk Reserve. E.D. 62, Page 103A, Household 95/97.

TARBELL, JOSEPH: (Iroquois) Age 32 was born in November 1867 in New York. Both of his parents were born in New York. Mary his wife age 17 born in August 1882 in New York. Both of her parents were born in New York. Elizabeth a daughter age 1 born in March 1899. St. Regis, Mohawk Reserve, E.D. 62, Page 115B, Household 184/186.

TARBELL, JOSEPH: (Iroquois) Age 52 was born in November in 1847 in New York. Both of his parents were born in New York. John a son age 20 was born in April 1880. George a son age 12 was born in July 1887. Jacob a son age 8 was born in August 1891. Nancy WOOD, a daughter age 23, was born in June 1876 in New York. Both of her parents were born in New York. Angus WOOD a grand son age 4 born in September 1895. All of the people in this household were listed as Iroquois. St. Regis, Mohawk Reserve. E.D. 62, Page 113A, Household 166/168.

TARBELL, MITCHELL: (Iroquois) Age 42 was born in February 1858 in New York. Both of his parents were born in New York. Ida STUMPS? OR STUMP?, a servant age 44, was born in March 1856 in Canada. Both of her parents were born in Canada. She immigrated in 1888. Both of the persons in this household were listed as Iroquois. Both of the parents of the persons in this household were Iroquois, St. Regis, Mohawk Reserve. E.D. 62, Page 91A, Household 9/9.

TARBELL, MITCHELL: (Iroquois) Age 56 was born in May 1844 in Canada. Both of his parents were born in Canada. He immigrated in 1845. Catharine his wife age 50, was born in April 1850 in Canada. Both of her parents were born in New York. She immigrated in 1864. St. Paul a son age 22 was born in March 1878. Margaret a daughter age 15 was born in March 1885. Peter a son age 12 was born in July 1887. Sarah a daughter age 11 was born in 1889. Mary TARBELL a daughter-in-law age 17 was born in January 1883 in New York. Her father was born in New York. Her mother was born in Canada. Catherine TARBELL a grand daughter age five months born in December 1899. Regis, Mohawk Reserve. E.D. 62, Page 109A, Household 138/140.

TARBELL, PHILLIP: (Iroquois) Age 51 was born in January? 1849 in New York. Both of his parents were born in New York. Nancy, his wife age 46, was born in March 18 in New York. His wife, Lucinda? age 21, was born in May 1871 in Canada. Both of her parents were born in Ontario, age 2. E.D. 62, Page 64, Household 402/407.

TARBELL, PHILLIP: (Iroquois) Age 51 was born in January? 1849 in New York. Both of his parents were born in New York. Nancy his wife age 46, was born in March 1854 in New York. Her father was born in Canada. Her mother was born in New York. John a son age 25 was born in July 1874. Charles a son age 22 was born in May 1878. Maggie a daughter age 12 was born in August 1887. Joseph a son age 10 was born in September 1889. Lewis a son age 8 was born in August 1891. Charlotte a daughter age 6 was born in November 1893. Peter a son age 4 was born in December 1895. Mary Ann COOK, mother-in-law (Of Phillip Tarbell) age 87, was born in March 1813 in New York. Both of her parents were born in Canada. All of the people in this household were listed as Iroquois. The parents of every one in this household were listed as Iroquois. St. Regis, Mohawk Reserve. E.D. 62, Page 92A, Household21/22.

TARBELL, THOMAS: (Iroquois) Age 34 was born in March 1866 in New York. His father was born in New York. His mother was born in Canada. Christie his wife age 23, was born in March 1877 in New York. Her father was born in New York. Her mother was born in Canada. Noah a son age 5 born in July 1894. Charlotte a daughter age 3 was born in April 1897. St. Regis, Mohawk Reserve. E.D. 62, Page 114B, Household 175/177.

TERANCE, FRANCIS: (Iroquois) Age 22 was born in July 1877 in New York. Both of his parents were born in New York. Annie his wife age 19, was born in April 1881 in New York. Both of her parents were born in New York. Sarah a daughter age 1 was born in October 1898. St. Regis, Mohawk Reserve. E.D. 62, Page 106B, Household 119/121.

TERANCE, FRANK: (Iroquois) Age 49 was born in November 1850 in New York. His father was born in New York. His mother was born in Canada. Mary his wife age 45 was born in April 1855 in Canada. Both of her parents were born in Canada. She immigrated in 1870. Abram a son age 10 was born in October 1889. Julia a daughter age 6 was born in July 1893. St. Regis Reserve, E.D. 62, Page 104B, Household 105/107.

TERANCE, GEORGE: (Iroquois) Age 34 was born in May 1866 in New York. Both of his parents were born in New York. Maggie his wife age 27, was born in September in 1872 in New York. Both of her parents were born in New York. Peter a son age 15 was born in October 1884. Frank a son age 12 was born in October 1887. Thomas a son age 2 was born in January 1898. Charlotte THOMPSON, a servant age 13, was born in August in 1880 in New York. Both of her parents were born in New York. Frank COOK, a servant age 20, was born in January 1880 in New York. Both of his parents were born in New York. David BRUCE a servant age 40, was born in June 1859 in New York. Both of his parents were born in New York. All of the people in this household were listed as Iroquois. St. Regis, Mohawk Reserve. E.D. 62, Page 103B, Household 99/101.

TERANCE, JOSEPH: (Iroquois) Age 45 was born in January 1855 in New York. Both of his parents were born in New York. Lizzie TARBELL, a cousin age 18, was born in May 1882 in New York. Both of her parents were born in New York. John TARBELL a cousin age 19 born in September 1880 in New York. Mary A. SMOKE, a servant age 19, was born in January 1881 in New York. Both of her parents were born in New York. Joseph HOPPS, an uncle (Of Joseph Terance) age 67, was born in April 1833 in Canada. Both of his parents were born in Canada. He immigrated in 1870. All of the people in this household were listed as Iroquois. St. Regis, Mohawk Reserve. E.D. 62, Page 98A, Household 62/64.

TERANCE, LEWIS: (Iroquois) Age 40 was born in January 1860 in New York. Both of his parents were born in New York. Minnie his wife age 31, was born in February 1869 in New York. Both of her parents were born in New York. John a son age 8 was born in April 1892. Joseph a son age 4 was born in June 1895. Francis a son age six months was born in November 1899. St. Regis, Mohawk Reserve. E.D. 62, Page 104A, Household 102/104.

TERANCE, LIZZIE: (Iroquois) Age 45 was born in March 1855 in New York. Both of his parents were born in New York. Agnes Terance a daughter age 16 was born in August 1883. Christie SIMONS, a cousin age 18, was born in August 1881 in Canada. Both of her parents were born in Canada. She immigrated in 1898. Louise JACKSON, a boarder age 23, was born in June 1876 in New York. Both of her parents were born in New York. Annie SMITH (A boarder?) age 18, was born in December 1881 in New York. Both of her parents were born in New York. All of the people in this household were listed as Iroquois. St. Regis, Mohawk Reserve. E.D. 62, Page 97B, Household 61/63.

TERANCE, MARY: (White) Age 41 was born in March 1859 in Canada. Both of her parents were born in Ireland. Peter a son age 21 born in July

1878, Ernest a son age 10 was born in September 1889. Grace a daughter age 5 was born in September 1894. All of the children of Mary Terance were listed as Iroquois. Their father was listed as Iroquois. He was born in New York. St. Regis, Mohawk Reserve. E.D. 62, Page 105A, Household 110/112.

TERANCE, MITCHELL: (Iroquois) Age 40 was born in March 1860 in New York. Both of his parents were born in New York. Margaret his wife age 31, was born in July 1868 in New York. Both of her parents were born in New York. Mary a daughter age 15 was born in March 1885. Susan a daughter age 12 was born in May 1888. John a son age 9 was born in May 1891. Thomas a son age 7 was born in August 1892. Angus a son age 5 was born in May 1895. Peter a son age 3 was born in April 1897. David age 1 was born in April 1899. Mary TERRENCE mother (Of Mitchell Terance) age 70 was born in January 1830 in New York. Both of his parents were born in Canada. St. Regis, Mohawk Reserve. E.D. 62, Page 95A, Household 38/38.

TERANCE, THOMAS: (Iroquois) Age 66 was born in June 1833 in New York. His father was born in New York. His mother was born in Canada. Francis a son age 40 was born in November 1859 in New York. His mother was born in Canada. St. Regis, Mohawk Reserve. E.D. 62, Page 107B, Household 129/131.

TEREANCE, RICHARD: (Iroquois) Age 52 was born in November 1847 in New York. Both of his parents were born in New York. Charlotte his wife age 44, was born in March 1856 in New York. Both of her parents were born in New York. Lewis a son age 23 was born in February 1877. Lizzie a daughter age 18 was born in January 1882. Joseph a son age 11 was born in July 1888. Moses a son age 5 was born in April 1895. St. Regis, Mohawk Reserve. E.D. 62, Page 103B, Household 100/102.

TERRANCE, HATTIE: (Iroquois) Age 53 was born in June 1846 in New York. Her father was born in New York. Her mother was born in Canada. Anice Terrance, mother-in-law (Of Hattie Terrance) age 68, was born in November in 1831 in French Canada (Quebec). Both of her parents were born in French Canada. She immigrated in 1835. Katie QUART an adopted daughter age 16 was born in December 1883 in New York. Both of her parents were born in New York. Lewis QUART an adopted son-in-law age 23 was born in April 1877 in New York. Both of his parents were born in New York. All of the people in this household were listed as Iroquois. St. Regis, Mohawk Reserve. E.D. 62, Page 110A, Household 145/147.

THOMAS, FRANK: (Iroquois) Age 40 was born in April 1860 in New York. Both of his parents were born in New York. Sarah his wife age 22, was born in February 1878 in Canada. Both of her parents were born in New York. She immigrated in 1891. Louisa a daughter age 7 was born in January 1873. St. Regis, Mohawk Reserve. E.D. 62, Page 117A, Household 193/194.

THOMAS, SIMON: (Iroquois) Age 26 was born in October 1873 in New York. Both of his parents were born in New York. Annie his wife age 24, was born in December 1875 in New York. Both of her parents were born in New York. Charles a son age 3 was born in December 1896. Mary a daughter age four months was born in January 1900. St. Regis, Mohawk Reserve. E.D. 62, Page 113A, Household 165/167.

THOMPSON, CHARLES: (Iroquois) Age 35 was born in November 1862 in New York. Both of his parents were born in New York. Margaret his wife age 37, was born in November 1862 in New York. Her father was born in New York. Her mother was born in Canada. Alexander a son age 12 was born in January 1888. George a son age 10 was born in December 1880. Thomas a son age 6 was born in March 1894. Louise a daughter age 4 was born in February 1896. Lewis a son age 2 was born in February 1898. St. Regis, Mohawk Reserve. E.D. 62, Page 107A, Household 124/126 or 123/124.

THOMPSON, LEWIS: (Iroquois) Age 84 was born in June 1815 in New York. Both of his parents were born in New York. Susan his wife age 78, was born in January 1822 in New York. Both of her parents were born in New York. Lillie BILLINGS a grand daughter age 18, was born in January 1882 in New York. Both of her parents were born in New York. Susan JACKSON, a grand daughter age 21, was born in April 1879 in New York. Both of her parents were born in New York. Frank JACKSON a grand son age 33 was born in November 1866. John JACKSON a grand son age 1 was born in August 1898. St. All of the grand children of Lewis Thompson were listed as Iroquois. Both of their parents were Iroquois. St. Regis, Mohawk Reserve. E.D. 62, Page 106B, Household 122/124.

THOMPSON, LORAN: (Iroquois) Age 39 was born in November 1860 in New York. Both of his parents were born in New York. Sarah his wife age 33, was born in October 1866 in New York. Both of her parents were born in New York. Louise a daughter age 10 was born in April 1890. James a son age 7 was born in July 1892. Mary a daughter age 5 was born in April 1895. Jacob a son age 3 was born in February 1897. Paul a son age 1 was born in July 1898. St. Regis, Mohawk Reserve. E.D. 62, Page 106A, Household 118/120 or 117/118.

VILLENEAUVE, MOSES: (Iroquois) Age 30 was born in February in 1870. The place of birth of Moses Villeneauve and his parents was listed as unknown. Jane his wife (She was listed as a white woman) age 19, was born in November in 1880 in New York. Both of her parents were born in New York. Lewis a son age 6 was born in June 1893. Alexander a son age 4 was born in July 1895. St. Regis, Mohawk Reserve. E.D. 62, Page 117B, Household 197/199.

WEBSTER, JOSHUA: (Iroquois) Age 45 was born in February 1855 in New York. Both of his parents were born in New York. Polly his wife age 50, was born in November 1849 in New York. Her father was born in New York. Her mother was born in Canada. Maggie LA FRANCE an adopted daughter age 18, was born in April 1882 in New York. Both of her parents were born in New York. Both of her parents were Iroquois. John WHITE an adopted son age 12, was born in March 1888 in New York. Both of his parents were born in New York. Both of his parents were Iroquois. St. Regis, Mohawk Reserve. E.D. 62, Page 100B, Household 77/79.

WHITE, ANNIE: (Iroquois) Age 52 was born in April 1848 in Canada. Her father was born in Canada. Her mother was born in New York. She immigrated in 1863. Joseph a son age 22 was born in June 1877. Peter a son age 16 was born in June 1883. David a son age 11 was born in April 1889. Margaret WHITE a daughter-in-law age 21 was born in November 1878 in New York. Her father was born in New York. Her mother was born in Canada. All of the people in this household were listed as Iroquois. All of the parents of the people in this household were listed as Iroquois. St. Regis, Mohawk Reserve. E.D. 62, Page 93A, Household 28/28.

WHITE, FELIX: (Iroquois) Age 32 was born in February 1863 in New York. His father was born in New York. His mother was born in Canada. Maggie his wife age 24, was born in November 1875 in New York. Both of her parents were born in New York. St. Regis, Mohawk Reserve. E.D. 62, Page 92A, Household 20/21.

WHITE, JOHN: (Iroquois) Age 77 was born in August 1822 in Canada. Both of his parents were born in Canada. He immigrated in 1865. Agatha his wife age 75, was born in December 1824 in Canada. Both of her parents were born in Canada. She immigrated in 1865. Angus a grandson age 37 was born in May 1863 in Canada. Both of his parents were born in Canada, he immigrated in 1863. Agnes a grand daughter age 32 was born in November 1867 in New York. Both of her parents were born in Canada, Charlotte a great grand daughter age 15 was born in November 1884 in New York. Christena a great grand daughter age 14 was born in May 1886. Minnie a great grand daughter age 12 was born in January 1888. Lewis a great grandson age 10 was born in April 1890. Loran a great grandson age 7 was born in April 1893. Susan a great grand daughter age 5 was born in April 1875. John a great grandson age 3 was born in January 1897. Maggie a great grand daughter age 8 was born in January 1899. All of the people in this household had the surname White. All of the people in this household were listed as Iroquois. All of the parents of the people in this household were Iroquois. The father of all of John White's great grandchildren was born in Canada. The mother was born in New York. St. Regis, Mohawk Reserve. E.D. 62, Page 93B, Household 30/30.

WHITE, JOHN: (Iroquois) Age 31 was born in October 1868 in New York. Both of his parents were born in New York. Annie his wife age 26, was born in December 1873 in New York. Both of her parents were born in New York. Melvin a son age 7 was born in December 1892. Agnes a daughter age 4 was born in October 1895. Abram a son age 1 was born in December 1898. George WHITE a nephew age 19 was born in February 1881. Alexander WHITE a nephew age 16 was born in June 1883. Moses WHITE a nephew age 14 was born in December 1885. Adaline WHITE a niece age 12 was born in November 1887. Michael WHITE a nephew age 10 was born in January 1890. Angeline WHITE a niece age 8 was born in February 1892. St. Regis, Mohawk Reserve. E.D. 62, Page 100B, Household 78/80.

WHITE, JOSEPH: (Iroquois) Age 35 was born in February 1865 in New York. Both of his parents were born in New York. Both of his parents were Iroquois. Annie his wife age 17, was born in July 1872 in New York. Both of her parents were born in New York. St. Regis, Mohawk Reserve. E.D. 62, Page 96A, Household 43/45.

WHITE, JOSEPH: (Iroquois) Age 38 was born in November in 1861 in New York. Both of his parents were born in New York. Annie, his mother age 76, was born in January in 1824 in New York. Both of her parents were born in New York. Susan WHITE a Niece age 7 was born in March 1893. St. Regis, Mohawk Reserve. E.D. 62, Page 112B, Household 160/162.

WHITE, LEWEY: (Iroquois) Age 39 was born in July 1860 in New York. Both of his parents were born in New York. Catharine his wife age 35, was born in October in 1864 in New York. Both of her parents were born in New York. Mary a daughter age 15 was born in October 1884. Frank a son age 13 was born in October 1886. Annie a daughter age 3 was born in October 1896. Sarah TERANCE, a niece age 9, was born in January 1891 in New York. Both of her parents were born in New York. St. Regis, Mohawk Reserve. E.D. 62, Page 95A, Household 42/44.

WHITE, LEWIS: (Iroquois) Age 40 was born in November 1859 in Canada. Both of his parents were born in Canada. He immigrated in 1895. Sarah his wife age 43, was born in November 1856 in Canada. Both of her parents were born in Canada. She immigrated in 1895. Jason a son age 1 was born in December 1898. Noah LA FRANCE, a boarder age 35, was born in September 1864 in New York. His father was born in Canada. His mother was born in New York. Alexander LA FRANCE a boarder age 17 was born in May 1883 in New York. His father was born in Canada. His mother was born in New York. All of the people in this household were Iroquois. All of the parents the people in this household were listed as Iroquois. St. Regis, Mohawk Reserve. E.D. 62, Page 103A, Household 97/99 or 96/97.

WHITE, LORAN: (Iroquois) Age 42 was born in March 1858 in New York. His father was born in Canada. His mother was born in New York. Christie his wife age 36 was born in December 1863 in Canada. Both of her parents were born in Canada. She immigrated in 1887. Elizabeth a daughter age 8 was born in May 1892. John a son age 4 was born in June 1895. Lizzie a daughter age 1 was born in January 1899. St. Regis, Mohawk Reserve. E.D. 62, Page 112A, Household 158/160 or 157/158.

WHITE, MARY: (Iroquois) Age 55 was born in October 1844 in New York. Both of her parents were born in Canada. Mitchell WHITE a son age 34 was born in September 1865. Annie SANDY, a daughter age 22, was born in November? 1877 in New York. Her father was born in Canada. Richard SANDY a son-in-law age 22, was born in August 1877 in Canada. Both of his parents were born in Canada. He immigrated in 1897. All of the people in this household were listed as Iroquois. All of the parents of the people in this household were listed as Iroquois. St. Regis, Mohawk Reserve. E.D. 62, Page 90A, Household 3/3.

WHITE, NELSON: (Iroquois) Age 25 was born in August 1874 in New York. Both of his parents were born in New York. Annie WHITE his mother age 68, was born in February 1832 in Canada. Both of her parents were born in Canada. She immigrated in 1845. St. Regis, Mohawk Reserve. E.D. 62, Page 101A, Household 82/84.

WILLIAMS, THOMAS: (Iroquois) Age 30 was born in December 1869 in Canada. Both of his parents were born in Canada. He immigrated in 1900. Sarah his wife age 29, was born in January 1871 in New York. Both of her parents were born in Canada. John a son age 3 was born in August 1896. Mary Ann a daughter age 1 was born in April 1899. Joseph GORROW, an uncle age 40, was born in May 1860 in New York. Both of his parents were born in Canada. Mitchell GORROW, a cousin age 19, was born in July 1880 in New York. His father was born in Canada. His mother was born in New York. All of the people in this household were listed as Iroquois. All of the parents of the people living in this household were listed as Iroquois. St. Regis, Mohawk Reserve. E.D. 62, Page 93B, Household 23/24.

WOOD, JOSEPH: (Iroquois) Age 57 was born in August 1842 in New York. Both of his parents were born in New York. Mary his wife age 50, was born in May 1850 in New York. Both of her parents were was born in New York. Annie a daughter age 25 was born in August 1874. Agatha a daughter age 20 was born in January 1880. Felicite a daughter age 17 was born in November 1882. Elizabeth a daughter age 14 was born in May 1886. Cecilia a daughter age 12 was born in August 1887. Loran a son age 10 was born in June 1889. Louisa a daughter age 9 was born in December 1890. Jacob a son age 7 was born in January 1893. Joseph a son age 3 was born in October 1896. Dorothy ARQUETTE, a grand daughter age 11, was born in September in 1888 in New York. Both of her parents were was born in New York. St. Regis, Mohawk Reserve. E.D. 62, Page 120A, Household 215/217.

WOOD, PETER: (Iroquois) Age 83 was born in February 1817 in New York. Both of his parents were born in New York. Catharine his wife age 80, was born in August in 1819 in New York. Both of her parents were born in New York. Lewis a son age 58 was born in October in 1841. Joachim a son age 49 was born in December 1850. William a son age 33 was born in May 1867. Peter a grand son age 8 was born in July 1891. Mathew a grand son age 6 was born in March 1894. Annie a grand daughter age 3 was born in April 1897. St. Regis, Mohawk Reserve. E.D. 62, Page 120B, Household 219/221.

1900 CENSUS OF ST. REGIS MOHAWK OF FRANKLIN COUNTY, NEW YORK CROSS INDEX	
SURNAME CROSS INDEX	HEAD OF HOUSEHOLD
ADAMS, John	Agnis Francis
ANGUS?, Margaret	Angus Smith
ARQUETTE, Dorothy	Joseph Wood
ARQUETTE, Mitchell	Charles Tarbell
BARRON, Margaret	Angus Gorrow
BENEDICT, John	Peter La Frence? (La France)
BENEDICT, Lizzie	Caroline Billings
BENEDICT, Mathew	Caroline Billings
BEVO, Thomas	Louise Smoke
BIGTREE, Louise	James Cook
BILLINGS, John	Christie Hoops
BILLINGS, Lillie	Lewis Thompson
BILLINGS, Sarah	Phillip Bigtree
BOOTS, Peter	William Lozor
BOOTS, Susan	Mitchell Oaks
BOVA, Sarah	Peter La Frence? (La France)
BOVAH, Ida	John Hoops
BRUCE, David	George Terance
CHUBB, Catherine	John Tarbell
CHUBB, Julia	Mitchell Laughing
CHUBB, Lewis	John Tarbell
CHUBB, Maria	William Lozor
CHUBB, Paul	Thomas Cree
CHUBB, Peter	John Rubado
COLE, Agnes	Abram Quart
COLE, Annie	Abram Quart
CONNORS, Daisy	Thomas Gray

COOK, Andrew	Angus Ransom
COOK, Annie	Margaret Ransom
COOK, Charles	Margaret Ransom
COOK, Francis	Margaret Ransom
COOK, Frank	George Terance
COOK, John	Phillip Bigtree
COOK, Mary	John Loran
COOK, Mary Ann	Phillip Tarbell
COREY, Ella	Frank Sawyer
COREY, James H.	Frank Sawyer
CUROOD, John	Michael Arquette
DAVID, Julia	Charles Tarbell
DEER, Nancy	Frank Hill
DEOME, Angus	Michael Arquette
DEOME, Frank	Michael Arquette
DEOME, Maggie	Michael Arquette
DEOME, Mary A.	Michael Arquette
EDWARDS, Lewis	Sarah Paul
EDWARDS, Susan	Sarah Paul
FRANCIS, Alexander	Agnes Laughing
FRIDAY, Annie	Abram Back
GARROW, John	Peter La Frence? (La France)
GARROW, Lewis	Peter La Frence? (La France)
GARROW, Sarah	Peter La Frence? (La France)
GORROW, Francis	Betsey Deome
GORROW, Joseph	Thomas Williams
GORROW, Loran	Betsey Deome
GORROW, Mary	Betsey Deome
GORROW, Mary	Thomas Ransom
GORROW, Mary	Joseph Connors
GORROW, Mary Ann	Abram Quart

GORROW, Mitchell	Thomas Williams
GRAY, Julia	William Lozor
GRAY, Margaret	Loran Ransom
GRAY, Margaret	Nancy Snow
GRAY, Mary	Lewis Quart
GRAY, Mary	Nancy Snow
HOOPS, Margaret	Sarah Bevo
HOPPS?, Joseph	Joseph Terance
ISAAC, Margaret	Mitchel Johnson
ISAAC, Sarah	Louise Smoke
JACKSON, Frank	Lewis Thompson
JACKSON, John	Lewis Thompson
JACKSON, Louise	Lizzie Terance
JACKSON, Mitchel	Mary Gorrow
JACKSON, Peter	Mitchell Armstrong
JACKSON, Richard	Lewis Cook
JACKSON, Sarah	Lewis Cook
JACKSON, Susan	Lewis Thompson
JACOB, Margaret	Lewis La France
JACOBS, Margaret	William Lozor
LA FRANCE, Alexander	Lewis White
LA FRANCE, Maggie	Joshua Webster
LA FRANCE, Mary A.	Lewis Jacobs
LA FRANCE, Noah	Lewis White
LA FRANCE, Susan	Lewis Cook
LA FRANCE, Thomas	Lewis Jacobs
LA FRENCE?, Catherine	Lewey Lazor
LAZOR, Paul	John McDonald
LEAF, Frank	Terance Ransom
LORAN, Annie	Frank Hart
LORAN, Mary	Frank Hart

LORAN, Mary	Mitchell Oaks
MARTIN, Loran	Frank Hill
MC DONALD, Sarah	Lewis Quart
MC DONALD, Thomas	Mary Gorrow
MC DONELL, John	Thomas Cornelius
MC DONELL, Mary	Peter Herrin
MITCHELL, David	Angus Gorrow
MITCHELL, John	Joseph Seymour
OAKS, Mitchell	Sarah Johndrow
PAPPINEAU, Andrew	David Cook
PAPPINEAU, John	David Cook
PETERS, George	Annie Gorrow
PETERS, Louise	Annie Gorrow
PETERS, Mitchel	Annie Gorrow
PHILLIPS, Mary	Sarah Johndrow
QUART, Annie	Abram Herrin
QUART, Ida	Abram Herrin
QUART, Joseph	Abram Herrin
QUART, Katie	Hattie Terrance
QUART, Lewis	Hattie Terrance
QUART, Teresia	Abram Herrin
SANDY, Annie	Mary White
SANDY, Richard	Mary White
SEARS, John	Mitchell Leaf
SEARS, Mary	Mitchell Leaf
SEARS, Minnie	Mitchell Leaf
SEARS, Teresia	Mitchell Leaf
SIMONS, Christie	Lizzie Terance
SIMONS, Margaret	Thomas Smoke
SMITH, Annie	Lizzie Terance
SMOKE, Lewis	John Cook

SMOKE, Mary A.	Joseph Terance
SQUIRES, George	Lewis Phillips
SQUIRES, Lewis	Lewis Phillips
SQUIRES, Teresia	Lewis Phillips
STUMPS?, Ida	Mitchell Tarbell
TARBELL, Catherine	Phillip Bigtree
TARBELL, John	Joseph Terance
TARBELL, Lizzie	Joseph Terance
TARBELL, Mary	Bazille Laughing
TARBELL, Peter	Thomas Cree
TERANCE, Sarah	Lewey White
THOMPSON, Betsey	Joseph Connors
THOMPSON, Charlotte	George Terance
THOMPSON, Richard	Paul Delorimer
THOMPSON, Vernece	Paul Delorimer
VILLENEAUVE, Mitchell	Peter Herrin
WHITE, Annie	John Loran
WHITE, Charles	Sarah Cook
WHITE, John	Thomas Gray
WHITE, John	Joshua Webster
WHITE, Lewis	Sarah Cook
WHITE, Mary	Sarah Cook
WHITE, Mary	Charles Gorrow
WHITE, Mitchell A.	Sarah Cook
WHITE, Sarah	Charlotte Beaubien
WILLIAMS, Annie	Sarah Johnson
WOOD, Angus	Joseph Tarbell
WOOD, Nancy	Joseph Tarbell
WOOD, Thomas	Thomas Smoke

THE SENECA IN NEW YORK

When Mohawk Chief Joseph Brant removed to Canada at the close of the American Revolution some of those who went with him had lived at Lewiston, New York. In 1784 the New York legislature passed an act appointing a Board of Commissioners or Indian Affairs. The first lands purchased of the Indians by the State of New York, included a tract lying between the Chenango and Unadilla Rivers. The tract of land comprising all the State of New York west of Seneca Lake, was in the possession of the Seneca Nation. A company was formed called the "New York Land Company," whose plan was to lease land from the Six Nations, for a period of nine hundred and ninety-nine years. A branch company, was organized in Canada. The combined members of the Six Nations agreed to a "Lessee Contract," in 1787. At this time some Seneca Reserves were located at, Kanawaugus, Jenesseo (Genessee) River, Big-Tree (Genessee River), Little Beard's Town (Genessee), Sqawkie Hill Town, Gardeau, Jenesse (Genessee) River, Allegheny River, Buffalo and Tonawanda Creek. Today the Allegany Reservation is tribally owned by the Seneca. The two Seneca Reservations Allegheny and Cattaraugus were established in 1784. The Seneca Nation adopted a constitution in 1848. The Cattaraugus Reservation together with the Allegany are jointly governed. The Cattaraugus Reservation is located in the area of Cattaraugus, Erie, and Chautauqua Counties, New York. Tribal membership is based on Matrilineal lines.

BIBLIOGRAPHY

ABRAMS, GEORGE H. J., "The Seneca People," Published by Indian Tribal Series, Phoenix, copyright 1976, page 32.

DRAPER, LYMAN COPELAND: (Manuscripts) Volume 22/F, part of the "Brant Manuscript Papers," contains the original diary (Account Book) by James Mc Corry, January 26th 1837. This book title reads: Property of Solomon Pierce and James Mc Corry, Allegheny Reservation state of New York. The diary contains many names of the residents of the Allegheny Reservation in 1837. Wisconsin Historical Society.

FEDERAL AND STATE INDIAN RESERVATIONS, U.S. DEPARTMENT OF COMMERCE, January 1971.

HOLLAND LAND COMPANY RECORDS: BUF 59--66, Supreme Court cases involving Land Claims 1851-1858. Original documents of the Buffalo and Erie County Historical Society.

O'RIELLY COLLECTION, New York, Historical Society.

ILLUSTRATED AND HISTORICAL ATLAS OF THE COUNTIES OF HASTINGS AND PRINCE EDWARD, ONTARIO, (CANADA) H. Belden & Company, Toronto, 1878, page 5, Third Offset Edition 1972, Edited by Mika Silk Screening Limited, Belleville, Ontario, Maracle Press, Oshawa.

JOSEPHY, ALVIN M., JR., Article entitled: "Cornplanter Can You Swim?" American Heritage Magazine's & Books, Volume XXX, Number 1, December 1868 issue, Berne and Pan-American Copyright Conventions, page 4. This article contains a detailed reference of the conception of the Alleghany Reserve and the history of the reserve past and present.

SENECA TREATIES

SURNAMES FOUND IN THE TREATY HELD IN ALBANY, NEW YORK 20TH OF AUGUST 1802 WITH THE SENECA INDIANS.

Farmers Brother, Red Jacket and Pollard

SURNAMES FOUND IN THE TREATY OF SEPTEMBER 12TH 1816 HELD AT BUFFALO WITH THE SENECA NATION

Red-Jacket, John Jamisen, Colonel Pollard, Sharp-Skins, Captain Shongo.

THE TREATY OF 26 OF MARCH 1830

Held at Albany, New York with the Seneca Nation residing at Buffalo in the county of Niagara now Erie. The Commissioner of Deeds Records, Erie County, Clerks Office 29th of March 1830, and the State of New York's Secretaries Office. Signed By: Twenty Canoes, Big Kettle, Pollard, White Seneca, John Snow, Destroy Town, Henry Two-Guns, Seneca White?

THE TREATY OF MAY 1842 BETWEEN SENECA NATION AND STATE OF NEW YORK

State of New York, Secretary's Office- Book of Deeds No. 42 page 491, 24Th of October 1842. The ratification by Massachusetts of the Treaty of the 20th of May 1842 between the Seneca Nation of Indians and Thomas Ogden and Joseph Fellow. The following surnames were found in the treaty: Armstrong, Bennett, Cook, Dennis, Doxtader, Governor Blacksnake, Halftown, Harris, Jemison, Jimison, John, Jones, Kennedy, Killbuck, Krouse, Little Johnson, Logan, Patterson, Seneca, Shongo, Silverheels, Tallchief, Turkey, Two Guns, White and Wilson. (Holland Land Records, BUF-96).

AWARDS ON THE TREATY OF MAY 20, 1842 PRESENTED MARCH 31, 1849

The surnames of owners of improvements on the Tonawanda Reservation of the Seneca Nation: Beaver, Bennet, Big Fire, Blackchief, Black Squirrel, Brooks, Buffalo, Canada, Caneseraga, Clute, Cone, Cooper, Doctor, Fish, Green, Griffin, Grounds, Harrison, Hill, Infant, Jack, Jemison, Jim, Johny-John? Johnson, Jonas, Little, Littlebeard, Loan? or Logan? Longhair, Mason, Miller, Mitten, Moses, Palmer, Parker, Peck, Small, Peters, Podry, Possum, Printup, Rueben, Sandford, Shanks, Shongo, Sky, Smith, Snyder, Spring, Stewart, Stone, Sundown, Taylor, Thomas, Washington, White and Young.

This census abstract is not in its original order. It has been alphabetized for this book. This abstract is arranged in alphabetical order by surname then given name. The age and roll number follows the given name. The surname of everyone in each household should be considered the same as the head of that household unless otherwise indicated. The surname of the head of each household has been highlighted. If a person living within a household had a different surname than the head of that household it was highlighted in capital letters and cross referenced at the end of this abstract. This abstract should be used only as a reference. It should not take the place of any original government records.

ABRAM, John age 52, Roll Number 6.

ARMSTRONG, Anna age 28, Roll Number 13. **ARMSTRONG**, Emma age 21, Roll Number 11. **ARMSTRONG**, GEORGE age 47, Roll Number 3. **ARMSTRONG**, JAMES age 32, Roll Number 14. **ARMSTRONG**, JESSE age 23, Roll Number 1. **ARMSTRONG**, John C. age 56, Susan wife age 57, Roll Numbers 8-9. **ARMSTRONG**, Joseph age 55, Roll Number 2. **ARMSTRONG**, Mrs. Sarah age 25, Roll Number 7.

ARNOLD, Henrietta age 33, Clara daughter 8, Roll Number 4-5.
BEAVER, Hiram age 35, Louisa daughter age 17? Roll Numbers 58-59.

BENNETT, Abigail age 84, Roll Number 80. **BENNETT**, Augustus age 34, Silvia wife age 29, Benjamin a son age 6, Linda a daughter age 5, Jacob a son age 3, Eliza a daughter age 1, Roll Numbers 64-69. **BENNETT**, Harriet W. age 35? Sarah Jane TALLCHIEF daughter age 8, Roll Numbers 78-79. **BENNETT**, Herman age 27, Laura wife age 28, Roll Numbers 30-31. **BENNETT**, John age ? Roll Number 32. **BENNETT**, Lewis? age 60, Roll Number 29. **BENNETT** Wallace age 48, Roll Number 36. **BENNETT**, William age 52, Roll Number 28.

BILLY, Deforest age 44, Roll Number 60.

BISHOP, Lester age 37, Albert son age 11, Lucius son age 8, Benjamin Franklin age 3, Roll Numbers 44-47. **BISHOP**, Kussuth? age 35, Ida wife age 24, Cora N. daughter age 3, Roll Numbers 82-84.

BLINKEY, Wagon? age 49, Roll Number 43.

BLUEYE, William age 45, Roll Number 42. **BLUE EYE**, William age 37, Roll Number 49.

BLUESKYE, Albert age 22, Lizzie wife age 22, Baby age two months, Roll Numbers 33-35.
BUCK, Augustus age 23, Roll Number 48.
BULLIS, Freddie age 22, Roll Number 81.

BUTTON, Fairbanks age 35 Roll Number 25. **BUTTON**, George age 30, Frances a wife age 28, Johnni a son age 5, Martha BUTTON age sister age 20, Roll Numbers 70-73. **BUTTON**, Gilbert age 63, Sarah his wife age

58, Laura WHITE Grand daughter age 15, Willet WHITE age 17, grandson, Abby KENNEDY age 16, grand daughter, Roll Numbers 19-23. **BUTTON**, James age 26, Roll Number 27. **BUTTON**, Jasper age 35, Roll Number 26. **BUTTON**, Josephine age 28, Ansley FOX a son age 6, Clarinda FOX? a daughter age 2, baby last name FOX? age two months, Roll Numbers 37-41. **BUTTON**, Lucy age 57, Roll Number 24. **BUTTON**, Lucy E. age 31, Moses MOHAWK Jr. age 4, Solon MOHAWK son age 2, Roll Numbers 74-76. **BUTTON**, Mary age 70, Roll Number 77. **BUTTON**, Susan age 37? or 57? Billy son age 12, Polly daughter age 9, Charles a son age 7, Roll Numbers 15-18.

BROOKS, Emily age 39, Rina daughter age 17? Mary GORDON mother age 79, Roll Numbers 61-63. **BROOKS**, James age 45, Roll Number 54. **BROOKS**, Lorinda age 22, Roll Number 53. **BROOKS**, Samuel age 61, Levi son age 15, Willis? son age 11, Roll Numbers 50-52. **BROOKS** Wellington age 27, Nancy age 22, Howard JOE? a stepson age 4. Roll Numbers 55-57.

COOK, Farnham age 28, Roll Number 135. **COOK**, Levi age 21, Roll Number 136.

COOPER, Hiram age 37, Lydia his wife age 30, Hannah a daughter age 2, Roll Number 111-113. **COOPER**, John age 52, Roll Number 114. **COOPER**, Mary age 67, Peter JIMISON age 9 a grand son. Roll Numbers 128, 129.

CORNPLANTER, Edward age 30, Nancy his wife age 22, Roll Numbers 115-116. **CORNPLANTER**, Ella age 39, Jimmie her husband age 49, Roll Numbers 133-134. **CORNPLANTER**, Jane age 20? or 26? Ines HEMLOCK daughter, age six months, Roll Numbers 131-132.

CROUSE, Alfred age 37, Julia age 30, Roy a son age 9, Lynn a son age 5, Baby a son age two months, Roll Numbers 91-95. **CROUSE**, Clarisa age 56, Lydia a daughter age 20, George a son age 18, Roll Numbers 96-98. **CROUSE**, Esther age 73, Roll Number 90. **CROUSE**, Griffin age 26, Roll Number 99. **CROUSE**, Jack age 37, Roll Number 86. **CROUSE**, Martha age 25, Roll Number 87. **CROUSE**, Marvin age 39, Roll Number 85. **CROUSE**, Mary age 33, Roll Number 89. **CROUSE**, Oscar age 30, Roll Number 88.

CROW, Charles age 59, Roll Number 130. **CROW**, James age 21, Phebe a wife age 16, baby a son age one month, Roll Numbers 107-109. **CROW**, James age 25, Roll Number 126. **CROW**, John age 54, Roll Number 110. **CROW**, Martha age 55, Sarah a daughter age 19, Lydia WHITE a grand daughter age 2, Roll Numbers 100-102. **CROW**, Wallace age 37, Roll Number 127. **CROW**, William age 50, Julia wife age 39, Ely a son age 16, Mary a daughter age 9, Willis a son age 7, Hiram a son age 6, Thomas J., age 4, Lewis age 3, Martha a daughter age 1, Roll Numbers 117-125.

CAYUGA, Elijah age 21, Roll Number 106. **CAYUGA**, Susan age 49, Caroline a daughter age 18, Nancy a daughter age 16. Roll Numbers 103-105.

DAVIS, Mary age 64, Roll Number 158. **DAVIS**, Lucy W., age 74, Roll Number 160. **DAVIS**, William age 49, Roll Number 157. **DAVIS**, Young or Davis Young? age 39, Roll Number 159

DEER, Emma age 42, Susan a daughter age 7, Lewis a son age 10. Roll Numbers 163. **DEER**, James Sr., age 52, Mary a wife age 24, John an adopted son age 12, Lucy a daughter age four months, Roll Numbers 164-

167. **DEER**, William age 26, Anna Jane? or June? wife age 24, Willie a son age five months, Roll Numbers 145-147.

DENNIS, Charles age 34, Effie a wife age 22, Bertha a daughter age ten months, Nancy mother (Of Charles Dennis) age 57, Roll Numbers 151-154. **DENNIS**, Louisa age 48, ARMSTRONG? Howard a son age 13, Roll Numbers 172-173.

DOCTOR, Lucinda age 46, Charles Jr., a son age 15, Kittie a daughter age 13, Roll Numbers 168-170.

DOLSON, Susan age ? Carrie SHANKS a daughter age ? Roll Numbers 180-181.

DOWDY, Addie age 30, Georgie NEWTON a son age 10, Wallace BENNETT Jr., a son age 5, Lillie STORY a daughter age 7, Baby BENNETT a son age 1, Roll Numbers 175-179. **DOWDY**, Betsey age 61? Roll Number 174. **DOWDY**, John age 65, Roll Number 171.

DOXTATOR, Daniel age 35, Roll Number 144. **DOXTATOR**, Jimmy? or Timmy? age 28, Olive wife age 29, Martha a daughter age two months, Roll Numbers 148-150. **DOXTATOR**, Moses Sr., age 64, Roll Number 137. **DOXTATOR**, Sarah age 25, Leroy G. BUTTON a son age 6, Jacob TAYLOR a son age 3, Lucinda DOXTATOR a sister age 19? or 17? Laura DOXTATOR a sister age 15, Sylvia TAYLOR a daughter age 1, Roll Numbers 138-143. **DOXTATOR**, THOMAS, age 65, Anna wife age 64, Roll Numbers 155-156.

EELS, George age 39, Louisa wife age 33, Lillie a daughter age 9, Linas LOGAN a nephew age 17, Roll Numbers 182-185. **EELS**, James, age 73, Betsey wife age 74, Roll Numbers 186-187. **EELS**, Thomas, age 41, Roll Number 189. **EELS**, William age 31, Roll Number 188.

FALTY, Fanny age 23, Roll Number 195. **FALTY**, Gordon age 56, Roll Number 191. **FALTY**, Thomas age 31, Susan wife age 41, Enos a son age 1, Moses CORNPLANTER a step son age 14, Jimmy CORNPLANTER a step son age 11, Roll Numbers 196-200.

FARMER, Ida age 29, Amanda daughter age 5, Roll Numbers 193-194. **FOX**, Madison age 37, Roll Number 192.

GEORGE, David age 54, Electa wife age 38, Samuel a son age 14, Helen a daughter age 9, Wallace a son age 6, Charlotte a daughter age 4, Mary a daughter age 1, Roll Numbers 225-231. **GEORGE**, Joslin age 50, Susan wife age 37, Almyra a daughter age 16, Francis a son age 12, Mable a daughter age 10, Willie a son age 7, Clinton a son age 1, Roll Number 218-224. **GEORGE**, Mary age 34, William JOHN a son age 4, Wilson JOHN a son age 1, Roll Numbers 257-259.

GORDON, Andrew age 31, Clara wife age 29, Theodore a son age 11, Sylvia a daughter age 6, Samuel a son age 4, Laura BROOKS an adopted daughters age 12, Baby Gordon a son age two weeks, Roll Numbers 204-210. **GORDON**, Amos age 25, Roll Number 217. **GORDON**, Nathan age 37? or 58?, Roll Number 211. **GORDON**, Stephen age 45, Polina? wife age 44, Felix a son age 18, Roll Numbers 203. **GORDON**, William Sr. Age 55, Mary wife age 55, William Jr., a son age 15, Sherman a son age 10, John BEAVER a nephew age 9, Roll Numbers 212-216.

GRANT, Albert age 32, Roll Number 255. **GRANT,** Flora age 29, Ora NEWTON a daughter age 3, Roll Numbers 251-252. **GRANT,** Jane? age 54, Roll Number 250.

GREEN, Amos age 33, Roll Number 256. **GREEN,** Chauncey age 41, Susan a wife age 35? Hattie a daughter age 15, Clara a daughter age 9, William a son age 7, Edward a son age 5, James a son age 1, Roll Numbers 235-241. **GREEN,** Chester age 20, Roll Number 249. **GREEN,** David age 49, Mary wife age 47, Peter a son age 19, George a son age 14, Sarah a daughter age 12, Thomas a son age 10, Roll Numbers 242-247. **GREEN,** Louisa? age 22, Jesse a son age 3, Mina a daughter age four months, Roll Numbers 232-234. **GREEN,** Louisa age 24, Lyman HARE, Roll Numbers 253-254. **GREEN,** Lucinda age 18, Roll Number 248. **GREEN,** Nancy age 24, Roll Number 10.

HALFTOWN, Jacob age 43, Roll Number 306. **HALFTOWN,** Jimmie age 31, Roll Number 285. **HALFTOWN,** Lucinda age 38, Amanda a daughter age 1, Roll Numbers 268-269. **HALFTOWN,** Martha age 39, Maria WILSON a daughter age 18, Charles WILSON age 16, Roll Numbers 307-309. **HALFTOWN,** Robert age 41, Nancy wife age 33, Caroline a daughter age 14, Johnson a son age 11, Eliza a daughter age 7, Francis a son age 4, Clarisa a daughter age three months, Roll Numbers 276-282. **HALFTOWN,** Truman age 56, Nancy wife age 46, Roll Numbers 283-284.

HALFWHITE, George, age 40, Roll Number 287. **HALFWHITE,** James Sr., age 45, Roll Number 286.

HARE, Alfred age 28, Roll Number 305. **HARE,** Asher age 24, Minnie a wife age 20, Roll Numbers 310-311. **HARE,** Hiram age 38, Roll Number 304.

HARRIS, Rebecca age? Roll Number 262.

HEMLOCK, George age 30, Filicia? or Leticia? wife age 29, Alice a daughter age 11, Jesse a son age 8, Lucinda a daughter age 2, Roll Numbers 263-267. **HEMLOCK,** John Jr., age 57, Mary wife age 39, Frank son age one month, Willie JONES a nephew age 14, Roll Numbers 270-273. **HEMLOCK,** Joseph age 74, Martha wife age 74, Roll Numbers 260-261. **HEMLOCK,** Sacket age 21, Roll Number 274.

HEWITT, Hattie CLARK, age 28, Roll Number 315. **HILLIKER,** Mrs. Florilla? age 29, Eva RUSSELL a daughter age 7, Roll Numbers 292-293.

HUDSON, Benjiman age 21, Roll Number 314. **HUDSON,** Chloe age 59, Mary a daughter age 13, Roll Numbers 312-313. **HUDSON,** Eliza age 24, Roll Number 294. **HUDSON,** George age 58, Lucy wife age 54, Nancy a daughter age 16, Stewart JONES a step son age 18, Roll Numbers 300-303. **HUDSON,** Jack, age 59, Sarah wife age 48, Robert a son age 10, Lena a daughter age 8. Roll Numbers 288-291. **HUDSON,** James age 28, Roll Number 275. **HUDSON,** Louisa age 22, Roll Number 295. **HUDSON,** Mary Ann age 41, Jennie a daughter age ? Johnnie a son age 5, Sophia EELS a daughter age 1, Roll Numbers 296-299.

ISAAC, Joseph age 41, Roll Number 316.

JACK, John age 66, Mary Ann wife age 54, Young a son age 16, Roll Numbers 468-470. **JACK**, John age 66, Mary Ann wife age 64? Young a son age 16, Roll Numbers 477-479 (A double entry?). **JACK**, Mary age 33, Isaac COOPER a son age 18, Cyrus SPENCER age 14, Roll Numbers 480-482.

JACKET, Abby age 65, Lewis PIERCE a grandson age 15, Roll Numbers 483-484. **JACKET**, John age 76, Sarah W., wife age 58, Roll Numbers 465-466.

JACKSON, Alvira age 42? Roll Number 448. **JACKSON**, Andrew age 22, Roll Number 367. **JACKSON**, Andrew age 25, Roll Number 428. **JACKSON**, Filmore age 34, Roll Number 416. **JACKSON**, Henry age 23, Eliza wife age 36, Louisa ABRAM a step daughter age 15, Willet ABRAM a step son age 13, Salina ABRAM a step daughter age 3, Roll Numbers 431-435. **JACKSON**, Horace age 48, Nancy wife age 38, Herman a son age 7, Betsey a daughter age 14, Alfred a son age 2, Sarah a daughter? age 5, Roll Numbers 436-441. **JACKSON**, John Sr., age 48, John Jr., a son age 9, William a son age 5, Roll Numbers 425-427. **JACKSON**, Julia age 33, Melinda a daughter age 1, Roll Numbers 429-430. **JACKSON**, Lewis age 39, Roll Number 442. **JACKSON**, Richard age 21, Roll Number 417.

JACOB, George Sr., age 42, Caroline wife age 41, Jasper a son age 16, Adam a son age 16, Austin a son age 9, Robert a son age 7, George a son age 5, Caroline a daughter age 11, James a son age 3, Jane a daughter age nine months Roll Numbers 449-458. **JACOB**, Jonah age 28, Roll Number 444. **JACOB**, Joseph age 22, Emily wife age 34, Roll Numbers 463-464. **JACOB**, Lewis age 25, Eli a son age 1, Roll Numbers 445-446. **JACOB**, Lucinda age 47, Anna a daughter age 5, Roll Numbers 461-462. **JACOB**, Mary Jane age 49, Roll Number 443. **JACOB**, Rufus age 46, William a son age 9, Roll Numbers 459-460. **JACOB**, Wallace age 21, Roll Number 550. **JACOBS** William age 21, Roll Number 550.

JAKE, John age 55, Roll Number 447.

JIMISON, Allen age 64, George a son age 20, Roll Numbers 350-351. **JIMISON**, Anson age 25, Roll Number 408. **JIMISON**, Anthony age 30, Mary wife age 28, Spencer a son age seven months, Roll Numbers 395-397. **JIMISON**, Augustus age 23, Roll Number 391. **JIMISON**, Charles age 38, Roll Number 368. **JIMISON**, Eli age 39, Roll Number 398. **JIMISON**, Eli age 27? Jennie wife age 29, Roll Numbers 400-401. **JIMISON**, Elijah age 64, Hanover BENNETT a grand son age 14, Newton BENETT a grand son age 17, Harrison KING a grand son age 12, George JIMISON a grand son age nine months, Roll Numbers 471-475. **JIMISON**, Eliza age 26, Roll Number 402. **JIMISON**, Fanny age 34, Thomas G., a son age 1? or 7? Roll Numbers 325-326. **JIMISON**, George age 41, Anna wife age 31, Clarinda a daughter age 15, Whirla? a son age 10, Richard a son age 3, Roll Numbers 369-373. **JIMISON**, Horace Jr., age 21, Roll Number 320. **JIMISON**, Horace Sr., age 53, Lydia his wife age 54, Roll Numbers 318-319. **JIMISON**, Howard age 26, Roll Number 409. **JIMISON**, Jake age 30? Roll Number 380. **JIMISON**, James age 24, Roll Number 339. **JIMISON**, Jane S., age 31, Roll Number 510. **JIMISON**, Jennie age 38, Roll Number 404. **JIMISON**, Jesse age 34, Roll Number 399. **JIMISON**, John age 54, Phinnie wife age 26, Roll Numbers 321-322. **JIMISON**, John age 21, Roll Number 345. **JIMISON**, Lee? or Lu? age 35, Roll Number 385. **JIMISON**, Lewis age 29, Roll Number 382. **JIMISON**, Lilly age 23, Arthur a son age 2, John Henry KENNEDY age two months, Roll Numbers 388-390. **JIMISON**, Lucy age 42, Lilly a daughter age 19, Katie Jimison mother age 67, Roll Numbers

392-394. **JIMISON**, Lydia age 29, Roll Number 381. **JIMISON**, Mary, age 46, Julia JACKSON a daughter age 15, Henry JACKSON a son age 12, Mary JACKSON a grand daughter age 1, Roll Numbers 363-366. **JIMISON**, Nancy age 35, Cora a daughter age 7, Sarah Williams age 4, Roll Numbers 405-407. **JIMISON**, Naomi age 31, Harry a son age 9, Roll Numbers 383-384. **JIMISON**, Nat? age 21, Roll Number 476. **JIMISON**, Nathan age 28, Avery a son age 3, Roll Numbers 386-387. **JIMISON**, Nick age 25, Roll Number 332. **JIMISON**, Orill age 35, Eli son age 9, Lorinca? ARMSTRONG a daughter age 6, Edith ARMSTRONG a daughter age 3, Etha? ARMSTRONG a daughter age 3, Ely ARMSTRONG a son age three months, Roll Numbers 352-357. **JIMISON**, Page age 33, Sadie wife age 29, Glennie? a daughter age 6, Nancy a daughter age 4, Roll Numbers 333-336. **JIMISON**, Peter age 46, Julia wife age 43, Roll Numbers 337-338. **JIMISON**, Reuben age 39, Roll Number 379. **JIMISON**, Rodgers age 32, Roll Number 403. **JIMISON**, Sally age 92? or 12? Roll Number 323. **JIMISON**, Samuel age 58, Lucy wife age 47, Lucy a daughter age 15, Betsey a daughter age 8, Alcie a daughter age 6, Roll Numbers 340-344. **JIMISON**, Stephen age 34, Roll Number 317. **JIMISON**, Susan age 32, Nettie a niece age 9, Roll Numbers 377-378. **JIMISON**, Sylvia age 28, Mary WASHINGTON daughter age 12, Albert GORDON a son age 14, Roll Numbers 374-376. **JIMISON**, Theodore age 18, Roll Number 831. **JIMISON**, Theodore Sr., age 48? Martha wife age 45, Orrin a son age 25? Theodore Jr., a son age 14, Eugenia a daughter age 6, Roll Numbers 358-362. **JIMISON**, Thomas Jr., age 23, Roll Number 410. **JIMISON**, Thomas Sr., age 67, Emeline wife age 47, Julia daughter age 17, Nehemiah Isreal son age 11, Roll Numbers 346-349. **JIMISON**, Thompson age 46, Roll Number 324. **JIMISON**, William age 30, Lucinda wife age 30, Scott a son age 8, Roll Numbers 327-329. **JIMISON**, William age 76, Jane wife age 48, Roll Numbers 330, 331.

JOE, George age 64, Roll Number 521. **JOE**, Jesse age 38, Jane wife age 26, Roll Numbers 516-517. **JOE**, Martin age 34, Sally wife age 32, Thomas a son age 4, Roll Numbers 525-527. **JOE**, Robert age 45, Hannah wife age 47, Roll Numbers 522-523. **JOE**, Samuel age 59, Hatch a son age 20, Hiram age son age 7, Roll Numbers 518-520. **JOE**, Simeon age 24, Emily wife age 16, Roll Number 511-512. **JOE**, Thomas age 41 Roll Number 524.

JOHN, Andrew Sr., age 65, Susan wife age 65, Abby daughter age 8, Roll Numbers 546-548. **JOHN**, Austin age 46, Olive wife age 29? Kingsley, NEPHEW a step son age 6, Victoria JIMISON a step daughter age 3, Roll Numbers 542-545. **JOHN**, Henry age 59, Sarah wife age 45, Raymond H. a son age 6, Lillian O. PARKER, Galen O. PARKER a son age 12, Ethelbertha PARKER a daughter age 10, Ely S. a son age 8, Roll Numbers 418-424. **JOHN**, Lorinda age 28, Olive BISHOP a sister age 20, Roll Numbers 411, 412. **JOHN**, Lucy age 38, Perry a son age 14, Roll Numbers 413-414. **JOHN**, Lucy age 59, Bertha WILLIAMS grand daughter age 14, Roll Numbers 530-531. **JOHN**, Minnie age 21, Roll Number 415. **JOHN**, William age 69, Roll Number 540. **JOHN**, William age 52, Roll Number 549. **JOHN**, Willie age 29, Roll Number 541.

JOHNSON, Alden age 28, Roll Number 500. **JOHNSON**, Electa age 62? Junietta a daughter age 19, Roll Numbers 501-502. **JOHNSON**, Gus age 35, Lawrence E. JOHNSON an adopted son age 3, James WHITE an adopted son age 10, Roll Numbers 513-515. **JOHNSON**, Jessie age 31? 37? Phebe wife age 30, Roll Numbers 503-504. **JOHNSON**, Julia age 26, Roll Number 505. **JOHNSON**, Lyttle age 24, Nettie wife age 21, Henry a son age 1, Roll

Numbers487-490. **JOHNSON**, Mary age 64, Isaac a son age 37, Roll Numbers 485-486. **JOHNSON**, Mary age 25, Roll Number 590. **JOHNSON**, Moses age 38? Lydia wife age 26, Matilda a daughter age 8, Jonathan a son age 6, Jesse a son age 6, Mable? age 5, Archibald age 2, Orphilia a daughter age six months, Roll Numbers 492-499. **JOHNSON**, Otis age 36 Roll Number 491. **JOHNSON**, Samuel age 40, Hannah his wife age 21, Lilly a daughter age 5, Sophilia a daughter age 4, Roll Numbers 506-509.

JOHNNY-JOHN, Abram age 78? Roll Number 584. **JOHNNY-JOHN**, Chauncey, age 46, Laura wife age 43, Bimer? a son age 19, Cornelius a son age 15, Jerome? a son age 12, Dora a daughter age 8, Mary a daughter age one month, Roll Numbers 592-598. **JOHNNY-JOHN**, Cyrus age 34, Louisa wife age 33, Alice a daughter age 13, Lewis a son age 10, Henry a son age 5, Roll Numbers 585-589. **JOHNNY-JOHN**, Eliza age 72, Roll Number 580. **JOHNNY-JOHN**, Lewis age 33, Lucy wife age 26, Isaac a son age 9, Maggie a daughter age 1, Roll Numbers 576-579. **JOHNNY-JOHN**, Lucinda age 33, Thomas FOX a son age 10, Roll Numbers 581-582. **JOHNNY-JOHN**, Lucy age 70, Roll Number 583. **JOHNNY-JOHN**, Sophia age 23, Roll Number 591.

JONAS, James age 40, Mary wife age 40, Louisa a daughter age 5, Albert a son age 2, Roll Numbers 536-539. **JONAS**, John age 32, Jennie age? Roll Numbers 528-529. **JONAS**, Julia Ann age 45, Louisa TAYLOR a daughter age 12, Izora? a daughter age 8, Frank TALLCHIEF age 14, Roll Numbers 532-535.

JONES, Albert age 21, Polly KING mother, age 66, Roll Numbers 599-600. **JONES**, Amanda age 63, Sophia LAY a niece age 19, Roll Numbers 559-560. **JONES**, George? or Henry? or Henrgy? age 56, Roll Number 565. **JONES**, Hannah age 69, Roll Number 566. **JONES**, Harry? or Garry? age 31, Lydia wife age 26, Minnie a daughter age 7, Carrie a daughter age 4, Philip a son age 2, Roll Numbers 570-574. **JONES**, Horatio age 43, Roll Number 558. **JONES**, Jabez age 65, Lucy wife age 53, Minnie a daughter age 18, Willie a son age 15, Roll Numbers 561-564. **JONES**, Julia age 30, Roll Number 554. **JONES**, Lewis age 26, Roll Number 575. **JONES**, Mary age 36, Nancy BUTTON, Roll Numbers 555-556. **JONES**, Orrine age 25, Helen a daughter age 5, Flora a sister age 19, Roll Numbers 567-569. **JONES**, William age 56, Mary wife age 56, Irine a daughter age 14, Roll Numbers 551-553. **JONES**, Willie age 25, Roll Number 557.

KENJOCKETY, Ida age 27, Laura a daughter age four months, Roll Numbers 616-617. **KENJOCKETY**, Isaac age 38, Cynthia wife age 31, Henry a son age 13, Frediie a son age 8, Ely a son age 4, Roll Numbers 618-622. **KENJOCKETY**, Jesse age 43, Roll Number 603. **KENJOCKETY**, Levi age 39, Lydia wife age 34, Florence? a daughter age 1, Minnie HARRIS a step daughter age 17, Roll Numbers 624-627. **KENJOCKETY**, Moses age 50, Mary wife age 40, Annauas? a son age 17, Roll Numbers 605-607. **KENJOCKETY**, Sidney age 25, Flora a wife age 20, Lenard a son age 3, Roll Numbers 613-615.

KENNEDY, Clarles Sr., age 67, Fidelia wife age 47, Charles Jr., a son age 20, Newton a son age 15, Livingston a son age 9, Roll Numbers 628-632. **KENNEDY**, Fidelia age 22, Minnie M., a daughter age one month, Roll Numbers 646-647. **KENNEDY**, Franklin age 29, Rosetta wife age 32, Cora SNYDER a step-daughter age 12, Roll Numbers 665-667. **KENNEDY**, George age 36, Roll Number 623. **KENNEDY**, Jerome age 45, Alvira wife age 45, Albert a son age 19, Julia daughter age 6, Roll Numbers 659-

662. **KENNEDY**, John Sr., age 71, Roll Number 645. **KENNEDY**, Lucy age 70, Roll Number 668. **KENNEDY**, Mary, age 57, Betsey mother age 91 (Born about 1794), Roll Numbers 663-664. **KENNEDY**, Nathaniel age 56, Julia wife age 47, Roll Numbers 657-658. **KENNEDY**, Porter? or Doctor? age 38, Mary wife age 38, Roll Number 648-649. **KENNEDY**, Steeprock age 33, Abby wife age 33, Leroy a son age 12, Nellie a daughter age 10? or 18? Frank a son age ? Warren a son age 5, Amelia a daughter age nine months, Roll Numbers 650-656. **KENNEDY**, Thomas age 43, Sarah wife age 48, Ulyses a son age 18, Ruth JIMISON mother-in-law age 71, Roll Numbers 641-644. **KENNEDY**, Walter age 22, Roll Number 601. **KENNEDY**, Walter age 40, Sarah a daughter age 10, Walter Lee a son age ? Roll Numbers 669-671.

KETTLE, John age 50, Mrs. John wife age 46, Delos? a son age 18, Mary a daughter age 14, Alexander a son age 12, Johnnie a son age 4, Fanny a daughter age 7, Jane a daughter age 2, Roll Numbers 633-640.

KING, Hannah age 47? or 49? Roll Number 608. **KING**, James age 25, Roll Number 609. **KING**, Job age 49, Roll Number 612. **KING**, John age 27, Roll Number 610. **KING**, Lucina age 30, Roll Number 602. **KING**, Wallace age 55, Roll Number 611. **KING**, Young age 43, Roll Number 604.

LAY, Chester C., age 38, Roll Number 693. **LAY**, Elizabeth age 28, Emma SNOW a niece age 11, Roll Numbers 708-709. **LAY**, John C. age 40, Rhoda wife age 20, Percival a son two months, Roll Numbers 683-685. **LAY**, John age 41, Elizabeth wife age 38, Nancy a daughter age 15, Hattie a daughter age 13, Kelly a son age 9, Lyman a son age 2, Roll Numbers 687-692. **LAY**, Joseph age 21, Roll Number 673. **LAY**, Moses age 61, Julia wife age 49, Roll Numbers 674-675. **LAY**, Skidmore age 33, Roll Number 686. **LAY**, Sylvester C. Sr., age 64, Lucinda wife age 40, Rachel a daughter age 9, Roll Numbers 680-682. **LAY**, Sylvister C., age 25, Jennie wife age 18, Fidelia B. a daughter age 1, Roll Number 705-707. **LAY**, Thomas age 41, Roll Number 672. **LAY**, Young M., age 21, Rose wife age 20, Lydia a daughter age 1, George a son age one month, Roll Numbers 676-679.

LEWIS, Elliott, age 29, Roll Number 704.

LOGAN, Alfred age 26, Jane wife age 17, Roll Numbers 718-719. **LOGAN**, Alphous? age 27? or 29? Roll Number 739. **LOGAN**, A. S? age 52, Roll Number 710. **LOGAN**, Benjamin age 42, Roll Number 734. **LOGAN**, Daniel age 34, Roll Number 737. **LOGAN**, Georgianna age 21, Jerome A. a son Roll Numbers &35-736, **LOGAN**, Harry age 25, Alice a daughter age 3, Roll Number 721-722, **LOGAN**, Hattie age 27, Albert age 5, Roll Numbers 716-717. **LOGAN**, Henderson age 23, Roll Number 723. **LOGAN**, Isaac age 47, Roll Number 733. **LOGAN**, John age 33, Phebe wife age 37, Jasper a son age 13, Jesse a son age 13, Phenie a daughter age 5, Lydia a daughter age 3, Roll Numbers 724-729. **LOGAN**, John Roll Number 735. **LOGAN**, Joseph age 64, Mary wife age 55, Josephine a daughter age 15, Roll Numbers 713-715. **LOGAN**, Louisa age 29, Roll Number 720. **LOGAN**, Lucinda age 46, Roll Number 738. **LOGAN**, Nancy G. age 58, Adda a daughter age 18, Frank a son age 16, Roll Numbers 730-732. **LOGAN**, Saxon age 52, Roll Number 710. **LOGAN**, Widow Mary age 67, Ethel JIMISON a grand daughter age 8, Roll Numbers 711-712.

LONG-FINGER? Hannah age 75? or 15? Roll Number 703. **LONG-FINGER,** Lewis age 22, Roll Number 740.

LUKE, Hannah age 62, Louisa JACK a daughter age 19, Sarah TALL-JOHN mother age 94 (Boun about 1791) Hoagg? SNOW a grand son age 1, Roll Numbers 694-697. **LUKE,** John age 31? Anna wife age 31? James a son age 13, Salina a daughter age 2, Richard a son age 6, Roll Numbers 698-702.

MAYBEE, Alex age 21, Roll Number 770. **MAYBEE,** Esther age 59, Roll Number 769. **MAYBEE,** Solomon Sr., age 27, Herbert a son age 9, Solomon Jr., a son age 5, Salina a daughter age 3, Florence a daughter age seven months. Roll Numbers 771-775.

MILLER, Aurelia age 39, Edith a daughter age 5, Amos JOHNSON a son age 13, Roll Numbers 776-778.

MOHAWK, Allen Sr., age 64, Orlando a son age 20, Allen Jr., age 15, Roll Number 745-747. **MOHAWK,** Christie age 13, Roll Number 759. **MOHAWK,** Eliza age 48, Christine WINNIE a daughter age 18, John WINNIE a son age 20, Roll Numbers 756-758. **MOHAWK,** Jesse age 28, Nancy wife age 22, Betsey a daughter age 1, Willie JACKSON a step son age 7, Roll Numbers 741-744. **MOHAWK,** Moses age 25, Eliza wife age 29? Bertha FALTY step daughter age 7, Roll Numbers 748-750. **MOHAWK,** William age 34, Louisa wife age 30, Alice daughter age 8, Clara Belle daughter age 5, Mary Maria daughter age 3, Roll Numbers 751-755.

MOSES, Amos age 52, Herman a son age 18, John age son age 13, Roll Numbers 760-762. **MOSES,** George age 46, Lucinda wife age 46, Eleanor a daughter age 7, Jacob PHILIPS a step son age 4? or 11? Eliza THOMPSON mother-in-law age 76, Roll Numbers 764-768. **MOSES,** Mary age 39, Roll Number 763.

NEPHEW, Jerome age 26, Roll Number 782. **NEPHEW,** Perserval age 24, Sophia wife age 22, Loyd W. a son age 1, Roll Numbers 784-786. **NEPHEW,** Willet, age 28, Roll Number 783. **NEPHEW,** William age 57, Nancy wife age 56, Ulyses a son age 16, Roll Numbers 779-781.

OBAIL, Crawford Sr., age 53, Julia wife age 35, Helen daughter age 19, Polina a daughter age 15, Ella a daughter age 12, Crawford a son age 10, Jimison RILEY? or KILEY? or Keley? adopted son age 6, Roll Numbers 790-796. **OBAIL,** Solomon age 72, Abbie wife age 48, Hannah mother age 91, Roll Numbers 787-789.

PARKER, William age 35, Roll Number 861.

PATTERSON, David age 52, Roll Number 855. **PATTERSON,** Frank age 26, Nancy wife age 27, Louisa daughter age 3, Roll Numbers 858-860. **PATTERSON,** John age 59, Mary age 49, Laura a daughter age 18, Martha a daughter age 15, Roll Numbers 850-853. **PATTERSON,** Nathaniel age 37, Roll Number 857. **PATTERSON,** Sarah age 28, Roll Number 854. **PATTERSON,** Thomas age 32, Roll Number 856.

PHILLIPS, Henry age 84, Roll Numbers 866. **PHILLIPS,** Jennie age 23, Roll Number 865. **PHILLIPS,** Jesse age 65, Hanover a son age 18, Anna a daughter age 8, Roll Numbers 862-864. **PHILLIPS**, Sarah age 53, Roll Number 867.

PIERCE, Adam age 54, Lucy wife age 53, Joseph a son age 18, Elon a son age 14, John a son age 12, Emily PARKER a step daughter age 31, Roll Numbers 835-840. **PIERCE**, Adam age 32, Nancy wife age 36, Reuben a son age 13, Electa a daughter age 9, Mary Jane a daughter age 2, Roll Numbers 841-845. **PIERCE**, Alfred age 23, Roll Number 820. **PIERCE**, Charles age 26, Lydia wife age 23, Laura daughter age 5, Roll Numbers 797-799. **PIERCE**, Ely S., age 26, Roll Number 848. **PIERCE**, Freddie age 27, Roll Number 819. **PIERCE**, George age 53, Martha wife age 51, Jennie MOSES a niece age 17, Lewis MOSES a nephew age 15, Henry MOSES a nephew age 12, Roll Numbers 801-805. **PIERCE**, Henry C. age 28, Roll Number 800. **PIERCE**, Jabez age 53, Roll Number 849. **PIERCE**, Jacob Sr., age 52, Jane wife age 36, Bermus? or Bernus? a son age 13, Hawley a son age 12, Delia a daughter age 10? Jerry a son age 7, Jacob Jr., a son age 5, Frank a son age 3, Theodore JIMISON, Roll Numbers 823-831. **PIERCE**, Jane age 42, Roll Number 808. **PIERCE**, Jennie age 22, Lena REDEYE daughter age 1, Roll Numbers 806-807. **PIERCE**, John age 62, Sarah A. wife age 45, Jane daughter age 19, Newton a son age 14, Bela a son age 10, Rena a daughter age 6, Peter a son age 16, Roll Numbers 810-816. **PIERCE**, Josephine age 20, Phennie a daughter age 5, Roll Numbers 846-847. **PIERCE**, Laura J., age 22, Roll Numbers 870. **PIERCE**, Lillie age 31, Lillie daughter age 17, Watson a son age 12, Lewis a son age 5, Moses JIMERSON a grand son age four months Roll Numbers 873-878.. **PIERCE**, Louisa age 29, Rachel a daughter age 3. Roll Numbers 817-818. **PIERCE**, MRS. Jane age 42, Roll Number 808. **PIERCE**, Reuben age? Roll Number 809. **PIERCE**, Sylvester, age 25, Alice wife age 19, Roll Numbers 821-822. **PIERCE**, Sylvia age 22, John a son age 2, Mary Jane a daughter age five months, Roll Numbers 832-834. **PIERCE**, Thomas age 44, Laura wife age 36, Roll Number 871, 872.

PLUMMER, Susan age 53, Roll Number 868.
PRATT, Eunice age 60, Roll Number 869.

REDEYE, Charles Sr., age 21? or 27? Lydia wife age 23, Florence a daughter age 1, Charles Jr., a son age 5, Roll Numbers 888-891. **REDEYE**, Emily age 25, Leroy JOHN a son age 5, Roll Numbers 885-886. **REDEYE**, Fuller age 23, Ida wife age 22, Roll Numbers 883-884. **REDEYE**, Henry age 32, Roll Number 887. **REDEYE**, James age 28, Roll Number 881. **REDEYE**, Martha age 54, Betsey GORDON mother age 80 Roll Numbers 892-893. **REDEYE**, Sally age 59, Roll Number 882.

REID, Sophia age 46, Charles JOHNSON a son age 19, Roll Numbers 879, 880.

SCOTT, Cyrus age 33, Hattie wife age 22, Edward son age 2, Baby age six months, Roll Numbers 943-946. **SCOTT**, Frank age 11, Roll Number 1071. **SCOTT**, GEN'L William age 75? Roll Number 940. **SCOTT**, Jacob age 37, Roll Number 941. **SCOTT**, KING age 31, Roll Number 934. **SCOTT**, Sarah age 28, Anna a daughter age 11, Felix a son age 10, Jane a daughter age 7, Skye a son age 5, Roll Numbers 935-939. **SCOTT**, Wallack age 47, Louisa wife age 44, Ella POODRY age 15, step daughter age 15, Crouse HARRISON age 6 (No Relationship given) Roll Numbers 935-933.

SCROGGS, Thomas S. age 28, Roll Number 1063.

SENECA, Emily age 63, Lucinda JIMISON daughter age 19, Ollie Ann JIMISON a grand daughter age ten months, Roll Numbers 1049-1050. **SENECA**, Frank Sr., age 35, Frank Jr., a son age 5, Letha a daughter age 3, Roll Numbers 1043-1045. **SENECA**, Isaac Sr., age 32, Laura wife age 32, Isaac Jr., a son age 12, Victor M. a son age 7, Bertha PIERCE a step daughter age 6, Roll Numbers 1038-1042. **SENECA**, Johnny age 27, Martha wife age 17, Roll Numbers 1046-1047. **SENECA**, Margaret age 69, Roll Number 998. **SENECA**, Sarah age 30, Roll Number 997. **SENECA**, Thomas age 30, Betsey wife age 27, Betsey a daughter age 5, Frank a son age 2, Roll Numbers 1034-1037. **SENECA**, Thomas age 47, Roll Number 1062.

SHANKS, Benjamin age 38, Roll Number 1057.

SHONGO, Moses age 30, Alice wife age 25, Wilber C. a son age 3, Mandy? L. a daughter age 2, Roll Numbers 1066-1069.

SILVERHEELS, Eliza age 64, Roll Numbers 1030. **SILVERHEELS**, Henry age 75, Nancy wife age 65, Sarah daughter age 17, Nancy SENECA grand daughter age 10, Roll Numbers 1026-1029. **SILVERHEELS**, Joseph age 47, Roll Numbers 1033. **SILVERHEELS**, Julia age 69, Roll Numbers 1031. **SILVERHEELS**, Oliver age 39, Roll Numbers 1032. **SILVERHEELS**, Robert age 86, Roll Number 1022. **SILVERHEELS**, Thomas age 32, Sarah wife age 28, Grace a daughter age 2, Roll Numbers 1023-1025.

SIRLEY? OR SEELEY? William age 65, Roll Number 1065.

SMITH, Betsey age 26, Roll Number 985. **SMITH**, Charlie age 28, Roll Number 984. SMITH, Eliza age 32, Roll Number 1021. **SMITH**, Joe age 48, Roll Number 981. **SMITH**, Louisa age 45, Lizzie a daughter age 17, Jane a daughter age 10, Roll Numbers 986-988. **SMITH**, Lyman age 24, Roll Number 996. **SMITH**, Silver age 46, Abby wife age 41, Jane a daughter age 15, Frank a son age 11, Phinie a daughter age 8, Della a daughter age 1, Roll Numbers 990-995. **SMITH**, Willie age 23, Roll Number 989.

SMOKE, Charles age 64, Roll Number 1064.

SNOW, Amos age 36, Roll Number 924. **SNOW**, Andrew age 94? Roll Number 958. **SNOW**, Austin age 26, Roll Number 913. **SNOW**, Deforest age 25, Delaney JOHN brother age 11, Roll Numbers 975-976. **SNOW**, Esau age 25, Roll Number 903. **SNOW**, George age 57, Roll Number 902. SNOW, George age 24, Roll Number 919. **SNOW**, Hattie age 38, Roll Number 977. **SNOW**, Hattie C. age 46, Charley a son age 15, Iva a daughter age 13, Roll Numbers 925-927. **SNOW**, Hiram age 27, Roll Number 978. **SNOW**, Jake age 39, Anna wife age 31, Etha LOGAN a step daughter age 11, Peter SNOW a step son age 2, Roll Numbers 969-972. **SNOW**, James age? Roll Number 190. **SNOW**, Jane age 60, Athalinda a daughter age 11, Viola a daughter age 16, George JIMISON a nephew age 18, Roll Numbers 907-910. **SNOW**, John age 52, Roll Number 974. **SNOW**, John Sr., age 32, Jane wife age 39, John Jr., a son age 5, Alta? or Atta? a daughter age 3, Willie COOPER a step son age 19, Green? JIMISON a step son age 17? Emma Snow a daughter age 1, David a son age one month, Roll Numbers 894-901. **SNOW**, Joseph age 26, Roll Number 928. SNOW, Joseph Jr., age 27, Roll Number 914. **SNOW**, Julia age 43, Isreal husband age 65, Jason a son age 18, Roll Numbers 904-906. **SNOW**, Lucy age 30, Roll Number 963. **SNOW**, Mary age 65, Roll Number 917. **SNOW**, Mary age 73, Frances LAY a grand son? or a step son? age 14, Alice YOUNG a daughter, Cornelius YOUNG a son age 10, Roll Numbers 920-923. **SNOW**, Nellie age 23, Roll Number 915. **SNOW**, Nicholas age 54, Roll Number 911. **SNOW**, Sally age 67, Roll Number 973. **SNOW**, Silas age 23, Roll Number 929. **SNOW**, Thomas age 45, Roll Number 916. **SNOW**, Wallace age 45, Hannah wife age 39, Willie a son age 15, Berman? a son age 9, Roll Numbers 959-962. **SNOW**, Ward age 30, Louise wife age 27, James a son age 7, Frank a son age 6, Lucinda a daughter age 1, Roll Numbers 964-968. **SNOW**, William age 23, Roll Number 912. **SNOW**, Young Joe Sr., Roll Number 918.

SNYDER, Absalom age 38, Roll Number 1009. **SNYDER**, Eliza age 51, Roll Number 980. **SNYDER**, Emily age 80, Roll Number 1007. **SNYDER**, Laura age 43, Willie a son age 18, Absalom a son age 15, Ella a daughter age 13, Philapina a daughter age 10?, Roll Numbers 1011-1015. **SNYDER**, Lewis age 42, Roll Number 979. **SNYDER**, Melinda age 49, Hattie PLUMER a daughter age 11, Roll Numbers 982-983. **SNYDER**, Peter age 22, Roll Number 1016. **SNYDER**, Polly age 55, Roll Number 1008. **SNYDER**, Sophia age 36, Mary Jane a daughter age 19? Leroy a son age 16, Clarence a son age 15? Roll Numbers 1017-1020. **SNYDER**, William age 47, Roll Number 1010.

SPENCE, Charley age 48, Roll Number 1053.
SPRING, Hanover age 45, Roll Number 1070.
STEEPROCK, Rose age 30, Virginia a daughter age ten months, Roll Numbers 1058-1059.

STEVENS, Charles age 49, Willie a son age 15, Roll Numbers 1001-1002. **STEVENS**, Henry age 47, Lucy wife age 40, Madison a son age 16, Wilson age 9, Roll Numbers 1003-1006. **STEVENS**, John age 75, Eliza wife age 71, Roll Numbers 999-1000.

STEVENSON, David age 69, Eliza wife age 47, Young age 7? Roll Numbers 1054-1056.
STEVENSON, Moses age 72, Mary Ann STEVENSON sister age 69, Roll Numbers 1060-1061.

SUNDOWN, Asa age 57, Susan wife age 57, Roll Numbers 954-955. **SUNDOWN**, Betsey age 74, John JOE? or Joe JOHN? husband age 77, Roll Numbers 956-957. **SUNDOWN**, Charley age 27, Simeon SUNDOWN a brother age 19, Roll Numbers 1051-1052. **SUNDOWN**, Henry age 51? Laura wife age 34, Albert a son age 16, Charley a son age 3, Roll Numbers 947-950. **SUNDOWN**, Lucy age 49, Parson a son age 17? or 19? Cordelia a daughter age 14, Roll Numbers 951-953. **SUNDOWN**, Peter age 45? Roll Number 942.

TALLCHIEF, Alexander age 61, Martha a wife age 56, Levi a son age 17, Hattie LOGAN a step daughter age 20? Roll Numbers 1101-1104. **TALLCHIEF**, Anna age 23, Roll Number 1115. **TALLCHIEF**, Asa age 64, Maria wife age 54, Delia a daughter age 16? Maggie a daughter age 14, Roll Numbers 1110-1113. **TALLCHIEF**, Charles age 22, Cordelia wife age 23, Mary a daughter age 1, Roll Numbers 1072-1074. **TALLCHIEF**, Charles Jr., age 21, Roll Number 1169. **TALLCHIEF**, Charley age 71, Roll Number 1116. **TALLCHIEF**, Chester age 25, Roll Number 1096. **TALLCHIEF**, Clara age 25, Roll Number 1114. **TALLCHIEF**, Clarence age 21, Roll Number 1105. **TALLCHIEF**, Eliza age 45, Roll Number 1117. **TALLCHIEF**, Emily age 52, Roll Number 1098. **TALLCHIEF**, George age 56, Roll Number 1097. **TALLCHIEF**, Sarah age 49, King a son age 18, Roll Number 1099-1100.

TALLCHIEF, William age 29, Susanah wife age 27, Jennie a daughter age 10, Minnie a daughter age 2, Roll Numbers 1106-1109.

TANDY? OR SANDY? Betsey age 34, Amanda JOHN a daughter age 6, Roll Number 1143-1144.
TAYLOR, Moses age 32, Roll Number 1147. **TAYLOR**, Sarah age 25, Warren JONES a son age 3, Roll Numbers 1148-1149.

THOMAS, David age 40, Sarah wife age 40, Phebe a daughter age 13, Lillie a daughter age 6, Roll Number 1135-1138. **THOMAS**, Eliza age 34, Roll Number 1142. **THOMAS**, Howard age 24, Roll Number 1145. **THOMAS**, Isaac age 71, Roll Number 1139. **THOMAS**, Jack age 39, Roll Number 1141. **THOMAS**, Jimeson age 52, Roll Number 1121. **THOMAS**, Lucy age 45, Alice TWOGUNS, niece age 12, Roll Numbers 1132, 1133. **THOMAS**, Moses age 49, Roll Number 1134.

THOMPSON, Charles age 31, Margaret age 25, Henry brother age 19, Emma sister age 17, Baby ISAAC niece age seven months, Roll Numbers 1123-1127. **THOMPSON**, Hawley age 25, Laura wife age 22, Roll Number 1119-1120. **THOMPSON**, Jimeson age 52, Roll Number 1121. **THOMPSON**, Lewis age 44, Roll Number 1118. **THOMPSON**, Lyo? age 23, Roll Number 1122. **THOMPSON**, Mary age 40, Philip JACKSON a son age 14, Lina Thompson a daughter age 9, Jerry THOMPSON a son age 7, Dora THOMPSON a daughter age 4, Elmer THOMPSON a son age six? months, Roll Numbers 1171-1176.

TOMMY? George Sr., age 47, Fidelia a daughter age 16, Lerisa age 7? Mary age 10, Roll Numbers 1128-1131. **TOMMY**, John Sr., age 47, Fedelia a daughter age 16, Louisa a daughter age 7, Mary a daughter age 10, Roll Numbers 1128-1131.

TITUS, Betsy age 31, Roll Number1146. **TITUS**, George age 85, Roll Number 1145.

TURKEY, Elijah age 30, Mary wife age 25, John DAVID a step son age 8, Roll Numbers 1158-1160. **TURKEY**, Foster age 62, Roll Number 1150. **TURKEY**, Freemont age 34, Roll Number 1151. **TURKEY**, Isaac age 29, Roll Number 1166. **TURKEY**, Jane age 41, Minnie age daughter age 19, Laura a daughter age 17, Minerva a daughter age 13, Wesley a son age 3, Clarisa KING a grand daughter age 1, Roll Numbers 1152-1157. **TURKEY**, Jesse age 41, Susan wife age 41, Johnnie COOPER adopted son age 5, Roll Number 1163-1165. **TURKEY**, John age 52, Roll Number 1161. **TURKEY**, John age 39, Roll Number 1162. **TURKEY**, Jones age 24, Roll Number 1168. **TURKEY**, Rolly? or Polly? age 69, Roll Number 1167.

TWOGUNS, Cephus age 65, Roll Number 1079. **TWOGUNS**, Cephus age 23, Hattie wife age 19, Bela ISAAC brother in law age 18, Young ISAAC brother in law age 17, Jacob ISAAC brother in Law age 11, Della TWOGUNS a daughter age six months, Roll Numbers 1087-1092. **TWOGUNS**, Daniel age 60? Roll Number 1170. **TWOGUNS**, George age 64, Lemuel C. a son age 19, Hattie C. a daughter age 16, Harry a son age 11, Roll Numbers 1083-1086. **TWOGUNS**, Hattie E. age 45, Irene JIMISON a niece age 19, Rose POODRY a daughter age 6, Roll Numbers 1093-1095. **TWOGUNS**, Louis? or Lorenzo? G. age 25, Ida wife age 19, Henry a son age two months, Roll Numbers 1080-1082. **TWOGUNS**, Noah age 54? or 34? Julia wife age 37, Mina daughter age 10, Eveline daughter age 2, Roll Numbers 1075-1078.

WARREN? OR WARRIOR? Anna age 44, Louisa JOHN age 18, niece, Frances THOMAS a great or grand niece age five months, Roll Numbers 1196-1198. **WARREN? OR WARRIOR,** Charles age 41, Roll Number 1181. **WARREN? OR WARRIOR,** Elizabeth age 29, Abby a daughter age 6, Rhoda a daughter age 2, Roll Numbers 1189-1191.

WARRIOR, Alice age 15, Roll Number 1240. **WARRIOR,** Emma age 24, Roll Number 1255. **WARRIOR,** George Sr., age 64, Roll Number 1179. **WARRIOR,** Hattie C., age 31, Freddie HARE a son age 9, Nelson a son age 7, Olive LOGAN a son? age 15, Roll Numbers 1192-1195. **WARRIOR,** Joslin age 33, Roll Number 1185. **WARRIOR,** Nancy age 35, David a son age 14, Lucy P., a daughter age 8, Sarah a daughter age 6, Ella KING age 18, Roll Numbers 1221-1225. **WARRIOR,** Peter age 35, Roll Number 1220. **WARRIOR,** Titus age 27, Roll Number 1182.

WASHINGTON, James age 37, Carl a son age 15, Roll Numbers 1246-1247.

WATERMAN, Betsey age 23, Lillian a daughter age 4, Ina a daughter age 3, John Jr., a son age 1, Roll Numbers 1256-1259. **WATERMAN,** Mary age 27, Charles a son age 6, Cornelius V., a son age 4, Glennie a daughter age 2, Roll Numbers 1250-1253.

WHEELER, Martha age 22, Rena PHILIPS a daughter age four months, Roll Numbers 1177-1178. **WHEELER,** Wilson age 37, Martha wife age 33, Ira a son age 12, Clara a daughter age 10, Minnie a daughter age 3, Sylvester a son age 1, Roll Number 1183-1188.

WHITE, BERNICE? age six months, Roll Number 12. She appears enumerated with Nancy Green Roll Number 10. No relationships was given. **WHITE,** Cyrus age 39, Roll Number 1214. **WHITE,** David age 68, Betsey a wife age 68, Roll Numbers 1215-1216. **WHITE,** George Jr., age 43, Julia wife age 43, Roll Numbers 1218-1219. **WHITE,** George Sr., age 73, Lucy wife age 72, Roll Numbers 1208-1209. **WHITE,** Hannah age 25, Clarence C. a son age 4, Frances a son age 2, Roll Numbers 1211-1213. **WHITE,** Jerry age 39, Roll Number 1210. **WHITE,** John age 41, Almyra wife age 25, Roll Numbers 1200-1201. **WHITE,** Louisa age 46, Roll Numbers 1199. **WHITE,** Mary Ann age 32, Abby JONAS a daughter age 14, Jerimiah a son age 11, Roll Numbers 1260-1262. **WHITE,** Peter, age 77, Roll Number 1202. **WHITE,** Mary Jane age 27, Maggie TALLCHIEF a daughter age 3, Baby a son age nine months, Roll Numbers 1205-1207. WHITE, Sarah age 74? Emma THOMAS an adopted daughter age 10? Roll Numbers 1203-1204. **WHITE,** Willie age 24, Roll Number 1217.

WILLIAMS, Charles age 21, Roll Number 1244. **WILLIAMS,** Christopher age 28, Roll Number 1249. **WILLIAMS,** David age 61, Lucy wife age 59, Richard a son age 5, Roll Numbers 1241-1243. **WILLIAMS,** George age 43, Roll Numbers 1245. **WILLIAMS,** Griffith, age 34, Roll Number 1254. **WILLIAMS,** William age 28, Agnes wife age 25, Spencer son age 5, Eunice J., a daughter age 2, Roll Numbers 1236-1239.

WILSON, Caroline age 38, Ada Pierce a daughter age 9, Roll Numbers 1232-1233. **WILSON,** Francis age 33, Roll Number 1235. WILSON, Hannah age 35, Sylvia SHANKS a daughter age 20, Frank WILSON Jr., a grand son age 2, Edith SHANKS a daughter age 16, Carrie SHANKS a daughter age 13, Lina WILSON a grand daughter age three months, Roll Numbers-1226-1231. **WILSON,** James age 28, Roll Numbers 1234.

WINNIE, David age 34, Roll Number 1248.

YELLOWBLANKET, John age 63, Roll Number 1274. **YELLOWBLANKET**, Moses age 55, Rebecca a daughter age 17, Roll Numbers 1272-1273.

YORK, C. Stephen age 50, Nancy wife age 37, Berusha a daughter age 19, Adell C., a daughter age 5, Marie? L., a daughter age 3, Orlando DOXTATOR a step son age 19, George DOXTATOR a step son age 16, Maggie DOXTATOR a step daughter age 14, Matie L., YORK a step daughter age 3, Roll Numbers 1263-1271.

CATTARAUGUS RESERVE BIA ROLL 1886
CROSS INDEX

SURNAME CROSS INDEX	RELATION/HEAD OF HOUSEHOLD	BIA ROLL #
ABRAM, Louisa	Step Dau. of Henry Jackson	#431-435
ABRAM, Salina	Step Dau. of Henry Jackson	#431-435
ABRAM, Willett	Step Son of Henry Jackson	#431-435
ARMSTRONG, Edith	Dau. of Orill Jimison	#352-357
ARMSTRONG, Ely	Son of Orill Jimison	#352-357
ARMSTRONG, Etha?	Dau. of Orill Jimison	#352-357
ARMSTRONG, Howard	Son of Lousia Dennis	#172-173
ARMSTRONG, Lorinca?	Dau. of Orill Jimison	#352-357
BEAVER, John	Nephew of William Gordon Sr.	#212-216
BENNETT, Baby	Son of Addie Dowdy	#175-179
BENNETT, Hanover	Gr. Son of Elijah Jimison	#471-475
BENNETT, Newton	Gr. Son of Elijah Jimison	#471-475
BENNETT, Wallace Jr.	Son of Addie Dowdy	#175-179
BROOKS, Laura	Adpt. Dau. of Andrew Gordon	#204-210
BUTTON, Leroy G.	Son of Sarah Doxtator	#138-143
BUTTON, Nancy	Household of Mary Jones	#555-556
COOPER, Isaac	Son of Mary Jack	#280-282
COOPER, Johnnie	Adpt. Son of Jessie Turkey	#1163-1165
COOPER, Willie	Step Son of John Snow Jr.	#894-901
CORNPLANTER, Jimmie	Step Son of Thomas Falty	#182-185
CORNPLANTER, Moses	Step Son of Thomas Falty	#182-185
DAVID, John	Step Son of Elijah Turkey	#1158-1160
DOXTATOR, George	Step Son of Stephen C. York	#1263-1271
DOXTATOR, Maggie	Step Dau. of Stephen C. York	#1263-1271
DOXTATOR, Orlando	Step Son of Stephen C. York	#1263-1271
GORDON, Albert	Son of Sylvia Jimison	#374-376
GORDON, Mary	Mother of Emily Brooks	#61-63

HARE, Freddie	Son of Hattie C. Warrior	#1192-1195
HARE, Lyman	Household of Louisa Green	#253-254
HARRIS, Minnie	Step Dau. of Levi Kenjockety	#624-627
HARRISON, Crouse	Household of Wallack Scott	#930-933
HEMLOCK, Ines	Dau. of Jane Cornplanter	#131-132
ISAAC, Baby	Niece of Charles Thompson	#1123-1127
ISAAC, Bela	Brother-in-law/Cephus Twoguns	#1087-1092
ISAAC, Jacob	Brother-in-law/Cephus Twoguns	#1087-1092
ISAAC, Young	Brother-in-law/Cephus Twoguns	#1087-1092
JACKSON, Henry	Son of Mary Jimison	#363-366
JACKSON, Julia	Dau. of Mary Jimison	#363-366
JACKSON, Mary	Gr. Dau. of Mary Jimison	#363-366
JACKSON, Phillip	Son of Mary Thompson	#1171-1176
JACKSON, Willie	Step Son of Jessie Mohawk	#741-744
JIMERSON, Moses	Gr. Son of Lillie Pierce	#817-818
JIMISON, George	Nephew of Jane Snow	#907-910
JIMISON, Green?	Step Son of John Snow Jr.	#894-901
JIMISON, Irene	Niece of Hattie E. Twoguns	#1093-1095
JIMISON, Lucinda	Dau. of Emily Seneca	#1049-1050
JIMISON, Ollie Ann	Gr. Dau. of Emily Seneca	#1049-1050
JIMISON, Peter	Gr. Son of John Cooper	#128-129
JIMISON, Ruth	Mother-in-law/Thomas Kennedy	#641-644
JIMISON, Victoria	Step Dau. of Austin John	#542-545
JOE?, Howard	Step Son of Wellington Brooks	#55-57
JOHN, Delany	Brother of Deforest Snow	#975-976
JOHN, Leroy	Son of Emily Redeye	#885-886
JOHN, Louisa	Niece of Anna Warrior	#1196-1198
JOHN, William	Son of Mary George	#257-259
JOHN, Wilson	Son of Mary George	#257-259
JOHNSON, Amos	Son of Aurelia Miller	#776-778
JOHNSON, Charles	Son of Sophia Reid	#879-880

JONAS, Abby	Dau. of Mary Ann White	#1260-1262
JONES, Stewart	Step Son of George Hudson	#300-303
JONES, Warren	Son of Sarah Taylor	#1148-1149
JONES, Willie	Nephew of John Hemlock Jr.	#270-273
KENNEDY, Abby	Gr. Dau. of Gilbert Button	#19-23
KENNEDY, John Henry	Son of Lilly Jimison	#388-390
KING, Ella	Household of Nancy Warrior	#1221-1225
KING, Harrison	Gr. Son of Elijah Jimison	#471-475
KING, Polly	Mother of Albert Jones	#599-600
LAY, Frances	Household of Mary Snow	#920-923
LOGAN, Hattie	Stp Dau./Alexander Tallchief	#1101-1104
LOGAN, Linas	Nephew of George Eels	#182-185
LOGAN, Olive	Son? of Hattie C. Warrior	#1192-1195
MOHAWK, Moses Jr.	Son of Lucy E. Button	#74-76
MOHAWK, Solon	Son of Lucy E. Button	#74-76
MOSES, Henry	Nephew of George Pierce	#801-805
MOSES, Jennie	Niece of George Pierce	#801-805
MOSES, Lewis	Nephew of George Pierce	#801-805
NEPHEW, Kingsley	Step Son of Austin John	#542-545
NEWTON, Georgie	Son of Addie Dowdy	#175-179
NEWTON, Ora	Dau. of Flora Grant	#251-252
PARKER, Emily	Step Dau. of Adam Pierce	#835-840
PHILIPS, Jacob	Step Son of George Moses	#764-768
PHILIPS, Rena	Dau. of Martha Wheeler	#1177-1178
PIERCE, Bertha	Step Dau. of Isaac Seneca Sr.	#1038-1042
PIERCE, Lewis	Gr. Son of Abby Jacket	#483-484
PLUMER, Hattie	Dau. of Melinda Snyder	#982-983
POODRY, Ella	Step Dau. of Wallack Scott	#930-933
POODRY, Rose	Dau. of Hattie E. Twoguns	#1093-1095
REDEYE, Lena	Dau. of Jennie Pierce	#806-807
RILEY?, Jimison	Adp. Son of Crawford Obail Sr.	#790-796

RUSSELL, Eva	Dau. of Mrs. Florilla Hilliker	#292-293
SENECA, Nancy	Gr. Dau. of Henry Silverheels	#1026-1029
SHANKS, Carrie	Dau. of Susan Dolson	#180-181
SHANKS, Carrie	Dau. of Hanna Wilson	#1226-1231
SHANKS, Edith	Dau. of Hanna Wilson	#1226-1231
SHANKS, Sylvia	Dau. of Hanna Wilson	#1226-1231
SNOW, Hoagg?	Gr. Son of Louisa Jack	#694-697
SPENCER, Cyrus	Household of Mary Jack	#280-282
STORY, Lillie	Dau. of Addie Dowdy	#175-179
TALLCHIEF, Frank	Son of Julia Ann Jonas	#532-535
TALLCHIEF, Maggie	Dau. of Mary Jane White	#1205-1207
TALLCHIEF, Sarah Jane	Dau. of Harriett W. Bennett	#78-79
TALL-JOHN, Sarah	Mother of Louisa Jack	#694-697
TAYLOR, Jacob	Son of Sarah Doxtator	#138-143
TAYLOR, Louisa	Dau. of Julia Ann Jonas	#532-535
TAYLOR, Sylvia	Dau. of Sarah Doxtator	#138-143
THOMAS, Emma	Adpt. Dau. of Sarah White	#1203-1204
THOMAS, Frances	Gr. Niece of Anna Warrior	#1196-1198
THOMPSON, Eliza	Mother-in-law of George Moses	#764-768
TWOGUNS, Alice	Niece of Lucy Thomas	#1132-1133
WASHINGTON, Mary	Dau. of Sylvia Jimison	#374-376
WHITE, Laura	Gr. Dau. of Gilbert Button	#19-23
WHITE, Lydia	Gr. Dau. of Martha Crow	#100-102
WHITE, Willett	Gr. Son of Gilbert Button	#19-23
WILLIAMS, Bertha	Gr. Dau. of Lucy John	#530-531
WILSON, Charles	Son of Martha Halftown	#307-309
WILSON, Maria	Dau. of Martha Halftown	#307-309
WINNIE, Christine	Dau. of Eliza Mohawk	#756-758
YOUNG, Alice	Dau. of Mary Snow	#920-923
YOUNG, Cornelius	Son of Mary Snow	#920-923

THE BUREAU OF INDIAN AFFAIRS CENSUS OF THE SENECA INDIANS RESIDING UPON THE ALLEGANY RESERVATION JULY 1886.

This census abstract is not in its original order. It has been alphabetized for this book. It is arranged in alphabetical order by surname, then given name. The age and roll number for each individual follows the given name. The surname of everyone in each household should be considered the same as the head of that household unless otherwise indicated. The surname of the head of each household has been highlighted. If a person living in a household had a different surname from the head of that household it was highlighted in capital letters and cross referenced at the end of this abstract. When the spelling of a name was in doubt a question mark was placed after that entry. This abstract should be used only as a reference. It should not take the place of any government records.

ABRAM, George age 44, Mary wife age 41, Freddie a son age 18, Frank a son age 18, George Jr., a son age 6, Roll Numbers 4-8. **ABRAM**, Henry age 24, Roll Number 9. **ABRAM**, Mary age 23, Alexander a son age 1, Roll Numbers 14-15. **ABRAM**, William age 48, Roll Number 3.

AMADON, Mary Jane age 31, Walter L. or Lee? JIMESON a son age 9, Roll Numbers 1-2.

ARMSTRONG, Johny age 28, Sarah wife age 27, Georgie a son age 8, Willie JIMISON a step son age 2, Roll Numbers 10-13.

BARNAM? or BARMAN? Maria age 37, Roll Number 27.

BENNETT, Dwight age 33, Betsey wife age 26, Lina a daughter age 5, Leroy a son age 1, Roll Numbers 16-19. **BENNETT**, John age 57, Roll Number 61. **BENNETT**, Martha age 23, Roll Number 74.

BIG-KETTLE, Eleanor age 61, Betsy a daughter age 19, Roll Numbers 59-60.
BILLY, George age 78, Nancy wife age 74, Hannah a grand daughter age 11, Roll Numbers 49-51.
BISHOP, Thomas age 32, Roll Number 62.

BLACKCHIEF, Simon age 40, Rebecca wife age 34, Marcus ABRAM a step son age 12, Luke ABRAM a step son age 8, Helen BLACKCHIEF a daughter age 3, Roll Numbers 63-67.

BLACKSNAKE, Dolly or Polly age 77, Roll Number 52. **BLACKSNAKE**, Jackson age 44, Roll Number 20. **BLACKSNAKE**, Susan age 34, Eliza a daughter age 4, Charles W. a son age 2, Joseph a son age four months, Roll Numbers 55-58.

BLINKEY, Hawley age 37, Mary Jane wife age 35, Roll Numbers 22-23. **BLINKEY**, Lutitia age 62, Roll Number 21.

BONE, Edmund age 38, Clarasa wife age 36, Loritta? or Lorilla a daughter age 9, Freddie JIMISON a cousin age 20, Nicholas BONE a nephew age 5, Roll Numbers 32-36. **BONE**, Daniel age 43, Amanda wife age 38, Jerome a son age 20, Amelia a daughter age 15, Dina a daughter age 12, Roll Numbers 43-47. **BONE**, Hiram age 47, Roll Number 31. **BONE**,

Horace age 26, Roll Number 26. **BONE**, Madison age 22, Roll Number 41.
BONE, William age 64, Hannah wife age 65, Emmet a son age 20, Edmund
a grand son age 7, Roll Numbers 37-40.

BROOKS, Ida age 17, Roll Number 80.

BUCKTOOTH, Abbie age 41, Roll Number 30. **BUCKTOOTH**, Abel age 28,
Lillie wife age 16, Roll Numbers 53-54. **BUCKTOOTH**, Eliza age 69, Roll
Number 48. **BUCKTOOTH**, Harriet age 55, Roll Number 26. **BUCKTOOTH**, James
age 78, Roll Number 24. **BUCKTOOTH**, Lucy age 45, Lindsey a son age 16,
Roll Numbers 28-29. **BUCKTOOTH**, Sally age 49, Roll Number 25.
BUCKTOOTH, Truman age 28, Lydia wife age 19, Grace a daughter age 3,
Lurie? a daughter age 1, Alice a daughter age one month, Roll Numbers
75-79.

BUTLER, Orpha age 27, Dora a daughter age 7, Freddie a son age 5, Adam
a son age 1, Della a daughter age one month, Roll Numbers 68-72.
BUTLER, Minnie age 29, Roll Number 73.

COOPER, Hannah age 39? or 59? Cyrus a son age 14, Roll Numbers 111-
112. **COOPER**, James age 59, Lucy wife age 46, William a son age 14,
Roll Numbers 81-83. **COOPER**, Julia age 34, Anna NEPHEW niece age 4,
Roll Numbers 128-129. **COOPER**, Lewis age 27, Roll Number 113. **COOPER**,
Mary age 32, Wallace a son age 7, Sherman a son age 2, Roll Numbers
119-121.

CORNFIELD, Ida age 22, Rhoda a daughter age 3, Clarence a son age 1,
Roll Numbers 131-133.

CROUSE, Alonzo age 38, Ida wife age 32, Chester a son age 18, Frank a
son age 8, Roll Numbers 122-125. **CROUSE**, Charles age 26, Roll Number
93. **CROUSE**, Cyrus age 55, Betsey a wife age 55, Jerusha a daughter age
19, Jerome a son age 13, Frank a son age 9, Roll Numbers 84-88.
CROUSE, Esther age 47, Willie a son age 17, Roll Numbers114-115.
CROUSE, Eugene age 29, Roll Number 130. **CROUSE**, Jones? or James age
28, Electa a wife age 24, Louisa a daughter age 1, Roll Numbers 90-92.
CROUSE, Martin age 21, Roll Number 89. **CROUSE**, Sylvester age 25,
Malinda wife age 16, Roll Numbers 94-95. **CROUSE**, William age 45,
George a son age 14, Ella a daughter age 13, Roll Numbers 46-48.

CROW, Rebecca age 42, Emma THOMAS a niece age 10, Roll Numbers 126-
127.

CURRY, Gibson age 28, Ida wife age 28, Laura a daughter age 1? or 7?
Roll Numbers 96-98. **CURRY**, James age 46, Roll Number 101. **CURRY**, John
age 50, Emily wife age 50, Roll Numbers 99-100. **CURRY**, Kennedy age 37,
Nancy wife age 37, Samuel a son age 14, Joseph a son age 12, Annie a
daughter age 8, Richard a son age 5, Lewis a son age 4, Eliza a
daughter age 2, Roll Numbers 103-110. **CURRY**, William age 51, Roll
Number 102.

DEER, Mary age 53, Esther JIMISON sister age 38, Roll Numbers 147-148.
DICKEY, Asa age 61, Roll Number 153.
DOWDY, James age 21, Roll Number 155. **DOWDY**, Lewis age 24, Roll Number
154.

DOXTATOR, Emma age 29, Roll Number 152. **DOXTATOR**, Henry age 35, Roll Number 142. **DOXTATOR**, Howard age 31, Roll Number 143. **DOXTATOR**, John age 59, Sarah wife age 50, Frank a son age 16, Roll Numbers 134-136. **DOXTATOR**, Lucinda age 27, Comadore a son age 4, Theodore a son age 4, Roll Numbers 144-146. **DOXTATOR**, Phebe age 33, Jane a daughter age 17? Rhoda a daughter age 10, Roll Numbers 149-151. **DOXTATOR**, William age 25, Roll Number 137.

DUDLEY, Allen age 54, Louisa wife age 41, Richard a son age 17, Edward a son age 19? Roll Numbers 138-141.

FALTY, George age 40, Cornelius a son age 3, Roll Numbers 163-164. **FALTY**, Philip age 39, Jurana? wife age 39, Lucinda a daughter age 12, Emma a daughter age 7, Roll Numbers 156-159. **FALTY**, Samuel age 34, Betsey wife age 25, Esther daughter age 6, Roll Numbers 160-162.

FARMER, Eli age 29, Jane wife age 29, Alice JIMISON a step daughter age 7, Minnie FARMER a daughter age three months, Roll Numbers 165-168.

GEORGE, James age 45, Lucy wife age 47, Sadie Redeye a step daughter age 4, Roll Numbers 221-223. **GEORGE**, Spencer age 39, Julia wife age 34, Charles ABRAM a step son age 16, Willie ABRAM a step son age 12, Bela a son age 9, Clara a daughter age 7, Amos a son age 1, Roll Numbers 202-208.

GORDON, Charles age 31, Rosa Lee wife age 26, Monroe a son age 11, Clarence a son age 1, Roll Numbers 217-220. **GORDON**, David age 61, Lucy wife age 56? Christiana a grand daughter age 8, Rosa a grand daughter age 2, Roll Numbers 213-216. **GORDON**, Emma age 22, James a son age 3, Cordlia a daughter age two months, Roll Numbers 210-212. **GORDON**, George age 43, Acsah wife age 25, Della a daughter age 10, Edwin a son age 5, Joseph a son age 2, Roll Numbers 169-173. **GORDON**, George age 25, Ella wife age 22, Bennett a son age 3, Adam a son age 1, Roll Numbers 183-186. **GORDON**, Hattie age 19, Peter WHITE a brother age 13, Roll Numbers 199-200. **GORDON**, Henry age 58, Roll Number 201. **GORDON**, Jack age 29, Philanda wife age 24, Gibson a son age 12, Sarah a daughter age 5, William a son age 2, Lucy a daughter age one month, Roll Numbers 177-182. **GORDON**, John age 41, Roll Number 187. **GORDON**, Joseph age 53, Roll Number 194. **GORDON**, Joseph age 65, Lydia wife age 55, Phebe a daughter age 18, Hattie NEPHEW a grand daughter age 7, Roll Numbers 195-198. **GORDON**, Julia age 40, Lucy a daughter age 14, Joseph a son age 12, Clara a daughter age 1, Roll Numbers 190-193. **GORDON**, Mary age 58, Nathan a son age 17, Roll Numbers 188-189. **GORDON**, Samuel age 51, Sally wife age 49, Franklin a son age 12, Roll Numbers 174-176. **GORDON**, Thomas age 26, Roll Number 209.

HALFTOWN, Alfred age 43, Hannah wife age 43, Nancy a daughter age 19, Jefford a son age 16, Alvin? a son age 10, Cordelia a daughter age 6, Alfred Jr., a son age 3, Roll Numbers 285-291. **HALFTOWN**, Amanda age 22, Electa THOMAS a daughter age 2, Willie JACOB a son age two months, Roll Numbers 292-294. **HALFTOWN**, Ann age 71, Roll Number 251. **HALFTOWN**, Elizabeth age 28, Lucy daughter age 3, Roll Numbers 231-232. **HALFTOWN**, Lucinda age 37, Amanda BUCK a daughter age 2, Roll Numbers 295-296. **HALFTOWN**, Harrison age 58, Mary wife age 50? Hamilton a son age 18, William H., a son age 14, Emily B., a daughter age 9, Roll Numbers

254-258. **HALFTOWN**, Henry age 28, Roll Number 235. **HALFTOWN**, James age 21, Roll Number 229. **HALFTOWN**, James age 29, Roll Number 230. **HALFTOWN**, James age 27, Esther wife age 28, Elizabeth JIMISON niece age 8, Willie P. JIMISON a nephew age 20, Roll Numbers 241-244. **HALFTOWN**, John age 45, Roll Number 265. **HALFTOWN**, Martha age 29, Roll Number 236. **HALFTOWN**, Rebecca age 67, Loura a grand daughter age 19, Roll Numbers 268-269. **HALFTOWN**, Robert age 39, Roll Number 266. **HALFTOWN**, Sarah Jane age 35, Roll Number 252. **HALFTOWN**, Susan age 45, Jerome a son age 14, Laura a daughter age 12, Roll Numbers 248-250. **HALFTOWN**, Wallace age 43, Martha wife age 39, Grace JIMISON a grand daughter age 7, Mary JIMISON a grand daughter age 5, Theodore JIMISON a grand son age 3, Roll Numbers 224-228.

HALFWHITE, Benjamin age 32, Roll Number 253. **HALFWHITE**, Charlie age 25, Roll Number 238. **HALFWHITE**, Eliza age 37, Sarah a daughter age 16, Georgie a son age 11, Martha a daughter age 7, Bertis? or Bertie? a daughter age four months, Roll Numbers 259-263. **HALFWHITE**, Joseph age 74? Roll Number 264.

HANSON, Jane B., age 25, Roll Number 267.

HARE? Mary age 49, Robert JIMISON a son age 16, Roll Numbers 280-281.

HARRIS, Alvira age 35, Malachi DOXTATOR a son age 2, Elvin? DOXTATOR a son age one month, Roll Numbers 282-284. **HARRIS**, Edward age 37, Nellie a daughter age 15, Willie a son age 12, Roll Numbers 245-247.

HILL, Mary Ann age 31, Roll Number 237.
HOAGG, William C., age 26, Dora wife age 26, Roll Numbers 233-234.
HOWE, Emily age 39, Roll Number 239. **HOWE**, Mary age 49, Robert Jimison a son age 16, Roll Numbers 280-281.

HUFF, Abram S., age 36, Emeline wife age 21, Elmore a son age 11, Michael a son age 2, Isreal a son age 1, Roll Numbers 270-274. **HUFF**, Henry Jr., age 40, Laura wife age 41, Nelson R., a son age 19, Gertrude JACKSON niece age 16, Evelyn a nephew age 14, Roll Numbers 275-279. **HUFF**, Hiram age 39, Roll Number 240.

JACK, John age 58, Lucy wife age 68, Roll Numbers 366-367.

JACKSON, Ansilia age 29, Josephine a daughter age 15, Lindsey a son age 8, Franklin a son age 5, Addlie a daughter age 4, Stonewall a son age 1, Roll Numbers 360-365. **JACKSON**, Jesse age 67, Roll Number 355. **JACKSON**, Moses age 45, Caroline wife age 45, Roll Numbers 352-353. **JACKSON**, Nancy age 21, Roll Number 354.

JACOB, Alfred Esq. age 44, Roll Number 381. **JAOCOB**, Allen age 42, Susan wife age 45, Roll Numbers 379-380. **JACOB**, Ella age 21, Twoguns CLUTE? or Clute TWOGUNS? a son age 4, Roll Numbers 486-487. **JACOB**, George age 50, Sally wife age 50, Amanda a daughter age 14, Roll Numbers 483-485. **JACOB**, Hiram age 25, Roll Number 385. **JACOB**, Isaac age 63, Roll Number 334. **JACOB**, James age 37, Mary wife age 54, Sophia a daughter age 15, Eliza a daughter age 11, Ella a daughter age 6, Roll Numbers 503-507. **JACOB**, John age 58, Lucy his wife age 68, Roll Numbers 366-367. **JACOB**, John Jr., age 26, Amanda wife age 25, Roll Numbers 426-427. **JACOB**, Margaret age 42, Percilla R., a daughter age

15? Roll Numbers 383-384. **JACOB**, Owen age 42, Emma a daughter age 12, Ezra a son age 11, William a son age 3, Harvey a son age 16, Roll Numbers 488-492. **JACOB**, Ruth age 65, Roll Number 481. **JACOB**, Thomas age 100? Roll Number 333. **JACOB**, Thomas W. age 39, Eleanor wife age 43, Skidmore a son age 11, Sabrina a daughter age 8, Roll Numbers 375-378.

JACKSON, Laura age 29? Peter a son age 9, Heber a son age 6, Hattie a daughter age 4, Roll Numbers 493-496. **JACKSON**, Moses age 45, Caroline wife age 45, Roll Number 352-353.

JIMISON, Adam age 29? Hattie wife age 24, Maranda a daughter age 6, Carrie a daughter age 4, Phnia a daughter age two months, Roll Numbers 457-467. **JIMISON**, Alexander age 34, Jacob a son age 12, Roll Numbers 446-447. **JIMISON**, Alfred B., age 29, Roll Number 482 **JIMISON**, Allen age 34, Roll Number 448. **JIMISON**, Allen G., age 24, Roll Number 436. **JIMISON**, Charles age 29, Julia wife age 29, Alexander a son age 4, Peter a son age 2, Charles HALFTOWN brother-in-law age 16, Georgie HALFTOWN brother-in-Law age 18, Roll Number 315-320. **JIMISON**, Charles age 21, Roll Number 406. **JIMISON**, Cordelia age 37, Roll Number 303. **JIMISON**, David B., age 58, Effie wife age 48, David B., Jr., a son age 28? or 20? Joel a son age 12, Daniel KILLBUCK adopted son age 10, Roll Numbers 395-399. **JIMISON**, Delila age 45, Bailey a son age 18, Nathan a son age 17? Nelson a son age 14, Roll Numbers 407-410. **JIMISON**, Dwight age 28, Quiltin? a son age 6, Roll Number 401-402. **JIMISON**, Ephraim age 33, Roll Numbers 497. **JIMISON**, Foster? or Lester? age 25, Claranda wife age 21, Roll Numbers 429-430. **JIMISON**, Frank age 30, Roll Number 468. **JIMISON**, HELLY? age 43, Mary wife age 25, Roll Numbers 342-343. **JIMISON**, Hiram age 32, Roll Number 455. **JIMISON**, Horace E. age 40, Emily wife age 31, Lillie a daughter age 11, Willet a son age 8, Roll Numbers 337-340. **JIMISON** Howard J. age 25, Roll Number 307. **JIMISON**, Isreal Scott age 31, Roll Number 302. **JIMISON**, Jacob age 29, Emily wife age 31, Cora DOXTATOR a step daughter age 10, Luther JIMISON a son age four months, Roll Numbers 308-311. **JIMISON**, HELLY? age 43, Mary wife age 25, Roll Numbers 342-343. **JIMISON**, Hiram age 32, Roll Number 455. **JIMISON**, Horace E. age 40, Emily wife age 31, Lillie a daughter age 11, Willet a son age 8, Roll Numbers 337-340. **JIMISON** Howard J. age 25, Roll Number 307. **JIMISON**, Jacob age 24, Eliza wife age 17? or 19? Dora a daughter age 2, Roll Numbers 417-419. **JIMISON**, James age 38, Ella wife age 31, Mary a daughter age 11, Roger A son age 4, Cora a daughter age 1, Roll Numbers 328-332. **JIMISON**, Jasper age 50, Roll Number 327. **JIMISON**, John age 84, Roll Number 341. **JIMISON**, John age 28, Lorinda wife age 18, Flora a daughter age six months, Roll Numbers 433-435. **JIMISON**, John A., age 51, Betsey wife age 31, Roll Numbers 305-306. **JIMISON**, John P., age 47, Lucy wife age 43, Phebe a daughter age 18, Eliza a daughter age 15, Lavinia a daughter age 12, Solon C., a son age 11, Roll Numbers 420-425. **JIMISON**, Joseph age 60, Roll Number 431. **JIMISON**, King L. age 40, Roll Number 400. **JIMISON**, Martha age 47, Roll Number 304. **JIMISON**, Martin age 37, Roll Number 382. **JIMISON**, Mary C., age 30, Roll Number 405. **JIMISON**, Polly L., age 58, James husband age 64, Lafayette a grand son age 8, Roll Numbers 443-445. **JIMISON**, Richard age 31, Susan wife age 31, Chauncey a son age 8, Berthie a daughter age five months, Roll Numbers 499-502. **JIMISON**, Sacket age 39, Roll Number 432. **JIMISON**, Sally W., age 43, Willie JIMISON a nephew age 18, Anna TITUS a niece age 18, Roll Numbers 312-314. **JIMISON**, Sarah age 30, Moses COOPER a son age 12, Thomas COOPER a son age 10, Clara COOPER age daughter age 8, Alice CORNFIELD a daughter age 6, Fannie CORNFIELD a daughter age 4, Walter CORNFIELD a son age 1, Roll Numbers 456-462. **JIMISON**, Solon age 28, Roll Number 437. **JIMISON**, Solon W., age 44, Roll Number 442. **JIMISON**, Susan age 54, Ada a grand daughter age 14, Roll Numbers 415-416. **JIMISON**, (Bih) Stephen age 49, Roll Number 428. **JIMISON**, Willet R. age 39, Amelia wife age 21, Alonzo a son age 17, Carrie a daughter age 13, Cyrus W., a son age three months, Roll Numbers 449-453. **JIMISON**, Wilson age 29, Roll Number 404. **JIMISON**, Wilson W., age 40, Laura wife age 39, Roll Numbers 479-480.

JOHN, Alexander age 37, Mary wife age 32, Oliver a son age 15, Jesse a son age 10, Hattie a daughter age 9, Truman? or Freeman? a son age one month, Roll Numbers 321-326. **JOHN**, Alphonse age 23, Roll Number 403. **JOHN**, Andrew Jr., age 39? Rosa A., age 24, Roll Number 335-336. **JOHN**, Ascah age 79? or 99? Roll Number 297. **JOHN**, Casler age 34, Elizabeth wife age 32, Lucius a son age 11, Hattie a daughter age 7, Roll Numbers 298-301. **JOHN**, Cordelia age 37? or 39? Roll Number 303. **JOHN**, Joseph age 52, Eliza wife age 42, Henry a son age 16, Lillie a daughter age 2, Roll Numbers 386-389. **JOHN**, Lewis age 42, Lucy wife age 42, Joseph a son age 19, Emily a daughter age 8, Perry a son age 6, Roll Numbers 370-374. **JOHN**, Mary age 58, Austin a son age 14, Roll Numbers 368-369. **JOHN**, Richard age 38, Anna wife age 25, Jerry? or Perry? a son age 7, Cora M., a daughter age three months, Roll Numbers 469-472. **JOHN**, Stephen age 28, Melvina wife age 25, Clarence a son age 5, Lydia a daughter age 4, Delora a daughter age 2, Chester a son age one month, Roll Numbers 473-478. **JOHN**, William age 40, Claranda wife age 29, Cynthia a daughter age 9, Hamilton a son age 7, Roll Numbers 411-414.

JOHNATHAN, John age 46, Roll Number 498.

JOHNSON, Archibald age 33, Hattie wife age 25, Archibald Jr., a son age 5, Freddie a son age 1, Roll Numbers 438-441. **JOHNSON**, Moses age 30, Mary wife age 28, Betsey a daughter age 4, Salina a daughter age 2, Roll Numbers 348-351.

JONES, Francis age 53, Elizabeth wife age 34, Franklin a son age 12, Sarah a daughter age 9, Elmor a son age 7, Roll Numbers 390-394. **JONES**, Hannah age 45, Roll Number 454. **JONES**, Josiah age 52, Mary wife age 32, Orrin a son age 13, Ruby C., JONES a grand daughter age 2, Roll Numbers 344-347.

KENJOCKETY, Samuel age 38, Louisa wife age 31, Mattie a daughter age 11, Joslyn a son age 6, Roll Numbers 508-511.

KILLBUCK, Anna? or Amie: age 42, Laura a daughter age 13, Jane a daughter age 15, Lucie ABRAM a grand daughter age one month, Roll Numbers 513-516. **KILLBUCK**, David age 35, Roll Number 526. **KILLBUCK**, Jesse age 69, Roll Number 512. **KILLBUCK**, John age 51, Annie wife age 40, Minnie a daughter age 12, Roll Numbers 523-525. **KILLBUCK**, Mary age 44, Roll Number 519. **KILLBUCK**, Peter age 27, Roll Number 517.

KING, Betsey age 69, Roll Number 521. **KING**, Jennie age 25, Roll Number 520. **KING**, Mary age 44, Roll Number 519. **KING**, Mary O., age 48, Roll Number 522. **KING**, Wooster age 47, Roll Number 518.

LAMPSON? Or SAMPSON, Abram, age 47, Roll Number 534. **LAMPSON? or SAMPSON**, John age 84, Julia wife age 65, Roll Numbers 531-532. **LAMPSON? or SAMPSON**, Thomas age 52, Alice wife age 40, Wallace a son age 10, Ira a son age 8, Roll Numbers 527-530.

LEE, George age 25, Elizabeth wife age 24, Georgia a daughter age 2, Chester a son age two months, Roll Numbers 566-569. **LEE**, Morris age 21, Roll Number 543. **LEE**, William age 39, Eliza wife age 32, Belinda a daughter age 1, Roll Numbers 548-550.

LEWIS, Benjamin age 63, Lucy wife age 58, Nella REDEYE grand daughter age 16, Freddie REDEYE a grand son age 9, Sheldon REDEYE a grand son age 14, Fidelia CROUSE a grand daughter age six months, Roll Numbers 551-556. **LEWIS**, Eliza age 50, Louisa a daughter age 19, Benjamin a son age 12, Peter B., a son age 4, Sally a daughter age 1, Roll Numbers 561-565. **LEWIS**, Hattie age 24? or 29? Joshua a son age 4, Loransa? a daughter age 1, Roll Numbers 539-541. **LEWIS**, John J., age 29, Julia wife age 20, Minnie a daughter age 4, William a son age 2, Roll Numbers 557-560.

LOGAN, Alfred age 48, Lucy wife age 45, Charles a son age 20, Acsah a daughter age 16, Howard a son age 14, Louisa a daughter age 12, Saxon a son age 10, Joseph age son age 8, Alfred WILLIAMS a son age two months, Roll Numbers 570-578. **LOGAN**, Charles age 26, Roll Number 542. **LOGAN**, Henry age 25, Louisa wife age 20? or 26? Roll Numbers 579-580. **LOGAN**, Jesse age 59, Susan wife age 52, James a son age 20, William DOWDY a grand son age 8, Roll Numbers 544-547. **LOGAN**, John age 88, Roll Number 533. **LOGAN**, Samuel age 41, Eliza wife age 35, Lucy a daughter age 9, Jesse a son age 1, Roll Numbers 535-538.

NEPHEW Robert age 45, Philo a son age 13? or 15? Crawford age 12, Cora a daughter age 10, Roll Numbers 581-584.

OBAIL, Susan age 85, Roll Number 585.
OBRAN? OR OBAIL? Della age 21, Lulia a daughter age one month, Roll Number 586-587.

PATTERSON, Polly age 90, Roll Number 614. **PATTERSON**, Mary age 60, Samuel JIMISON a grand son age 4, Roll Numbers 616-617. **PATTERSON**, Sacket age 50, Roll Number 615. **PATTERSON**, William age 39, Mary wife age 35, George a son age 11, Jennie a daughter age 9, Percilla daughter age 5, Cora a daughter age 4, Flora a daughter age 2, Roll Numbers 607-613.

PIERCE, Able age 68, Eda a daughter age 13, Roll Numbers 655-656. **PIERCE**, Adam age 31, Roll Number 632. **PIERCE**, Amos age 23, Roll Number 626. **PIERCE**, Benjamin age 84, Abagail wife age 63, Roll Numbers 661-662. **PIERCE**, Charles age 25, Roll Number 664. **PIERCE**, Clinton age 42, Roll Number 623. **PIERCE**, Cora age 22, Roll Number 657. **PIERCE**, Elizabeth age 28, Roll Number 622. **PIERCE**, Esther age 32, Roll Number 650. **PIERCE**, Fidelia age 36, Elmore? a son age 15, Ona a daughter age 13, Roll Numbers 633-635. **PIERCE**, Frank age 30, Roll Number 621. **PIERCE**, Gibson age 30, Roll Number 636. **PIERCE**, Hannah age 55, Nathan Jimison a son age 15, Roll Number 624-625. **PIERCE**, Hannah age 32, Ellen a daughter age 11, Burnis a son age 5, Harvey a son age 3, Peter JOHN a nephew age 20, Eliza JOHN a niece age 16, Malinda JOHN a niece age 11, Roll Numbers 639-645. **PIERCE**, Harrison age 46, Roll Number 593. **PIERCE**, Henry B., age 30, Lillian C., wife age 26, Roll Numbers 648-649. **PIERCE**, Howard age 38? or 58? Roll Number 654. **PIERCE**, Ira age 45, Adelaide a wife age 41, Gideon a son age 13, Roll Numbers 658-660. **PIERCE**, James age 49, Roll Number 651. **PIERCE**, John B., age 32, Roll Number 646. **PIERCE**, Katie R., age 28, Roll Number 647. **PIERCE**, King age 72, Roll Number 619. **PIERCE**, Lewis age 31, Roll Number 620. **PIERCE**, Lucinda age 52, Roll Number 666. **PIERCE**, Lydia age 63, Roll Number 665. **PIERCE**, Lyman age 44, Emma wife age 26, Burty a son age 10, Sadie a daughter age 4, Amelia a daughter age 1, Roll Numbers 588-592. **PIERCE**, Marina Jennie age 25, Roll Number 638. **PIERCE**, Marsh age 65, Topla? or Sopla? a son age 17, Windsor a son age 15, Roll Numbers 667-669. **PIERCE**, Martha age 21, Roll Number 663. **PIERCE**, Mary age 33, Roll Number 618. **PIERCE**, Oakley age 28, Julia wife age 19, Florence a daughter age 2, Burtha a daughter age 1, Roll Numbers 627-630. **PIERCE**, Thomas H., age 39, Lucy W., wife age 27, Roll Numbers 596-597. **PIERCE**, Seneca age 27, Roll Number 637. **PIERCE**, Wallace W., age 53, Roll Number 652. **PIERCE**, Wilson Jr., age 25, Roll Number 670.

PLUMMER, Amelia age 25, Roll Number 598. **PLUMMER**, Elvira age 26, Roll Number 599. PLUMMER, Lewis age 28, Roll Number 600. **PLUMMER**, Nathaniel age 38, Mary Jane wife age 32, Lewis a son age 14, John a son age 6, Cornelius a son age 4, Roll Numbers 602-606. **PLUMMER**, Sally age 65, Sophelia JOHNSON a grand daughter age 12, Roll Numbers 594-595. **PLUMMER**, William age 61, Roll Number 601.

PIERCE, Lyman age 44, Emma wife age 26, Burty a son age 10, Sadie a daughter age 4, Amelia a daughter age 1, Roll Numbers 588-592.

PRINTUP, Russel age 22, Roll Number 631.

RAY, Acsah age 50, Roll Number 704. **RAY**, Stephen age 46, Lucy wife age 43, Griffith a son age 9, James a son age 1, Roll Numbers 682-685.

REDEYE, Bennett age 47, Lucinda wife age 51, Roll Numbers 698-699. **REDEYE**, Casler age 57, Lucy wife age 43, Carrie a daughter age 12, Jerome H. JIMISON a nephew age 18, Roll Number 671-674. **REDEYE**, Hiram age 34, Betsey B., wife age 23, Amos a son age 11, Roll Numbers 675-677. **REDEYE**, James age 61, Caroline wife age 55, Mary daughter age 18, James Jr., a son age 10, Roll Numbers 686-689. **REDEYE**, Jones age 32, Emma wife age 30, Jones Jr., a son age 3, George a son age 1, Roll Numbers 678-681. **REDEYE**, Lillie age 5, Roll Number 695. **REDEYE**, Lucy age 64, Pason JIMISON a grand son age 15, William JIMISON a grand son age 17, Roll Numbers 700-702. **REDEYE**, Sacket age 45, Susan wife age 45, Henry a son age 14, Elizabeth a daughter age 10, Howard a son age 5, Roll Numbers 690-694. **REDEYE**, Willis age 21, Roll Number 703.

RITTENOUR, Eveline age 35, Anna JIMISON a daughter age 11, Roll Numbers 696-697.
SCROGG, Jack age 57, Roll Number 783. **SCROGG**, Thomas age 60, Roll Number 784.

SENECA, Julia age 49, Roll Number 779. **SENECA**, Lay? or Say? age 27, Julia a daughter age one month, Roll Numbers 777-778. **SENECA**, Sally age 52, Clarence PLUMMER a son age 12, Roll Numbers 772-773. **SENECA**, William age 26, Roll Number 786.

SHANKS, Hannah age 43, Roll Number 765.

SHONGO, Amos age 49, Roll Number 782. **SHONGO**, Anderson B., age 24, Roll Number 771. **SHONGO**, Bennett age 49, Roll Number 776. **SHONGO**, Daniel E., age 27, Roll Number 780. **SHONGO**, Eli age 25, Roll Number 767. **SHONGO**, Emma age 28, Roll Number 716. **SHONGO**, Emma age 25, Roll Number 785. **SHONGO**, Howard age 22, Roll Numbers 715. **SHONGO**, Jane age 48, Roll Number 766. **SHONGO**, James age 46, Nettie a daughter age 8, Lerinda a daughter age 17, Lyford a son age 19, Roll Numbers 739-742. **SHONGO**, James (Doctor) Age 70, Roll Number 781. **SHONGO**, Lyman age 49, Lucy wife age 57, Ida a daughter age 17, Louisa HALFTOWN a niece age 10, William H. CORNFIELD a nephew age 9, Roll Numbers 708-712. **SHONGO**, Peter age 37, Mary a wife age 34, Philanda a daughter age 14, Henry W., a son age 10, Cora a daughter age 1, Roll Numbers 729-733. **SHONGO**, Silas age 59, Jane wife age 45, Elmore a son age 14, Lina a daughter age 9, Roll Numbers 735-738. **SHONGO**, Victoria age 21, Roll Numbers 734. **SHONGO**, William age 47, Minnie a daughter age 15, Roll Numbers 760-761.

SILVERHEELS, Alfred age 35, Bella a daughter age 8, Roll Numbers 729-728. **SILVERHEELS**, Joel age 25, Roll Number 757. **SILVERHEELS**, Laura age 45, Charles BLACKSNAKE a son age 14, Roll Numbers 758-759. **SILVERHEELS**, Ruth age 83, Roll Number 756. **SILVERHEELS**, Myron age 49, Cynthia wife age 44, Elias a son age 9, Roll Numbers 705-707.

SKY, Alice age 32, Lillie JIMISON a daughter age 14, Roll Number 774-775.

SNOW, Amos age 47, Lucy a daughter age 35, Emma a daughter age 12, Annie a daughter age 9, James a son age 7, Jones? or Jonas? a son age 5, Hudson a son age 2, Lafayette GREEN a step son age 15, Alice SNOW a daughter age five months, Roll Numbers 745-753. **SNOW**, David age 62, Roll Number 764. **SNOW**, Hannah age 72, Roll Number 763. **SNOW**, Hiram age 27, Roll Number 788. **SNOW**, Jerome age 29, Jane wife age 25, Rena a daughter age 8, Roll Numbers 721-723. **SNOW**, Joseph age 27, Roll Number 787. **SNOW**, Margaret age 39, Moses a son age 10, Roll Numbers 754-755. **SNOW**, Mary age 51, John B., a son age 19, Roll Numbers 743-744. **SNOW**, Nelson age 30, Roll Number 762. **SNOW**, Sally age 48, Roll Number 770.

SNYDER, Cordelia age 29, John a son age 9, Della a daughter age 5, Susie? or Lusie? a daughter age 3, Roll Numbers 717-720. **SNYDER**, William age 45, Roll Number 789.

STRONG, Nathaniel age 45, Jane wife age 49, Roll Numbers 724-725. **STRONG**, Sarah age 76, Roll Number 726.

SUNDOWN, Hannah age 65, Roll Number 768. **SUNDOWN**, Louisa age 53, Roll Number 769.
SUTTON, Louisa age 23, Elliot a son age four months, Roll Numbers 713-714.

THOMAS, David age 25, Silas PIERCE, a nephew age 8, Roll Numbers 816-817. **THOMPSON**, Caroline age 30, Sally a daughter age 1, Roll Numbers 803-804. **THOMAS**, Lyman age 33? Roll Numbers 818. **THOMAS**, Martha age 58, Ephraim a son age 16, William E. MOULTON, a grand son age 9, Joseph MOULTON a grand son age 6, Roll Numbers 794-797. **THOMPSON**,

Sally age 52, Lydia a daughter age 17, Jane a daughter age 9, Roll Numbers 798-800.

TITUS, Dennis age 45, Roll Number 813. **TITUS**, Dennis Jr., age 22, Roll Number 814. **TITUS**, George age 64? or 67? Polly wife age 73, Roll Numbers 805-806. **TITUS**, George Jr., age 24, Roll Number 807. **TITUS**, Jackson age 57, Jane R., wife age 44, Minnie REDEYE a step daughter age 16, Malinda a daughter age 4, Roll Numbers 809-812. **TITUS**, Julia age 52, Roll Number 808.

TWOGUNS, George Jr., age 32, Roll Number 815. **TWOGUNS**, John age 35, Laura wife age 30, Myrtie a daughter age 4, Phebe a daughter age 1, Roll Numbers 790-793. **TWOGUNS**, Lewis age 28, Mary wife age 28, Roll Numbers 801-802.

VAN ARNAM, Lutitia age 27, Louvina? or Louisa? a daughter age 8, Henry a son age 5, John a son age 4, Betsey a daughter age 1? or 2? Roll Numbers 820-824. **VAN ARNAM** William age 29, Roll Number 819.

WADE, Ethie age 25, Roll Number 845.

WARRIOR, George Jr., age 29, Susie wife age 24, Roll Numbers 840-841. **WARRIOR**, William age 27, Betsey D., wife age 26, Rosina JIMISON a step daughter age 9, Roll Numbers 842-844.

WATT, Hiram age 24, Phebe wife age 16, Roll Numbers 846-847. **WATT**, James age 24, Ida wife age 25, Roll Numbers 828-829. **WATT**, Sarah age 69, Roll Number 830.

WAUDELL, George age 22, Roll Number 848.

WHITE, James age 43, Lucy wife age 43, Wesley a son age 8, Roll Numbers 825-827. **WHITE**, Reuben age 28, Jane wife age 22, Roll Numbers 835-836. **WHITE**, Robert age 29, Caroline wife age 27, Willie a son age 6, Roll Numbers 837-839. **WHITE**, Wesley age 22, Hattie wife age 21, Wesley Jr., a son age 4, Lillie a daughter age 1, Roll Numbers 831-834.

WILLIAMS, Augustus age 21, Roll Number 849.
YELLOWBLANKET, Moses age 56, Roll Number 850.

THE SENECA RESIDING ON THE ALLEGANY RESERVE-1886 CROSS INDEX		
SURNAME CROSS INDEX	**RELATION/HEAD OF HOUSEHOLD**	**BIA ROLL #**
ABRAM, Charles	Step Son of Spencer George	#202-208
ABRAM, Luke	Step Son of Simon Blackchief	#63-67
ABRAM, Marcus	Step Son of Simon Blackchief	#63-67
BLACKSNAKE, Charles	Son of Laura Silverheels	#758-759
COOPER, Clara	Dau. of Sarah Jimison	#456-462
COOPER, Moses	Son of Sarah Jimison	#456-462
COOPER, Thomas	Son of Sarah Jimison	#456-462
CORNFIELD, Alice	Dau. of Sarah Jimison	#456-462
CORNFIELD, William H.	Nephew of Lyman Shongo	#708-712
CROUSE, Fidelia	Gr. Dau. of Benjamin Lewis	#551-556
DOWDY, William	Gr. Son of Jesse Logan	#544-547
DOXTATOR, Cora	Step Dau. of Jacob Jimison	#308-311
DOXTATOR, Elvin?	Son of Alvira Harris	#282-284
DOXTATOR, Malachi	Son of Alvira Harris	#282-284
GREEN, Lafayette	Step Son of Amos Snow	#745-753
HALFTOWN, Charles	Brother-in-law/Charles Jimison	#315-320
HALFTOWN, George	Brother-in-law/Charles Jimison	#315-320
HALFTOWN, Louisa	Niece of Lyman Shongo	#708-712
JACKSON, Gertrude	Niece of Henry Huff Jr.	#275-279
JACOB, Willie	Son of Amanda Halftown	#292-294
JIMESON, Walter L.	Son of Mary Jane Amadon	#1-2
JIMISON, Alice	Step Dau. of Eli Farmer	#165-168
JIMISON, Anna	Dau. of Eveline Rittenour	#696-697
JIMISON, Elizabeth	Niece of James Halftown	#241-244
JIMISON, Esther	Sister of Mary Deer	#147-148
JIMISON, Freddie	Cousin of Edmund Bone	#32-36
JIMISON, Grace	Gr. Dau. of Wallace Halftown	#224-228

JIMISON, Jerome	Nephew of Casler Redeye	#671-674
JIMISON, Mary	Gr. Dau. of Wallace Halftown	#224-228
JIMISON, Pason	Gr. Son of Lucy Redeye	#700-702
JIMISON, Robert	Son of Mary Hare	#280-281
JIMISON, Rosina	Step Dau. of William Warrior	#842-844
JIMISON, Samuel	Gr. Son of Mary Patterson	#616-617
JIMISON, Theodore	Gr. Son of Wallace Halftown	#224-228
JIMISON, William	Gr. Son of Lucy Redeye	#700-702
JIMISON, Willie	Step Son of Johny Armstrong	#10-13
JIMISON, Willie P.	Nephew of James Halftown	#241-244
JOHN, Eliza	Niece of Hannah Pierce	#639-645
JOHN, Malinda	Niece of Hannah Pierce	#639-645
JOHN, Peter	Nephew of Hannah Pierce	#639-645
KILLBUCK, Daniel	Adpt. Son of David B. Jimison	#395-399
MOULTON, William E.	Gr. Son of Martha Thomas	#794-797
NEPHEW, Anna	Niece of Julia Cooper	#128-129
NEPHEW, Hattie	Gr. Dau. of Joseph Gordon	#195-198
PIERCE, Silas	Nephew of David Thomas	#816-817
PLUMMER, Clarence	Son of Sally Seneca	#772-773
REDEYE, Freddie	Gr. Son of Benjamin Lewis	#551-556
REDEYE, Minnie	Step Dau. of Jackson Titus	#809-812
REDEYE, Nella	Gr. Dau. of Benjamin Lewis	#551-556
REDEYE, Sadie	Step Dau. of James George	#221-223
REDEYE, Sheldon	Gr. Son of Benjamin Lewis	#551-556
THOMAS, Electa	Dau. of Amanda Halftown	#292-294
TITUS, Anna	Niece of Sally W. Jimison	#312-314
TWOGUNS, Clute?	Son of Ella Jacob	#486-487
WHITE, Peter	Brother of Hattie Gordon	#199-200
WILLIAMS, Alfred	Son of Alfred Logan	#570-578

This census abstract is not in its original order. It has been alphabetized for this book. It is arranged in alphabetical order by surname then given name. The age and roll number follows each given name or family group. The surname of everyone in each household should be considered the same as the head of that household unless otherwise indicated. The surname of the head of each household has been highlighted. If a person living in a household had a different surname from the head of that household it was highlighted in capital letters and cross referenced at the end of this abstract. A question mark was place after a name or date that was in doubt. Use caution with the surname Miller. In some cases it may have been mistaken for the surname Mitten. This abstract should be used only as a reference. It should not take the place of any original government records.

ABRAM, Barber B., age 24, Roll Number 3. **ABRAM**, Chauncey age 48, Sarah wife age 44, Roll Numbers 1-2. **ABRAM**, Milton age 49, Albert a son age 15, Henry a son age 14, Harry a son age 12, Lute? or Luke? a son age 4, Roll Numbers 4-8.

ALICK, Emeline age 57? or 59? Hattie daughter age 9, Roll Numbers 12-13. **ALICK**, William age 68, Sally wife age 48, Ida SKYE a niece age 18, Roll Numbers 9-11.

BAPTIST, Sararh age 40, Isaac a son age 20, Robert a son age 12, John SCROGGS a son age 2, Roll Numbers 41-44.

BENNETT, Harriet age 69, Roll Number 32.

BIGFIRE, Charles age 41, Roll Number 31. **BIGFIRE**, Jane age 62, Susan SUNDOWN a grand daughter age 19, Lucinda CHARLES a grand daughter age 2, Roll Numbers 52-54.

BILLY, David age 47, Roll Number 45. **BILLY**, John age 30, Roll Number 21. **BILLY**, Leon? or Lian? age 27, Roll Number 23. **BILLY**, Silas age 23, Roll Number 22.

BLACK, John age 49, Mary a daughter age 15, Roll Numbers 46-47.

BLACKCHIEF, Andrew age 64, Andrew BILLY a nephew age 16, Roll Numbers 15-16. **BLACKCHIEF**, Charles age 32, Roll Number 14. **BLACKCHIEF**, Herman age 24, Roll Number 30. **BLACKCHIEF**, Jennie age 27, Allen a son age 10, Hiram a son age 7, Lyman a son age 4, Roll Numbers 17-20. **BLACKCHIEF**, Nancy age 18, Lenard? SNYDER brother age 15, Lucy BLACKCHIEF age 8, sister, Roll Numbers 34-36.

BLACKSQUIRREL, Mary age 89, Roll Number 24.
BLUESKY, Samuel age 55, Salina a daughter age 14, Roll Numbers 28-29.
BLUESKY, Thomas age 29, Emma wife age 25, Anna daughter age 5, Roll Numbers 37-39.

BROOKS, Anna age 21? or 29? Helen JONES a daughter age 4, Electa **BROOKS** a daughter age nine months, Roll Numbers 49-51. **BROOKS**, Elijah age 29, Roll Number 40. **BROOKS**, Joel? Age 28, Roll Number 33. **BROOKS**,

John age 49, Mary age 15 a daughter Roll Numbers 46-47. **BROOKS**, John age 39, Roll Number 48. **BROOKS**, John W., age 39, Eunice wife age 42, Fannie PRINTUP a grand daughter age 6, Roll Numbers 25-27.

CARPENTER, Cornelius age 24, Ida wife age 23, Elias a son age 1, Roll Numbers 58-60. **CARPENTER**, Harvy? age 31, Laura wife age 27, Herbert BLACKCHIEF a step-son age 7, Roll Numbers 75-77. **CARPENTER**, Laura age 22, Roll Number 68 & 78? **CARPENTER**, Moses age 46, Emily? wife age 48, Ida a daughter age 9, Roll Numbers 55-57.

CHARLES, Addison age 57, Roll Number 67. **CHARLES**, Anderson age 24, Roll Number 66. **CHARLES**, John age 32, Roll Number 64. **CHARLES**, Joseph age 36, Anna wife age 30, William a son age 9, Elias a son age 6, Daniel a son age 4, Reuben a son age 2, Roll Numbers 69-74. **CHARLES**, Solomon age 30, Roll Number 65.

CLUTE, Charles age 56, Elizabeth wife age 36, David S. FISH step-son age 13, Phebe D. FISH a step daughter age 11, Lydia CLUTE a daughter age 6, Alex CLUTE a son age 3, Louisa CLUTE a daughter age 1, Roll Numbers 79-85.

COOPER, William age 32, Sarah wife age 38, Roll Numbers 61-62.
CROW, George age 53, Roll Number 63.

DAVID, John age 36, Roll Number 102. **DAVID**, Louisa age 41, Roll Number 107. **DAVID**, Sally age 31? Roll Number 111.

DESTROYTOMI, Samuel age 48, Phebe wife age 42, Frances a daughter age 13, Elijah a son age 9, Roll Numbers 103-106.

DOCTOR, Charles age 53, Roll Number 96. **DOCTOR**, Frank A., age 36, Moses a son age 9, Rose a daughter age 7, Milo a son age 4, Roll Numbers 92-95. **DOCTOR**, Frederick age 37, Mary wife age 21? or 27? Roll Numbers 109-110. **DOCTOR**, Isaac age 73, Maria wife age 74, Benjamin grand son age 13, Roll Numbers 86-88. **DOCTOR**, Jacob age 41, Laura wife age 40, Dasie adopted daughter age 7, Roll Numbers 112-114. **DOCTOR**, Laura B., age 31, Herman a son age 11, Charles a son age 5, Roll Numbers 89-91. **DOCTOR**, Peter age 25, Roll Number 108.

DOXTATOR, Isaac age 71, Jane wife age 59, Roll Numbers 97-98. **DOXTATOR**, James age 24, Sarah wife age 23, Roll Numbers 100-101. **DOXTATOR**, Mary age 22, Roll Number 99.

FISH, Daniel age 56, Eliza wife age 62, Roll Numbers 120-121. **FISH**, Eliza age 30, Jane a daughter age 9, Mary MOSES a daughter age 1, Roll Numbers 124-126. **FISH**, Harriet age 28, Roll Number 118. **FISH**, Johnny age 28, Nancy wife age 23, Roll Numbers 122-123. **FISH**, Thomas age 27? Roll Number 119. **FISH**, William age 58, Daniel a son age 12, Elizabeth a daughter age 9, Roll Numbers 115-117.

GANSWORTH, Carrie age 29, Howard a son age 11, Leander a son age 9, Newton a son age 6, Albertie a daughter age 3, Osamer a son age 1, Roll Numbers 134-139.

GEORGE, Eliza age 27, Roll Number 141. **GEORGE**, James age 46, Mary wife age 42, Simon son age 15, Solomon a son age 9, Jane a daughter age 2,

Halbern? a son age one month, Roll Numbers 167-172. **GEORGE**, Thomas age 36, Roll Number 140.

GREEN, Jane age 57, Wallace a son age 17, Alice PARKER a niece age 15, Roll Numbers 150-152. **GREEN**, Mary age 9, Roll Number 142. **GREEN**, Sally age 39, Martha SUNDOWN niece age 18, Roll Numbers 162-163.

GRIFFIN, John age 66, Roll Number 133. **GRIFFIN**, Mary age 37, Katie WHITE daughter age 5, Roll Numbers 148-149.

GROUND, Andrew age 31, Roll Number 147. **GROUND**, Asa age 66, Wife age 47, Alexander a son age 11, George a son age 8, Roll Numbers 129-132. **GROUND**, Asa G., Jr., age 26, Roll Number 127. **GROUND**, Benjamin age 25, Louisa wife age 28, Gertie daughter age 3, Roll Numbers 173-175. **GROUND**, Betsey (Widow) age 73, Roll Number 146. **GROUND**, Caroline age 22, Roll Number 128. **GROUND**, Celia age 30, Hattie a daughter age 11, Lillie a daughter age 8, Roll Numbers 143-145. **GROUND**, Emiline age 33, Charles a son age 15, Josephine a daughter age 9, Myron a son age 7, Roll Numbers 158-161. **GROUND**, Moses age 36, Lucinda wife age 44, Charles a son age 18, Sally a daughter age 16, William a son age 11, Minervie? a daughter age 6, Roll Numbers 176-181. **GROUND**, Sarah age 34, Ella B., a daughter age 14, James B., a son age 12, Solomon a son age 4, Eli BILLY? a son age ten months, Roll Numbers 153-157.

HATCH? OR HUTCH? OR HALCH? George age 33, Roll Number 197. **HATCH**, Howard age 39, Charlotte wife age 37, Willie a son age 14, Sillie a daughter age 5, Roll Numbers 198-201. **HATCH**, Jacob age 46, Affie a grand daughter age 13, Roll Numbers 202-203. **HATCH**, James age 36, Roll Number 204. **HATCH**, Sarah age 23, Julia a daughter age 5, Simon? BILLY a son age two months, Roll Numbers 194-196 .**HATCH? or HUTCH?** Mary age 67, Jerry SUNDOWN a grand son age 15, Roll Numbers 185-186.

HILL, Ella age 33, Roll Number 206. **HILL**, Frederick age 36, Roll Number 205. **HILL**, Hannah age 62, Roll Number 210. **HILL**, Isaac age 56, Mary wife age 45, Benjamin JIMISON a step son age 20, Willie JIMISON Jr., a step son age 15, Herman JIMISON a step son age 6, Roll Numbers 249-253. **HILL** James age 23, Roll Number 183. **HILL**, John age 65, Roll Number 182. HILL, Sarah age 25, Roll Number 184. **HILL**, William age 49, Nancy wife age 34, Laura a daughter age 15, Huzzy? a son age 12, Asa a son age 9, Herman a son age 6, Jennie a daughter age 3, Roll Numbers 187-193.

HIRAM, Eliza age 47, Anna PARKER niece age 5, James C., SKYE adopted son age 20, Roll Numbers 207-209.

HOTBREAD, Charles age 31, Roll Number 164. **HOTBREAD**, Lewis age 65, Roll Number 165. **HOTBREAD**, William age 23, Roll Number 166.

INFANT, Amos age 31, Eliza wife age 39, Lizzie niece age 18, Amanda MOSES age 16, Roll Numbers 216-219. **INFANT**, Henry age 37, Nancy wife age 42, Peter S. a son age 20? or 23? Newton S. a son age 18, Ella a daughter age 7, Roll Numbers 211-215.

JACK, Thomas age 54? or 64? Roll Number 223.
JACKSON, Mary P., age 63, Julia a daughter age 18, Roll Numbers 276-277.

JIMISON, George age 47, Louisa wife age 47? Roll Numbers 226-227. **JIMISON**, Joe age 93, Roll Number 248. **JIMISON**, Johnathan age 34, Susan wife age 29, Silas a step son age 13, Cordelia a daughter age 8, Abbie a daughter age 4, Nat a son age 2, Roll Numbers 268-273. **JIMISON**, John age 63, Roll Number 263. **JIMISON**, John age 63, Roll Number 267. **JIMISON**, Polly age 53, John L., a son age 13, Jennie Mc PHERSON a grand daughter age 10 Roll Numbers 236-238. **JIMISON**, Wallace age 30? or 38? Nellie a daughter age 9, Wyman a son age 7, Roll Numbers 243-245.

JOHNSON, Charles A., age 27, Roll Number 275. **JOHNSON**, Charley age 33, Martha wife age 34, Lyman a son age 13, Lina a daughter age 2, Roll Numbers 256-259. **JOHNSON**, Eli age 52, Roll Number 225. **JOHNSON**, Eli A., age 29, Roll Number 246. **JOHNSON**, Henry age 56, Roll Number 224. **JOHNSON**, Herbert age 27, Roll Number 274. **JOHNSON**, James age 84, Nancy wife age 79, Roll Numbers 228-229. **JOHNSON**, Lucy age 36, Roll Number 247.

JOHNA-JOHN, Betsey age 39, Elijah a son age 17, Abby BROOKS a daughter age 2, Roll Numbers 220-222.

JONAS, Monroe age 63, Mary Ann, Roll Numbers 260-261.

JONES, Caroline age 35, Amelia a daughter age 3, Roll Numbers 240-241. **JONES**, Hiram age 25, Roll Number 230. **JONES**, Jennie age 37, Roll Number 254. **JONES**, John age 74, Roll Number 262. **JONES** Julia age 74, Roll Number 255. **JONES**, Louisa age 28, Aggie WHITE a daughter age eight months, Maggie WHITE a daughter age eight months, Roll Numbers 264-266. **JONES**, Maria age 52, Martha a daughter age 28, Young a son age 18, Jennie a daughter age 11, Caleya? a grand daughter age 3, Roll Numbers 231-235. **JONES**, Moses age 37, Roll Number 242. **JONES**, Thomas age 29, Roll Number 239.

KENNEDY, Charles C., age 24, Roll Number 279. **KENNEDY**, Charles J., age 28, Roll Number 280. **KENNEDY**, John age 28, Roll Number 281. **KENNEDY**, Widow age 72, Roll Number 278.

LINDSLEY, Harriet age 41? Roll Number 283.
LONE, Chauncey age 49, Roll Number 282.

MASON, William age 42, Rose wife age 32, Billy a son age 5, Alphia a son? age 2, Roll Numbers 292-295.

MILLER? OR MITTEN? Jacob age 47, Mary wife age 48, Roll Numbers 310-311. **MILLER? OR MITTEN?** Mary age 54, Roll Number 291.

MITTEN, George age 29, Roll Number 309. **MITTEN**, James age 79, Roll Number 308.

MOSES, Atelbert age 23, Roll Number 306. **MOSES**, Clinton age 57, Roll Number 299. **MOSES**, David age 47, Hiram a son age 9, Hattie a daughter age 7, Roll Numbers 303-305. **MOSES**, George age 32, Roll Number 288. **MOSES**, Louisa age 37, Roll Number 287. **MOSES**, Melorna age 54, Roll Number 300. **MOSES**, Philip age 24, Roll Number 301. **MOSES**, Robert age 27, Roll Number 285. **MOSES**, Susan age 37, Roll Number 298. **MOSES**, William age 57, Roll Number 287. **MOSES**, Widow Sally age 62, Lilly a grand daughter age 9, Roll Numbers 289-290. MOSES, Widow H? age 78? Roll Number 284. **MOSES**, William age 31, Roll Number 307.

MT. PLEASANT, Caroline age 55, Eli S. PARKER brother age 57, Roll Numbers 296-297.

PARKER, Clara age 42, Charlie MOSES a son age 12, Eliza JOHNSON a daughter age 5, Roll Numbers 346-348. **PARKER**, Eliza age 66, Roll Number 372. **PARKER**, Frank age 30, Roll Number 383. **PARKER**, Ida age 22, Simon a son age 9, Roll Numbers 374-375. **PARKER**, Levi age 66, Julia wife age 57, Jerry SNYDER a grand son age 8, Roll Numbers 354-356. **PARKER**, Louisa age 43, Dora a daughter age 16, Isaac a son age 14, Lucinda a daughter age 12, Roll Numbers 326-329. **PARKER**, Lucy age 69, Roll Number 357. **PARKER**, Maria age 58, Fred a son age 20, Carrie a daughter age 18, Phebe POODRY mother age 86, Roll Numbers 330-333. **PARKER**, Olive L., age 39, Roll Number 373. **PARKER**, Otto age 36, Mary wife age 37, Mollie SMITH a step daughter age 14, Morris PARKER a son age 6, Spencer PARKER a son age five months, Roll Numbers 349-353. **PARKER**, Thomas age 28, Roll Number 334.

PETER, Betsey age 36, Emma a daughter age 13, Elijah a son age 12, Libbie a daughter age 7, Eliza a daughter age 2, Roll Numbers 367-371.

POODRY, Anna age 31, Gaby? or Galy? a son age 6, Girdie a daughter age 4, Roll Numbers 314-316. **POODRY**, Electa age 57, Peter age 20, Roll Numbers 377-378. **POODRY**, E. M., age 53, Amanda wife age 47, Barnam a son age 20, Anna a daughter age 17, E. M. Jr., a son age 15, Stafford a son age 10, Fannie a daughter age 8, Henriette a daughter age 5, Dora a daughter age 3, Roll Numbers 317-325. **POODRY**, Nellie age 22, Roll Number 379. **POODRY**, Samson age 24, Roll Number 376. **POODRY**, Thomas age 25, Roll Number 313. **POODRY**, William age 47, Eliza wife age 40, Roll Numbers 358-359. **POODRY**, Willie S. age 22, Roll Number 312.

PRINTUP, Eli age 22, Roll Number 335. **PRINTUP**, Emma age 52, Roll Number 360. **PRINTUP**, Erastus, age 51, Cephua BLACKCHIEF a nephew age 20, Simon BLACKCHIEF a nephew age 16, Abbie BLACKCHIEF a niece age 13, Roll Numbers 336-339. **PRINTUP**, Harrison age 52, Roll Number 361. **PRINTUP**, John age 32, Nancy wife age 28, Horatio son age 10, Olive a daughter age 7, Lena a daughter age 5, Roll Numbers 362-366. **PRINTUP**, Lucinda age 26, Alphia a son age 3, Truman JOHNSON? or Johnson TRUMAN? a son age six months, Roll Numbers 380-382. **PRINTUP**, Marshall age 47, Martha wife age 42, Clara a daughter age 18, Herman a son age 15, Cordelia a daughter age 10, Silas a son age 5, Roll Numbers 340-345.

REUBEN, Jacob age 36, Lucy wife age 31, Young CHARLES? or Charles YOUNG? a step son? age 11, Roll Numbers 388-390. **REUBEN**, Nancy age 52, Caroline a daughter age 18, Elizabeth a daughter age 11, Thomas a son age 7, Roll Numbers 384-387. **REUBEN**, Nancy S. age 26, Roll Number 391.

SCROGG, Henry age 60, Roll Number 461. **SCROGG**, James age 40, Julia wife age 31, Solomon a son age 7, Orlando a son age 15, Herman a son age 3, Francis a son age three months, Roll Numbers 409-414. **SCROGG**, Thomas age 28, Roll Number 479. **SCROGGS**, Carlos age 27, Roll Number 398. **SCROGGS**, Mary age 49, Roll Number 451.

SHANKS, Charles age 42, Phebe wife age 35, Solon son age 17, Souisa a daughter age 14, Roll Numbers 504-507. **SHANKS**, Eliza age 44, Sarah a daughter age 19, Truman a son age 13, Daniel age son age 11, Morgan a son age 7, Isaac Jr., a son age 6, Roll Numbers 392-397. **SHANKS**, James age 39, Nancy wife age 39, Robert a son age 15, Georgiana a daughter age 11, Simon a son age 9, Oscar a son age 5, Abba a daughter age 2, Roll Numbers 454-460.

SHONGO, Mary age 39, Salina a daughter age 10, Roll Numbers 435-436. **SHONGO**, Susan age 37, Jesse a son age 12, Roll Numbers 463-464.

SILVER, Charles age 44, Roll Number 434. **SILVER**, Lucinda age 42, Samuel a son age 19, Chauncey THOMAS age son age 5, Roll Numbers 466-468.

SILVERHEELS, Alice age 35, Cora a daughter age 14, Kittie a daughter age 6, Stephen a son age 4, Henry a son age six months, Roll Numbers 400-404.

SKYE Asa age 21, Roll Number 416, Sarah wife age 24, Roll Numbers 416-417. **SKYE**, Elon age 69, Roll Number 437. **SKYE**, Eunice age 37, Sadie POODRY a daughter age 11, Alphia SKYE a son? age 7, Roll Numbers 467-471. **SKYE**, Harriet age 58, Roll Number 415. **SKYE**, James age 23, Roll Number 494. **SKYE**, Jerome age 25, Roll Number 418. **SKYE**, Louisa age 24, Moses a son age eleven months, Roll Numbers 486-487. **SKYE**, Noah age 28, Roll Number 485. **SKYE**, Robert age 27, Roll Number 521. SKYE, Stephen age 37, Lucy wife age 27, Yankie? a son age 7, Adam SPRING a step son age 8, Roll Number 490-493. **SKYE**, Thomas age 42, Roll Number 489. **SKYE**, Warren age 50, Melina? or Melvina? wife age 28, Simeon SKYE a nephew age 16, Simeon? a son age 1, Libbie a daughter age six months, Roll Numbers 420-424.

SMITH, Julia Ann age 72, Solon SKYE a grand son age 17, Roll Numbers 452-453. **SMITH**, Lucy age 23, Roll Number 508. **SMITH**, Mary, age 36, Nicholson age 10, Emeline a daughter age 7, Lydia a daughter age 3, Roll Numbers 440-443. **SMITH**, Sally age 55, Sophia SMITH a grand daughter age 18, Roll Numbers 495-496. **SMITH**, William age 40, Roll Number 488.

SNOW, George age 46, Roll Number 520.

SNYDER, Alexander age 49, Mary wife age 40, Emma a daughter age 20, Salina a daughter age 15, Rose a daughter age 5, Minnie CHARLES a grand daughter age four months, Roll Numbers 444-449. **SNYDER**, Amos age 67, Eliza wife age 58, Susan a daughter age 18, Philip a son age 15, John a grand son age two months, Roll Numbers 425-429. **SNYDER**, GILSON? age 63, Nancy BLACKCHIEF step-daughter age 17, Lenard BLACKCHIEF step son age 15, Roll Numbers 512-514. **SNYDER**, Lafayette age 55, Roll Number 462. **SNYDER**, Peter H., age 48, Roll Number 478. **SNYDER**, Margaret age 22, Roll Number 450. **SNYDER**, William age 42, Roll Number 465. **SNYDER**, Willie age 21, Roll Number 430.

SPRING, Henry age 36, Albert a son age 9, Roll Numbers 438-439. **SPRING**, Jessie age 71? Roll Number 399. **SPRING**, Solomon age 27, Alida B., wife age 24, Helen daughter age 3, Hanover a son age eight months, Roll Numbers 405-408.

STEEPROCK, Cynthia age 31, Josephine a daughter age 10, Ulysses a son age 7, Lester SKYE a son age seven months, Roll Numbers 575-578.

STONE, Charles Jr., age 21, Roll Number 522. **STONE**, Charles age 39, Hanah wife age 41, Henry a son age 12, Eliza a daughter age 6, Jennie a daughter age 7, Addie a daughter age 2, Roll Numbers 479-484. **STRONG**, William age 45, William Strong Jr., a son age 16, Salina a daughter age 9, Strong? a son age 4, Roll Numbers 472-475.

SUNDOWN, Blodget age 62, Nancy wife age 35, Roll Numbers 476-477. **SUNDOWN**, Louisa age 21, Roll Number 497. **SUNDOWN**, Mary age 47, Jane BLUEYE a daughter age 18, William BLUEYE a son age 10, Roll Numbers 431-433. **SUNDOWN**, Mary A., age 23, Alexander a brother age 18, Jacob a brother age 16, Charles a brother age 14, Edward a brother age 9, Martha KENNEDY a daughter age 4, Roll Numbers 498-503. **SUNDOWN**, Newton age 35, Charlotte wife age 39, Willie MOSES a nephew age 18, Roll Numbers 508-511. **SUNDOWN**, Peter age 26, Roll Number 579. **SUNDOWN**, Sarah age 32, Roll Number 419.

TAYLOR, John G. age 33, Roll Number 523. **TAYLOR**, Mary age 30, Jane age 12 daughter, Lillie daughter age 9, Roll Numbers 524-526.

WALTER, Thomas age 24, Roll Number 527.

WHITE, Eliza age 58, Jerome a son age 19, Roll Numbers 533-534. **WHITE**, James age 21, Roll Number 535. **WHITE**, Seneca age 42, Roll Number 532.

WILSON, John age 83, Mary wife age 67, George a son age 17, Fanny WILSON a grand daughter age 15? Roll Numbers 528-531.

CROSS INDEX TO TONAWANDA SENECA RESERVE-1886 CROSS INDEX		
SURNAME CROSS INDEX	**RELATION/HEAD OF HOUSEHOLD**	**BIA ROLL #**
BILLY, Andrew	Nephew of Andrew Blackchief	#15-16
BILLY, Simon?	Son of Sarah Hatch	#194-196
BILLY?, Eli	Son of Sarah Ground	#153-157
BLACKCHIEF, Cephus	Nephew of Erastus Printup	#336-339
BLACKCHIEF, Lenard	Step Son of Gilson Snyder	#512-514
BLACKCHIEF, Nancy	Step Dau. of Gilson Snyder	#512-514
BLACKCHIEF, Simon	Nephew of Erastus Printup	#336-339
BLACKHCHIEF, Abbie	Niece of Erastus Printup	#336-339
BLUEYE, Jane	Dau. of Mary Sundown	#431-433
BROOKS, Abby	Dau. of Betsey Johna-John	#220-222
CHARLES, Lucinda	Gr. Dau. of Jane Bigfire	#52-54
CHARLES, Minnie	Gr. Dau. of Alexander Snyder	#444-449
CHARLES, Young	Step of Jacob Reuben	#388-390
FISH, David S.	Step Son of Charles Clute	#79-85
JIMISON, Benjamin	Step Son of Isaac Hill	#249-253
JIMISON, Herman	Step Son of Isaac Hill	#249-253
JIMISON, Willie Jr.	Step Son of Isaac Hill	#249-253
JOHNSON, Eliza	Dau. of Clara Parker	#346-348
JOHNSON, Truman	In h'hold of Lucinda Printup	#380-382
JONES, Helen	Dau. of Anna Brooks	#49-51
KENNEDY, Martha	Dau. of Mary A. Sundown	#498-503
MOSES, Amanda	In household of Amos Infant	#216-219
MOSES, Mary	Dau. of Eliza Fish	#124-126
MOSES, Willie	Nephew of Newton Sundown	#508-511
PARKER, Allice	Niece of Jane Green	#150-152
PARKER, Anna	Niece of Eliza Hiram	#207-209
PARKER, Eli S.	Brother/Caroline Mt. Pleasant	#296-297

POODRY, Phebe	Mother of Maria Parker	#330-333
POODRY, Sadie	Dau. of Eunice Skye	#467-471
PRINTUP, Fannie	Gr. Dau. of John W. Brooks	#25-27
SCROGGS, John	Son of Sarah Baptist	#41-44
SKYE, Ida	Niece of William Alick	# 9-11
SKYE, James C.	Adpt. Son of Eliza Hiram	#207-209
SKYE, Solon	Gr. Son of Julia Ann Smith	#452-453
SMITH, Mollie	Step Dau. of Otto Parker	#349-353
SNYDER, Jerry	Gr. Son of Levi Parker	#354-356
SNYDER, Lenard	Brother of Nancy Blackchief	#34-36
SUNDOWN, Jerry	Gr. Son of Mary Hatch	#185-186
SUNDOWN, Martha	Niece of Sally Green	#162-163
SUNDOWN, Susan	Gr. Dau. of Jane Bigfire	#52-54
WHITE, Maggie	Dau. of Louisa Jones	#264-266

THE JULY 1886 BUREAU OF INDIAN AFFAIRS CENSUS OF THE CAYUGA RESIDING UPON THE CATTARAUGAS RESERVATION IN NEW YORK

The Allegany Reservation is located in Cattaraugus County, New York. The 1794 Pickering Treaty established the boundaries of the Seneca Nation of which the Allegany Reservations is a part. Reference Sources: "Federal And State Indian Reservations Handbook", U.S. Department of Commerce, January 1971. "Cayuga Indians Enumerations of Indians for Payment of Annuities," June 1969, Cayuga Tribe 1971, on one microfilm reel. This reel provides names, birth dates, and addresses. A copy is available at the Church of Jesus Christ of Latter-day Saints (Mormon) Family History Library. "The Cayuga Reservation and Colonel John Harris," by John Van Sickle, Ann Arbor, Michigan University Microfilms International, published in Ithaca New York, by Dewitt Historical Society of Tompkins County (New York) 1965, 19 pages. The following census abstract is not in its original order. It has been alphabetized for this book. Everyone in each household has the same surname as the head of that household unless otherwise stated. The roll numbers follows the given name or family group. The surname of the head of each household has been highlighted. If a individual living in a household had a different surname from the head of that household it was highlighted in capital letters. A question mark was placed after a name or age that was in doubt. This census abstract should be used only as a reference. It should not take the place of any original government records.

ARMSTRONG, Mary, age 41 mother, Ebenezer son age 19, Ami a daughter age 24, Roll Numbers 1-3.

BENNETT, Elizabeth mother age 22, Lorenza a daughter age 2, Roll Numbers 17-18. **BENNETT**, Helen age 26, Frances a daughter age 2, Roll Numbers 15-16. **BENNETT**, Nancy age 44 mother, Ulysis a son age 12, Obed a son age 2, Roll Numbers 12-14.

BILLY, Eleanor age 29, Eliza a daughter age 10, Louisa a daughter age 6, Nancy a daughter age 3, De forest a son age one month, Roll Numbers 19-23.

BONE, Jonathan age 58, father, Charles a son age 22, Hiram a son age 12, Roll Numbers 24-26.

BROOKS, Julia age 52, Roll Number 4. **BROOKS**, Orpha age 53, mother, Jerry a son age 23, Elmer a son age 21, Melinda a daughter age 18, Gertie a daughter age 15, James a son age 9, Martha a daughter age 11, Roll Numbers 5-11.

CHARLES, Lillie A., age 28, mother, Clarinda a daughter age 7, Orman a son age 5, Geneva a daughter age 3, Roll Numbers 32-35.

CROW, Clara Thompson mother age 51, Willie a son age 7, Roll Numbers 30-31. **CROW**, David age 79, Roll Number 79. **CROW**, Polly age 84, Roll Number 28. CROW, Herman age 54, Roll Number 29.

DOXTATOR, Joseph age 50, Roll Number 36.

GEORGE, Jane mother age 38, Chauncey a son age 13, Roll Numbers 37-38.

GORDON, Cassie a mother age 33, Rush a son age 10, Gertie a daughter age 4, Lulie? a daughter age one month, Roll Numbers 39-42.

GRIFFIN, Margaret age 56, mother, Lyman a son age 20, Ulysses a son age 18, Lena a daughter age 16, Charles a son age 11, Roll Numbers 152-156.

GROUND, Susan a sister age 17, Susie GROUND a cousin age 14, James GROUND a brother age 11, Jemima GROUND a sister age 8, Roll Numbers 43-46.

JACKSON, L. W., age 50, Roll Number 151.

JIMISON, Lewis age 36, Roll Number 65.

JOHN, Alexander age 39, Roll Number 51. **JOHN**, Lewis age 42, Roll Number 49. **JOHN**, Perry age 54, Roll Number 50. **JOHN**, Susan age 74, Roll Number 48. **JOHN**, William age 64, Roll Number 47.

JOHNSON, Austin D., age 48, Roll Number 66. **JOHNSON**, Hannah W., age 41 mother, Helena R., a daughter age 13, Roll Numbers 58-59.

JOHNY-JOHN, Louisa age 28, mother, Jesse WARRIOR brother age 17, Helen CROW a daughter age two months, Roll Numbers 55-57. **JOHNY-JOHN**, Mary, mother age 31, Nancy a daughter age 12, Betsey a daughter age 7, Roll Numbers 52-54.

JONES, Elizabeth age 46, mother, Charles a son age 19, Louisa a daughter age 12, Thomas a son age 9, Anna a daughter age 18, Roll Numbers 60-64.

JOSHUA, James age 44, Roll Number 67. **JOSHUA**, Phebe age 29, Roll Number 68.

KENJOCKETY, Sarah age 38, mother, Frank a son age 15, Josephine a daughter age 12, Amelia a daughter age 10, Jessie a daughter age 7, Richard a son age 4, Roll Numbers 69-74.

LAY, Clara E., mother age 32, Florence E., a daughter age 11, Roll Numbers 77-78.
LOGAN, Phebe S., age 41, mother, Avery Q. LOGAN adopted son age 8, Roll Numbers 75-76.

PARKER, Abbie S., age 31, mother, Carrie G., a daughter age 7, Ashe W., a son age 5, Mattie E., a daughter age 3, Grover C., a son age six months, Roll Numbers 100-104.

PATTERSON, James a brother age 12, mother, Florence a sister age 10, Helen a sister age 9, Roll Numbers 79-81.

PIERCE, Dora age 24, Roll Number 87. **PIERCE**, Elizabeth age 37, mother, Dana a son age 13, Carl A., age five months, Louisa PIERCE? age 6 (No relation given) Roll Numbers 94-97. **PIERCE**, Ida age 31, mother, Sidney a son age 13, Roll Numbers 84-85. **PIERCE**, Helen L. age 23, Roll Number

98. **PIERCE**, Jesse age 29, Roll Number 99. **PIERCE**, Julia age 54, Roll Number 86. **PIERCE**, Lucy age 45, mother, Ulyses a son age 12, Roll Numbers 88-89. **PIERCE**, Melinda age 28, mother, Lillian a daughter age 6, Samuel a son age 4, Roll Numbers 91-93. **PIERCE**, Richard J., age 26, Roll Number 90. **PIERCE**, Mary mother (No age given) Ira a son age 12, Roll Numbers 82-83.

SENECA, Catherine (Adopted) age 25, Roll Number 150. **SENECA**, Jacob G., age 70, Roll Number 109.
SNOW, Anna age 29, Roll Number 107. **SNOW**, Jacob age 28, Roll Number 105. SNOW, Maria age 27, Roll Number 108.

SNYDER, Torance age 7, Alice sister age 6, Oscar brother age 4, Roll Numbers 114-116.

SPRING, Edwin M., age 24, Roll Number 111. **SPRING**, Hattie L., mother age 43, Ernest a son age 18, Roll Numbers 112-113.

STAFFORD, Austin G., age 42, Roll Number 110.

SUNDOWN, Abagail age 80, Roll Number 106.

TALLCHIEF, Amelia age 34, mother, Jennie a daughter age 15, George a son age 13, Elon a son age 9, Roll Numbers 123-126. **TALLCHIEF**, Carrie age 33, mother, Fidelia a daughter age 11, Lillie a daughter age 10, Myria a daughter age 7, Roll Numbers 127-130. **TALLCHIEF**, Cyrus age 29, Roll Number 121. **TALLCHIEF**, Ezra age 31, Roll Number 122. **TALLCHIEF**, Hiram age 41, Roll Number 120.

TAYLOR, Charles age 50, Roll Number 117.
THOMPSON, Albert age 53, Roll Number 119. **THOMPSON**, Moses age 50, Roll Number 118.

TURKEY, Eliza age 24, mother, Levi a son age 1, Roll Numbers 138-139. **TURKEY**, Jennie age 27, Roll Number 137. **TURKEY**, Joseph age 47, Roll Number 136. **TURKEY**, Nancy age 40, mother, Lyman a son age 19, Emma a daughter age 15, Jennie a daughter age 12, Loura a daughter age 11, Roll Numbers 131-135.

WARRIOR, David age 40, Roll Number 140. **WARRIOR**, Samuel age 13, Roll Number 142. **WARRIOR**, William age 33, Roll Number 141.

WHEELBARROW, Smith age 64, Roll Number 149.

WILSON, Esther age 29, mother, Louisa? a daughter age 5, William Jr., a son age 4, Clinton a son age 4 months, Roll Numbers 144-147. **WILSON**, L? or S? Rush age 28, Roll Number 148.

THE 1886 BUREAU OF INDIAN AFFAIRS CENSUS OF THE CAYUGA INDIANS RESIDING UPON TONAWANDA RESERVATION IN NEW YORK.

This census abstract is not in its original order. It has been alphabetized for this book. This census abstract should be used only as a rerference. It should not take the place of any original government records.

BLUESKY, Mary age 51, mother, John a son age 17, Eliza a daughter age 14, Major a son age 12, Sarah a daughter age 2, Roll Numbers 1-5.

JONES, Susanna (Adopted in 1885) age 79, Roll Number 6. (Into the tribe?)

MOSES, Lucy age 5, mother, Ely a son age 27, Augustus a son age 27, Stansil age 9. (Omitted last year). Roll Numbers 7-10.

TAYLOR, Joseph age 56, Roll Number 11. **TAYLOR**, Olive age 30, mother, Lewis a son age 8, Amos a son age 11, Hattie a daughter age 2, Mollie a daughter age three months, Roll Numbers 12-16.

THE 1886 BUREAU OF INDIAN AFFAIRS CENSUS OF THE CAYUGAS AT THE L. O. ASYLUM FROM TONAWANDA IN NEW YORK

MITTEN, Arson age 7, R17, **MITTEN**, Ida age 10, R19, **MITTEN**, Minerva age 5, R18, **MITTEN**, Phina age 4, R25, **MITTEN**, Selina age 12, Roll Number 21.

THE 1886 BUREAU OF INDIAN AFFAIRS CENSUS OF THE ONEIDA INDIANS RESIDING UPON THE ONEIDA RESERVATION IN NEW YORK

The following census abstract is not in its original order. This abstract is arranged in alphabetical order by surname, then given name. The age and roll numbers follows the given name. The surnames of each head of household was highlighted. Everyone in each household had the same surname as the head of that household unless otherwise stated. If an individual in a household had a different surname than the head of that household that surname was highlighted with capital letters an cross indexed at the end of this abstract. This abstract should only be used as a reference. It should not take the place of any original government records. Oneida Reference Sources: "The Oneida Indian Experience," by Jack Campisi, Ed., 1988. "The Oneida People," by Cara F. Richards, Published by Indian Tribal Series, Phoenix, 1974. "The History of Madison County," by Mrs. L. M. Truair, State of New York, Smith & Company, 1872, pages 120-122.

ANTONE, Aaron age 35, Roll Number 3. **ANTONE**, CHRISTY, age 46, Alexander a son age 14, Charlotte a daughter age 17, Sophia a daughter age 13, MOSES POWELS? (Or Powles?) a step son age 8, PETER WHITE a step son age 10, Roll Numbers 4-9. **ANTONE**, DOLLIE age 64, Elizabeth daughter age 43, Roll Numbers 1-2.

BREAD, Daniel, Mary wife, Roll Numbers 22-23. **BREAD**, DOLLIE age 79, Roll Number 15. **BREAD**, JACOB, Lucy wife, Carrie daughter, Martin a son, Phebe a daughter, Baby (No name given) a daughter, Roll Numbers 16-21.

BURNING, ALEXANDER age 22, Lillie wife age 23, Baby (No name given) a son age 2, Roll Numbers 12-14. **BURNING**, AUGUSTUS age 50, Catherine wife age 44, Roll Numbers 10-11.

CHRIS-JOHN, JAMES, Mary (Wife?) Roll Numbers 34-35. No ages were given.

CORNELIUS, JONAS age 42, Hannah wife age 39, Hattie a daughter age 16, Wilson a son age 6, Babe a son (No name or age was given) Roll Numbers 25-29. **CORNELIUS**, JOSHUA, (No age given) Mrs. wife (No name or age given) a Child (No name or age was given) Roll Numbers 31-33. **CORNELIUS**, PHEBE age 28, Roll Number 24. **CORNELIUS**, THOMAS JR., age 42, Roll Number 30.

DANA, JOHN age 23, Roll Number 37. **DANA**, MARY age 31, Roll Number 36. **DANA**, THOMAS age 51, Roll Number 38.

DAY, BAPTIST? age 44, ELECTA BEECHTREE wife age 43, LEWIS a son age 15, Roll Numbers 39-41. **DAY**, HENRY age 36, Lucy wife age 27, Gertie a daughter age 3, Lucinda a daughter age 5, Roll Numbers 53-56. **DAY**, LEWIS age 32, Margaret wife age 34, Lizzie a daughter age 4, Simon ELM step-son age 15, Roll Numbers 57-60. **DAY**, MOSES age 65, Susan wife age 61, Louisa a daughter age 27, Roll Numbers 50-52.

DOXTATOR, ELECTA age 25, Roll Number 49. **DOXTATOR**, LEWIS age 31, Nancy wife age 20, Estella a daughter age 3, Roll Numbers 42-44. **DOXTATOR**,

LYDIA age 27, Roll Number 48. **DOXTATOR**, WILLIAM age 55, Mary a wife age 57, Susie a step-daughter age 19, Roll Numbers 45-47.

ELM, ABRAM, Maggie, Charlie, Horton, Elias, Elsie, Babe, Roll Numbers 61-67. No ages were given.

GEORGE, ELIJAH age 30, Roll Number 68. **GEORGE**, HENRY age 29, Mary wife age 19, Roll Numbers 71-72. **GEORGE**, JAMES age 29, Roll Number 69. **GEORGE**, WILLIAM age 26, Roll Number 70.

GOULD, MARY, Katie, Gould? CHARLES WHITE, ALEX WHITE, MARY ANN WHITE, Roll Numbers 73-77. These people were all listed in the same household. No ages or relationships were given.

HONYOST, ISAAC age 31, Roll Number 80. **HONYOST**, MARGARET age 41, William Jr., a son age 16, Roll Numbers 78-79. **HONYOST**, MARY age 47, ALBERT SCANONDOAH a son age 20, Chapman a son age 20, Nicholas a son age 14, Roll Numbers 83-86. **HONYOST**, NICHOLAS age 39, Mary wife age 34, Louisa a daughter age 15, Silira? or Silvia? a daughter age 13, Daniel a son age 20, Katie a daughter age 8, Nicholas a son age 4, Roll Numbers 87-93. **HONYOST**, SIMON age 36, Roll Number 82. **HONYOST**, WILLIAM age 31, Roll Number 81.

JOHN, DAVID age 29, Roll Number 100. **JOHN**, JOHN age 31, Roll Number 99. **JOHN**, MARTIN age 28, Roll Number 95. **JOHN**, MELINDA age 35, Marshall a son age 8, Roll Number 97, 98. **JOHN**, SARAH age 53, Roll Number 94. **JOHN**, SOLOMON age 41, Roll Number 96.

JOHNSON, BAPTIST age 51, Lizzie wife age 49, Phebe a daughter age 27, Libbie a daughter age 16, Estella a daughter age 18, Joseph a son age 10, Josiah a son age 6, Roll Numbers 120-126. **JOHNSON**, BETSEY age 49, LOUVINA? GEORGE a daughter age 3, HELEN GEORGE a daughter age 1, Roll Numbers 104-106. **JOHNSON**, DOLLIE age 79, Roll Number 107. **JOHNSON**, HANNAH age 81, MOSES POWELS? or POWLES? a grand son age 15, Roll Numbers 111-112. **JOHNSON**, JAMES age 59, Sarah wife age 55, Angeline a daughter age 26, Roll Numbers 101-103. **JOHNSON**, NICHOLAS age 45, Roll Number 110. **JOHNSON**, THOMAS age 44, Betsey wife age 38, Lillie a daughter age 10, Emma a daughter age 8, Lewis a son age 6, Jennie a daughter age 4, Nelson a son age 2, Roll Numbers 113-119. **JOHNSON**, WILLIAM age 41, Melinda wife age 38, Roll Numbers 108-109.

JORDON, HENRY, Sophia, John, Henry Jr., Roll Numbers 127-130. **JORDON**, NICK, Roll Number 131. No ages or relationships were given.

KENNEDY, ELIZABETH, Eli, Mary Roll Numbers 132-134. No ages or relationships were given.

POWELS? OR POWLES? JAMES age 56, Kate wife age 57, Roll Numbers 135-136. **POWELS**, MARTIN age 46, Roll Number 139. **POWELS**, SARAH age 49, Thomas a son age 11, Roll Numbers 137-138. **POWELS**, THOMAS (A notation was provided that seven members existed in the family of Thomas Powels but the names were not given) Roll Number 167.

SCONONDOAH, DANIEL age 74, Roll Number 156. **SCONONDOAH**, DANIEL JR., age 40, Mary wife age 41, Frank a son age 15, George a son age 15, Maria a daughter age 12, Nelson a son age 10, Nancy a daughter age 6,

Roll Numbers 160-166. **SCONONDOAH**, PHEBE age 46, Josiah a son age 16, Joel a son age 9, Roll Numbers 157-159. **SCONONDOAH**, THOMAS age 49, Roll Number 155.

WEBSTER, DANIEL age 56, Hannah wife age 46, Roll Numbers 140-141. **WEBSTER**, ElIJAH 29, Lydia wife age 24, Maud a daughter age 7, Nellie a daughter age 5, Gilbert a son age 2, Roll Numbers 142-146. **WEBSTER**, JOSIAH age 29, Roll Number 147. **WEBSTER**, MARY age 60, Eliza a daughter age 20, Roll Numbers 149-150. **WEBSTER**, MOSES age 36, Hannah wife age 32, Roll Numbers 151-152. **WEBSTER**, THOMAS age 29, Roll Number 153.

WHEELOCK, Joe age 81, Roll Number 154.

WHITE, David age 38, Roll Number 148

THE 1886 BUREAU OF INDIAN AFFAIRS CENSUS OF THE ONEIDA INDIANS RESIDING UPON THE ONONDAGA RESERVATION IN 1886.

Only the names of the heads of each family or household was provided for this census abstract. No roll numbers were given. This abstract should be used only as a reference. It should not be used in the place of any original government records.

ADAMS, John, **CANADA**, Daniel, **ELM**, Peter, **GEORGE**, George, **GEORGE**, John, **GEORGE**, Adam, **HILL**, Nancy, **HILL**, Mary, **HILL**, Abram, **IRELAND**, Abram, **JOHN**, Phebe, **JONES**, Joshua, **JONES**, Melinda, **JACOB**, Thomas, **JOHNSON**, Joseph, **JONES**, Sally, **JACOBS**, David, **JONES**, Mary, **POWELS**, Peter, **SCONONDOAH**, Ida, **THOMAS**, Lewis, **THOMAS**, Elizabeth, **WILLIAMS**, Adam, **WATERMAN**, Charles.

THE 1887 BUREAU OF INDIAN AFFAIRS CENSUS OF THE ONONDAGA INDIANS RESIDING ON THE ONONDAGA RESERVATION IN NEW YORK

Onondaga reference sources: "Onondaga Indians," 1803-1869, by Joshua V. Clark, Millwood, New York, Kraus reprint, 1973, original published Syracuse, New York, Stoddard and Babcock. "Onondaga a Portrait of a Native People," by Dennis Connors, Onondaga County, Department of Parks and Recreation, Syracuse University Press, 1986, 110 pages. "Onondaga Iroquois Prehistory, by James Tuck 1971. "Onondaga: Portrait of a Native People," by Fred Wolcott, 1986. This census is not in its original order. It has been alphabetized for this book. This census abstract should only be used as a reference. It should not be used in place of any original government records.

ADAMS, Margaret Roll Number 1. **BECKMANN**, Melissa Roll Number 98. **BIG-BRAVE?** Jacob Roll Number 47. **BILLINGS**, David Roll Number 62. **BILLINGS**, Sally Roll Number 53. **BILLINGS**, Webster Roll Number 43. **BROWN**, Martha Roll Number 78. **BROWN**, Thomas Roll Number 70. **BROWN**, Widow Roll Number 37. **CANADA**, Albert Roll Number 9. **CANADA**, Susan Roll Number 48. **CROUSE**, Susanna Roll Number 19. **CROW**, George Roll Number 106. **CUSICK**, Albert Roll Number 56. **DAY**, Lizzie Roll Number 60. **DAY**, Maggie Roll Number 61. **DAXEN**, Ellex Roll Number 91 **DRAKE**, Julius Roll Number 118. **ELIJAH**, William Roll Number 115. **ELM**, Christie Roll Number 63. **FARMER**, Avis? or Orris? Roll Number 71. **FARMER**, James Roll Number 102. **FARMER**, Thomas Jackson Roll Number 103. **FISH**, Eliza Roll Number 104. **FROST**, Mary Roll Number 45. **FROST**, Solomon Roll Number 44. **GEORGE**, Carrie Roll Number 119. **GEORGE**, Daniel Roll Number 12. **GEORGE**, Mary Roll Number 74. **GEORGE**, Peter Roll Number 76. **GEORGE**, Sally Roll Number 13. **GIBSON**, Andrew Roll Number 72. **GREEN**, Charles Roll Number 84. **GREEN**, George Roll Number 5. **GREEN**, John Roll Number 83. **GREEN**, Joseph Roll Number 93. **GREEN**, JONES? Roll Number 34. **GRIFFIN**, Esther, Roll Number 51. **HOVNEN?** or **HAVNEN?** Elizabeth Roll Number 46. **HILL**, Avice Roll Number 24. **HILL**, Davie Roll Number 52. **HILL**, Elijah Roll Number 2. **HILL**, Emily Roll Number 64. **HILL**, Hawley Sen., Roll Number 7. **HILL**, Hawley J., Roll Number 28. **HILL**, John Roll Number 4. **HILL**, Unis Roll Number 82. **HILL**, William Jr. Roll Number 3. **ISAACS**, Benjamin Roll Number 105. **ISAACS**, Harry Roll Number 116. **ISAACS**, Mary Jane Roll Number 100. **ISAACS**, Samuel G., Roll Number 23. **ISAACS**, William Roll Number 33. **JACOBS**, Miss David? Roll Number 97. **JACOBS**, Isaac Roll Number 49. **JACOBS**, John Roll Number 50. **JACOBS**, Ulett, Roll Number 58. **JACOBS**, Wilson Roll Number 25. **JOE**, William Roll Number 41. **JOHN**, Thomas Roll Number 6. **JOHNSON**, Cornelius Roll Number 65. **JOHNSON**, Elizabeth Roll Number 96. **JOHNSON**, Frank, Roll Number 32. **JOHNSON**, John Roll Number 109. **JOHNSON**, William Roll Number 92. **JOHNSON**, Wilson Roll Number 108. **JONES**, Alexes Roll Number 54. **JONES**, Abbatt Roll Number 10. **JONES**, Henry Roll Number 35. **JONES**, Mary Roll Number 59. **JONES**, Sarah Roll Number 88. **JONES**, Unis Roll Number 77. **LA FORTE**, Abram Roll Number 21. **LA FORTE**, Charlotte Roll Number 95. **LA FORTE**, Daniel Roll Number 29. **LA FORTE**, Thomas Roll Number 15. **LOFT**, Mary Roll Number 8. **LOGAN**, Frank Roll Number 69. **LOGAN**, George Roll Number 89. **LYON**, Chalres Roll Number 113. **LYON**, William Roll Number 31. **OBEDIAH**, John Roll Number 38. **OBEDIAH**, Sally Roll Number 68. **PATTERSON**, Phebe Roll Number 101. **PIERCE**, Jaris Roll Number 30. **PIERCE**, Joshua Roll Number 27. **POWLES**, Hattie Roll Number 14. **POWLES**, Isaac Roll Number 22. **PRINTUP**, Abram Roll Number 85. **REDEYE**, Git-Toh Roll Number 117. **RUEBIN**, Wilson Roll Number 73. **SCANNADOAH**, David Roll Number 18. **SCANNANDOAH**, Jacob Roll

Number 79. **SCANNADOAH**, Mary Roll Number 36. SMITH, Chris John Roll Number 86. **SMITH**, Levi Roll Number 78. **SMITH**, Moses, Roll Number 11. **THOMAS**, Baptist Roll Number 81. **THOMAS**, Hattie Roll Number 111. **THOMAS**, James Roll Number 42. **THOMAS**, Joe Roll Number 67. **THOMAS**, J. L., Roll Number 20. **THOMAS**, Phebe Roll Number 40. **THOMPSON**, Sarah Roll Number 114. **VARNEY**, George Roll Number 99. **WHITE**, John Roll Number 110. **WHITE**, Silas Roll Number 94. **WEBSTER**, Eliza Roll Number 80. **WEBSTER**, Ida Roll Number 57. **WEBSTER**, David Roll Number 55. **WEBSTER**, Richard Roll Number 66. **WEBSTER**, Samuel, Roll Number 112. **WEBSTER**, Thomas Roll Number 87. Wheelbarrow, Emily Roll Number 107.

THE 1886 BUREAU OF INDIAN AFFAIRS CENSUS OF THE ONONDAGA RESIDING ON THE ALLEGANY RESERVATION IN NEW YORK

This census is not in its original order. It has been alphabetized for this book.

BUCKTOOTH, Lydia age 68, Freeman a son age 29, Roll Numbers 1, 2. **BLACKSNAKE**, Joseph age 36, Roll Number 3. **BIRGLER?** Cordelia age 30, Roll Number 85. **CROUSE**, Minnie Age 28, Bertha a daughter age 1, Roll Numbers 11-12. CROUSE, Sophia age 44, Lena a daughter age 15, Roll Number 4-5. **CROW**, Mary age 86, Roll Number 6. CROW, Oscar age 37, Roll Number 10. **CURRY**, Eliza age 40, To-De-Wah a son age one month, Willet a son age 20, Roll Numbers 7-9. **CURRY**, Thomas age 19, Roll Number 13. **DOLSON**, Eliza C., age 26, Ellen a daughter age 3, James a son age 1, Roll Numbers 14-15 (James Dolson the last child in this household was not counted. Cynthis Gordon in the next household was given Roll Number 16 instead). **GORDON**, Cynthia age 49, Willie a son age 28, Roll Numbers 16-17. GORDON, Julia age 34, Kate a daughter age 10, Birdie a daughter age 6, Roll Number 18-20. **HALFTOWN**, Anna age 24, Kate a daughter age 6, Lena a daughter age 3, Nellie a daughter age 1, Roll Numbers 21-24. **HALFWHITE**, Robert age 41, Roll Number 25. **HUFF**, Bennie age 22, Roll Number 27. **HUFF**, V. E., age 45, Roll Number 26. **JACOB**, Abigail age 38, Fanny a daughter age 8, Helen a daughter age 3, Olive a daughter age two months, Roll Numbers 40-43. **JACOB**, Lucinda age 22, Howard a son age 1, Roll Numbers 38-39. **JACOB**, Sally age 56, Roll Number 44. **JACKSON**, Jesse age 36, Albert a son age 19, Roll Number 32-33. **JACKSON**, Jos., age 43, Roll Number 30. **JACKSON**, Lewis age 27, Willie a son age 1, Roll Numbers 34-35. **JACKSON**, Lucy age 61, Roll Number 31. **JACKSON**, Orlando age 40, Roll Number 28. **JACKSON**, Reuben age 34, Roll Number 29. **JONES**, Hannah age 58, Samuel a son age 20, Roll Numbers 36-37. **PIERCE**, Abel age 39, Roll Number 59. **PIERCE**, Albert age 36, Roll Number 58. **PIERCE**, Amelia age 38, Emerson a son age 17, Leroy a son age 6, Harry a son age 6, Russel a son age 1, Lewis a son age 1, Roll Numbers 54-55. **PIERCE**, Eliza age 41, Roll Number 60. **PIERCE**, Elizabeth age 29, Ross a son age 1, Roll Numbers 56-57. **PIERCE**, Esther W., age 23, Walter a son age 6, Willie a son age 3, Wilson a son age 1, Roll Numbers 46-49. **PIERCE**, Lydia age 25, Mattie a daughter age 1, Roll Number 63-64. **PIERCE**, Willet age 45, Roll Number 61. **PIERCE**, Wilson age 47, Roll Number 62. **REDEYE**, Robert age 38, Lucinda wife age 29, Henry a son age 17, Eliza a daughter age 15, Chester a son age 8, Willet age son age 6, Harrison a son age 3, Hattie a daughter age 1, Jennie a daughter age one month, Roll Numbers 65-73. **SNOW**, Esther age 20, Louvina a daughter age 5, George a son age 3, Clinton a son age 2, Jasper a son age six months, Roll Numbers 75-79. **SNOW**, Moses age 96, Roll Number 74. **THOMPSON**, Ebeneazor age 48, Roll Number 80. **YELLOWBLANKET**, Jane age 48, Lewis age 26, Ida a daughter age 15, Roll Numbers 81-85. **SNOW**, Moses age 96, Roll Number 94. **SAMPSON**, Sylvia age 41, Roll Number 45.

THE 1886 BUREAU OF INDIAN AFFAIRS CENSUS OF ONONDAGA INDIANS RESIDING UPON THE TUSCARORA RESERVATION IN NEW YORK

This Census is not in its original order. It has been alphabetized for this book.

CHEW, Oziah age 51, Roll Number 5. **CUSICK**, Elizabeth age 32, Charles age 11, Libbie age 7, Lillie age 5, Roll Numbers 1-4. **GARLOW**, Martha age 23, Minnie A., age 6, Hatzel? age 5, Philip age 4, William age 1, Roll Numbers 10-14. **GREEN**, Jonas age 19, Phebe age 17, Lena age 15, Morris? age 26, Roll Numbers 6-9. **JACK**, Catherine age 52, Meyer age 11, Marion age 8, Roll Numbers 16-18. **JACOBS**, Oziah age 15, Roll Number 15. **Mt. PLEASANT**, Charlotte age 57, Roland age 30, Lucy age 35, Amos age 13, Nelson age 3, Roll Numbers 19-23. **PATTERSON** TITUS age 23, Roll Number 24. **PEMBLETON**, Mary A., age 58, Roll Number 34. **PEMBLETON**, Simon age 32, Roll Number 25. **PRINTUP**, Elizabeth age 53, William age 24, Moses age 23, Charles age 22, Eleazor age 20, Harrison age 18, Ezikiel age 16, Daniel age 11, Roll Numbers 33. **SMITH**, Amos age 38, Roll Number 35. **THOMPSON**, Jennie age 34, Leah age 15, Moses age 11, Anna age 9, Roll Numbers 36-39.

THE 1886 BUREAU OF INDIAN AFFAIRS CENSUS OF THE ONONDAGA CHILDREN AT L.O. (ORPHAN) ASYLUM IN NEW YORK

BILLINGS, Irving age 6, Roll Number 1. **BILLY**, Lyman age 11, Roll Number 2. **JIMISON**, Benjamin age 16, Roll Number 3. **MAYBEE**, Alice age 11, Roll Number 6. **MAYBEE**, Harvey age 9, Roll Number 4. **MAYBEE**, Wilson age ? Roll Number 5. **PIERCE** Susie age 12, Roll Number 7. **PIERCE**, Smith age 10, Roll Number 8.

THE 1886 BUREAU OF INDIAN AFFAIRS CENSUS OF THE ONONDAGA INDIANS RESIDING UPON THE CATTARAUGUS RESERVATION IN NEW YORK

This census is not in its original order. It has been alphabetized for this book.

JACKSON, Hattie age 19, Roll Number 6. **JAKEY**, Betsey age 49, Roll Number 7. **JAKEY**, Mary age 26, Roll Number 8. **JAKEY**, Peter age 24, Roll Number 9. **JAKEY**, William age 22, Roll Number 10. **JIMISON**, Laura Q., age 40, Horatio a son age 18, Amanda a daughter age 21, Josie WARRIOR a daughter age 4, Roll Numbers 1-4. **JIMISON**, Sidney age 19, Roll Number 5. **LOGAN**, George age 53, Roll Number 13. **LOGAN**, Jack age 50, Moses a nephew age 16, Roll Numbers 11-12. **PATTERSON**, Lucy J., age 25, a baby daughter age six or one months, Roll Numbers 17-18. **PATTERSON**, Martha age 41, Rhoda a daughter age 18, Mildred a daughter age 14, Abner a son age 13, Cappie a son age 5, Carrie a daughter age six or one months, Roll Numbers 20-25. **PIERCE**, Elkinton age 55, Roll Number 19. **PIERCE**, Lydia age 30, Gertie a daughter age 1, Clarence BILLINGS a son age 10, Roll Numbers 14-16. **REDEYE**, Lucinda age 29, Chester a son age 8, Spencer a son age 6, Harrison a son age 4, Hattie a daughter age 1, Roll Numbers 26-30. **STAFFORD**, Susan age 31, Bertie a son age 11, Austin a son age 3, Roll Numbers 31-33. **TURKEY**, Melinda age 42, Lucinda a daughter age 20, Roll Numbers 34-35. **YELLOW-BLANKET**, John age 50, Roll Number 36.

THE CATTARAUGUS RESERVATION
1900 FEDERAL CENSUS CATTAURAGUS & ALLEGANY COUNTIES

The Allegany Reservation was established in 1794. The reservation land is owned by the Seneca Nation. Over 10,000 acres were taken for the Kinsau Dam and Reservoir. Tribal membership is based on matrilineal lines. Only children of women who are members of the Seneca nation are permitted to inherit allotment rights. The Allegany Reservation is in Cattaraugus County, New York. Tribal Headquarters is in Irving, New York. "Handbook of Federal and State Indian Reservations," U.S. Department of Commerce, January 1971. The census abstract below is not in its original order. It has been alphabetized for this book. All of the people in each of the following households were members of the same tribe as the head of that household. Exceptions were noted where individuals were members of another tribe, or race. Everyone in each household was born in New York unless otherwise stated. Everyone in each household has the same surname as the head of household. If an individual in a household has a different surname than the head of household that surname was highlighted by capital letters. The following names were recorded as they were spelled in the original records. The accuracy of the genealogy information represented in the following census abstract depends on how that information was provided and recorded for the creation of the original census. A question mark was placed after the names, ages and dates where the spelling was in doubt. This census abstract starts with Enumeration District 131, page 131. One town mentioned in this census appears as either Red Horse? or Red House? The Munci or Munsee are a division of the Delaware. The Abanaka or Abanaki native group reside today in Vermont and Quebec. The town Red Horse also appeared as Red House. Use the term "Adopted," with caution. This term appeared very similar to the term used to indicate grandchildren.

ABRAM, FRED: (Seneca) Age 33 was born in September 1866 in New York. Both of his parents were born in New York. Both of his parents were Seneca. Sarah his wife age 39 was born in June 1860 in New York. She was listed as a Seneca. Her father was an Onondaga. Her mother was a Seneca. Henry SHERLOCK (He was listed as a white man) a boarder age 12 was born in May 1888 in New York. Both of his parents were of Irish descent. Both of his parents were born in New York. Cattaraugus County, Elko Town, E.D. 131, Page 211A, Household 164/164.

ABRAM, MARCUS: (Seneca) Age 26 was born in September 1873 in New York. Both of his parents were born in New York. Both of his parents were Seneca. Lina his wife age 23 was born in July 1876 in New York. Both of her parents were Seneca. Florence ABRAM an adopted? daughter age 2 was born in May 1898. both of her parents were Seneca. Cattaraugus County, Elko Town, E.D. 131, Page 213B, Household 192.

ABRAM, MARY: (Seneca) Age 53 was born in March 1847 in New York. Both of her parents were born in New York. Both of her parents were Seneca. George Abram a son age 19 was born in July 1880 in New York. Both of his parents were born in New York. Both of his parents were Seneca. Mary WASHINGTON a daughter-in-law age 22 was born in July 1877 in New York. Both of her parents were Seneca. Courisa? ABRAM a grand daughter was born in May 1899 in New York. Both of her parents were Seneca.

Cattaraugus County, Coldspring Town, E.D. 131, Page 206B, Household 120/120.

ABRAMS, CHARLES: (Seneca) Age 39 was born in February 1861 in New York. Both of his parents were born in New York. Both of his parents were Seneca. Agnes his wife age 24 was born in April 1876 in New York. Both of her parents were born in New York. Both of her parents were Seneca. Blanche a daughter age five months was born in December 1899. Cattaraugus County, Elko Town, E.D. 131, Page 213A, Household 186.

ABRAMS, FRANK: (Seneca) Age 27 was born in January 1873 in New York. Both of his parents were born in New York. Both of his parents were Seneca. Hannah his wife age 25 was born in April 1875 in New York. Both of her parents were born in New York. Both of her parents were Seneca. Geneva a daughter age 10 was born in May 1890. Lee a son age 6 was born in February 1894. Lena a daughter age 4 was born in January 1896. Cattaraugus County, Cold Spring Town, E.D. 131, Page 209A, Household 145/145.

ABRAMS, LUKE: (Seneca) Age 22 was born in January 1878 in New York. Both of his parents were born in New York. Both of his parents were Seneca. Anna his wife age 22 was born in June 1877 in New York. Both of her parents were born in New York. Both of her parents were Seneca. Elko Town. Cattaraugus County, E.D. 131, Page 212B, Household 180/180.

ABRAMS, WILLIAM: (Seneca) Age 60 was born in May 1890 in New York. Both of his parents were born in New York. Both of his parents were Seneca. Margaret his wife age 50 was born in March 1850 in New York. Both of her parents were born in New York. She was listed as a Seneca. Her father was an Onondaga. Her mother was a Seneca. Moses PATTERSON a step son (Of William ABRAM) age 23 was born in February 1877 in New York. Both of his parents were born in New York. Both of his parents were Seneca. Louise GORDON a grand daughter age 11 was born in January 1889 in New York. Both of her parents were born in New York. She was listed as a Seneca. Her father was an Onondaga. Her mother was a Seneca. Cattaraugus County, Elko Town, E.D. 131, Page 212B, Household 182/182.

ABRAMS, WILLIE: (Seneca) Age 24 was born in April 1876 in New York. Both of his parents were born in New York. Both of his parents were Seneca. Sally his wife age 16 was born in July 1883 in New York. Both of her parents were born in New York. Both of her parents were Seneca. Cattaraugus County, Elko Town, E.D. 131, Page 212B, Household 178/178.

ARMSTRONG, JOHN: (Seneca) Age 41 was born in December 1858 in New York. Both of his parents were born in New York. Both of his parents were Seneca. Sarah his wife age 40 was born in July 1859 in New York. Both of her parents were born in New York. Both of her parents were Seneca. Carrie a daughter age 11 was born in March 1888. Hattie a daughter age 8 was born in November 1891. Jessie a son age 2 was born in September 1897. Willie a son age 16 was born in March 1884. Cattaraugus County. Coldspring Town, E.D. 131, Page 208A, Household 138/138.

BEAVER? HIRAM: (Seneca) Age 32 was born in January 1850 in New York. Both of his parents were born in New York. Both of his parents were

Seneca. Phebe his wife age 42 was born in September 1857 in New York. Both of her parents were born in New York. Both of her parents were Seneca. Cattaraugus County, Coldspring Town, E.D. 131, Page 206A, Household 119/119.

BENNETT, HANOVER: (Seneca) Age 29 was born in March 1871 in New York. Both of his parents were born in New York. Both of his parents were Seneca. Minnie his wife age 27 was born in September 1872 in New York. Both of her parents were born in New York. Both of her parents were Seneca. Lyman a son age 9 was born in March 1891. Sadie a daughter age 7 was born in May 1893. Clarence a son was born in February 1900. Cattaraugus County, Elko Town, E.D. 131, Page 212B, Household 183/183.

BILLINGS, CLARANCE: (Onondaga) Age 22 was born in December 1878 in New York. Both of his parents were born in New York. He was listed as an Onondaga. Both of his parents were Onondaga. Lucinda his wife age 28 was born in October 1871 in New York. Both of her parents were born in New York. Both of her parents were Seneca. David a son age 3 was born in November 1896 in New York. Alfaretta? a daughter age 1 was born in December 1898. The children of Clarence BILLINGS were listed as Seneca. Cattaraugus County, Red Horse Town, Allegany Indian Reservation, E.D. 131, Page 204A, Household 97/97.

BISHOP, THOMAS: (Seneca) Age 46 was born in February 1854 in New York. Both of his parents were born in New York. Both of his parents were Seneca. Priscilla his wife age 29 was born in May 1871 in New York. Both of her parents were born in New York. Both of her parents were Seneca. Tracy BISHOP age 9 a grand son was born in May 1891 in New York. Both of his parents were born in New York. Both of his parents were Seneca. Margaret JACOBS mother-in-law of Thomas BISHOP age 56 was born in May 1844 in New York. Both of her parents were born in New York. Both of her parents were Seneca. Cattaraugus County, Coldspring Town, E.D. 131, Page 205B, Household 113/113.

BLACK, CHARLES: (Seneca/Onondaga) Age 60 was born in May 1840 in New York. Both of his parents were born in New York. He was listed as a Seneca. His father was an Onondaga. His mother was a Seneca. Betsy JIMISON his wife age 55 was born in March 1845 in New York. Both of her parents were born in New York. Both of her parents were Seneca. Victoria JIMISON a step daughter (Of Charles Black) was age 10 born in May 1890 in New York. Both of her parents were born in New York. Both of her parents were Seneca. Cattaraugus County, Elko Town, E.D. 131, Page 212A, Household 175/175.

BLACKSNAKE, JOSEPH: (Seneca/Onondaga) Age 48 was born in May 1852 in New York. Both of his parents were born in New York. He was listed as an Onondaga. His father was a Seneca. His mother was an Onondaga. Cattaraugus County, Elko Town, E.D. 131, Page 213A, Household 184.

BONE, DANIEL: (Seneca/Onondaga) Age 57 was born in July 1842 in New York. Both of his parents were born in New York. He was listed as a Seneca. His father was an Onondaga. His mother was a Seneca. Amanda his wife age 52 was born in July 1842 in New York. Both of her parents were born in New York. Both of her parents were Seneca. Jerome L., a son age 35 born in May 1865 in New York. Cattaraugus County, South Valley Town, E.D. 131, Page 217A, Household 225.

BONE, EDWARD: (Seneca) Age 52 was born in May 1848 in New York. Both of his parents were born in New York. Both of his parents were Seneca. Clarissa his wife age 50 was born in January 1850 in New York. Both of her parents were born in New York. Both of her parents were Seneca. Lorilla? a daughter age 23 was born in February 1877. Charles S. HANSON (He was listed as a white man) a son-in-law age 25 was born in May 1835 in Germany. Both of his parents were born in Germany. Cattaraugus County, South Valley Town, E.D. 131, Page 216A, Household 218/218.

BONE, MADISON: (Seneca) Age 39 was born in April 1861 in New York. Both of his parents were born in New York. Both of his parents were Seneca. Cora his wife age 37 was born in April 1863 in New York. Both of her parents were born in New York. Both of her parents were Seneca. Cattaraugus County, South Valley Town, E.D. 131, Page 216A, Household 219/219.

BOWEN, WILLIAM: (Seneca/Onondaga) Age 81 was born in January 1819 in New York. Both of his parents were born in New York. He was a Seneca. His father was an Onondaga. His mother was a Seneca. Hannah his wife age 81 was born in September 1818 in New York. Both of her parents were born in New York. Both of her parents were Seneca. Emmet a son age 30 born in February 1870. Martha a daughter-in-Law age 21 was born in August 1878 in New York. Both of her parents were Seneca. Eli BOWEN a grand son age 4 was born in June 1895. Laura BOWEN a grand daughter was born in January 1897. Sanders BOWEN a grand son age ten months was born in July 1899. Cattaraugus County, Elko Town, E.D. 131, Page 211B, Household 171/171.

BUCK, AUGUSTUS: (Seneca) Age 36 was born in October in New York. Both of his parents were born in New York. Both of his parents were Seneca. Axie his wife age 29 was born in November 1870 in New York. Both of her parents were born in New York. Both of her parents were Seneca. Lucinda a daughter age 11 was born in August 1888. Cordelia a daughter age 8 was born in September 1891. Delia a daughter age 4 was born in May 1896. Ella a daughter age four months born in February 1900. Cattaraugus County, Cold Spring Town, E.D. 131, Page 207B, Household 133/133.

BUCKTOOTH, ABLE: (Seneca) Age 38 was born in March 1862 in New York. Both of his parents were born in New York. Both of his parents were Seneca. Hanah his wife (She was listed as a white woman) age 41 was born in February in 1859 in New York. Her father was born in Germany. Her mother was born in New York. Her mother was of French descent. Wallace PIERCE a boarder age 63 was born in April 1837 in New York. Both of his parents were born in New York. Both of his parents were Seneca. Cattaraugus County, E.D. 131, Page 197A, Household 11.

CLARK, NELLIE: (Seneca) Age 24 was born in March 1876 in New York. Both of her parents were born in New York. Both of her parents were Seneca. Daniel SHONGO a boarder age 39 was born in December 1860 in New York. Both of his parents were born in New York. Both of his parents were Seneca. Cattaraugus County, E.D. 131, Page 199B. Household 18.

CLESMAN, LOUIS: (Seneca) Age 35 was born in February 1865 in New York. Both of his parents were born in New York. Both of his parents were Seneca. Minnie his wife age 30 was born in March 1870 in New York. Both of her parents were born in New York. Both of her parents were Seneca. Cattaraugus County, South Valley Town, E.D. 131, Page 217B, Household 231/231.

COOPER, CYRUS: (Seneca) Age 27 was born in January 1872 in New York. Both of his parents were born in New York. Both of his parents were Seneca. Emily his wife age 22 was born in February 1878 in New York. Both of her parents were born in New York. Both of her parents were Seneca. Myrtle a daughter age 3 was born in March 1897. Floyd a son age six months was born in December 1899. Cattaraugus County, Cold Spring Town, E.D. 131, Page 207B, Household 134/134.

COOPER, HIRAM: (Seneca) Age 47 was born in April 1853 in Pennsylvania. Both of his parents were born in Pennsylvania. Both of his parents were Seneca. Lydia his wife age 37 was born in September 1862 in New York. Both of her parents were born in New York. Both of her parents were Seneca. Laurence a son age 18 was born in July 1881. Cattaraugus County, Cold Spring Town, E.D. 131, Page 208B, Household 143.

COOPER, JOHN: (Seneca) Age 63 was born in October 1836 in New York. He was listed as a Seneca. His father was born in England. His mother was born in New York. His father was a white man. His mother was a Seneca. Charlotte his wife (She was listed a white woman) age 67 was born in August 1832 in New York. Both of her parents were born in New York. Chautauqua County, Town of Hanover, Cattaraugus Reservation, E.D. 135, Page 220A, Household 1, or 167//168.

COOPER, LEWIS: (Seneca) Age 44 was born in April 1856 in Pennsylvania. Both of his parents were born in Pennsylvania. Both of his parents were Seneca. Louisa his wife age 36 was born in April 1864 in New York. Both of her parents were born in New York. Mande? A. ALLEN a step-daughter age 13 was born in June 1876 in New York. Both of her parents were born in New York. Claude ALLEN a step daughter? age 11 was born in August 1878 in New York. Both of her parents were born in New York. Irene ALLEN a step-daughter age 10 was born in February 1890 in New York. Both of her parents were born in New York. Cattaraugus County, E.D. 131, Page 198A, Household 22.

CORNPLANTER, JAMES: (Seneca) Age 62 was born in 1837 in New York. Both of his parents were born in New York. Both of his parents were Seneca. Ella his wife age 53 was born in September 1846 in New York. Both of her parents were born in New York. Both of her parents were Seneca. Perrysburg, Cattaraugus County, E.D. 135, Page 29, Household 219/221.

CROUSE, BETSY: (Seneca) Age 67 was born in March 1833 in New York. Both of her parents were born in New York. Both of her parents were Seneca. Jerome a son age 28 was born in June 1872 in New York. Hannah a daughter-in-law age 17 was born in October 1882 in New York. Emeline a grand daughter age six months was born in December 1899 in New York. Martin a son age 35 was born in April 1865 in New York. Frank a son age 23 was born in June 1876 in New York. Cattaraugus County, Coldspring Town, E.D. 131, Page 206A, Household 118/118.

CROUSE, CHAUNCEY: (Seneca) Age 26 was born in January 1874 in New York. Both of his parents were born in New York. Both of his parents were Seneca. Sadie his wife age 18 was born in New York in May 1882. Both of her parents were born in New York. Both of her parents were Seneca. Cattaraugus County, Coldspring Town, E.D. 131, Page 210A, Household 154/154.

CROUSE, GEORGE: (Seneca) Age 31 was born in May 1869 in New York. Both of his parents were born in New York. Both of his parens were Seneca. Cattaraugus County, South Valley Town, E.D. 131, Page 215A, Household 209.

CROUSE, IDA: (Seneca) Age 30 was born in March 1870 in New York. Both of her parents were born in New York. Both of her parents were Seneca. Cattaraugus County, E.D. 131, Page 198A, Household 24.

CROUSE, JAMES: (Seneca) Age 42 was born in January 1858 in New York. Both of his parents were born in New York. Both of his parents were Seneca. Electa his wife age 37 born in June 1862? in New York. Both of her parents were born in New York. Both of her parents were Seneca. Marian a daughter age 7 was born in April 1893. Florence a daughter age 2 was born in January 1898. Cattaraugus County, E.D. 131, Page 205B, Household 113/113.

CROUSE, JOHN: (Seneca) Age 50 was born in February 1850 in New York. Both of her parents were born in New York. Both of her parents were Seneca. Martha his wife age 39 was born in New York. Both of her parents were Born in New York. Both of her parents were Seneca. Perrysburg, Cattaraugus County, E.D. 135, Page 223A, Household 24 or 191/192.

CROUSE, JULIA: (Seneca) Age 30 was born in May 1870 in New York. Both of her parents were born in New York. Both of her parents were Seneca. George Crouse a son age 1 was born in February 1899. Chester Crouse the husband of Julia CROUSE age 27 was born in April 1873 in New York. Both of his parents were born in New York. Both of his parents were Seneca. Edward HARRIS a boarder age 45 born in February 1855 in New York. Both of his parents were born in New York. Both of his parents were Seneca. Cattaraugus County, Salamanca Town, Allegany Indian Reservation, Page 199B, Household 43/43.

CROUSE, SOLON: (Seneca) Age 26 was born in January 1874 in New York. Both of his parents were born in New York. Both of his parents were Seneca. Lena his wife age 20 was born in January 1880 in New York. Both of her parents were born in New York. Both of her parents were Seneca. Evelina a daughter was born in August 1899. Cattaraugus County, South Valley Town, E.D. 131, Page 215A, Household 208.

CROUSE, SYLVESTER: (Seneca) Age 37 was born in February 1863 in New York. Both of his parents were born in New York. Both of his parents were Seneca. Malinda his wife age 32 was born in August 1867 in New York. Both of her parents were born in New York. Both of her parents were Seneca. Sophia a daughter age 13 was born in May 1887. Addison a son age 8 was born in April 1892. Loyd a son age 5 was born in June 1894. Denna a daughter age 3 was born in January 1897. Elon a son age one month was born in May 1900. Cattaraugus County, Cold Spring Town, E.D. 131, Page 208B, Household 142/142.

CROW, OSCAR: (Onondaga/Seneca) Age 50 was born in January 1850 in New York. Both of his parents were born in New York. He was listed as an Onondaga. His father was a Seneca. His mother was an Onondaga. Ida his wife age 35 was born in May 1865 in New York. Both of her parents were born in New York. Both of her parents were Seneca. Seneca a son age 10 was born in April 1890. Sadie a daughter age 8 was born in January 1892. Arthur a son age 6 was born in August 1893. The children in this family were all listed as Seneca. Cattaraugus County, Elko Town, E.D. 131, Page 214A, Household 196.

CURRY, CANADA: (Seneca) Age 54 was born in May 1846 in New York. Both of his parents were born in New York. Both os his parents were Seneca. Lucy his wife age 29 was born in August 1870 in New York. Both of her parents were born in New York. Both of her parents were Seneca. Eunice a daughter age 20 was born in May 1880. Lewis a son age 16 was born in March 1884. John JIMISON a son-in-law age 34 was born in April 1866 in New York. Both of his parents were born in New York. Both of his parents were Seneca. Sampson JIMISON a grand son age 5 was born in May 1895. Amos JIMISON a grand son age 3 was born in January 1897. Harrison JIMISON a grand son age 2 was born in May 1898. Cattaraugus County, Elko Town, E.D. 131, Page 213B, Household 190.

CURRY, GIBSON: (Seneca) Age 42 was born in February 1858 in New York. Both of his parents were born in New York. Both of his parents were Seneca. Ida his wife age 42 was born in February 1858 in New York. Both of her parents were born in New York. Both of her parents were Seneca. John a son age 11 was born in April 1889. Robert a son age 8 was born in May 1891. Mary a daughter age 5 was born in February 1895. Cattaraugus County, Cold Spring Town, E.D. 131, Page 209B, Household 152/152.

CURRY, JAMES: (Seneca) Age 60 was born in April 1840 in New York. Both of his parents were born in New York. Both of his parents were Seneca. Eliza his wife age 54 was born in December 1845 in New York. Both of her parents were born in New York. She was listed as an Onondaga. Her father was a Seneca. Her mother was an Onondaga. Mary CROW mother-in-law, (Of James Curry) age 98 was born in January in 1802 in New York. Both of her parents were born in New York. She was listed as a Onondaga. Her father was a Seneca. Her mother was a Onondaga. Cattaraugus County, Elko Town, E.D. 131, Page 211A, Household 173/173.

CURRY, THOMAS: (Onondaga/Seneca) Age 32 was born in June 1867 in New York. Both of his parents were born in New York. He was listed as a Onondaga. His father was a Seneca. His mother was a Onondaga. Amanda his wife age 35 was born in January 1865 in New York. Both of her parents were born in New York. Both of her parents were Seneca. Amanda a daughter age 6 was born in February 1894. Dora a daughter age 4 was born in May 1896. Richard a son age 2 was born in June 1897. Cattaraugus County, South Valley Town, E.D. 131, Page 215B, Household 212/212.

CURRY, WILLIAM: (Seneca) Age 59 born in July 1840 in New York. Both of his parents were born in New York. Both of his parents were Seneca.

Josephine his wife (She was listed as a white woman) age 39 was born in April 1860 in New York. Both of her parents were born in New York. Both of her parents were of English ancestry. Edgar a son age 10 was born in February 1890. Daisy a daughter age 8 was born in August 1891. Cattaraugus County, Elko Town, E.D. 131, Page 214A, Household 197.

CURRY, WILLIE: (Onondaga/Seneca) Age 32 born in March 1868 in New York. Both of his parents were born in New York. He was listed as a Onondaga. His father was a Seneca. His mother was a Onondaga. Maggie his wife age 17 was born in November 1882 in New York. Both of her parents were born in New York. She was listed as a Seneca. Her father was a Cayuga. Her mother was a Seneca. Cattaraugus County, Elko Town, E.D. 131, Page 212A, Household 174/174.

DOCKSTADER, HOWARD: (Seneca) Age 45 born in October 1854 in New York. Both of his parents were born in New York. Both of his parents were Seneca. Deforest a son age 6 was born in July 1893. Howard a son age 3 was born in March 1897. Cattaraugus County, Red Horse Town, Allegany Indian Reservation, E.D. 131, Page 204A, Household 98/98.

DOCKSTADER, SARAH: (Seneca) Age 66 born in January 1834 in New York. Both of her parents were born in New York. Both of her parents were Seneca. Frank a son age 33 was born in August 1866. Both of his parents were born in New York. Both of his parents were Seneca. Mary AMADEN? a daughter age 43 was born in September 1856 in New York. Both of her parents were born in New York. Both of her parents were Seneca. Walter AMADEN a grandson age 23 was born in May 1877 in New York. Both of his parents were born in New York. Both of his parents were Seneca. Cattaraugus County, Red House Town, Allegany Indian Reservation, E.D. 131, Page 202A, Household 68/68.

DOCKSTADER, WILLIAM: (Seneca) Age 39 born in May 1861 in New York. Both of his parents were born in New York. Both of his parents were Seneca. Sarah his wife age 42 was born in October 1847 in New York. Both of her parents were born in New York. Both of her parents were Seneca. Cattaraugus County, Red House Town, Allegany Indian Reservation, E.D. 131, Page 202A, Household 69/69.

DOCTOR, PETER: (Seneca) Age 38 born in February 1862 in New York. Both of his parents were born in New York. Both of his parents were Seneca. E.D. 131, Page 198B, Household 31.

DOWDY, JOSEPH: (Seneca) Age 36 born in March 1864 in New York. Both of his parents were born in New York. Both of his parents were Seneca. Jennie his wife age 30 was born in May 1870 in New York. Both of her parents were born in New York. Both of her parents were Seneca. Liney a son age 7 was born in June 1892. Wesley a son age 3 was born in May 1897. Cattaraugus County, Coldspring Town, E.D. 131, Page 210A, Household 158/158.

DOXTATOR, PETER: (Seneca/Cayuga) Age 24 born in February 1876 in New York. Both of his parents were born in New York. He was listed as a Seneca. His father was a Cayuga. His mother was a Seneca. Jennie JIMISON mother (Of Peter?) age 52 was born in 1847 in New York. Both of her parents were born in New York. Both of her parents were Seneca. Julia BROOKS a boarder age 72 was born in 1827 in New York. Both of her parents were born in New York. She was listed as a Cayuga. Both of her parents were Cayuga, Cattaraugus County, Perrysburg, E.D. 135, Page 221A, Household 5? or 172/173.

EELS, GEORGE: (Seneca) Age 52 born in 1847 in New York. Both of his parents were born in New York. Both of his parents were Seneca. Louise his wife age 47 was born in 1857 in New York. Both of her parents were born in New York. Both of her parents were Seneca. Alberta EELS? a grand daughter age 3 was born in February 1897 in New York. Both of her parents were born in New York. Both of her parents were Seneca. Lena PARKER a grand daughter age ten months was born in July 1899? in New York. Both of her parents were born in New York. Both of her parents were Seneca. Willie Parker a son-in-law age 28 was born in February 1877 in New York. Both of his parents were born in New York. Both of his parents were Seneca. Cattaraugus County, Perrysburg, E.D. 135, Page 224A, Household 25 or 215/217.

FALTY, PHILLIP: (Seneca) Age 54 born in February 1846 in New York. Both of his parents were born in New York. Both of his parents were Seneca. Serena his wife age 53 was born in May 1847 in New York. Both of her parents were born in New York. Both of her parents were Seneca. Anna a daughter age 23 was born in May 1877. Cattaraugus County, Salamanca Town, Alleghany Indian Reservation, E.D. 131, Page 203A, Household 87/87.

FUN? OR FIN? WILLIAM: (Mohawk) Age 41 born in August 1858 in Canada. Both of his parents were born in Canada. He was listed as a Mohawk. Both of his parents were Mohawks. Sally his wife age 50 was born in May 1850 in New York. Both of her parents were born in New York. Both of her parents were Seneca. George Titus a boarder age 91 was born in 1808 in Pennsylvania. Both of his parents were born in Pennsylvania. Both of his parents were Seneca. William White a boarder age 22 was born in May 1878 in New York. Both of his parents were born in New York. Both of his parents were Seneca. Webster WHITE a grandson (Of William Fun?) age 9 was born in April 1891 in New York. Both of his parents were born in New York. Both of his parents were Seneca. Coldspring Town, E.D. 131, Page 206B, Household 123/123.

GEORGE, JAMES: (Seneca) Age 58 born in September 1841 in New York. Both of his parents were born in New York. Both of his parents were Seneca. Julia his wife age 78 was born in October 1821 in New York. Both of her parents were born in New York. Both of her parents were Seneca. Cattaraugus County, Cold Spring Town, E.D. 131, Page 208B, Household 140/140.

GORDON, JACK: (Seneca) Age 48 born in August 1851? in New York. Both of his parents were born in New York. Both of his parents were Seneca. Philinda his wife age 43 was born in August 1856 in New York. Both of her parents were born in New York. Gibson a son age 21 was born in April 1879. Sarah a daughter age 19 was born in May 1881. William a son age 17 was born in April 1883. Lucinda a daughter age 14 was born in August 1885. Aurelia a daughter age 12 was born in January 1888. Horatio a son age 3 was born in May 1897. Julia TITUS mother-in-law (Of Jack Gordon) age 67 was born in July 1832 in New York. Both of her parents were born in New York. Both of her parents were Seneca.

Cattaraugus County, No town was given. Allegany Indian Reservation,
E.D. 131, Page 204B, Household 103/103.

GORDON, JOHN: (Seneca) Age 53 was born in January 1867 in New York.
Both of his parents were born in New York. Both of his parents were
Seneca. Louise his wife age 59 was born in february 1841 in New York.
Both of her parents were born in New York. Both of her parents were
Seneca. Chas. W. BLACKSNAKE (Seneca) a nephew age 16 was born in
January 1884 in New York. Both of his parents were Seneca. Cattaraugus
County, Coldspring Town, E.D. 131, Page 210A, Household 155/155.

GORDON, JOSEPH: (Seneca) Age 25 born in October 1874 in New York. Both
of his parents were born in New York. Both of his parents were Seneca.
Lilly his wife age 17 was born in June 1882 in New York. Both of her
parents were born in New York. She was listed as a Seneca. Her father
was a Onondaga. Her mother was a Seneca. Josephine a daughter age 2
was born in march 1898. Jabez SAMPSON a cousin (Of Joseph Gordon) age
21 was born in June 1878 in New York. Both of his parents were born in
New York. Both of his parents were Seneca. Julia GORDON mother (Of
Joseph Gordon) age 50 was born in May 1850 in New York. Both of her
parents were born in New York. Both of her parents were Seneca.
Cattaraugus County, Elko Town, E.D. 131, Page 212B, Household 177/177.

GORDON, JOSEPH: (Seneca) Age 78 born in August 1821 in New York. Both
of his parents were born in New York. Both of his parents were Seneca.
Lydia his wife age 68 was born in December 1831 in New York. Both of
her parents were born in New York. Both of her parents were Seneca.
Benjamin Halfwhite a nephew age 45 was born in July 1854 in New York.
Both of his parents were born in New York. Both of his parents were
Seneca. Cattaraugus County, Coldspring Town, E.D. 131, Page 208A,
Household 135/135.

GORDON, SALLY: (Seneca) Age 62 born in December 1838 in New York. Both
of her parents were born in New York. Both of her parents were Seneca.
Charles JIMISON jr., a grandson age 9 was born in September 1890 in
New York. Both of his parents were born in New York. Harriet JIMISON
a grand daughter age 5 was born in December 1894 in New York. Both of
her parents were born in New York. The parents of the grand children
of Sally Gordon were all Seneca. Cattaraugus County, Coldspring Town,
E.D. 131, Page 208A, Household 137/137.

GRANT, ALBERT: (Seneca) Age 46 born in January 1853 in New York. His
father was born in Pennsylvania. His father was listed as a white man.
His mother was born in New York. She was listed as a Seneca. Minnie
his wife age 40 was born in 1859 in Germany. Both of her parents were
born in Germany. Chautauqua County, Hanover Town, Cattaraugus
Reservation, E.D. 135, Page 220A, Household 3 or 169/170.

HALFTOWN, AUSTIN: (Oneida/Seneca) Age 58 born in May 1842 in New York.
Both of his parents were born in New York. He was listed as a Oneida.
His father was a Seneca. His mother was a Oneida. Susan his wife age
60 was born in January 1840 in New York. Both of her parents were born
in New York. Both of her parents were Seneca. Rachel HILL a grand
daughter was born in January 1895 in New York. Both of her parents
were born in New York. Both of her parents were Seneca. Cattaraugus

County, E.D. 131, Page 204A, Red House Town, Allegany Indian Reservation, Household 93/93.

HALFTOWN, FORMAN? (Seneca) Age 69 born in 1830 in New York. Both of his parents were born in New York. Both of his parents were Seneca. Nancy his wife age ? was born in 1840 in New York. Both of her parents were born in New York. Both of her parents were Seneca. Cattaraugus County, Perrysburg, E.D. 135, Page 224B, Household 38.

HALFTOWN, HAMILTON: (Seneca) Age 31 born in November 1868 in New York. Both of his parents were born in New York. Both of his parents were Seneca. Emma his wife age 30 was born in May 1870 in New York. Both of her parents were born in New York. Mable a daughter age 8 was born in December 1891. Irene a daughter age 4 was born in April 1896. Rachel a daughter age 2 was born in April 1898. Cattaraugus County, Coldspring Town, E.D. 131, Page 210A, Household 159/159.

HALFTOWN, HARRISON: (Seneca) Age 71 born in August 1828 in New York. Both of his parents were born in New York. Both of his parents were Seneca. Mary his wife age 64 was born in May 1836 in New York. Both of her parents were born in New York. Both of her parents were Seneca. Emily a daughter age 22 was born in September 1877 in New York. Ava Halftown? a grand daughter age 2 was born in April 1898 in New York. Cattaraugus County, Coldspring Town, E.D. 131, Page 209A, Household 147/147.

HALFTOWN, MARTIN: (Seneca) Age 45 born in April 1855 in New York. Both of his parents were born in New York. Both of his parents were Seneca. Alice his wife age 35 was born in May 1865 in New York. Both of her parents were born in New York. Both of her parents were Seneca. E.D. 131, Page 198A, Household 25.

HALFWHITE, CHARLES: (Seneca) Age 39 born in January 1861 in New York. Both of his parents were born in New York. Both of his parents were Seneca. Laura his wife age 43 was born in February 1857 in New York. Both of her parents were born in New York. Both of her parents were Seneca. Hetty a daughter age 17 was born in August 1882. Solomon a son age 6 was born in May 1894. Orrin a son age 4 was born in February 1896. Clara a daughter age 8 was born in May? 1891. Cattaraugus County, Cold Spring Town, E.D. 131, Page 209A, Household 148/148.

HALFWHITE, GEORGE: (Seneca) Age 40 born in May 1860 in New York. Both of his parents were born in New York. Both of his parents were Seneca. James HALFWHITE a brother age 35 was born in January 1865 in New York. Cattaraugus County, South Valley Town, E.D. 131, Page 217B, Household 232/232.

HALFWHITE, JAMES: (Seneca) Age 38 born in May 1862 in New York. Both of his parents were born in New York. Both of his parents were Seneca. Ester his wife age 43 was born in July 1856 in New York. Both of her parents were born in New York. Both of her parents were Seneca. Cattaraugus County, Red House Town, Allegany Indian Reservation, E.D. 131, Page 202A, Household 67/67.

HALFWHITE, JEROME: (Seneca) Age 28 born in February 1872 in New York. Both of his parents were born in New York. Both of his parents were

Seneca. Laura his wife age 26 was born in March 1874 in New York. Both of her parents were born in New York. She was listed as a Seneca. her father was a Cayuga. Her mother was a Seneca. Rachael HILL a step daughter age 6 was born in January 1894 in New York. Both of her parents were born in New York. She was listed as a Seneca. Her father was a Mohawk. Daniel THOMAS a nephew? age 45 was born in March 1855 in New York. Both of his parents were born in New York. Both of his parents were Seneca. Cattaraugus County, South Valley Town, E.D. 131, Page 217A, Household 230.

HALFWHITE, ROBERT: (Seneca/Onondaga) Age 60 born in January 1840 in New York. Both of his parents were born in New York. He was listed as a Onondaga. His father was a Seneca. His mother was a Onondaga. Eliza his wife age 50 was born in August 1849 in New York. Both of her parents were born in New York. Both of her parents were Seneca. George a son age 25 was born in March 1875, Flora a daughter-in-law age 24 was born in October 1875. Rosetta a grand daughter was born in January 1900. Josephen a daughter age 17 was born in June 1882. Mack a son age 16 was born in March 1884. All of the children of Robert Halfwhite were listed as Seneca. Cattaraugus County, Coldspring Town, E.D. 131, Page 206B, Household 122/122.

HANSON, LOUIS: (White) Age 44 born in July 1855 in Denmark. Both of his parents were born in Denmark. He immigrated in 1873. Jennie his wife age 38 was born in May 1862 in New York. She was listed as a Seneca. Her father was a Seneca. Her mother was probably a Seneca. The original census has the word Seneca written over the word Onondaga for her mother's tribal information. Lucy Bucktooth mother-in-law (Of Louis Hanson) age 70 born in February 1830 in New York. Both of her parents were born in New York. Both of her parents were Seneca. Cattaraugus County, South Valley Town, E.D. 131, Page 217A, Household 227.

HENHAWK, WILLIAM: (Munsi/Munsee or Delaware) Age 86 born in December 1813 in New York. Both of his parents were born in New York. Both of his parents were Munsi (A division of the Lenni Lenapi or Delaware). Electa his wife age 77 was born in January 1823 in New York. Both of her parents were born in New York. Both of her parents were Seneca. E.D. 131? Page 201A, Household 57.

HOAG, WILLIAM: (Seneca) Age 39 born in August 1860 in New York. Both of his parents were born in New York. Both of his parents were Seneca. Dora his wife age 41 was born in July 1858 in New York. Both of her parents were born in New York. Both of her parents were Seneca. Arthur HOAG a grandson age 7 was born in April 1893 in New York. Both of his parents were born in New York. Both of his parents were Seneca. Mabel TALLCHIEF a niece age 11 was born in April 1889 in New York. Both of her parents were born in New York. Both of her parents were Seneca. Jennie TALLCHIEF a niece age 22 was born in September 1877 in New York. Both of her parents were born in New York. Both of her parents were Seneca. William BOMBERRY a servant age 31 was born in April 1869 in New York. Both of his parents were born in New York. Both of his parents were Seneca. Cattaraugus County, E.D. 131, Red House Town, Allegany Indian Reservation, Page 204A, Household 92/92.

HOWE, MARY R.: (Seneca) Age 62 born in October 1837 in New York. Both of her parents were born in New York. Both of her parents were Seneca. Cattaraugus County, Colspring Town, E.D. 131, Page 206B, Household 125/125.

HUDSON, MARY: (Seneca) Age 56 born in March 1844 in New York. Both of her parents were born in New York. Both of her parents were Seneca. William a son age 19 was born in March 1881. Sophia E., a daughter age 15 was born in December 1884 in New York. The father of the children of Mary Hudson was listed as a Seneca. Cattaraugus County, Perrysburg, E.D. 135, Page 224B, Household 30 or 220/222.

HUFF, HENRY JR: (Seneca) Age 56 born in May 1844 in New York. Both of his parents were born in New York. His father was a white man. His mother was a Seneca. Nelson R., a son age 32 was born in September 1867. He was listed as a Seneca. Both of his parents were Seneca. Jennie a daughter-in-law age 23 was born in August 1876 in New York. Both of her parents were born in New York. Both of her parents were Seneca. Cattaraugus County, South Valley Town, E.D. 131, Page 216B, Household 221/221.

HUFF, HENRY: (White) Age 85 born in April 1815 in New York. He was listed as a white man. His father was born in Germany. His mother was born in Pennsylvania. Harriet his wife age 76 was born in January 1824 in New York. Both of her parents were born in New York. Both of her parents were Seneca. Elmer HUFF a grandson age 25 was born in April 1875 in New York. Both of his parents were born in New York. Both of his parents were Seneca. Marie BARNUM? a step daughter age 52 was born in January 1848 in New York. Both of her parents were born in New York. Both of her parents were Seneca. Cattaraugus County, Elko Town, E.D. 131, Page 211A, Household 167/167.

JACKSON, ANDREW: (Seneca/Cayuga) Age 38 born in September 1861 in New York. Both of his parents were born in New York. He was listed as a Seneca. His father was a Cayuga. His mother was a Seneca. Abbie his wife age 23 was born in 1876 in New York. Both of her parents were born in New York. Both of her parents were Seneca. E.D. 135, Page 224B, Household 37.

JACKSON, EVELINN?: (Male Onondaga/Seneca) Age 29 born in January 1871 in New York. Both of his parents were born in New York. He was listed as a Seneca. His father was a Onondaga. His mother was a Seneca. Marilla? his wife age 29 was born in October 1870 in New York. Both of her parents were born in New York. Both of her parents were Seneca. Theodore a son age 2 was born in February 1898. Alma a daughter age two months was born in April 1900. Job JACKSON father (Of Evelinn? Jackson) age 56 was born in January 1844 in New York. He was listed as a Onondaga. Both of his parents were Onondaga. Cattaraugus County, South Valley Town, E.D. 131, Page 216B, Household 222.

JACKSON, FILLMORE: (Seneca) Age 50 born in January 1850 in New York. Both of his parents were born in New York. Both of his parents were Seneca. Eliza his wife age 39 was born in New York. Both of her parents were born in New York. She was listed as a Munsee (Delaware). Her father was a Seneca. Her mother was a Munsee. Marjorie a daughter age 11 was born in April 1889. Philo a son age 2 was born in June

1898. All of the children of Fillmore Jackson were listed as Munsee. Cattaraugus County, Perrysburg, E.D. 135, Page 233A, Household 23 or 190/191.

JACKSON, HENRY: (Seneca) Age 38 born in February 1862 in New York. Both of his parents were born in New York. Both of his parents were Seneca. Emily his wife age 42 was born in November 1857 in New York. Both of her parents were born in New York. Both of her parents were Seneca. Peter a son age 6 was born in March 1894. Cattaraugus County, Red House Town, Allegany Indian Reservation, E.D. 131, Page 201B, Household 64/64.

JACKSON, MOSES: (Seneca) Age 58 born in October 1841 in New York. Both of his parents were born in New York. Both of his parents were Seneca. Cornelius his wife age 57 was born in January 1843 in New York. Both of her parents were born in New York. Both of her parents were Seneca. Leon a son age 21 was born in January 1879 in New York. Stonewall JACKSON a grandson age 15 was born in February 1885 in New York. Both of his parents were born in New York. Both of his parents were Seneca. Cattaraugus County, Coldspring Town, E.D. 131, Page 205A, Household 107/107.

JACKSON, RICHARD: (Seneca) Age 30 born in January 1870 in New York. Both of his parents were born in New York. Both of his parents were Seneca. Jennie his wife age 27 was born in May 1873 in New York. Both of her parents were born in New York. She was listed as a Cayuga. Her father was a Seneca. Her mother was a Cayuga. Benjamin a son age 8 was born in May 1892. He was listed as a Cayuga. Cattaraugus County, Elko Town, E.D. 131, Page 214A, Household 195.

JACOB, JAMES: (Seneca) Age 49 born in May 1851 in Pennsylvania? His father was born in New York. His mother was born in Pennsylvania. Both of his parents were Seneca. Mary his wife age 35 was born in December 1860 in Pennsylvania. Her father was born in New York. Her mother was born in Pennsylvania. Both of her parents were Seneca. Sherman a son age 16 was born in March 1884 in New York. Bertha a daughter age 9 was born in November 1890 in New York. Cattaraugus County, Cold Spring Town, E.D. 131, Page 210B, Household 162/162.

JACOB, JOHN: (Seneca) Age 24 born in May 1876 in New York. Both of his parents were born in New York. Both of his parents were Seneca. Minnie his wife age 24 was born in May 1876 in New York. Both of her parents were born in New York. Both of her parents were Seneca. Thomas a son age 5 was born in March 1895. Allen a son age 2 was born in October 1898. Alphus a son was born in August 1899. Cattaraugus County, Elko Town, E.D. 131, Page 214A, Household 194.

JACOBS, ALFRED: (Seneca) Age 59 born in January 1841 in New York. Both of his parents were born in New York. Both of his parents were Seneca. Abigail his wife age 47 was born in May 1853 in New York. Both of her parents were born in New York. Both of her parents were Onondaga. Helen a daughter age 17 was born in February 1883 in New York. She was listed as a Onondaga. Geneva WARRIOR a grand daughter age 3 was born in May 1897 in New York. Both of her parents were born in New York. She was listed as a Onondaga. Her father was a Cayuga. Her mother was a Onondaga. Fedelia JEMISON a grand daughter age 1 was born in June

1898. She was listed as a Onondaga. Her father was a Seneca. Her mother was a Onondaga. Cattaraugus County, Coldspring Town, E.D. 131, Page 205B, Household 114.

JACOBS, GEORGE: (Seneca) Age 61 born in July 1838 in New York. Both of his parents were born in New York. Both of his parents were Seneca. Amanda JIMISON a daughter age 27 was born in May 1873 in New York. Both of her parents were born in New York. Both of her parents were Seneca. Ada JIMISON age 9 a grand daughter was born in May 1891. Lunus? JIMISON age 5 a grandson was born in January 1895. Nora JIMISON a grand daughter age 3 was born in January 1897. Haddy JIMISON age nine months a grandson was born in August 1899. Robert JIMISON a son-in-law (No age or birth information was given) was born in New York. Both of his parents were born in New York. Both of his parents were Seneca. All of the grandchildren in George Jacobs household were listed as Seneca. Cattaraugus County, Cold Spring Town, E.D. 131, Page 207A, Household 127/127.

JACOBS, HIRAM: (Seneca) Age 37 born in August 1862 in New York. Both of his parents were born in New York. Both of his parents were Seneca. Jane his wife age 48 was born in January 1852 in New York. Both of her parents were born in New York. She was listed as a Cayuga. Both of her parents were Cayuga. Chauncey WARRIOR a step son age 31 was born in April 1869. Both of his parents were born in New York. He was listed as a Cayuga. His father was a Seneca. His mother was a Cayuga. Clarence JACOBS a son age 15 was born in May 1885 in New York. He was listed as a Onondaga. His mother was a Onondaga. Borman? or Barnum? JACOBS a son age 8 was born in June 1891 in New York. He was listed as a Onondaga. His mother was a Onondaga. Roda WARRIOR a step daughter age 17 was born in May 1883 in New York. Both of her parents were Seneca. Dena WARRIOR a step grand daughter age 2 was born in April 1898 in New York. Both of her parents were born in New York. She was listed as a Seneca. Her father was a Cayuga? Her mother was a Seneca. Cattaraugus County, Elko Town, E.D. 131, Page 211A, Household 166/166.

JEMISON, JOEL: (Seneca) Age 26 born in October 1873 in New York. Both of his parents were born in New York. Both of his parents were Seneca. Della his wife age 20 was born in March 1880 in New York. Both of her parents were born in New York. Both of her parents were Seneca. Earl a son age 4 was born in August 1895. He was listed as a Cayuga. His father was a Seneca. His mother was a Cayuga. Elfie? of Effa? mother (Of Joel Jemison) was age 63 born in September 1836 in New York. She was born in New York. Both of her parents were born in New York. She was listed as a Seneca. Both of her parents were Seneca. Cattaraugus County, Cold Spring Town, E.D. 131, Page 210B, Household 160/160.

JEMISON, LUCY: (Onondaga/Seneca) Age 59 born in April 1841 in New York. Both of her parents were born in New York. She was listed as a Seneca. Her father was a Onondaga. Her mother was a Seneca. Leroy SNOW a grandson age 9 was born in February 1891. Both of his parents were Seneca. Cattaraugus County, Elko Town, E.D. 131, Page 211B, Household 168/168.

JIMISON, ALEXANDER: (Seneca) Age 48 born in February 1852 in New York. Both of his parents were born in New York. Both of his parents were Seneca. E.D. 131, Page 197A, Household 13.

JIMISON, ALFRED: (Seneca) Age 43 born in July 1856 in New York. Both of his parents were born in New York. Both of his parents were Seneca. Mary his wife age 48 was born in March 1856 in New York. Both of her parents were born in New York. Both of her parents were Seneca. Eva B. JIMISON was listed as a adopted daughter born in ? She was listed as white. Her parents were of English ancestry. E.D. 131, Page 198B, Household 29.

JIMISON, ALLEN: (Seneca) Age 38, born in June 1861 in New York. Both of his parents were born in New York. Both of his parents were Seneca. Helen his wife age 38 was born in January 1862 in New York. Both of her parents were born in New York. Both of her parents were Seneca. Clinton JIMISON an adopted son age 14 was born in May 1886 in New York. Both of his parents were born in New York. Both of his parents were Cayuga. Elso JIMISON an adopted daughter age 1 was born in June 1898 in New York. Both of her parents were born in New York. Both of her parents were Seneca. Cattaraugus County, Red House Town, Allegany Indian Reservation, Page 201A, Household 56/56.

JIMISON, ALONZO: (Seneca) Age 31 born in May 1869 in New York. Both of his parents were born in New York. Both of his parents were Seneca. Serinda? his wife age 29 was born in November 1870 in New York. Both of her parents were born in New York. Both of her parents were Seneca. Mande a daughter age 9 was born in July 1890. Allen a son age 4 was born in July 1895. Salina a daughter age 1 was born in October 1898. Cattaraugus County, E.D. 131, Salamanca Town, Allegheny Indian Reservation, Page 203B, Household 89/89.

JIMISON, BELA: (Seneca) Age 34 born in January 1866 in New York. Both of his parents were born in New York. Both of his parents were Seneca. Roda his wife age 32 was born in March 1868 in New York. Both of her parents were born in New York. Both of her parents were Seneca. E.D. 131, Page 199A, Household 39.

JIMISON, CHARLES: (Seneca) Age 39 born in March 1861 in New York. Both of his parents were born in New York. Both of his parents were Seneca. Donna his wife age 27 was born in May 1873 in New York. Both of her parents were Seneca. Cattaraugus County, South Valley Town, Page 217A, Household 229.

JIMISON, CHARLES: (Seneca) Age 37 born in August 1862 in New York. Both of his parents were born in New York. Both of his parents were Seneca. Josephine his wife age 38 was born in January 1862 in New York. Both of her parents were born in New York. Both of her parents were Seneca. William GARLOW a boarder age 28 was born in September 1871 in New York. Both of his parents were born in New York. Both of his parents were Seneca. Page 200B, Household 53.

JIMISON, CHARLES: (Seneca) Age 60 born in May 1840 in New York. Both of his parents were born in New York. Both of his parents were Seneca. E.D. 131, Page 197A, Household 14.

JIMISON, EMELINE: (Seneca) Age 59 born in June 1840 in New York. Both of her parents were born in New York. Both of her parents were Seneca. Isreal a son age 23 was born in March 1877 in New York. Both of his parents were born in New York. Both of his parents were Seneca. Martha

THOMAS age 70 a boarder was born in May 1830 in New York. Both of her parents were born in New York. Both of her parents were Seneca. No town name was given. Allegany Indian Reservation, Cattaraugus County, E.D. 131, Page 204B, Household 99/99.

JIMISON, EPHRAIM: (Seneca) Age 45 born in April 1855 in New York. Both of his parents were born in New York. Both of his parents were Seneca. Cattaraugus County, Red House Town, Allegany Indian Reservation, E.D. 131, Page 202A, Household 66/66.

JIMISON, FRANK: (Seneca) Age 46 born in May 1854 in New York. Both of his parents were born in New York. He was listed as a Seneca. Both of his parents were Seneca. Ida his wife age 40 was born in February 1860 in New York. Both of her parents were born in New York. Both of her parents were Seneca. Frank Jr., a son age 20 was born in December 1879 in New York. Cattaraugus County, E.D. 131, Page 215B, Household 211/211.

JIMISON, FRED: (Seneca) Age 35 born in February 1865 in New York. Both of his parents were born in New York. Both of his parents were Seneca. Malinda his wife age 29 was born in March 1871 in New York. Both of her parents were born in New York. Both of her parents were Seneca. E.D. 131, Page 200B, Household 54.

JIMISON, GEORGE: (Seneca) Age 30 born in July 1870 in New York. Both of his parents were born in New York. Maggie his wife age 27 was born in October 1872 in New York. Both of her parents were born in New York. Lewellen YORK a sister-in-law age 17 was born in August 1882 in New York. E.D. 131, Page 214B, Household 197A.

JIMISON, HEWLEY: (Seneca) Age 56 born in May 1844 in New York. Both of his parents were born in New York. Both of his parents were Seneca. Mary his wife age 50 was born in December 1849 in New York. Both of her parents were Seneca. Cattaraugus County, Red House Town, Allegany Indian Reservation, E.D. 131, Page 201B, Household 63/63.

JIMISON, HORACE: (Seneca) Age 54 born in January 1846 in New York. Both of his parents were born in New York. Both of his parents were Seneca. Emily his wife age 46 was born in January 1854 in New York. Both of her parents were born in New York. Both of her parents were Seneca. Cattaraugus County, Coldspring Town, E.D. 131, Page 205B, Household 112/112.

JIMISON, HOWARD: (Seneca) Age 50 born in February 1850 in New York. Both of his parents were born in New York. Both of his parents were Seneca. Betsy his wife age 44 was born in March 1856 in New York. Both of her parents were born in New York. Both of her parents were Seneca. Lucy RED-EYE a step daughter age 13 was born in July 1886 in New York. Both of her parents were born in New York. Both of her parents were Seneca. Eva RED-EYE a step daughter age 5 was born in October 1894 in New York. Both of her parents were born in New York. Both of her parents were Seneca. Cattaraugus County, Elko Town, E.D. 131, Page 214B, Household 200.

JIMISON, JAMES: (Seneca) Age? born in New York. Both of his parents were born in New York. Both of his parents were Seneca. Ella his wife age 40 was born in April 1860 in New York. Both of her parents were born in New York. Both of her parents were Seneca. Mary a daughter age 25 was born in November 1874. Roger a son age 17 was born in December 1882. Clara a daughter age 16 was born in May 1884. Cattaraugus County, Cold Spring Town, E.D. 131, Page 207B, Household 131.

JIMISON, JANE: (Seneca) Age 80 born in February 1820 in New York. Both of her parents were born in New York. Both of her parents were Seneca. Hawley JIMISON a grandson age 17 was born in March 1883 in New York. Both of his parents were born in New York. Both of his parents were Seneca. No town name was given. Allegany Indian Reservation, E.D. 131, Page 204B, Household 101/101.

JIMISON, JENNY: (Seneca) Age 46 born in March 1854 in New York. Both of her parents were born in New York. Both of her parents were Seneca. Matilda A. JIMISON age 20 a adopted? or grand daughter? was born in February 1880 in New York (She was listed as white). Both of her parents were of English ancestry. Both of her parents were born in New York. Cattaraugus County, Salamanca Town, Allegany Indian Reservation, E.D. 131, Page 203A, Household 81/81.

JIMISON, JOHN: (Seneca) Age 52 born in March 1848 in New York. Both of his parents were born in New York. Both of his parents were Seneca. Malinda his wife age 32 was born in June 1867 in New York. Both of her parents were born in New York. Both of her parents were Seneca. Sadie a daughter age 12 was born in September 1887. Gertie a daughter age 10 was born in May 1890. Alice a daughter age 7 was born in August 1892. Silas a son age 3 was born in June 1896. Arthur a son age 1 was born in September 1898. Letitis BLINKEY mother-in-law (Of John Jimison) age 70 born in February 1830 in New York. Both of her parents were born in New York. Both of her parents were Seneca. George Gordon brother-in-law (Of John Jimison) age 55 was born in August 1844 in New York. Both of his parents were born in New York. Both of his parents were Seneca. Cattaraugus County, Red House Town, Allegany Indian Reservation, E.D. 131, Page 201B, Household 62/62.

JIMISON, JOSEPH: (Seneca) Age 66 born in May 1834 in New York. Both of his parents were born in New York. Both of his parents were listed as Seneca. E.D. 131, Page 197A, Household 10.

JIMISON, KING: (Seneca) Age 54 born in October 1845 in New York. Both of his parents were born in New York. Both of his parents were Seneca. Ursilla his wife age 49 was born in July 1850 in Canada. Both of her parents were born in Canada. She immigrated in 1865. Both of her parents were Abanaka (Abenaki). Chauncey JIMISON an adopted? son or grandson? age 18 was born in April 1882 in New York. Both of his parents were born in New York. Both of his parents were Seneca. Cattaraugus County, Salamanca Town, Alleghany Indian Reservation, E.D. 131, Page 203A, Household 86/86.

JIMISON, LORINDA: (Seneca) Age 20 was born in February 1880 in New York. Both of her parents were born in New York. Both of her parents were Seneca. Carrie Jimison, a sister, age 17 was born in March 1883 in New York. Uusie? JIMISON a niece age five months born in January 1900 in New York. Both of her parents were born in New York. Both of her parents were Seneca. Jennie CROUSE a boarder age 20 born in March

1880 in New York. Both of her parents were born in New York. Both of her parents were Seneca. Cattaraugus County, Red House Town, Allegany Indian Reservation, E.D. 131, Page 200A, Household 50/50.

JIMISON, LUCY: (Seneca) Age 65 was born in January 1835 in New York. Both of her parents were born in New York. Both of her parents were Seneca. William JOHN a son age 30 was born in May 1870 in New York. Both of his parents were born in New York. Both of his parents were Seneca. Olive JOHN a daughter-in-law age 20 was born in March 1880 in New York. Both of her parents were born in New York. Both of her parents were Seneca, Eva JOHN a grand daughter age 2 was born in February 1898. Margaret JOHN a grand daughter born in May 1900. Nettie? SHONGO a boarder was 24 was born in May 1876 in New York. Both of her parents were born in New York. Both of her parents were Seneca. William SHONGO a boarder was born in January 1900 in New York. Both of his parents were born in New York. Both of his parents were Seneca. Cattaraugus County, Salamanca Town, E.D. 131, Page 199B, Household 41/41.

JIMISON, MARTIN: (Seneca) Age 50 was born in January 1850 in New York. Both of his parents were born in New York. Both of his parents were Seneca. Anna his wife age 39 was born in September 1860 in New York. Both of her parents were born in New York. She was listed as an Onondaga. Her father was a Seneca. Her mother was an Onondaga, Clara a daughter age 11 was born in April 1889. Rebecka a daughter age 6 was born in July 1893. Andrew a son age 4 was born in April 1896. Claude a son age ten months was born in July 1899. The children of Martin Jimison were listed as Onondaga. Cattaraugus County, Cold Spring Town, E.D. 131, Page 209B, Household 149/149.

JIMISON, MATILDA: (Abanaka/Abenaki) Age 41 was born in August 1858 in Canada. Both of her parents were born in Canada. Both of her parents were listed as Abanaka. Clunde? a daughter age 12 was born in February 1888 in New York. Her father was born in New York. She was listed as an Abanaka. Her father was a Seneca. Her mother was an Abanaka. John a son age 8 was born in December 1891. Cattaraugus County, Red House Town, Allegany Indian Reservation, Page 201A, Household 58/58.

JIMISON, NATHAN: (Seneca) Age 31 was born in September 1868 in New York. Both of his parents were born in New York. Both of his parents were Seneca. Lucinda his wife age 31 was born in March 1869 in New York. Both of her parents were born in New York. She was listed as an Onondaga. Her father was a Seneca. Her mother was a Seneca? Carrie TURKEY a sister-in-law (Of Nathan Jimison) age 13 was born in March 1869 in New York. Both of her parents were born in New York. She was listed as an Onondaga. Her father was a Seneca. Her mother was an Onondaga. E.D. 131, Page 199A, Household 40.

JIMISON, NELSON: (Seneca) Age 27 was born in March 1878 in New York. Both of his parents were born in New York. Both of his parents were Seneca. Monroe a son age 9 was born in May 1891 in New York. Both of his parents were born in New York. Both of his parents were Seneca. Delilah JIMISON mother (Of Nelson JIMISON) age 67 was born in January? or June? in 1833 in New York. Both of her parents were born in New York. Both of her parents were Seneca. Cattaraugus County, Red House Town, Allegany Indian Reservation, Page 200A, Household 4/47.

JIMISON, QUILLTIS? (Male Seneca) Age 20 was born in May 1880 in New York. Both of his parents were born in New York. Both of his parents were Seneca. Cattaraugus County, E.D. 131, Page 199A, Household 32.

JIMISON, ROGER: (Seneca) Age 48 was born in May 1852 in New York. Both of his parents were born in New York. Both of his parents were Seneca. Mary A., his wife age 47 was born in April 1853 in New York. Both of her parents were born in New York. Both of her parents were Seneca. Blanche BOMBERY a grand daughter age 7 was born in September 1892 in New York. Both of her parents were born in New York. Both of her parents were Seneca. Cattaraugus County, E.D. 131, Salamanca Town, Allegheny Indian Reservation, Page 203B, Household 90/90.

JIMISON, SUSAN: (Seneca) Age 65 was born in May 1835 in New York. Both of her parents were born in New York. Both of her parents were Seneca. Jennett DOCKSTADER a boarder age 75 was born in December 1824 in New York. Both of her parents were born in New York. Both of her parents were Oneida. Cattaraugus County, Red House Town, Allegany Indian Reservation, E.D. 131, Page 201A, Household 61/61.

JIMISON, THOMAS: (Seneca) Age 40 was born in April 1860 in New York. Both of his parents were born in New York. Both of his parents were Seneca Cattaraugus County, Allegany Indian Reservation, E.D. 131, Page 204B, Household 100/100.

JIMISON, WILLET: (Seneca) Age 52 was born in May 1848 in New York. Both of his parents were born in New York. Both of his parents were Seneca. Amelia his wife age 34 was born in August 1865 in New York. Both of her parents were born in New York. Both of her parents were Seneca. Eugene JIMISON a grand son age 8 born in September 1891. Page 201A, Household 59/59.

JIMISON, WILLETT: (Seneca) Age 22 was born in March 1878 in New York. Both of his parents were born in New York. Both of his parents were Seneca. Carrie his wife age 19 was born in December 1880 in New York. Both of her parents were born in New York. Both of her parents were Seneca. Cattaraugus County, Coldspring Town, E.D. 131, Page 205B, Household 111/111.

JIMISON, WILLIAM: (Seneca) Age 43 was born in August 1856 in New York. Both of his parents were born in New York. Both of his parents were Seneca. Lucinkey? his wife age 45 was born in 1854 in New York. Both of her parents were born in New York. Both of her parents were Seneca. Winfiled JIMISON age 22 an adopted son was born in December 1877 in New York. Both of his parents were born in New York. Both of his parents were Seneca. Cattaraugus County, Perrysburg, E.D. 135, Page 224B, Household 32 or 222/224.

JIMISON, WILLIS: (Seneca) Age 40 was born in May 1860 in New York. Both of his parents were born in New York. Both of his parents were Seneca. Mary his wife age 35 was born in April 1865 in New York. Both of her parents were born in New York. Both of her parents were Seneca. Alex ABRAM a step son age 15 was born in May 1885 in New York. Both of his parents were born in New York. Both of his parents were Seneca. Cattaraugus County, E.D. 131, Page 198A, Household 23.

JOE, JESSE: (Seneca) Age 50 was born in January 1850 in New York. Both of his parents were born in New York. Both of his parents were Seneca. Jane his wife was age 49. No birth date information was given. Both of her parents were born in New York. Both of her parents were Seneca. Rachel KING age 9 a grand daughter was born in March 1891 in New York. Both of her parents were born in New York. Both of her parents were Seneca. Cattaraugus County, Leon Town, E.D. 48, Page 20A, Household 255/257.

JOHN, ALPHONS? OF ALPHEUS? (Seneca) Age 38 was born in February 1862 in New York. Both of his parents were born in New York. Both of his parents were Seneca. Anna his wife age 39 was born in February 1879 in New York. Both of her parents were born in New York. Both of her parents were Seneca. Layfaett (As spelled) a son age 21 was born in February 1879. Perry a son age 19 was born in September 1880. Cora a daughter age 14 was born in April 1886. Beander? a son age 12 was born in February 1888. Jennie a daughter age 7 was born in April 1893. Alpheus Jr., a son age 5 was born in March 1895. Louncey? a daughter age 2 was born in March 1895. Cattaraugus County, South Valley Town, E.D. 131, Page 215A, Household 210.

JOHN, AUSTIN: (Seneca) Age 58 was born in February 1842 in New York. Both of his parents were born in New York. Both of his parents were Seneca. Olive his wife age 40 was born in May 1860. Cattaraugus County, Perrysburg, E.D. 135, Page 221B, Household 12 or 179/180.

JOHN, CALRINDA? (OR CLARINDA?) (Seneca) Age 43 was born in New York. Both of her parents were born in New York. Both of her parents were Seneca. E.D. 131, Page 199A, Household 37.

JOHN, CASLER: (Seneca) Age 54 was born in August 1845 in New York. Both of his parents were born in New York. Both of his parents were Seneca. Elizabeth his wife age 47 was born in December 1852 in New York. Both of her parents were born in New York. Both of her parents were Seneca. Leonard a son age 10 was born in January 1880. Marcus a son age 6 was born in June 1893. Cattaraugus County, Red House Town, Allegany Indian Reservation, E.D. 131, Page 202B, Household 79/79.

JOHN, CORDELIA: (Seneca) Age 55 was born in New York. Both of her parents were born in New York. Both of her parents were Seneca. Harrison STOCKWELL (He was listed as a white man) a boarder age 59 was born in March 1841 in New York. Both of his parents were of Scotch descent. Frank STOCKWELL adopted son (Of Harrison Stockwell?) age 4 born in May 1896 in New York. Both of his parents were born in New York. He was listed as an Indian. Both of his parents were Seneca. Charles PLUMMER a boarder was age 5 born in 1895. Both of his parents were Seneca. Cattaraugus County, Red House Town, Allegany Indian Reservation, E.D. 131, Page 202A, Household 72/72.

JOHN, DANIEL: (Seneca) Age 24 was born in February 1876 in New York. Both of his parents were born in New York. He was listed as a Seneca. His father was a Seneca. His mother was a white woman. Martha his wife age 23 was born in December 1876 in New York. Both of her parents were born in New York. She was listed as a Cayuga. Her father was a Seneca. Her mother was a Cayuga. Gertrude BROOKS sister-in-law (Of Daniel John) age 25 was born in May 1875 in New York. Both of her parents were born in New York. She was also listed as a Cayuga. Perrysburg, Cattaraugas County, Cattaraugus Reservation, E.D. 135, Page 221A, Household 4 or 171//172.

JOHN, FRANK: (Seneca) Age 28 was born in February 1872 in New York. Both of his parents were born in New York. Both of his parents were Seneca. Carrie his wife age 26 was born in April 1874 in New York. Both of her parents were born in New York. Both of her parents were Seneca. Ulyses J., a son age 3 was born in June 1896. Leland a son age 1 was born in September 1898. Louella a daughter was born in May 1900. Cattaraugus County, Coldspring Town, E.D. 131, Page 205A, Household 108/108.

JOHN, HENRY: (Seneca) Age 24 was born in April 1876 in New York. Both of his parents were born in New York. Both of his parents were Seneca. Lucy his wife age 20 was born in May 1880 in New York. Both of her parents were born in New York. Both of her parents were Seneca. E.D. 131, Page 199B. Household 18.

JOHN, JOSEPH: (Seneca) Age 70 was born in May 1830 in New York. Both of his parents were born in New York. Both of his parents were Seneca. Mary (Seneca) his wife age 65 was born in February 1825 in New York. Both of her parents were born in New York. Both of her parents were Seneca. E.D. 131, Page 196B, Household 8.

JOHN, LEWIS: (Seneca) Age 57 was born in March 1843 in New York. Both of his parents were born in New York. Both of his parents were Seneca. Eliza his wife age 48 was born in February 1852 in New York. Both of her parents were born in New York. Both of her parents were Seneca. Perry a son age 20 born in June 1879. Cattaraugus County, Coldspring Town, E.D. 131, Page 210A, Household 157/157.

JOHN, LUCINDA: (Seneca) Age 25 was born in February 1875 in New York. Both of her parents were born in New York. Both of her parents were Seneca. Lilly DYE (No relationship was given) age 30 was born in February 1870 in New York. Both of her parents were born in New York. Both of her parents were Seneca. Jerome HALFTOWN a boarder age 29 was born in June 1870 in New York. Both of his parents were born in New York. Both of his parents were Seneca. Cornelius FALTY age 20 was born in February 1880 in New York. Both of his parents were born in New York. Both of his parents were Seneca. Cattaraugus County, Red House Town, Allegany Indian Reservation, E.D. 131, Page 202A, Household 73.

JOHN, MARY A.: (Seneca) Age 53 was born in January 1847 in New York. Both of her parents were born in New York. Both of her parents were Seneca. Cattaraugus County, E.D. 131, Page 204A, Red Horse Town, Allegany Indian Reservation, Household 96/96.

JOHN, MARY: (Seneca) Age 71 was born in August in 1828 in New York. Both of her parents were born in New York. Both of her parents were Seneca. Austin a son age 27 was born in February 1873 in New York. Both of his parents were born in New York. Both of his parents were Seneca. Cattaraugus County, Cold Spring Town, E.D. 131, Page 208B, Household 141/141.

JOHN, OLIVER: (Seneca) Age 28 was born in February 1872 in New York. Both of his parents were born in New York. Both of his parents were Seneca. Lilly his wife age 24 was born in June 1875 in New York. Both of her parents were born in New York. Both of her parents were Seneca. Richard a son age 2 born in September 1897. Cattaraugus County, Coldspring Town, E.D. 131, Page 205A, Household 106/106.

JOHN, STEPHEN: (Seneca) Age 42 was born in March 1858 in New York. Both of his parents were born in New York. Both of his parents were Seneca. Malfina? or Malbina? his wife age 39 was born in May 1861 in New York. Both of her parents were born in New York. Both of her parents were Seneca. Clarence a son age 14 was born in July 1880. Fleta a daughter age 17 was born in July 1882. Delara a daughter age 15 was born in June 1884. Clinton a son age 12 was born in December 1882. Lena a daughter age 7 was born in March 1893. Eva a daughter age 4 was born in March 1896. Cattaraugas County, Red House Town, Allegany Indian Reservation, E.D. 131, Page 200A, Household 52/52.

JOHN, WILLIAM: (Seneca) Age 58 was born in ? 1849 in New York. Both of his parents were born in New York. Both of his parents were Seneca. Mary his wife age 47 was born in January 1852 in New York. Both of her parents were born in New York. Both of her parents were Seneca. Lydia CROUSE a sister-in-Law (Of William John) age 34 was born in May 1866 in New York. Both of her parents were born in New York. Ulta or Alta DOXTATOR a niece age 6 was born in January 1893 in New York. Ellen DOXTATOR a niece age 6 was born in May 1894 in New York. Harold JOHN a nephew age 1 was born in May 1899 in New York. Cattaraugus County, Perrysburg, E.D. 135, Page 221A, Household 9 or 176/177.

JOHN, WILLIE: (Seneca) Age 43 was born in March 1857 in New York. Both of his parents were born in New York. Both of his parents were Seneca. William his father age 65 was born in ? 1834 in New York. Both of his parents were born in New York. Both of his parents were Seneca. Cattaraugus County, Perrysburg, E.D. 135, Page 222B, Household 18 or 185/186.

JOHNNYJOHN (OF JOHNNY JOHN) CYRUS: (Seneca) Age 56 was born in January 1843 in New York. Both of his parents were born in New York. Both of his parents were Seneca. Louisa his wife age 55 was born in March 1845 in New York. Both of her parents were born in New York. Both of her parents were Seneca. Lewis a son age 28 was born in June 1876. Mary JOHNSON a grand daughter age 9 was born in September 1890. Cattaraugus County, Perrysburg, E.D. 135, Page 224A, Household 27, Page 216/217.

JOHNSON, LYDIA: (Seneca) Age 35 was born in January 1864 in New York. Both of her parents were born in New York. Both of her parents were Seneca. Johnathan a son age 22 was born in May 1878. Mabel a daughter was born in January 1881. Bertha a daughter age 13 was born in January 1887. Arthur a son age 9 was born in February 1890. Emma daughter age 4 was born in June? 1895. Harvey a son age 3 was born in May 1897. Joseph SILVERHEELS a boarder age 60 was born in ? 1839 in New York. both of his parents were born in New York. Both of her parents were Seneca. E.D. & Page information unclear.

JONES, ALIN? OR ALUMN? (Seneca) Age 31 was born in May 1869 in New York. Both of his parents were born in New York. Both of his parents were Seneca. Hattie his wife age 21 was born in New York. Both of her parents were born in New York. Both of her parents were Seneca. E.D. 131, Page 202B, Household 76.

JONES, FRANCIS: (Seneca) Age 68 was born in May 1832 in New York. Both of his parents were born in New York. Both of his parents were Seneca. Elizabeth his wife age 48 was born in October 1851 in New York. Both of her parents were born in New York. Both of her parents were Seneca. Frank a son age 25 was born in May 1875. Cristine GREEN a grand daughter age 3 was born in September 1896 in New York. Both of her parents were born in New York. Both of her parents were Seneca. Cattaraugus County, Red House Town, Allegany Indian Reservation, E.D. 131, Page 202B, Household 75/75.

JONES, JOSIAH: (Seneca) Age 66 was born in June 1834 in New York. Both of his parents were born in New York. Both of his parents were Seneca. Mary his wife age 55 was born in May 1844 in New York. Both of her parents were born in New York. Both of her parents were Seneca. Orrin a son age 27 was born in March 1873. Ruby a daughter age 16 was born in November 1883. Cattaraugus County, Red House Town, Allegany Indian Reservation, E.D. 131, Page 202B, Household 77/77.

JONNEYJOHN (OR JOHNNY-JOHN) CHAUNCEY: (Seneca) Age 32 was born in May 1868 in New York. Both of his parents were Seneca. Amos a son age 10 was born in April 1890. Lydia JONNEY JOHN mother (Of Chauncey Jonney-John) age 80 was born in January 1820 in New York. Both of her parents were born in New York. Both of her parents were Seneca. Cattaraugus County, Elko Town, E.D. 131, Page 214B, Household 199.

KENJOCKETY, HENRY: (Seneca) Age 28 was born in May 1872 in New York. Both of his parents were born in New York. Both of his parents were Seneca. Nancy his wife age 33 was born in August in 1866 in New York. Both of her parents were born in New York. Both of her parents were Seneca. Harry a son age 11 was born in July 1888. Arthur a son age 5 was born in August 1894. A baby Kenjockety daughter age 2 was born in September 1897. Cattaraugus County, Cold Spring Town, E.D. 131, Page 207A, Household 130/130.

KENJOCKETY, ISAAC: (Seneca) Age 58 was born in May 1842 in New York. Both of his parents were born in New York. He was a Seneca. Both of his parents were Seneca. Sytha? his wife age 55 was born in July 1844 in New York. Both of her parents were born in New York. She was an Onondaga. Both of her parents were Onondaga. Fred a son age 22 was born in January 1878 in New York. Eli a son age 18 was born in March 1882 in New York. Both of the sons of Isaac Kenjockety were listed as Seneca. Both of their parents were listed as Seneca. Cattaraugus County, Cold Spring Town, E.D. 131, Page 207A, Household 129/129.

KENJOCKETY, JESSIE: (Seneca) Age 56 was born in March 1844 in New York. Both of his parents were born in New York. Both of her parents were Seneca. Julia his wife age 48 was born in May 1852 in New York. Both of her parents were born in New York. Both of her parents were Seneca. Cattaraugus County, Cold Spring Town, E.D. 131, Page 209A, Household 146/146.

KENJOCKETY, JOCLYN (Male Seneca) Age ? born in September 1889 in New York. Both of his parents were born in New York. Both of his parents were Seneca. Dora his wife age 25 was born in May 1875 in York. Both of her parents were born in New York. Both of her parents were Seneca. E.D. 131, Page 199A, Household 34.

KENNEDY, AUGUSTUS: (Seneca) Age 42 was born in December 1857 in New York. Both of his parents were born in New York. Both of his parents were Seneca. His father was a Seneca. His mother was a white woman. Town of Hanover, Chautauqua County, E.D. 135, page 225B, Household 41.

KENT, ABBY: (Seneca) Age 57 was born in March 1843 in New York. Both of her parents were born in New York. Both of her parents were Seneca. Marion KENT husband (Of Abby Kent) was age 56 was born in September 1843 in Pennsylvania. Both of his parents were born in Pennsylvania. He was listed as a white man. Cattaraugus County, E.D. 131, Red House Town, Allegany Indian Reservation, Page 204A, Household 95/95.

KILLBUCK, JOHN: (Seneca) Age 58 was born in September 1841 in New York. Both of his parents were born in New York. Both of his parents were Seneca. Emma his wife age 50 born in May 1850 in New York. Both of her parents were born in New York. Both of her parents were Seneca. Ida CURRY a boarder age 40 was born in April 1860 in New York. Both of her parents were born in New York. Both of her parents were Seneca. Eugene CURRY a cousin (Of Ida Curry?) age 1 was born in March 1899. Both of his parents were Seneca. Cattaraugus County, Elko Town, E.D. 131, Page 214A, Household 193.

KING, BETSEY: (Seneca) Age 83 was born in April 1817 in New York. Both of her parents were born in New York. Both of her parents were Seneca. Axy GORDON age 37 a daughter was born in May 1863 in New York. Both of her parents were born in New York. Both of her parents were Seneca. Cattaraugus County, Red House Town, E.D. 131, Page 202A, Household 70/70.

KING, JENNIE: (Seneca) Age 36 was born in July 1863 in New York. Both of her parents were born in New York. Both of her parents were Seneca. Augustus JOHNSON a boarder age 48 was born in April 1852 in New York. Both of his parents were born in New York. Both of his parents were Seneca. Richard JONES a half brother (Of Jennie King? or Augustus Johnson?) age 31 was born in April 1869 in New York. Both of his parents were born in New York. Both of his parents were Seneca. Cattaraugus County, Salamanca Town, Allegany Indian Reservation, E.D. 131 Page 199B, Household 42/42.

KING, MARY: (Seneca) Age 57 was born in February 1843 in New York. Both of her parents were born in New York. Both of her parents were Seneca. Cattaraugus County, Red House Town, Allegany Indian Reservation, E.D. 131, Page 200A, Household 48/48.

LEE, WILLIAM: (Seneca) Age 53 was born in January 1847 in New York. Both of his parents were born in New York. Both of his parents were Seneca. Eliza his wife age 46 was born in February 1854 in New York. Both of her parents were born in New York. Both of her parents were Seneca. Belinda a daughter age 15 was born in March 1885. Chauncey a son age 12 was born in April 1888. Cattaraugus County, Cold Spring Town, E.D. 131, Page 209B, Household 151/151.

LEWIS, ELLIOTT: (Seneca) Age ? born in October 1856 in New York. Both of his parents were born in New York. Both of his parents were Seneca. Lucinda his wife age 43 was born in September 1856 in New York. Both of her parents were born in New York. Both of her parents were Seneca. Wilson JIMISON a boarder age 43 was born in September 1856 in New York. Both of his parents were born in New York. Both of his parents were Seneca. E.D. 131, Page 199A, Household 36.

LEWIS, ELLIOTT: (Seneca) Age 43 was born in October 1856 in New York. Both of his parents were born in New York. Both of his parents were Seneca. Laura PIERCE a sister (Of Elliott Lewis) was age 37 born in August 1862 in New York. Both of her parents were born in New York. Both of her parents were Seneca. Cattaraugus County, Salamanca Town, Allegany Indian Reservation, E.D. 131, Page 203A, Household 83/83.

LEWIS, JOHN: (Seneca) Age 42 was born in April 1858 in New York. Both of his parents were born in New York. Both of his parents were Seneca. Julia his wife age 30 born in May 1870 in New York. Both of her parents were born in New York. Both of her parents were Seneca. E.D. 131, Page 197A, Household 9.

LOGAN, HENRY: (Seneca) Age 38 was born in January 1862 in New York. Both of his parents were born in New York. Both of his parents were Seneca. Lucy his wife age 40 was born in March 1860 in New York. Both of her parents were born in New York. She was listed as an Onondaga. Her father was a Seneca. Her mother was an Onondaga. Nelson a son age 22 was born in August 1877 in New York. Lucy JACKSON mother-in-law (Of Henry Logan) was age 70 was born in February 1830 in New York. Both of her parents were born in New York. She was listed as an Onondaga. Her father was a Seneca. Her mother was an Onondaga. Jessie JACKSON brother-in-Law (Of Henry Logan) age 44 was born in May 1856 in New York. He was listed as an Onondaga. His father was a Seneca. His mother was an Onondaga. All of the children of Henry Logan were listed as Onondaga. Cattaraugus County, South Valley Town, E.D. 131, Page 215A, Household 206.

LOGAN, HOWARD: (Seneca) Age 28 was born in January 1872 in New York. Both of his parents were born in New York. Both of his parents were Seneca. Rose his wife age 26 was born in January 1873 in New York. Both of her parents were born in New York. Both of her parents were Seneca. Cattaraugus County, Coldspring Town, Page 206B, Household 121/121.

LOGAN, JACK: (Seneca) Age 24 was born in January 1886 in New York. Both of his parents were born in New York. Both of his parents were Seneca. Eliza his wife age 22 was born in February 1878 in New York. Both of her parents were born in New York. Both of her parents were Seneca. Lorency a daughter was born in December 1899. Cattaraugus County, Cold Spring Town, E.D. 131, Page 207B, Household 132/132.

LOGAN, LEWIS: (Seneca) Age 30 was born in September 1869 in New York. Both of his parents were born in New York. Both of his parents were

Seneca. Perrysburg, Cattaraugus County, E.D. 135, Page 224B, Household 35.

LOGAN, LUCY: (Seneca) Age 52 was born in September 1847 in New York. Both of her parents were born in New York. Both of her parents were Seneca. James GORDON a grand son age 18 was born in April 1882 in New York. Both of his parents were born in New York. Both of his parents were Seneca. William COOPER a grand son age 9 was born in August 1890 in New York. Both of his parents were born in New York. Both of his parents were Seneca. Della GORDON a grand daughter age 24 was born in March 1876 in New York. Both of her parents were born in New York. Both of her parents were Seneca. Cattaraugus County, Coldspring Town, E.D. 131, Page 207A, Household 126/126.

LONG? OR LENZ? MARTHA: (Seneca) Age 32 was born in August 1867 in New York. both of her parents were born in New York. Both of her parents were Seneca. Benjamin her husband (He was listed as white) age 39 was born in December 1860 in Germany. Both of his parents were born in Germany. Cattaraugus County, Elko Town, E.D. 131, Page 214B, Household 203.

LONGFINGER, LEWIS: (Seneca) Age 36 was born in February 1864 in New York. Both of his parents were born in New York. Both of his parents were Seneca. Louisa his wife age 37 was born in March 1863 in New York. Both of her parents were born in New York. Both of her parents were Seneca. Cattaraugas County, Perrysburg, E.D. 135, Page 221A, Household 6 or 173/174.

LUKE, JAMES: (Seneca) Age 27 was born in June in 1872 in New York. Both of his parents were born in New York. Both of his parents were Seneca. Cordelia his wife age 29 was born in August 1875 in New York. Both of her parents were born in New York. Both of her parents were Seneca. Hannibal GORDON a step son age 7 was born in December 1892 in New York. Both of his parents were born in New York. Both were Seneca. Chautauqua County, Perrysburg, E.D. 135, Page 225B, Household 40

MAYBEE, HARPER: (Onondaga/Seneca) Age 24 was born in February 1876 in New York. Both of his parents were born in New York. He was listed as an Onondaga. His father was a Seneca. His mother was an Onondaga. Sarah his wife age 26 was born in May 1874 in New York. Both of her parents were born in New York. She was listed as an Abenaka. Her father was a Seneca. Her mother was an Abenaka. Lillie a daughter age 3 was born in July 1896. Beatrice a daughter age 1 was born in July 1898. The children of Harper MAYBEE were all listed as Abenaka. Cattaraugus County, South Valley Town, E.D. 131, Page 215A, Household 207.

MOHAWK, ELIZA: (Seneca) Age 61 was born in 1838 in New York. Both of her parents were born in New York. Both of her parents were Seneca. Christine WINNIE a daughter age 32 was born in June 1868 in New York. Both of her parents were born in New York. Both of her parents were Seneca. Lilah WATERMAN a grand daughter age 7 was born in April 1893. She was listed as a Seneca. Her father was a Munsee. Her mother was a Seneca. Opha WINNIE an adopted daughter (Of Christin WINNIE) age two months was born in March 1900. Both of her parents were Seneca.

Cattaraugus County, Perrysburg, E.D. 135, Page 223A, Household 21, or 188/189.

MOHAWK, ORLANDO: (Seneca) Age 39 was born in December 1869 in New York. Both of his parents were born in New York. Both of his parents were Seneca. Lydia his wife age 26 was born in May 1874 in New York. Both of her parents were born in New York. Her father was a Seneca. Her father was an Onondaga. Her mother was a Seneca. Perrysburg, Cattaraugus County, E.D. 135, Page 224B, Household 31 or 221/223.

MOHAWK, ORRIN: (Seneca) Age 27 was born in August 1872 in New York. Both of his parents were born in New York. Both of his parents were Seneca. Ida his wife age 43 was born in July 1856 in New York. Both of her parents were born in New York. Both of her parents were Seneca. Levi FARMER a stepson age 22 was born in December 1877. Harry FARMER a stepson age 20 was born in February 1880. Both Farmer children were listed as Seneca. Their father was a Seneca. Perrysburg, Cattaraugus County, E.D. 135, Page 224B, Household 33.

MOHAWK, WILLIAM: (Munsi of Munsee) Age 86 was born in December 1813 in New York. Both of his parents were born in New York. He was enumerated as a Munsi. Both of his parents were Munci. Electa his wife age 77 was born in January 1823 in New York. Both of her parents were born in New York. Both of her parents were Seneca. Cattaraugus County, Red House Town, E.D. 131, Page 201A, Household 57/57.

MOSES, AMOS: (Seneca) Age 65 was born in January 1835 in New York. Both of his parents were born in New York. Both of his parents were Seneca. Cattaraugus County, Perrysburg, Page 221A, Household 8 or 175/176.

NEPHEW, FILO: (Seneca) Age 27 was born in May 1878 in New York. Both of his parents were born in New York. Both of his parents were Seneca. Phobe his wife age 28 was born in October 1871 in New York. Both of her parents were born in New York. Both of her parents were Seneca. Hellen a daughter age 10 was born in January 1880? Lorena a daughter age 6 was born in May 1884? Oscar a son age 2 was born in May 1898. The dates or ages of Hellen NEPHEW and Lorena NEPHEW appear to be in error. Cattaraugus County, Cold Spring Town, E.D. 131, Page 210B, Household 163/163.

NEPHEW, JEROME: (Seneca) Age 39 was born in April 1861 in New York. Both of his parents were born in New York. Both of his parents were Seneca. Cattaraugus County, Perryburg, E.D. 135, Page 222A, Household 182/183.

NEPHEW, PERCIVAL: (Seneca) Age 35 was born in May 1865 in New York. Both of his parents were born in New York. Both of his parents were Seneca. Alice his wife age 28 was born in May 1872 in New York. Both of her parents were Seneca. Marion PIERCE a daughter age 10 was born in May 1889. Raymond NEPHEW a nephew age 7 was born in March 1893. Both of his parents were Seneca. Arthur a son age 3 was born in June ? 1896. Lester a son age 1 was born in September 1898. Cattaraugus County, Perrysburg, E.D. 135, Page 224A, Household 26 or 217/218.

176

NEPHEW, ROBERT: (Seneca) Age 59 was born in October 1840 in New York. Both of his parents were born in New York. Both of his parents were Seneca. Cattaraugus County, Elko Town, E.D. 131, Page 214B, Household 202.

NEPHEW, WILLETT: (Seneca) Age 41 was born in January 1858 in New York. Both of his parents were born in New York. Both of his parents were Seneca. Catherine his wife age 46 was born in May 1854 in New York. both of her parents were born in New York. Her father was a Seneca. Her mother was a white woman. Christopher a son age 3 was born in January 1897 in New York. He was listed as a Seneca. Lena JOHN a boarder age 5 was born in October 1894 in New York. Both of her parents were born in New York. She was listed as a Seneca. Her father was a Seneca. Her mother was listed as half white. Cattaraugus County, Perrysburg, E.D. 135, Page 221A, Household 10 or 179/178.

NEPHEW, WILLIAM: (Seneca) Age 70 was born in September 1829 in New York. Both of his parents were born in New York. Both of his parents were Seneca. Nancy his wife age 69 was born in March 1831 in New York. Both of her parents were born in New York. Both of her parents were Seneca. Ulyses a son age 30 was born in November 1869. Lorenza? a daughter-in-law age 27 was born in January in 1873 in New York. Both of her parents were born in New York. Both of her parents were Seneca. Cattaraugus County, Perrysburg, E.D. 135, Page 222A, Household 16 or 183/184.

PALMER, ELI: (Seneca) Age 40 was born in February 1860 in New York. Both of his parents were born in New York. Both of his parents were Seneca. Emma his wife age 44 was born in August 1855 in New York. Both of her parents were born in New York. Both of her parents were Seneca. E.D. 131, Page 198B, Household 26.

PATTERSON, DAVID: (Seneca) Age 55 was born in June? in 1844 in New York. Both of his parents were born in New York. Both of his parents were Seneca. Martha his wife age 54 was born in ? in New York. Both of her parents were born in New York. She was listed as an Onondaga. Her father was a Seneca. Her mother was an Onondaga. Carrie a daughter age 30. Mildred a daughter age 28. Abner a son age 27. (All children were listed as Seneca) Ethel M. PLUMMER a grand daughter age 3 was born in November 1896 in New York. Both of her parents were born in New York. She was listed as an Onondaga. Her father was a Seneca. Her mother was an Onondaga. Perrysburg, Cattaraugus County, E.D. 135, Page 221B, Household 11 or 178/179.

PATTERSON, SACKET: (Seneca) Age 61 was born in May 1839 in New York. Both of his parents were born in New York. Both of his parents were Seneca. Cattaraugus County, Coldspring Town, E.D. 131, Page 206A, Household 117/117.

PATTERSON, THOMAS: (Seneca) Age 44 was born in May 1856 in New York. Both of his parents were born in New York. Both of his parents were Seneca. Louisa his wife age 44 was born in June 1855 in New York. Both of her parents were born in New York. E.D. 131, Page 199A, Household 34.

PATTERSON, WILLIAM: (Seneca) Age 53 was born in March 1847 in New York. Both of his parents were born in New York. Both of his parents were Seneca. Mary his wife? age 50 was born in May 1850 in New York. Both of her parents were born in New York. Both of her parents were Seneca. George a son age 25 was born in May 1850. Susie a daughter age 20 was born in March 1880. Cora a daughter age 18 was born in April 1882. Ada a daughter age 16 born in July 1884. Ella a daughter age 9 was born in December 1890. Daniel a son age 6 born in October 1893. Cattaraugus County, Coldspring Town, E.D. 131, Page 206A, Household 116/116.

PIERCE, ABLE: (Onondaga/Seneca) Age 50 was born in March 1850 in New York. Both of his parents were born in New York. He was listed as an Onondaga. His father was a Seneca. His mother was an Onondaga. Ester his wife age 47 was born in March 1853 in New York. Both of her parents were born in New York. Both of her parents were Seneca. Cattaraugus County, South Valley Town, E.D. 131, Page 216A, Household 215/215.

PIERCE, ALBERT: (Onondaga/Seneca) Age 50 was born in February 1850 in New York. Both of his parents were born in New York. He was listed as an Onondaga. His father was a Seneca. His mother was an Onondaga. Hanah his wife age 46 was born in October 1853 in New York. Both of her parents were born in New York. She was listed as a Seneca. Her father was an Onondaga. Her mother was a Seneca. Harvey a son age 17 was born in April 1883. Alice M., a daughter age 16? was born in November 1888. Albert Jr., a son age 8 was born in March 1892. Anna B., a daughter age 5 was born in February 1895. Lilla E., a daughter age 2 was born in May 1898. All of the children were in this household were listed as Seneca. Cattaraugus County, South Valley Town, E.D. 131, Page 216A, Household 216.

PIERCE, CHARLES: (Seneca) Age 30 was born in May 1870 in New York. Both of his parents were born in New York. Both of his parents were Seneca. Lilly his wife (She was listed as a white woman) age 23 was born in February 1877 in New York. Both of her parents were born in New York.. Her parents were of English descent. Grace a daughter age 3 was born in July 1896. Bessie a daughter was born in January 1898. Bertha a daughter was born in January 1900. Abigail PIERCE mother (Of Charles Pierce) age 80 was born in April 1820 in New York. Both of her parents were born in New York. Both of her parents were Seneca. Cattaraugus County, South Valley Town, E.D. 131, Page 215A, Household 205.

PIERCE, CLINTON: (Seneca) Age 53 was born in July 1846 in New York. Both of his parents were born in New York. Both of his parents were Seneca. Amelia his wife age 51 was born in October 1848 in New York. Both of her parents were born in New York. She was listed as an Onondaga. Her father was a Seneca. Her mother was an Onondaga. Harry a son age 20 was born in May 1880. Lee a son age 17 was born in October 1882. Tip a son age 12 was born in August 1887. Clyde a son age 8 was born in January 1892. All the children of Clinton Pierce were listed as Onondaga. Cattaraugus County, South Vallley Town, E.D. 131, Page 217A, Household 226.

PIERCE, EDWIN: (Seneca/Onondaga) Age 29 was born in July 1870 in New York. Both of his parents were born in New York. His father was an Onondaga. His mother was a Seneca. Edna his wife age 22 was born in May ? in New York. His wife was listed as a Seneca. Cattaraugus County, Salamanca Town, Page 119A, E.D. 71.

PIERCE, FRANK: (Seneca) Age 46 was born in May 1854 in New York. Both of his parents were born in New York. Both of his parents were Seneca. Ida his wife age 40 was born in February 1860 in New York. Both of her parents were born in New York. Both of her parents were Seneca. Frank Jr., a son age 20 was born in December 1879 in New York. Cattaraugus County, South Valley Town, E.D. 131, page 215B, Household 211.

PIERCE, FRANK: (Seneca) Age 43 was born in June 1856 in New York. Both of his parents were born in New York. Both of his parents were Seneca. Elizabeth his wife age 41 was born in November 1858 in New York. Both of her parents were Seneca. Cattaraugus County, South Valley Town, E.D. 131, Page 215B, Household 213/213.

PIERCE, HENRY: (Seneca) Age 42 was born in February 1858 in New York. Both of his parents were born in New York. Both of his parents were Seneca. Lilly his wife age 40 was born in November 1859 in New York. Both of her parents were born in New York. Both of her parents were Seneca. Serena a daughter age 12was born in September 1887. Christe? a son age 9 was born in September 1890. Cattaraugus County, South Valley Town, E.D. 131, Page 216A, Household 220/220.

PIERCE, LUCINDA: (Seneca) Age 68 was born in February 1832 in New York. Both of her parents were born in New York. Both of her parents were Seneca. James a brother age 62 was born in May 1838 in New York. Cora CROUSE a daughter-in-law age 24 was born in March 1876 in New York. Both of her parents were born in New York. Both of her parents were Seneca. Iva CROUSE a grand daughter age 5 was born in February 1895 in New York. Both of her parents were born in New York. Cattaraugus County, Elko Town, E.D. 131, Page 211B, Household 170/170.

PIERCE, LYDIA: (Seneca) Age 70 was born in May 1830 in New York. Both of her parents were born in New York. Both of her parents were Seneca. Cattaraugus County, Elko Town, E.D. 131, Page 214B, Household 204.

PIERCE, LYMAN: (Seneca) Age 56 was born in January 1844 in New York. Both of his parents were born in New York. Both of his parents were Seneca. Emma his wife age 46 was born in May 1854 in New York. Both of her parents were born in New York. Fred RED-EYE a son in law age 24 was born in May 1876 in New York. Both of his parents were born in New York. Both of his parents were Seneca. Harrison PIERCE a brother (Of Lyman Pierce) age 58 was born in June 1842 in New York. Both of his parents were born in New York. Both of his parents were listed as Seneca. Cattaraugus County, E.D. 131, Page 196A.

PIERCE, MARINA? OR MARIAN? (Seneca) Age 40 was born in May 1860 in New York. Both of her parents were born in New York. Both of her parents were Seneca. Webster PIERCE (He was listed as white?) an adopted son age 27 was born in December 1892 in New York. Both of his parents were born in New York. Cattaraugus County, E.D. 131, Page 199A, Household 38.

PIERCE, MARY: (Seneca) Age 45 was born in March 1855 in New York. Both of her parents were born in New York. Both of her parents were Seneca. Floyd Pierce a grand son age 15 was born in May 1885. Both of his parents were Seneca. Cattaraugus County, South Valley Town, E.D. 131, page 215B, Household 214/214.

PIERCE, THOMAS: (Seneca) Age 55 was born in April 1845 in New York. Both of his parents were born in New York. Both of his parents were Seneca. Cattaraugus County, South Valley Town, E.D. 131, Page 216A, Household 217/217.

PIERCE, THOMAS: (Seneca) Age 58 was born in May 1842 in New York. Both of his parents were born in New York. Both of his parents were Seneca. Laura his wife age 42 was born in 1857 in New York. Both of her parents were born in New York. Both of her parents were Seneca. Wesley GOODSON a boarder age 11 was born in July 1888 in New York. Both of his parents were Seneca. Clara SUNDOWN age 4 a niece was born in January 1896 in New York. Rachel SUNDOWN a niece age 2 was born in November 1897. Foster JEMISON a boarder age 39 was born in March 1861 in New York. The parents of everyone in this household were Seneca. Cattaraugus County, Perrysburg, E.D. 135, Page 222B, Household 19 or 186/187.

PLUMMER, JOHN: (Seneca) Age 21 was born in May 1879 in New York. Both of his parents were born in New York. Both of his parents were Seneca. Cattaraugus County, Salamanca Town, Allegany Indian Reservation, E.D. 131, Page 199B, Household 45/45.

PLUMMER, NATHANIEL: (Seneca) Age 51 was born in October 1848 in New York. Both of his parents were born in New York. Both of his parents were Seneca. Mary J., his wife age 45 was born in September 1854 in New York. Both of her parents were born in New York. Both of her parents were Seneca. Cornelias a son age 19 was born in April 1881.Sally Plummer mother (Of Nathaniel Plummer) age 80 was born in June 1820 in New York. Both of her parents were born in New York. Both of her parents were Seneca, Louis PLUMMER brother-in-law (Of Nathaniel Phummer?) age 40 was born in March 1860 in New York. Both of his parents were born in New York. Both of his parents were Seneca. Louis PLUMMER brother-in-law (Of Nathaniel Plummer?). Cattaraugus County, Red House Town, Allegany Indian Reservation, E.D. 131, Page 200A, Household 46/46.

PLUMMER, SALLY: (Seneca) Age 69 was born in May 1831 in New York. Both of her parents were born in New York. Both of her parents were Seneca. Addison SHONGO a nephew age 36 was born in August in 1863 in New York. Both of his parents were born in New York. He was listed as a Seneca. His father was an Oneida. His mother was a Seneca. Dora TAYLOR a niece age 36 was born in February 1864 in New York. Both of her parents were born in New York. Both of her parents were Seneca. Cattaraugus County, Allegany Indian Reservation, E.D. 131, Page 204B, Household 104/104.

PRINTUP, WILLIAM: (Onondaga) Age 39 was born in October 1860 in New York. Both of his parents were born in New York. He was listed as an Onondaga. Both of his parents were Onondaga. Lena his wife age 22 was born in May 1878 in New York. Both of her parents were born in New York. Both of her parents were Seneca. Ernest a son age 6 was born in

December 1893. Rosa a daughter age 4 was born in February 1896. Ulyses a son age 2 was born in March 1898. Alice a daughter was born in May 1900. All of the children of William Printup were listed as Seneca. Cattaraugus County, Red House Town, Allegany Indian Reservation, E.D. 131, Page 201B, Household 65/65.

RAY OR ROY, AXIE: (Seneca) Age 63 was born in December 1856 in New York. Both of her parents were born in New York. Both of her parents were Seneca. Cattaraugus County, Cold Spring Town, E.D. 131, Page 208B, Household 139/139.

RED-EYE, BENNET: (Seneca) Age 50 was born in March 1850 in New York. Both of his parents were born in New York. Lucinda his wife age 48 was born in April 1852 in New York. Both of her parents were born in New York. Amelia FARMER a grand-daughter age 13 was born in January 1887 in New York. Both of her parents were born in New York. Cattaraugus County, E.D. 131, Page 197B, Household 16.

RED-EYE, CASLER: (Seneca) Age 73 was born in January 1827 in New York. Both of his parents were born in New York. Both of his parents were Seneca. Cattaraugus County, Coldspring Town, E.D. 131, Page 205A, Household 109/109.

RED-EYE, HENRY J. : (Onondaga/Seneca) Age 29 was born in May 1871 in New York. Both of his parents were born in New York. He was listed as an Onondaga. His father was a Seneca. His mother was an Onondaga. Orpha his wife age 35 was born in July 1864 in New York. Both of her parents were born in New York. She was listed as a Seneca. Her father was a white man. Her mother was a Seneca. Fred a son age 18 was born in November 1881. Adam a son age 16 was born in January 1884. Freeman a son age 11 was born in March 1889. Sherman a son age 9 was born in April 1891. Willie a son age 7 was born in March 1893. Ada a daughter age 1 was born in May 1899. All of the children in this household were listed as Seneca. Cattaraugus County, Elko Town, E.D. 131, Page 213A, Household 185.

RED-EYE, HENRY: (Seneca) He was age 29? was born in May 1873 in New York. Both of his parents were born in New York. Both of his parents were Seneca. William CORNFIELD a boarder was age 20 born in May 1880 in New York. Both of his parents were born in New York. Both of his parents were Seneca. Meet? (A Female) CORNFIELD a boarder age 18 was born in April 1882 in New York. Both of her parents were born in New York. Both of her parents were Seneca. E.D. 131, Page 196B, Household 7.

RED-EYE, HENRY: (Seneca) Age 45 was born in February 1855 in New York. Both of his parents were born in New York. He was listed as a Seneca. Both of his parents were Seneca. Lucinda his wife age 40 was born in September 1859 in New York. She was listed as an Onondaga. Her father was a Seneca. Her mother was an Onondaga. Chester a son age 21 was born in March 1879. Sarah a daughter-in-law age 23 was born in August 1876 in New York. Both of her parents were born in New York. Both of her parents were Seneca. Spencer age son age 19 was born in November 1880. Harrison a son age 17 was born in July 1882. Hattie a daughter age 15 was born in January 1885. Rena a daughter age 13 was born in December 1876. Clara a daughter age 10 was born in April 1890. Henry

Jr., a son age 6 was born in June 1894. All the children in this household were listed as Onondaga. Cattaraugus County, Elko Town, E.D. 131, Page 212A, Household 176/176.

RED-EYE, HOWARD: (Seneca) Age 21 was born in April 1879 in New York. Both of his parents were born in New York. Both of his parents were Seneca. Hattie his wife age 18 was born in May 1882 in New York. Both of her parents were born in New York. Both of her parents were Seneca. E.D. 131, Page 196B, Household 5.

RED-EYE, JAMES: (Seneca) Age 75 was born in February 1825 in New York. Both of his parents were born in New York. Both of his parents were Seneca. Caroline his wife age 70 was born in March 1830 in New York. Both of her parents were born in New York. Both of her parents were Seneca. Cattaraugus County, Red Horse Town, Allegany Indian Reservation, E.D. 131, Page 204A, Household 94/94.

RED-EYE, JAMES: (Seneca) Age 70 was born in May 1830 in New York. Both of his parents were born in New York. Both of his parents were Seneca. Carolina his wife age 65 was born in February 1835 in New York. Both of her parents were born in New York. Both of her parents were Seneca. Cattaraugus County, Salamanca Town, Allegany Indian Reservation, E.D. 131, Page 203A, Household 82/82.

RED-EYE, JONAS: (Seneca) Age 48 was born in February 1852 in New York. Both of his parents were born in New York. Both of his parents were Seneca. Emma his wife age 46 was born in February 1854 in New York. Both of her parents were born in New York. She was listed as a Seneca. Her father was an Onondaga. Her mother was a Seneca, Jonas Jr., a son age 17 was born in September 1883. Cornelius a son age 9 was born in June 1890. Cattaraugus County, Coldspring Town, E.D. 131, Page 210A, Household 156/156.

RED-EYE, LUCY: (Seneca) Age 79 was born in New York in October 1820. Both of her parents were born in New York. Both of her parents were Seneca. Payson? JIMESON a grandson age 33 was born in December 1866 in New York. Both of his parents were born in New York. Both of his parents were Seneca. Laura JIMESON (Wife of Payson JIMESON?) age 24 was born in January 1876 in New York. Both of her parents were born in New York. Both of her parents were Seneca. William JIMESON a grand-son age 23 was born in January 1876 in New York. Both of his parents were born in New York. Both of his parents were Seneca. Eli HILL a boarder age 33 was born in June 1867 in New York. Both of his parents were born in New York. Both of his parents were Mohawk. E.D. 131, Page 196B, Household 4.

RED-EYE, LUCY: (Seneca) Age 70 was born in January 1830 in New York. Both of her parents were born in New York. Both of her parents were Seneca. Fred RED-EYE a grandson age 23 was born in June 1876 in New York. Both of his parents were born in New York. Katie RED-EYE a grand daughter age 18 was born in February 1882 in New York. Both of her parents were born in New York. Shelden RED-EYE a grandson age 26 was born in December 1873 in New York. Both of his parents were born in New York. Both of his parents were Seneca. E.D. 131. Page 196B, Household 6.

RED-EYE, ROBERT: (Onondaga) Age 56 was born in October 1843 in New York. Both of his parents were born in New York. He was listed as an Onondaga. Both of his parents were Onondaga. Cattaraugus County, Elko Town, E.D. 131, Page 212B, Household 179/179.

RED-EYE, SACKETT: (Seneca) Age ? was born in June 1844 in New York. Both of his parents were born in New York. Both of his parents were Seneca. Elizabeth GARLOW? a daughter age 23 was born in March 1877 in New York. Both of her parents were born in New York. Both of her parents were Seneca. Lena HILL a grand daughter age 2 was born in September 1897 in New York. Both of her parents were born in New York. Samson HILL a grand son age? was born in July 1899 in New York. Both of his parents were born in New York. Both were Seneca. Cattaraugus County, E.D. 131, Page 195A, Household 3.

RED-EYE, WILLIS: (Seneca) Age 35 was born in May 1865 in New York. Both of his parents were born in New York. Both of his parents were Seneca. Eliza his wife age 30 was born in March 1870 in New York. Both of her parents were born in New York. Both of her parents were Seneca. Jennie a daughter age 11 was born in May 1889. Nora a daughter age 3 was born in March 1897. Cattaraugus County, Elko Town, E.D. 131, Page 211B, Household 169/169.

RITTENHOUSE, JOSEPH: (White) Age 60 was born in January in 1840 in New York. Both of his parents were born in Germany. Eveline his wife age 43 was born in March 1857 in New York. Both of her parents were born in New York. Her race was listed on the first census page as white. On the second page the tribal membership of Eveline Rittenhouse was listed as Seneca. Hiram BROWN a boarder (He was listed as a white) age 60 was born in May 1840 in New York. Both of his parents were born in Germany. Cattaraugus County, South Valley Town, E.D. 131, Page 216B, Household 223.

ROY, STEPHEN: (Seneca) Age 63 was born in March 1837 in New York. Both of his parents were born in New York. Both of his parents were Seneca. Lucy his wife age 58 was born in October 1841 in New York. Both of her parents were Seneca. Thomas SNOW a grand son? age 12 was born in December 1887. Both of his parents were Seneca. Cattaraugus County, Elko Town, E.D. 131, Page 213B, Household 189.

SCRUGGS (OR SCROGGS?), THOMAS: (Seneca) Age 64 was born in January 1836 in New York. Both of his parents were born in New York. E.D. 131, Page 197B, Household 15.

SEELEY, JASPER: (Seneca) Age 53 was born in August 1846 in New York. Both of his parents were born in New York. He was listed as a Seneca. His father was a Seneca. His mother was a white woman. Minnie his wife (She was listed as a white woman) age 34 was born in September 1865 in New York. Both of her parents were born in New York. Florence a daughter age 8 was born in August 1891. Flossie a daughter age 7 was born in April 1893. Jasper a son age 3 was born in July 1896. Georgia LEWIS a step daughter age 11 (She was Listed as white) was born in April 1889. Franklin SEELY brother (Of Jasper Seeley) age 40 was born in December 1859. Maria SEELY mother (Of Jasper Seeley) age 81 was born in September 1818 in New York. Both of her parents were born in New York. She was listed as a white woman. Albert TEBO a nephew (of

Jasper Seeley) age 20 was born in May 1880. He was listed as a white man. Chautauqua County, Town of Hanover, Cattaraugus Reservation, E.D. 135, Page 220A, Household 2 or 168/169.

SENECA, JULIA: (Seneca) Age 65 was born in March 1835 in New York. Both of her parents were born in New York. Both of her parents were Seneca. Hoy? a son age 39 was born in July 1860 in New York. Both of his parents were born in New York. Both of his parents were Seneca. William a son age 36 was born in May 1864. Cattaraugus County, Salamanca Town, Allegany Indian Reservation, E.D. 131, Page 199B, Household 44/44.

SHONGO, DANIEL: (Seneca) Age 39 was born in December 1860 in New York. Both of his parents were born in New York. Both of his parents were Seneca. He was listed as a boarder in the household of Nellie Clark. See: E.D. 131, Page 199B, Household 18.

SHONGO, ELI: (Seneca) Age 41 was born in June 1858 in New York. Both of his parents were born in New York. Both of his parents were Seneca. Laura his wife age 29 was born in May 1871 in New York. Both of her parents were born in New York. Both of her parents were Seneca. Lucy a daughter age 8 was born in January 1852 in New York. Mitchell a son age 4 was born in November 1895 in New York. Delana a daughter was born in November 1899 in New York. Amos KILLBUCK father-in-law (Of Eli Shongo) age 65 was born in April 1835. Both of his parents were born in New York. Both of his parents were Seneca. Cattaraugus County, Coldspring Town, E.D. 131, Page 205A, Household 105/105.

SHONGO, ELMER: (Seneca) Age 28 was born in February 1872 in New York. Both of his parents were born in New York. Both of his parents were Seneca. Hattie his wife age 28 was born in May 1875 in New York. Both of her parents were born in New York. Both of her parents were Seneca. Vernon a son age 8 was born in May 1892. Lilla? or Lillie? a daughter age 3 was born in August 1896. Herman a son age 2 was born in May 1898. Letha a daughter was born in April 1900. Herbert a son age 6 was born in February 1894. Cattaraugus County, E.D. 131, Salamanca Town, Allegheny Indian Reservation, Page 203B, Household 91/91.

SHONGO, HOWARD: (Seneca) Age 40 was born in August 1859 in New York. Both of his parents were born in New York. Betsy his wife age 40 was born in September 1859 in New York. Both of her parents were born in New York. Both of her parents were Seneca. E.D. 131, Page 198B, Household 28.

SHONGO, JAMES: (Seneca) Age 60 was born in August 1839 in New York. Both of his parents were born in New York. Both of his parens were Seneca. Howard a son age 23 was born in February 1877. Cattaraugus County, Salamanca Town, Allegany Indian Reservation, E.D. 131, Page 203A, Household 85/85.

SHONGO, LUCY: (Seneca) Age 60 was born in April 1840 in New York. Both of her parents were born in New York. Both of her parents were Seneca. James RED-EYE a boarder age 36 was born in October 1863 in New York. Both of his parents were born in New York. Both of his parents were Seneca. Cattaraugus County, E.D. 131, Page 199B, Household 19.

SHONGO, MARY: (Seneca) Age 51 was born in May 1849 in New York. Both of her parents were born in New York. Both of her parents were listed as Seneca. Cattaraugus County, Page 200B, Household 55.

SHONGO, PETER: (Seneca) Age 48 was born in September 1851 in New York. Both of his parents were born in New York. Both of his parents were Seneca. Cattaraugus County, Allegany Indian Reservation, E.D. 131, Page 204B, Household 102/102.

SILVERHEELS, JOEL: (Seneca) Age 38 was born in May 1862 in New York. Both of his parents were born in New York. Both of his parents were Seneca. Phebe his wife age 44 was born in April 1856 in New York. Both of her parents were born in New York. Both of her parents were Seneca. Rolly? or Polly? PLUMMER a step daughter age 23 was born in February 1877 in New York. Both of her parents were born in New York. Both of her parents were Seneca. E.D. 131, Page 199A, Household 33.

SILVERHEELS, UYLESE? H. (Seneca) Age 64 was born in March 1836 in New York. Both of his parents were born in New York. Both of his parents were Seneca. Cattaraugus County, Red House Town, E.D. 131, Page 202A, Household 71/71.

SMITH, LYMAN: (Seneca) Age 34 was born in September 1865 in New York. Both of his parents were born in New York. Both of his parents were Seneca. Laura his wife age 28 was born in January 1887 in New York. Both of her parents were born in New York. Both of her parents were Seneca. Leon Town, E.D. 48, Page 20A, Household 254/256.

SNOW, AMOS: (Seneca) Age 61 was born in August in 1838 in New York. Both of his parents were born in New York. Both of his parents were Seneca. Lucy his wife age 48 was born in June? 1852 in New York. Both of her parents were born in New York. Both of her parents were Seneca. Jonas a son age 23 was born in May 1877 in New York. Emma a daughter age 28 was born in February 1872 in New York. Hudson a son age 15 was born in May 1885 in New York. Alice a daughter age 13 was born in March 1887 in New York. Nellie LOGAN a grand daughter age 9 was born in May 1891 in New York. Carrie LOGAN a grand daughter age 5 was born in April 1895 in New York. Chloe LOGAN a grand daughter age two months was born in April 1900 in New York. Cold Spring Town, E.D. 131, Page 208B, Household 144/144.

SNOW, DAVID: (Seneca) Age 70 was born in April 1830 in New York. Both of his parents were born in New York. Both of his parents were Seneca. Joseph a son age 37 was born in January 1863. Sarah a daughter-in-law age 30 was born in May 1870. Both of her parents were Born in New York. Both of her parents were Seneca. Henry a grand son age 10 was born in March 1890. Elko Town, E.D. 131, Page 214B, Household 198.

SNOW, HIRAM: (Seneca) Age 37 was born in August 1862 in New York. Both of his parents were born in New York. Both of his parents were Seneca. Ester his wife age 35 was born in January 1865 in New York. Both of her parents were born in New York. She was listed as an Onondaga. Her father was a Seneca. Her mother was an Onondaga. Viola a daughter age 19 was born in January 1881. Philip a son age 13 was born in June 1886. Charley a son age 10 was born in June 1889. Albert WATERMAN a son-in-law age 20 was born in March 1880 in New York. Both of his parents were born in New York. He was listed as a Seneca. His father was a Stockbridge. His mother was a Seneca. All of the children of Hirman Snow were listed as Onondaga. Cattaraugus County, Elko Town, E.D. 131, Page 213A, Household 188.

SNOW, JULIA: (Seneca) Age 58 was born in March 1842 in New York. Both of her parents were born in New York. Both of her parents were Seneca. Esau a son age 39 was born in February 1861. Nellie a daughter age 37 was born in December 1862. Jason a son age 32 was born in January 1868. Nettie a grand daughter was born in November 1886. Agnes a grand daughter age 7 was born in April 1893. Phoebe a grand daughter age 4 was born in February 1896. Gideon a grand son age 1 was born in December 1898. Cattauragus County, Perrysburg, E.D. 135, Page 221B, Household 13 or 180/181.

SNYDER, ADELIA: (Seneca) Age 43 was born in March 1857 in New York. Both of her parents were born in New York. Both of her parents were Seneca. Susie a daughter age 17 was born in July 1883. Alvin? a son age 10 was born in April 1890. Cattaraugus County, Coldspring Town, E.D. 131, Page 209B, Household 153/153.

SNYDER, ELIZA: (Seneca) Age 65 was born in May 1835 in New York. Both of her parents were born in New York. Both of her parents were Seneca. Cattaraugus County, Salamanca Town, E.D. 131, Page 203A, Household 84/84.

SNYDER, LAURA: (Seneca) Age 55 was born in April 1845 in New York. Both of her parents were born in New York. Both of her parents were Seneca? Harry BURMASTER a son age 11 was born in January 1889 in New York. Both of his parents were born in New York. He was listed as a Seneca. His father was a white man. His mother was a Seneca. Chataugua County, Hanover Town, Cattaraugus Reservation, E.D. 135, Page 220A, Household 4 or 170/171.

SNYDER, TORRANCE: (Seneca) Age 23 was born in July 1876 in New York. Both of his parents were born in New York. Both of his parents were Seneca. Minnie his wife age 18 was born in July 1881 in New York. Both of her parents were born in New York. Both of her parents were Seneca. Gaylord a son age nine months was born in August 1899. Cattaraugus County, Cold Spring Town, E.D. 131, Page 209B, Household 150/150.

SPRAGUE, MARGERET: (Seneca) Age 26 was born in July 1873 in New York. Both of her parents were born in New York. Both of her parents were Seneca. Hazel a daughter age 1 born in May 1899. Both of her parents were born in New York. Both of her parents were Seneca. Cattaraugus County, Elko Town, E.D. 131, Page 213A, Household 187/187.

SPRING, URINA? (Seneca) Age 29 was born in September 1870 in New York. Both of her parents were born in New York. Both of her parents were Seneca. Alice a daughter age 10 was born in April 1890. William a son age 6 was born in August 1893. John a son age 3 was born in April 1897. Minnie a daughter was born in August 1899. James O'BRIEN a boarder age 41 was born in May 1859 in New York (He was listed as white). Both of his parents were born in Ireland. Della O'BRIEN a step daughter age 15 was born in April 1885 in New York. Both of her parents were born in New York. She listed as a white female of Irish descent. Cattaraugus County, Salamanca Town, Allegany Indian Reservation, E.D. 131, Page 203A, Household 88/88.

STEVENS, WILLIAM: (Seneca) Age 30 was born in May 1870 in New York. Both of his parents were born in New York. Both of his parents were Seneca. Dora his wife age 20 was born in November 1879 in New York. Both of her parents were born in New York. Both of her parents were Seneca. Bertha a daughter age ten months was born in August 1899. Cattaraugus County, Elko Town, E.D. 131, Page 211B, Household 172/172.

SUNDOWN, LOUISA? OR LOVICA? (Seneca) Age 66 was born in February 1834 in New York. Both of her parents were born in New York. Both of her parents were Seneca. E.D. 131, Page 198B, Household 30.

SUTTEN? EUGENE: (White) Age 35 was born in April 1865 in New York. Both of his parents were born in New York. Louisa his wife age 36 was born in July 1863 in New York. Both of her parents were born in New York. Both of her parents were Seneca. Martha a daughter age 14 was born in March 1886. Ernest a son age 11 was born in July 1888. Bertie a son age 9 was born in June 1890. Mertie a daughter age 6 was born in December 1893. Henry a son age 4 was born in November 1895. Gertie age 2 was born in October 1897. Charles a son age three months was born in March 1900. All of the children in this household were listed as Seneca. Cattaraugus County, South Valley Town, E.D. 131, Page 216B, Household 224.

TANDY, BETSY: (Seneca) Age 45 was born in August 1854 in New York. Both of her parents were born in New York. Both of her parents were Seneca. Gordon FALTY an uncle age 69 was born in October 1830 in New York. Both of his parents were born in New York. Both of his parents were Seneca. Harrison JOHN a son-in-law age 23 was born in December 1876 in New York. Both of his parents were born in New York. He was listed as a Seneca. His father was a Seneca. His mother was a white woman. Amanda daughter age 20 was born in April 1880 in New York. Both of her parents were born in New York. Both of her parents were Seneca. Benjamin a grand son age? John a grand son age 5 was born in August 1895. Harrison Jr., a grand son was born in May 1900. All of the children in this household were listed as Seneca. Perrysburg, Cattaraugus County, E.D. 135, Page 222A, Household 17 or 184/185.

TAYLOR, MOSES: (Seneca) Age 48 was born in May 1852 in New York. Both of his parents were born in New York. Both of his parents were Seneca. Pheobe J., his wife age 32 born in November 1867 in New York. Both of her parents were born in New York. Both of her parents were Seneca. Theodore? or Thadeus JIMISON a step son age 10 was born in November 1889 in New York. Both of his parents were born in New York. Both of his parents were Seneca. Cattaraugus County, Red House Town, Allegany Indian Reservation, E. D. 131, Page 200A, Household 51/51.

THOMAS, DAVID: (Seneca) Age 54 was born in July 1845 in New York. Both of his parents were born in New York. Both of his parents were Seneca. Sarah his wife age 54 was born in April 1846 in New York. Both of her parents were born in New York. Both of her parents were Seneca. Nellie a daughter age 19 was born in June 1880. George PIERCE a grand son age 10 was born in July 1889. Both of his parents were Seneca. Cattaraugus County, Perrysburg, E.D. 135, Page 224B, Household 33.

THOMAS, JOSEPHINE: (Seneca) Age 23 was born in November 1876 in New York. Both of her parents were born in New York. Both of her parents were Seneca. Ada a daughter age 1 was born in September 1898. Both of her parents were born in New York. Both of her parents were Seneca. Cattaraugus County, Salamanca Town, Allegany Indian Reservation, E.D. 131, Page 203A, Household 80/80.

TITUS, DENNIS: (Seneca) Age 34 was born in June 1865 in New York. Both of his parents were born in New York. Both of his parents were Seneca. Sophia his wife age 28 was born in May 1872 in New York. Both of her parents were born in New York. Both of her parents were Seneca. Elko Town, E.D. 131, Page 214B, Household 201.

TITUS, GEORGE: (Seneca) Age 40 was born in May 1860 in New York. Both of his parents were born in New York. Both of his parents were Seneca. E.D. 131, Page 199B, Household 21.

TITUS, JACKSON: (Seneca) Age 79 was born in April 1821 in New York. Both of his parents were born in New York. Both of his parents were Seneca. Jane his wife age 55 was born in May 1845 in New York. Both of her parents were born in New York. Both of her parents were Seneca. Amelia a daughter age 18 was born in March 1882 in New York. Abby VAN ARMAN? a grand daughter age one born in November 1888 in New York. Both of her parents were Seneca. Cattaraugus County, South Valley Town, E.D. 131, Page 217A, Household 228.

TITUS, JONAS: (Seneca) Age 37 was born in March 1863 in New York. Both of his parents were born in New York. Both of his parents were Seneca. Mary his wife age 38 was born in October 1861 in New York. Both of her parents were born in New York. Both of her parents were Seneca. Willie a son age 3 was born in September 1896 in New York. Lydia HALFWHITE a grand daughter age 16 was born in July 1883 in New York. Both of her parents were born in New York. Both of her parents were Seneca. Cattaraugus County, Coldspring Town, E.D. 131, Page 207A, Household 128/128.

TITUS, SARAH: (Seneca) Age 57 was born in December 1842 in New York. Both of her parents were born in New York. Both of her parents were Seneca. Charles RED-EYE a grand-son born in March 1891 in New York. Both of his parents were born in New York. Both of his parents were Seneca. Peter KILLBUCK age 42 a boarder was born in December 1857 in New York. Both of his parents were born in New York. Both of his parents were Seneca. Josephine ABRAM age 14 a boarder was born in June 1886. Both of her parents were Seneca. E.D. 131, Page 196A, Household 1.

TOMMY, GEORGE: (Seneca) Age 61 was born in May 1839 in New York. Both of his parents were born in New York. Both of his parens were Seneca. Annie his wife age 54 was born in October 1845 in New York. Both of her parents were born in New York. Both of her parents were Seneca. Sylvia WILSON a daughter age 34 was born in September 1865. Lucinda TOMMY a daughter age 13 was born in September 1886. Le Roy WILSON a grand son age 16 was born in December 1883. Lucinda LAY a grand daughter age 3 was born in March 1897. Eliza STEVENS mother-in-law (Of George Tommy) age 86 was born in December 1813 in New York. Both of her parents were born in New York. She was listed as a Seneca. Her father was a white man. Her mother was a Seneca. All of the children in this household were listed as Seneca. All of their parents were listed as Seneca. Cattaraugus County, Perrysburg, E.D. 135, Page 224B, Household 34.

TOMPKINS, EMELINE: (Seneca) Age 33 was born in June 1866 in New York. Both of her parents were born in New York. Both of her parents were Seneca. Michael HUFF a son age 16 was born in October 1883 in New York. Abram HUFF a son age 10 was born in March 1890 in New York. Flora HUFF a daughter age 9 was born in May 1891 in New York. Maurice HUFF a son age 7 was born in March 1893 in New York. Ely THOMPKINS a son age 3 was born in March 1897 in New York. All of the children in this household were listed as Seneca. Both parents of all of the children in this household were Seneca. Cattaraugus County, Coldsrping Town, E.D. 131, Page 205B, Household 110/110.

TWO-GUNS, LEWIS: (Seneca) Age 45 was born in April 1855 in New York. Both of his parents were born in New York. Both of his parents were Seneca. Cattaraugus County, Coldspring Town, E.D. 131, Page 206B, Household 124/124.

WADE, ETHIE? (Seneca) Age 38 was born in July in 1861 in New York. Both of her parents were born in New York. Both of her parents were listed as Seneca? Edward Wade an adopted son? (He was listed as an Indian) age 16 was born in July 1883 in New York. Both of his parents were born in New York. Both of his parents were Seneca. George WAUDALL? OR WARDELL? father (Of Ethie WADE) age 65 was born in May 1835 in New York. Both of his parents were born in New York. He was listed as a white man. Charles YAGER a boarder age 52 born in March 1848 in New York. Both of his parents were born in Massachusetts. He was listed as a white man of German descent. Cattaraugus County, Red House Town, Allegany Indian Reservation, Page 201A, Household 60/60.

WARRIOR, GEORGE: (Seneca) Age 42 was born in September 1857 in New York. Both of his parents were born in New York. Both of his parents were Seneca. Susan his wife age 40 was born in April 1860 in New York. Both of her parents were born in New York. Both of her parents were Seneca. Mable a daughter age 6 was born in March 1894. Grace a daughter age 3 was born in November 1896. Ruth a daughter was born in September 1899. Cattaraugus County, Red House Town, Allegany Indian Reservation, E.D. 131, Page 202B, Household 78/78.

WARRIOR, WILLIAM: (Seneca) Age 40 was born in August 1859 in New York. Both of his parents were born in New York. Both of his parents were Seneca. Betsy his wife age 40 was born in September 1859 in New York. Both of her parents were born in New York. Both of her parents were Seneca. E.D. 131, Page 198A, Household 28.

WASHINGTON, JAMES: (Seneca) Age 57 was born in ? in 1842 in New York. Both of his parents were born in New York. Both of his parents were Seneca. Jane his wife age 57 was born in ? 1842 in New York. Both of her parents were born in New York. Both of her parents were Seneca. John SNOW a step son age 18 was born in August 1881 in New York. Both of his parents were born in New York. Both of his parents were Seneca. Willie COOPER a step son age 33 was born in March 1867 in New York. Both of his parents were Seneca. Green JIMISON a step son age 31 was born in May 1869 in New York. He was listed as a Seneca. His father was a Cayuga. His mother was a Seneca. Lawrence COOPER a grand son age 4 was born in February 1896. Both of his parents were Seneca. Cattaraugus County, Perrysburg, E.D. 135, Page 224A, Household 28 or 218/219.

WATERMAN, JOHN: (Munsee/Munci or Delaware) Age 40 was born in ? March 1860 in Wisconsin. His father was born in New York. His mother was born in English Canada (Ontario). He was listed as a Munsee. His father was a Seneca. His mother was a Munsee. Elizabeth his wife age 37 was born in New York. Her father was born in English Canada (Ontario). Her mother was born in English Canada. She was listed as a Seneca. Her father was a White man. Her mother was a Seneca. Ina a daughter age 17 was born in August 1883 in New York. John Jr., age 15 was born in March 1885. Ralph a son age 13 was born in May 1881. Raymon a son age 8 was born in December 1891. Isaac a son age 1 was born in April 1899. All children is this household were born in New York. All of the children in this household were listed as Seneca. Cattaraugus County, Perrysburg, E.D. 135, Page 222B, Household 20 or 187/188.

WATERMAN, SARAH: (Munci/Oneida) Age 78 was born in ? 1821 in New York. Both of her parents were born in New York. She was listed as a Munci. Her father was an Oneida. Her mother was a Munci. Philip a son age 40 was born in September? 1859 in New York. He was listed as a Munci. His father was a Seneca. His mother was a Munci. Cattaraugus County, Perrysburg, E.D. 135, Page 221A, Household 7 or 174/175.

WATT, HIRAM: (Seneca) Age 40 was born in August 1859 in New York. Both of his parents were born in New York. Both of his parents were Seneca. Elizabeth his wife age 28 was born in October 1871 in New York. Both of her parents were born in New York. Both of her parents were Seneca. Cephus a son age 7 was born in August 1892. Clarence a son age 4 was born in October 1895. Celia a daughter age 1 was born in March 1899. Mary SNOW mother (Of Hiram Watt) age 63 was born in September 1836 in New York. Both of her parents were born in New York. Both of her parents were Seneca. Cattaraugus County, Coldspring Town, E.D. 131, Page 210B, Household 161/161.

WATT, JAMES: (Seneca) Age 37 was born in June 1862 in New York. Both of his parents were born in New York. Both of his parents were Seneca. Jane his wife age 24 was born in May 1876 in New York. Both of her parents were born in New York. She was listed as a Seneca. Her father was an Onondaga. Her mother was a Seneca. Ulyses a son age 3 was born in May 1897. Ebenezer THOMPSON father-in-law (Of James Watt) age 63 was born in March 1837 in New York. Both of his parents were born in New York. Both of his parents were Onondaga. Cattaraugus County, Elko Town, E.D. 131, Page 212B, Household 181/181.

WAUDELL? OR WARDELL?, GEORGE JR.: (Seneca) Age 40 was born in February 1860 in New York. Both of his parents were born in New York. Both of his parents were Seneca. Cattaraugus County, Red House Town, Allegany Indian Reservation, E.D. 131, Page 202B, Household 74/74.

WHITE, JOHN: (Seneca) Age 56 was born in July 1843 in New York. Both of his parents were born in New York. Both of his parents were Seneca. Cattaraugus County, Perrysburg, E.D. 135, Page 224B, Household 36.

WHITE, RUEBEN: (Seneca) Age 40 was born in May 1860 in New York. Both of his parents were born in New York. Both of his parents were Seneca. Jennie his wife age 40 was born in February 1860 in New York. Both of her parents were born in New York. Both of her parents were Seneca. Henry a son age 9 born in January 1890. Allie? a daughter age 7 born in July 1892. Eda? a daughter age 6 was born in September 1893. Louisa a daughter age 3 was born in July 1896. Cattaraugus County, Coldspring Town, E.D. 131, Page 208A, Household 136/136.

WHITE, WESLEY: (Seneca) Age 40 was born in March 1860 in New York. Both of his parents were born in New York. Hattie his wife age 35 was born in May 1865 in New York. Both of her parents were born in New York. E.D. 131, Page 197B, Household 17.

WINNIE, DAVID: (Seneca) Age 45 was born in August 1854 in New York. Both of his parents were born in New York. Both of his parents were Seneca. Rebecca his wife age 47 was born in February 1853 in New York. Both of her parents were born in New York. Both of her parents were Seneca. Helen BLACKCHIEF a step daughter age 16 was born in June 1883 in New York. Both of her parents were born in New York. Both of her parents were Seneca. Cattaraugus County, Elko Town, E.D. 131, Page 213B, Household 191/191.

WINNIE, MARY: (Seneca) Age 40 was born in August 1859 in New York. Both of her parents were born in New York. Both of her parents were Seneca. Cornelius WATERMAN a son age 18 was born in August 1881. Both of his parents were Seneca. Lula B. GREEN a daughter age 3 born in April 1897. Both of her parents were Seneca. John Winnie a brother age 34 was born in October 1865 in New York. Thomas GREEN husband (Of Mary Winnie) age 24 was born in 1875 in New York. Both of his parents were born in New York. Both of his parents were Seneca. Cattaraugus County, Perrysburg, E.D. 135, Page 223A, Household 189/190.

YELLOWBLANKET, JANE: (Onondaga) Age 70 was born in March 1830 in New York. Both of her parents were born in New York. Both of her parents were Onondaga. Ida a daughter age 28 was born in August 1871. Both of her parents were born in New York. Both of her parents were Onondaga. Edith YELLOWBLANKET a grand daughter age 7 was born in July 1892. Both of her parents were Onondaga. Irene YELLOWBLANKET a grand daughter age 1 was born in April 1899. Both of her parents were Onondaga. Cattaraugus County. Elko Town, E.D. 131, Page 211A, Household 165/165.

SURNAME CROSS INDEX	HEAD OF HOUSEHLD
ABRAM, Alex	Willis Jemison
ABRAM, Josephine	Sarah Titus
ALLEN, Claude	Lewis Cooper
ALLEN, Irene	Lewis Cooper
ALLEN, Maude A.	Lewis Cooper
AMADEN, Mary	Sarah Dockstader
AMADEN, Walter	Sarah Dockstader
BARNUM?, Marie	Henry Huff
BLACKCHIEF, Helen	David Winnie
BLACKSNAKE, Chas. W.	John Gordon
BLINKEY, Letitis	John Jimison
BOMBERRY, William	William Hoag
BOMBERY, Blanche	Roger Jimison
BROOKS, Gertrude	Daniel John
BROOKS, Julia	Peter Doxtator
BROWN, Hiram	Joseph Rittenhouse
BUCKTOOTH, Lucy	Louis Hanson
BURMASTER, Harry	Laura Snyder
COOPER, Lawrence	James Washington
COOPER, William	Lucy Logan
COOPER, Willie	James Washington
CORNFIELD, Meet?	Henry Red-Eye
CORNFIELD, William	Henry Red-Eye
CROUSE, Cora	Lucinda Pierce
CROUSE, Iva	Lucinda Pierce
CROUSE, Jennie	Lorinda Jimison
CROUSE, Lydia	William John

CROW, Mary	James Curry
CURRY, Eugene	John Killbuck
CURRY, Ida	John Killbuck
DOCKSTADER, Jenett	Susan Jimison
DOXTATOR, Alta	William John
DOXTATOR, Ellen	William John
DYE, Lilly	Lucinda John
FALTY, Cornelius	Lucinda John
FARMER, Amelia	Bennet Red-Eye
FARMER, Harry	Orrin Mohawk
FARMER, Levi	Orrin Mohawk
GARLOW, Elizabeth	Sackett Red-Eye
GARLOW, William	Charles Jeminson
GOODSON, Weley	Thomas Pierce
GORDAN, Louise	William Abrams
GORDON, Axy	Betsey King
GORDON, Della	Lucy Logan
GORDON, Falty	Betsy Tandy
GORDON, George	John Johnson
GORDON, Hannibal	James Luke
GORDON, James	Lucy Logan
GREEN, Cristine	Francis Jones
GREEN, Lula B.	Mary Winnie
GREEN, Thomas	Mary Winnie
HALFTOWN, Jerome	Lucinda John
HALFWHITE, Benjamin	Joseph Gordon
HALFWHITE, Lydia	Jonas Titus
HANSON, Charles S.	Edward Bone
HARRIS, Edward	Julia Crouse
HENRY, Sherlock	Fred Abram
HILL, Eli	Lucy Red-Eye

HILL, Lena	Sackett Red-Eye
HILL, Rachael	Jerome Halfwhite
HILL, Rachel	Austin Halftown
HILL, Samson	Sackett Red-Eye
HUFF, Abram	Emeline Thompkins
HUFF, Flora	Emeline Thompkins
HUFF, Maurice	Emeline Thompkins
HUFF, Michael	Emeline Thompkins
JACKSON, Jesse	Henry Logan
JACKSON, Job	Evelinn? Jackson
JACKSON, Lucy	Henry Logan
JACOBS, Margaret	Thomas Bishop
JEMISON, Ada	George Jacobs
JEMISON, Amada	George Jacobs
JEMISON, Betsey	Charles Black
JEMISON, Charles Jr.	Sally Gordon
JEMISON, Fedelia	Alfred Jacobs
JEMISON, Foster	Thomas Pierce
JEMISON, Haddy	George Jacobs
JEMISON, Harriet	Sally Gordon
JEMISON, Jennie	Peter Doxtator
JEMISON, Lora	Lucy Red-Eye
JEMISON, Lunus	George Jacobs
JEMISON, Nora	George Jacobs
JEMISON, Robert	George Jacobs
JEMISON, Thadeus	Moses Taylor
JEMISON, Victoria	Charles Black
JEMISON, William	Lucy Red-Eye
JIMISON, Amos	Canada Curry
JIMISON, Green	James Washington
JIMISON, Harrison	Canada Curry

JIMISON, John	Canada Curry
JIMISON, Sampson	Canada Curry
JIMISON, Wilson	Elliot Lewis
JOHN, Eva	Lucy Jimison
JOHN, Harrison	Betsey Tandy
JOHN, Lena	Willett Nephew
JOHN, Olive	Lucy Jimison
JOHN, William	Lucy Jimison
JOHNSON, Augustus	Jennie King
JOHNSON, Mary	Cyrus Johnny-John
JONES, Richard	Jennie King
KILLBUCK, Amos	Eli Shongo
KILLBUCK, Peter	Sarah Titus
KING, Rachel	Jesse Joe
LAY, Lucinda	George Tommy
LEWIS, Georgia	Jasper Seeley
LOGAN, Chloe	Amos Snow
LOGAN, Nellie	Amos Snow
O'BRIEN, Della	Urina? Spring
O'BRIEN, James	Urina? Spring
PARKER, Lena	George Eels
PARKER, Willie	George Eels
PATTERSON, Moses	William Abrams
PIERCE, George	David Thomas
PIERCE, Laura	Elliot Lewis
PIERCE, Marion	Percival Nephew
PIERCE, Wallace	Abel Bucktooth
PLUMMER, Charles	Cordelia John
PLUMMER, Ethel M.	David Patterson
PLUMMER, Polly	Joel Silverheels
RED-EYE, Charles	Sarah Titus

RED-EYE, Eva	Howard Jimison
RED-EYE, Fred	Lyman Pierce
RED-EYE, James	Lucy Shongo
RED-EYE, Lucy	Howard Jimison
SAMPSON, Jabez	Joseph Gordon
SHERLOCK, Henry	Fred Abram
SHONGO, Addison	Sally Plummer
SHONGO, Daniel	Nellie Clark
SHONGO, Nettie	Lucy Jimison
SHONGO, William	Lucy Jimison
SILVERHEELS, Joseph	Lydia Johnson
SNOW, John	James Washington
SNOW, Leroy	Lucy Jemison
SNOW, Mary	Hiram Watt
SNOW, Thomas	Stephen Roy
STEVENS, Eliza	George Tommy
STOCKWELL, Frank	Cordelia John
STOCKWELL, Harrison	Cordelia John
SUNDOWN, Clara	Thomas Pierce
SUNDOWN, Rachel	Thomas Pierce
TALLCHIEF, Jennie	William Hoag
TALLCHIEF, Mabel	William Hoag
TAYLOR, Dora	Sally Plummer
TEBO, Albert	Jasper Seeley
THOMAS, Daniel	Jerome Halfwhite
THOMAS, Martha	Emeline Jeminson
THOMPSON, Ebenezer	James Watt
TITUS, George	William Funn?
TITUS, Julia	Jack Gordon
TURKEY, Carrie	Nathan Jimison
VAN ARMAN?, Abby	Jackson Titus

WARRIOR, Chauncey	Hiram Jacob
WARRIOR, Dena	Hiram Jacob
WARRIOR, Geneva	Alfred Jacobs
WARRIOR, Roda	Hiram Jacob
WASHINGTON, Mary	Mary Abram
WATERMAN, Albert	Hiram Snow
WATERMAN, Cornelius	Mary Winnie
WATERMAN, Lilah	Eliza Mohawk
WAUDELL?, George	Ethie Wade
WHITE, Webster	William Funn?
WHITE, William	William Funn?
WILSON, Le Roy	George Tommy
WILSON, Sylvia	George Tommy
WINNIE, Christine	Eliza Mohawk
WINNIE, Opha?	Eliza Mohawk
YAGER, Charles	Ethie Wade
YORK, Lewellan	George Jeminson

QUAKER SCHOOL FOR INDIAN CHILDREN, ELKO TOWNSHIP
CATTARAUGUS COUNTY, NEW YORK

From the United States Federal Census taken on the 18th of June 1900. Enumberation District 39, beginning with page 131A. The place of birth of the parents of each student was not provided. The third column below lists each student's birthplace, then tribal origins, then father and mother's tribal origin. If only one Indian Nation was listed both parents and child belonged to the same tribe.

NAME	AGE	Birthplace/Student/Father/Mother
ALBUCK, Albert	14	New York Seneca
BUTTON, George	12	New York Seneca
CROUSE, Lovina	15	New York Seneca
CROUSE, Miloina?	10	New York Seneca
CROUSE, Sophia	13	New York Seneca
CURRY, Rhoda	11	New York Sen/Onon/Sen
DOLSON, Elon	17	New York Seneca
DOLSON, James	14	New York Cay/?/Cay
DOXTATOR, Marthy	14	New York Seneca
GORDON, Clarence	15	Penn. Onon/Sen/Onon
GORDON, Josephine	13	New York Seneca
GORDON, Leslie	14	New York No information
GORDON, Lucinda	15	New York Seneca
GORDON, Victor	11	Penn. Seneca
JACKSON, Hellan	10	New York Onon/Sen/Onon
JIMESON, Geneva	13	New York Seneca
JAMESON, Clinton	14	New York Seneca
JAMESON, Charles	10	New York Onon/Sen/Onon
JAMESON, Hattie	10	New York Seneca
JAMESON, LaFayette	12	New York Seneca
JOHN, Meranda	13	New York Seneca
KENNEDY, Geneva	12	New York Seneca

KENNEDY, John	13	New York Seneca
LOGAN, Ealie	17	New York Seneca
MOHAWK, Solon?	16	New York Seneca
O'BRIEN, Della	14	New York Seneca
PATTERSON, Ella	10	New York Seneca
PIERCE, Alva	9	New York Seneca
PIERCE, Rosetta	11	New York Seneca
REDEYE, Florance	15	New York Seneca
REDEYE, Rena	13	New York Seneca
SCOTT, Felax	23	New York Seneca
SCOTT, Solon	12	New York Sen/Onon/Sen
SNOW, Tomy	11	New York Seneca
TALLCHIEF, Elmar	13	New York Seneca
THOMPSON, Albert	10	New York Seneca
THOMPSON, Eliner	14	New York Seneca
TURKEY, Levi	15	New York Cay/Sen/Cay
TWOGUNS, Della	14	New York Seneca
TWOGUNS, Sabina?	11	New York Seneca
WATT, Tasher?	13	New York Seneca
WHITE, Clara	12	New York Seneca
WHITE, Bura?	17	New York Seneca

THE TUSCARORAS RESIDING ON THE
TUSCARORA RESERVATION, NIAGARA COUNTY,
NEW YORK

The Tuscarora originally came from North Carolina. About 1718 they were adopted as the Sixth Nation to belong to the Iroquois Confederacy. The Tuscarora Reservation is located in Niagara County, New York. They obtained their reserve in 1784 from the Senecas and the Holland Land Company. The reserve was purchased from the money acquired by giving up their lands in North Carolina. Only those who are born of an Iroquois mother is considered a member of the tribe. The Tuscarora have a matrilineal society. Source: "Federal and State Indian Reservations Handbook," U. S. Department of Commerce 1971. The early location of the Tuscarora in North Carolina is defined in the following maps.

"The South Part of Virginia, Now the North Part of Carolina," drawn by Nicholas Comberford in 1657, showing the Tuscarora towns between the Neus, Pamtico and Chowan Rivers. Source: New York Public Library, Map List Number 50.

"A New Description of Carolina," drawn by John Ogilby, Ca., 1672. The Map is often called the First Lords Proprietors Map. Source: Map Collection, Yale University Library, Map List Number 70.

A map titled "Carolina 1729," Drawn by Herman Moll. Source: W.P. Cumming, Davidson, North Carolina, Map List Number 206, "The Southeast in Early Maps," by William P. Cumming, The University of North Carolina Press, Chapel Hill, North Carolina, Copyright 1962.

"A Map of the British and French Dominions in North American 1755." drawn by John Mitchell prepared before the outbreak of the French and Indian War. Reference: Reproduction: Fite, E.D. and A. Freeman. Op. cit., Plate 47 (British Museum "George III," Copy; Fourth English Edition). Shown in "The Southeast in Early Maps," by William P. Cumming, The University of North Carolina Press, Chapel Hill, North Carolina, Plate 59, Copyright 1962.

"A New and Correct Map of the Province of North Carolina, 1733," drawn by Edward Moseley. Source: Map Collection, Yale University Library. Map List 217. Shown in "The Southeast in Early Maps," by William P. Cumming, The University of North Carolina Press, Chapel Hill, North Carolina, Copyright 1962, Plate Number 51, 53 & 54.

Edward Moseley's map of 1733 of North Carolina, shows areas designated as "Part of the Country Formerly Inhabited by the Tuscarora Indians in Bertie and Edgecomb Precinct." The area today includes approximately part of the counties of Beaufort, Bertie, Halifax, Greene, and Pitt. Also shown is the location of the Meherrin and Nasemond Indian treaty land.

200

JOSEPH CUSICK A TUSCARORA INDIANS
1812 MILITARY PENSION APPLICATION

Notes from the War of 1812 Military Service of Joseph Cusick a Tuscarora Indian from New York. Abstracted from the original pension statements of Joseph Cusick and his widow on file at the National Archives, Washington D.C.

Joseph Cusick stated that he served in Simon Longboard's Company commanded by Little Billy Printup. He was part of a company raised at the Tuscarora Reservation in New York of volunteers to fight on the American side. Solomon Longboard was a principal war chief at that time. This company which comprised mainly of Tuscaroras reported to Fort George and soon were in "The Battle of Fort George." They also fought British backed Indians from Canada. In the fall of 1813 they fought near Fort Niagara and acted as scouts. Joseph Cusick was born about 1790. He volunteered in July 1813 and served one and a half years. He married Susan Pemberton (Or Pembleton) the daughter of James Pemberton a British deserter during the Revolutionary War and Seneca woman. Joseph and Susan were married on the 20th of June 1813 at Lewiston, New York, by Sacharega head Chief of the Tuscarora Nation. Joseph died on July the 15th 1878. His wife died in the fall of 1886. On the sixth of August 1858 a report was filed by the U. S. Indian Agency that stated Samuel Wilson age sixty-eight an Indian belonging to the Seneca tribe, a resident of the Cattaraugus Indian Reservation received "Bounty Land Wrrant Number 72329." William Johnson age Seventy Three, a Seneca of the same reservation received "Bounty Land Warrant Number 72326." They knew of their own knowledge of Joseph Cusick's service with Solomon Longboard. Isaac Miller a Tuscarora from Niagara County, New York stated he had also served with Joseph Cusick in the War with Britain. Sworn the 15th day of December 1857. Farmer's Brother was also mentioned as being in command. Some of the other individual's mentioned in Joseph Cusick's papers who served in his company included the following men:

William? Alvis, Jim Basket, John Beach or Birch, Big-Fish, Blacksnake, George Cusick, John Fox, Grouse? or Crouse? (Sergeant), Isaac Grouse? or Crouse? John Henry, Jacob (Colonel), Aron Johnson, Washington Lewis, Little-Fish, Seth Lyon, Isaac Miller, Adam Patterson, John Patterson, Samuel Pembleton, George Printup, John Printups, William Printups, Thomas Smith, Isaac Thompson, John Tobacco and Henry Williams.

Another source for the service of Joseph Cusick appeared in the Chicago Times Newspaper in 1888 in an article entitled "A Brave Indians Services," A letter from Lockport New York.

During the War of 1812 some engagements in Canada, Michigan, Ohio and near the Canadian, New York border included: Beaver Dams, Black Rock, Brownstown, Buffalo, Butler's Farm, Chateaugay, Chippewa, Chyrsler's Farm, Cross Roads, Fort Erie, Fort George, Fort Meigs, Fort Niagara, Frenchman's Creek, Lewiston, Lundy's Lane, Lyon's Creek, Machinac, Malcolm's Mills, Maquaga, Miami, Moravian Town, Nottawasaga, Prarie-du-Chien, York, Sandusky, Rock River Rapids and York.

THE BUREAU OF INDIAN AFFAIRS CENSUS OF THE TUSCARORA INDIANS, NEW YORK AGENCY IN JULY 1886.

This census abstract is not in its original order. it has been alphabetized for this book. Family relationships were not provided in this census. The ages of some of the entries indicates that several families with similar surnames may be grouped together. This abstract should be used only as a reference. It should not take the place of any original government records.

ALVIS, Amanda age 56, Roll Number 9.

ANDERSON, Edward, 38, Sarah age 40, Willis age 17, Belle age 8, Florence age 19, Geneva age 2, Chauncey age 13, Nellie age 15, Roll Numbers 1-8.

BEAVER, Helen age 38, George W., age 3, Roll Numbers 16, 17.

BISSELL, Elias age 21, James age 19, William age 15, Edwin age 12, Hattie age 9, Francis age 37, Roll Numbers 10-15.

BRALEY? or **BRABEY?** Amelia age 25, Roll Number 18.
CARRIER, William age 39, Roll Number 65.

CHEW, Silas age 24, Emily G. age 26, Hawley age 42, Lucy age 43, Jefferson age 18, Elvira age 12, Sidney age 10, Carolina age 6, Eliza age 46, Olive age 21, Frank age 36, Cornelius age 40, John H., age 18, Roll Numbers 19-31.

CUSICK, Hiram age 28, Lucy age 67, Esther age 34, Wilkins age 25, Sarah age 18, Enos? or Emos? age 2, Albert age one month, James age 41, Nancy age 48, Nickolas age 27, Lucinda age 28, Baby age one month, Wilson age 1, William age 23, Emeline age 26, David age 25, Cassie age 21, Elias age 4, Josephine age 6, Eli age 36, Roll Numbers 45-64.
CUSICK, Peter age 65, Levi age 11, Susannah age 91, Anna age 36, Delos age 17, Leah age 17, Samson age 40, Sarah Ann age 40, David age 20, William age 16, Rostha? age 4, Baby age six months, Lydia age 28, Roll Numbers 32-44.

DOUGLAS, George age three months, Delia age 4, Roll Numbers 66-67.
FISH, Sally age 79, Roll Number 68.
GANSWORTH, John age 75, John Jr., age 35, Roll Numbers 105-106.

GARLOW, Henry age 23, Alex age 61, Emeline age 35, Eunice age 20, Julia age 26, Roll Numbers 91-95. **GARLOW**, Minnie age 22, Hattie age 17, Isaac age 28, Alex age 14, John age 31, William age 58, Louisa age 52, Andrew age 22, Eleazor age 1, Roll Numbers 96-104.

GREEN, Dinah age 30, Amelia age 7, Bacheriah? or Zachariah? age 44, Sarah age 53, Helen age 18, Sarah age 14, Eliza age 64, Leander age 4, George age 65, Sally age 66, Frank age 2, Peter age 30, Jacob age 30, Hannah age 19, Julia age 46, Isaac age 16, Leah age 17? or 14? Hiram age 26, Eunice age 23, Romer age 2, Baby age six months, John age 4, Roll Numbers 69-90.

HENRY, Noah age 34, Mary age 36, Eli age 14, Timothy age 60, Lester age 5, Viola age 7, Ethel age 3, Emeline age 1, Roll Numbers 396-403.

HEWETT, Abagail age 19, Alvis age 39, Roll Numbers 121-122. **HEWETT,** David M.D. (Doctor?) age 71, John age 29, Aaron age 24, Frank age 22, Casanda age 20, Hattie age 12, Avis age 27? or 29? Silas age 19, Roll Numbers 113-120.

HILL, Ida age 22, Cinderella age 1, Eunice age 48, Annie age 23, Baby age six days, Hiram age 23, Roll Numbers 107-112.

ISAAC, Justice age 10, Thomas age 7, Roll Numbers 123-124.

JACK, Anderson age 22, Luther N. age 27? Louisa age 23, Elizabeth age 64? or 4? Andy age 33, Isaac N., age 54, Sam age 23, Roll Numbers 188-194.

JACOBS, Samuel age 71, Emily age 46, Jacob age 13, Thomas age 7, Maria age 53, Wilbert age 18, Adeline age 26, Roll Numbers 125-131.

JIMISON, John age 22, Helen age 29, Roll Numbers 179-180.

JOHNATHAN, Isalam? age 6, Roll Number 195.

JOHNSON Ely age 34, Eunice age 31, Alida age 8, Arther? age 6, Chester age 3, Mary age 60, Isiah age 19, Mathew age 17, Elias age 48, Julia A., age 47, Farmer? age 20, Alice age 18, Dexter age 22, Philip age 26, Josephine age 21, James age 54, Elizabeth age 55, Althia age 22, Martha age 22, Foster age 19, Nellie age 14, Wilkinson age 12, Wlliam J., age 28, Lucy age 30, Cora age 3, Margaret age 29, Melissa age 10, Roll Numbers 146-172. **JOHNSON,** Enos age 41, Lewis age 23, Frank? age 5, Lillie age 6, Bertha age 4, Gilbert age 1, Roll Numbers 173-178. **JOHNSON,** William age 58, Nancy age 71, Eli age 31, Adeline age 31, Eliza age 11, Frank age 5, Newton age 2? Sarah Ann age 2, Levi age 28, Elizabeth age 39, Charles age 3, Dennis age 1, Laura age 16, Enos? or Emos? age 11, Roll Numbers 132-145.

JONES, Helen age 29, Minervia age 10, Harriet age 3, Adophus abe 7, Elvira age 5? or 15? Lucy age 13, Eliza age 11, Roll Numbers 181-187.

MILLER, Simeon age 57, Eliza age 49, Ida age 12, Leander age 7, Rachael age 17, Clara age 4, Rachael age 19? or 17? Daniel age 14, Joslyn age 5, Roll Numbers 196-203.

MT. PLEASANT, CHIEF JOHN age 76, Rachael age 33, Frank age 30, Minnie age 25, William age 4, Frank Jr., age 2, Grant age 19, Emily age 56, Walter age 26, Roll Numbers 204-212.

NATH? OR NASH? Celia age 44, Roll Number 213.

PATTERSON, Holland age 30, Asa age 8, Catherine age 6, Mary age 27, Mary age 43, Elmer age seven months, George age 30, Elmer age 27, Guy age 9, Clara Jane age seven months, Wilson age 5, Minerva age 4, John age 10, Selinda age 39, Noah age 30, Hattie age 1, Lewis age 45, Mary J., age 40, Mary age 10, Jane age 60, William H., age 49, Margaret age 42, Sophronia age 17, Jesse age 15, Moses age 13, Homer age 9, Amelia age 1, Roll Numbers 247-273. **PATTERSON**, Susan age 83, Mary age 27, Augusta age 12, Hattie age 10, Nancy age 52, Racheale age 10, Eddie age 3, Ely age 49, Lucy age 44, Isaac age 49, Lizzie age 58, Jacob age 22, Emeline age 9, Emma age 12, Delia age 57, Michael age 28, Althea age 16, Philima age five months, **PATTERSON**, W. Tory? age 60, Joseph age 30, Roll Numbers 274-293.

PEMBLETON, James Sr., age 56, Eliza age 56, James Jr., age 22, Ruth age 27, Enoch age 4, Lovina age 1, Avis age 33, Louisa age 3, Eliza age 36, Josephine age 11, Daniel age 8, Caroline age 6, Elvira age 3, Alice age 2, James age 56, Roll Numbers 219-233. **PEMBLETON**, Samuel J., age 60? Melinda age 23, Dennis age 27? Levi age 7, Sarah age 44, Roll Numbers 214-218.

PETER, Levi age 27, Lucy age 26, Harrison age 4, Louisa age 2, baby one month, Joshua age 43, Roll Numbers 294-299. **PETER**, Marcus age 39, Lucy age 37, Jasper age 12, Samuel age 3, Jerimiah age 45, John age 11, Marcus age 39, Lucy age 37, Eugene age 15, Wilber age 11, Alice age 9, Roll Numbers 300-310.

PRINTUP, Racheal age 70, Roll Number 246. **PRINTUP**, William age 76, Lafayette age 37, Kate age 32, Sabrina age 11, Lafayette age 7, Lerverne? age 5, Daniel age 46, Stephen age 31, Lydia age 23, Amos age 29, Mary age 21, Sarah age 35, Roll Numbers 234-245.

RACKET, Aaron age 30, Emily age 17, George age 28, Lucy age 25, Edgar age 7, Fred age 5, Clinton age 4, Chester age 3, John age 38, Minnie P. age 17, Roll Numbers 311-320.

SENECA, Sarah age 36, Roll Number 321.

SMITH, Elias age 41, Hannah age 70, Hanah age 11, Hasley age 8, Daniel age 6, Isaac age 65, Rachael age 48, Lucinda age 38, Daisy age 19, Jennie D., age 15, Spencer age 11, Ediie age 6, Mary age 39, Roll Numbers 326-337.

SYLVESTER, EMMA age 25, Oscar age 5, Cora age 2, Hubbard age five months, Roll Numbers 322-325.

THOMPSON, Lena age 10, (See Nat Thompson?) E. Adell age 6, Amane age 4, Cleveland age 1, Samuel age 21, Joseph age 36, Melissa age 7, Sarah a., age 49, Samuel age 53, Eliza age 45, Jerimiah age 21, Enos? or Emos? age 7, Beckey age 27, Eunice age 24, Effie age 20, Sally age 58, Lucinda age 36, Mary age 21, Baby age one months, Roll Numbers 347-365. **THOMPSON**, Nat age 26, Amelia age 22, Edward age 4, De Forest age 1, Minnie age 1, Lafayette age 17, Simeon age 57, Susan age 44, Martha age 16? Roll Numbers 338-346.

WILLIAMS, Daniel age 27, Althia age 15, Lucy age 10, Abagail age 25, Frank age 9, Albert age 6, Alex age 26, Lucius age 27, Roll Numbers 366-373. **WILLIAMS**, Lillie age 20, Bilmous? age 2, Adam age 44, Hayes age 9, Joseph age 70, Louisa age 56, Emma age 17, George age 20, Lucy age 49, Samson age 25, John age 18, Emma age 10, Thomas age 31, Lucinda age 29, Eleazor age 8, Theodore age 7, Hattie age 5, Anna Maria age five months, Daniel age 28, Josiah age 29, Roll Numbers 374-394.

WHITE, Avis age 23, Roll Numbers 395.

THE 1900 UNITED FEDERAL CENSUS OF THE TUSCARORA RESERVE IN NIAGARA COUNTY, NEW YORK.

The census abstract below is not in its original order. It has been alphabetized for this book. All of the people in each of the following households were Tuscarora. Exceptions were noted where individuals were members of the another tribe, or race. Everyone in each household was born in New York unless otherwise stated. Everyone in each household has the same surname as the head of household. If an individual in a household had a different surname than the head of household that surname was highlighted by capital letters. The following names were recorded as they were spelled in the original records. The accuracy of the genealogy information represented in the following census abstract depends on how that information was provided and recorded for the original census. A question mark was placed after the names, ages and dates where the spelling was in doubt. This 1900 Federal Census of the Tuscarora Reservation, Niagara County, Lewiston, New York begins with Enumeration District Number 138, Page 81A.

ANDERSON, ATWOOD: (Cayuga/Tuscarora) Age 50 born in June 1849 in English Canada (Ontario). His father was born in English Canada. His mother was born in New York. He was listed as a Tuscarora. His father was a Cayuga. His mother was a Tuscarora. Geneva a daughter age 17 was born in March 1883. Her mother was born in New York. Both of her parents were listed as Tuscarora. E.D. 138, Page 83A, Household 22/22.

ANDERSON, WILLIS? (Tuscarora) Age not given. He was born in New York. His father was born in English Canada (Ontario). His mother was born in New York. Both of his parents were Tuscarora. Alvis his wife age 25 was born in August 1874 in New York. Both of her parents were born in New York. Both of her parents were Tuscarora. Robert a son age 8 was born in May 1892. Malisse a daughter age 4 was born in March 1898. Nettle? or Nellie? a daughter age 2 was born in January 1898. An infant daughter with no name listed was age four months born in January 1890. E.D. 138, Page 82B/83A, Household 19/19.

BEAVER, HELEN M.: (Tuscarora) Age 52, born in March 1848 in New York. Both of her parents were born in New York. Both of her parents were Tuscarora. John H., CHEW a son age 32 was born in May 1868 in New York. George W. BEAVER a son age 18, was born in Sept 1881 in New York. Thomas A. CUSICK a boarder (Age not given). He was born in September in New York. Both of his parents were born in New York. Both of his parents were Tuscarora. Everyone in this household was listed as Tuscarora. Page 82B, Household 18/18.

BISSEL, WILLIAM: (Tuscarora) Age 30 born in ? 1870 in New York. Both of his parents were born in New York. Both of his parents were Tuscarora. E.D. 138, Page 89A, Household 87/87.

BISSELL, ELIAS: (Tuscarora) Age 33, born in Mary 1867 in New York. Both of his parents were born in New York. Both of his parents were listed as Tuscarora? Harry a son age 10 was born in December 1889 in New York. Both of his parents were born in New York. Joseph BISSELL (He was listed as a white man) father (Of Elias Bissell) age 69 was born in November 1830 in English Canada (Ontario). Both of his parents were born in New York. Both of the parents of Joseph BISSELL were listed as Tuscarora? Lensy? DOCTOR (A female servant) age 28 was born in August 1871 in English Canada (Ontario). Both of her parents were born in English Canada (Ontario). She was listed as a Mohawk, however both of her parents were listed as Tuscarora? E.D. 138, Page 84B, Household 36/36.

CHEW, CORNELIUS: (Tuscarora) Age 50 born in ? 1850 in New York. Both of his parents were born in New York. Both of his parents were Tuscarora. E.D. 138, Page 88B, Household 78/78.

CHEW, DAVID: (Tuscarora) Age 34, born in May 1866 in New York. Both of his parents were born in New York. Both of his parents were Tuscarora. Ruth his wife age 41 was born in February 1859 in New York. Both of her parents were born in New York. Both of her parents were Tuscarora. Enoch PAMELTON (This surname may be a corruption of the surname Pembleton) age 17 was born in December 1882 in New York. Both of his parents were born in New York. He was listed as a Tuscarora. Both of his parents were Tuscarora. Barbara CHEW a daughter age 6 was born in October 1893 in New York. Amelia CHEW a daughter age 3 was born in June 1896 in New York. Sampson a son age 1 was born in March 1899 in New York. Myron PATERSON (He was listed as a servant) age 15 was born in August 1889 in New York. Both of his parents were born in New York. He was listed as a Tuscarora, both of his parents were Tuscarora. E.D. 183, Page 81A, Household 1.

CHEW, ELIZA: (Oneida/Tuscarora) Age 58 born in July 1841 in New York. Both of her parents were born in New York. She was listed as a Tuscarora. Her father was an Oneida. Her mother was a Tuscarora. Olive a daughter age 35 was born in February 1865 in New York. Both of her parents were born in New York. Both of her parents were Tuscarora. E.D. 183, Page 86A, Household 54/54.

CHEW, FRANK: (Tuscarora) Age 46 born in August 1853 in New York. Both of his parents were born in New York. Both of his parents were Tuscarora. Charles a son age 17 was born in 1883 in English Canada (Ontario). His father was born in New York. His mother was born in English Canada. Both of his parents were Tuscarora. Sarah J., a daughter age 3 was born in August 1896 in New York. Her father was born in New York. Her mother was born in English Canada (Ontario). Bell his wife (Of Frank?) age 20 was born in 1880 in New York. Both of her parents were born in New York. Both of her parents were Tuscarora. E.D. 183, Page 82A, Household 9/9.

CHEW, HOLLY: (Tuscarora) Age 66 born in May 1834 in New York. Both of his parents were born in New York. Both of his parents were Tuscarora. Althia WILLIAMS a servant age 31 was born in May 1869 in New York. Both of her parents were born in New York. Both of her parents were Tuscarora. Fillman CHEW a son age 14 was born in March 1886. George CHEW a son age 8 was born in March 1892. Matilda CHEW a daughter age 6 was born in March 1894. Delia CHEW a daughter age 3 was born in March 1897. E.D. 183, Page 88B, Household 80/80.

CHEW, OSIAS: (Onondaga/Tuscarora) Age 63 was born in ? 1837 in New York. Both of his parents were born in New York. He was listed as an Onondaga. His father was a Tuscarora. His mother was an Onondaga. Lucy his wife age 55 was born in ? 1845 in New York. Both of her parents were born in New York. Both of her parents were Tuscarora. Garfield a son age 20 was born in 1880. E.D. 183, Page 87B, Household 73/73.

CHEW, SAMPSON: (Indian) Age 53 born in August 1846 in New York. Both of his parents were born in New York. Both of his parents were Tuscarora. Sarah A., his wife age 55 was born in March 1845 in New York. Both of her parents were born in New York. Both of her parents were Tuscarora. Lusaltha? a daughter age 18 was born in June 1882 in New York. Emily a daughter age 15 was born in December 1884 in New York. Both of the parents of Lusaltha and Emily Chew were born in New York. Both parents were listed as Tuscarora. E.D. 138, Page 86A, Household 58/58.

CHEW, SILAS: (Tuscarora) Age 38 born in March in 1862. The place of birth of Silas Chew and his parents was listed as unknown. Both of his parents were Tuscarora. Mary PATTERSON a servant. Her age and birthplace was listed as unknown. Both of her parents were born in New York. Both of her parents were Tuscarora. Mable PATTERSON a niece (Of Mary?) age 18 was born in New York. Both of her parents were born in New York. Both of her parents were Tuscarora. Page 88A, Household 74/74.

CUSICK, LYDIA: (Tuscarora) Age 40 born in November 1859 in New York. Both of her parents were born in New York. Both of her parents were Tuscarora. Webster a son age was 17 born in November 1882 in New York. Both of his parents were born in New York. Both of his parents were Tuscarora. E.D. 138, Page 88B, Household 82/82.

CUSICK, PETER: (Tuscarora) Age 79 born in May 1821 in New York. Both of his parents were born in New York. Both of his parents were Tuscarora. Levi a son age 25 was born in October 1874 in New York. Both of his parents were born in New York. Both of his parents were Tuscarora. E.D. 138, Page 83B, Household 24/24.

CUSICK, WILLIAM: (Tuscarora) Age 38, born in August 1861 in New York. Both of his parents were born in New York. Both of his parents were Tuscarora. Emaline his wife age 39 was born in August 1860 in New York. She was listed as a Tuscarora. Both of her parents were Tuscarora. E.D. 138, Page 83B, Household 27/27.

GANSWORTH, JOHN: (Tuscarora) Age 49 born in November 1850 in New York. Both of his parents were born in New York. Both of his parents were Tuscarora. Elizabeth his wife age 46 was born in July 1853 in New York. Both of her parents were born in New York. She was listed as an Onondaga. Her father was a Tuscarora. Her mother was an Onondaga. Orasmus a son age 16 was born in September 1883 in New York. He was listed as a Seneca. His father was a Tuscarora. His mother was listed as a Seneca? Elmer a son age 6 was born in March 1894 in New York. He was listed as an Onondaga. His father was a Tuscarora. His mother was an Onondaga. E.D. 138, Page 86A, Household 55/55.

GARLOW, ALEXANDER: (Tuscarora/Oneida) Age 77 was born in April 1823 in New York. Both of his parents were born in New York. He was listed as a Tuscarora. His father was an Oneida. His mother was a Tuscarora. Emaline a daughter was age 49 was born in August 1850 in New York.

Both of her parents were born in New York. Both of her parents were Tuscarora. E.D. 183, Page 81B, Household 7/7.

GARLOW, HENRY: (Tuscarora) Age 36 was in 1864 in New York. Both of his parents were born in New York. Both of his parents were Tuscarora. E.D 138, Page 88B, Household 79/79.

GARLOW, ISAAC: (Tuscarora) Age 42 born in February 1858 in New York. Both of his parents were born in New York. Both of his parents were Tuscarora. Martha his wife age 36 born in July 1863 in New York. Both of her parents were born in New York. Both of her parents were Tuscarora. Winnifred a daughter age 9 was born in September 1890. Ethel a daughter age 8 was born in October 1893. Mary a daughter age two months was born in March 1900. E.D. 138, Page 86A/86B, Household 59/59.

GARLOW, JOHN: (Tuscarora) Age 48, born in June 1851 in New York. Both of his parents were born in New York. Both of his parents were Tuscarora. Marthy his wife age 36 was born in June 1864? in New York. Both of her parents were born in New York. Both of her parents were Tuscarora. Minnie a daughter age 20 was born in March 1880. Hederl? a son age 18 was born in March 1882. Philip a son age 16 was born in March 1884. James a son age 14 was born in November 1885. William a son age 12 was born in January 1888. Claudie a son age 9 was born in July 1860. Florence M. a daughter age 7 was born in June 1892. Theodore a son age 3 was born in August 1896. Hattie a daughter age 1 was born in May 1899. E.D. 183, Page 81B, Household 6/6.

GARLOW, WILLIAM: (Tuscarora) Age 75 born in October 1824 in New York. Both of his parents were born in New York. Both of his parents were Tuscarora. Andrew a son age 29 was born in March 1871 in New York. Mollie a daughter-in- law (She was listed as white) age 28 was born in September 1871 in Alabama. Both of her parents were born in New York. E.D. 138, Page 85A, Household 42/42.

GREEN, ELIZA: (Tuscarora) Age 55 born in March 1845 in New York. Both of her parents were born in New York. Both of her parents were Tuscarora. Zackery GREEN her husband age 52 was born in March 1848 in New York. Both of his parents were born in New York. Both of his parents were Tuscarora. Jerrymiah THOMPSON a son (Of Eliza) age 35 was born in September 1864 in New York. Both of his parents were born in New York. Both of his parents were Tuscarora. E.D. 138, Page 88A, Household 75/75.

GREEN, ELIZA: (Tuscarora) Age 78, born in February 1822 in New York. Both of her parents were born in New York. Both of her parents were Tuscarora. E.D. 183, Page 82A, Household 13/13.

GREEN, GEORGE: (Tuscarora) Age 78 born in February 1822 in New York. Both of his parents were born in New York. Both of his parents were Tuscarora. Nancy his wife age 62 was born in December 1837 in New York. Both of her parents were born in New York. Both of her parents were Tuscarora. George Junior a grand son age 9? or 19? was born in April 1881. Anna a step-daughter age 33 was born in March 1867. Thomas a son age 14 was born in December 1885. All were born in New York. All of the members of this household were listed as Tuscarora. All of the parents of everyone in this household were listed as Tuscarora. E.D. 183, Page 85A, Household 44/44.

GREEN, ISAAC: (Onondaga/Tuscarora) Age 30, born in March 1870 in New York. Both of his parents were born in New York. He was listed as a Tuscarora. His father was an Onondaga. His mother was a Tuscarora. E.D. 183, Page 83B, Household 28/28.

GREEN, JONAS: (Onondaga/Tuscarora) Age 31 born in June 1868 in New York. Both of his parents were born in New York. He was listed as an Onondaga. His father was a Tuscarora. His mother was an Onondaga. Berthy his wife age 24 was born in August in 1875 in New York. Both of her parents were born in New York. John J., a son was born in July 1891. Phebe a daughter age 6 was born in August 1893. Benjamin H., a son age 4 was born in January 1896. Lawrence age four months was born in January 1900. E.D. 183, Page 84B, Household 39/39.

HENRY, ELI: (Tuscarora) Age 28 born in March in 1872 in New York. Both of his parents were born in New York. Both of his parents were Tuscarora. Nellie his wife age 29 was born in June 1870 in New York. Both of her parents were born in New York. Both of her parents were Tuscarora. Noah a son age 7 was born in February 1893. Lillian a daughter age eleven months was born in June 1899. E.D. 138, Page 85A, Household 43/43.

HENRY, TIMOTHY: (Tuscarora) Age 24, born in August 1875 in New York. Both of his parents were born in New York. He was listed as a Tuscarora. Nellie his wife age 28 was born in August 1871 in New York. Her father was born in Canada. Her mother was born in New York. Elizabeth HENRY? mother-in-law (Of Timothy Henry) age 67 was born in July 1832 in New York. Both of her parents were born in New York. Both of her parents were Tuscarora. Lucinda WILLIAMS a sister-in-law (Of Timothy Henry?) age 59 was born in April 1841 in New York. Both of her parents were born in New York. Althia JOHNSON a sister-in-law (Of Timothy Henry?) age 39 was born in April 1861 in New York. Both of her parents were born in New York. The parents of Lucinda Williams and Althia Johnson were listed as Tuscarora. E.D. 183, Page 82B, Household 15/15.

HEWETT, ALVIS: (Tuscarora) Age 56, born in May 1844 in New York. Both of his parents were born in New York. Both of his parents were Tuscarora. Avis C., his wife age 43 born in March 1857 in New York. Both of her parents were born in New York. Both of her parents were Tuscarora. Fremont a son age 16, born in March 1884, Minnie a daughter age 11 was born in December 1888. Amelia HEWETT a grand daughter age 6 was born in April 1894 in New York. Her father was born in English Canada (Ontario). Her mother was born in New York. Both of her parents were Tuscarora. E.D. 138, Page 83B/84A, Household 31/31.

HEWETT, SILAS M: (Tuscarora) Age 33, born in May 1867 in New York. Both of his parents were born in New York. Both of his parents were Tuscarora. Emily his wife age 31, was born in March 1869 in New York. Both of her parents were born in New York. Both of her parents were Tuscarora. Ethel S., a daughter age 8 was born in September 1891. David B., a son age 6 was born in July 1893. Wilkison P., a son age 4 was born in September 1895. E.D. 138, Page 83B, Household 30/30.

HILL, ANNA: (Tuscarora) Age 38, born in August 1861 in New York. Both of her parents were born in New York. Both of her parents were Tuscarora. John HILL her husband age 56 was born in March 1844 in New York. Both of his parents were born in New York. He was listed as a Iroquois. Both of his parents were listed as Iroquois. Edith a daughter age 13 was born in June 1886. John Jr. a son age 11 was born in April 1889. Robert a son age 9 was born in April 1891. Joseph a son age 5 was born in April 1895. Anna Hill was listed as the Head of this household. All of the children of Anna Hill were listed as Tuscarora. E.D. 138, Page 82B, Household 16/16.

HILL, EUNICE: (Tuscarora) Age 64 born in December 1835 in English Canada (Ontario). Both of her parents were born in New York. Both of her parents were Tuscarora. Elizabeth PETERS a sister age 42 was born in June 1857 in New York. Her father was born in English Canada. Her mother was born in New York. Both of her parents were Tuscarora. John JIMISON a nephew age 31 was born in New York. His father was born in English Canada. Both of his parents were born in New York. Both of his parents were Tuscarora. E.D. 138, Page 86B, Household 62/62.

HILL, HERMAN W: (Tuscarora) Age 37 born in July 1863 in New York. The birthplace of his father was unknown. His mother was born in New York. Both of his parents were Tuscarora. Avis his wife age 32 was born in October 1867 in New York. Both of her parents were born in English Canada (Ontario). Avis Hill was listed as a Tuscarora. No tribal origin was given for her parents. Dewey a son age one was born in July 1898 in New York. E.D. 138, Page 85B, Household 48/48.

ISAAC, THOMAS: (Tuscarora) Age 22 born in 1878 in New York. His father was born in English Canada (Ontario). His mother was born in New York. He was listed as a Tuscarora. His father's tribal origins was listed as unknown. His mother was a Tuscarora. Minnie GREEN (Relationship not given) age 30 was born in 1870 in New York. Her father was born in English Canada. Her mother was born in New York. Both of her parents were Tuscarora. Mary GREEN a sister (Of Thomas Isaac? or Minnie Green?) age 7 was born in 1893 in New York. Carrie GREEN a sister age 5 was born in 1895 in New York. Marthy GREEN a sister age 1 was born in 1899 in New York. Everyone in this household was listed as a Tuscarora. All of the parents of everyone in this household except the father of Thomas Isaac was listed as Tuscarora. E.D. 138, Page 87A, Household 67/67.

JACK, ANDERSON: (Tuscarora) Age 47 born in New York. Both of his parents were born in New York. Both of his parents were Tuscarora. E.D. 138, Page 87A, Household 64/64.

JACK, ISAAC: (Tuscarora) Age 66 born in August 1833 in New York. The birthplace of his father was unknown. His mother was born in New York. Both of his parents were Tuscarora. Catherine his wife age 66 was born in 1874 in New York. Both of her parents were born in New York. She was listed as an Onondaga. Her father was a Tuscarora. Her mother was an Onondaga. Wavemyer? or Havemyer? a son age 25 was born in March 1875 in New York. Marvin a son age 22 was born in March 1878 in New York. Havemyer and Marvin Jack were listed as Onondaga. E.D. 138, Page 86B, Household 63/63.

JACK, LUTHER: (Tuscarora) Age 44, born in July 1855 in New York. Both of his parents were born in New York. Both of his parents were Tuscarora. Louise his wife age 36, was born in August 1863 in New York. Both of her parents were born in New York. Both of her parents were Tuscarora. Warren JACK a nephew age 13 was born in 1887 in New York. Both of his parents were born in New York. He was a Tuscarora. Both of his parents were Tuscarora. E.D. 138, Page 83A, Household 20/20.

JACOB, JOSIAH: (Onondaga) Age 28 born in January 1872 in New York. Both of his parents were born in New York. Both of his parents were Onondaga. Caroline his wife age 20 was born in 1880 in New York. Both of her parents were born in New York. Both of her parents were Tuscarora. Viola a daughter age 2 was born in September 1898. Louise a daughter age nine months was born in August 1899. E.D. 138, Viola and Louise Jacob were listed as Tuscarora. E.D. 138, Page 85B, Household 50/50.

JACOB, MERIE (MARIE): (Tuscarora) Age 67 born in May 1833 in New York. Both of her parents were born in New York. Both of her parents were Tuscarora. Wilber a son age 33 was born in June 1866 in New York. Both of his parents were born in New York. Both of his parents were Tuscarora. E.D. 138, Page 87B, Household 69/69.

JACOBS, WILSON: (Onondaga/Tuscarora) Age 55 born in November 1844 in New York. He was listed as an Onondaga. His father was born in Oneida, New York. His mother was born in New York. His father was a Tuscarora. His mother was an Onondaga. Dennis a son age 17 was born in March 1883. Edward a son age 15 was born in March 1885. Eunice HILL a servant age 25 was born in June 1875 in English Canada (Ontario). Both of her parents were born in English Canada. She was listed as an Onondaga. No further information was given about her parents. Alice HILL age 31 was born in 1863 in English Canada. She was listed as an Onondaga. Both of her parents were born in English Canada (Ontario). Both Alice and Eunice Hill immigrated in 1899. E.D. 138, Page 81B, Household 5/5.

JOHNSON, ELI S.: (Tuscarora) Age 49 born in April 1851 in New York. Both of his parents were born in New York. Both of his parents were Tuscarora. Enice? or Eunice? his wife age 45 was born in November 1854 in New York. Both of her parents were born in New York. Both of her parents were Tuscarora. Alida a daughter age 22 was born in March 1878. Arthur G., a son age was 19 born in June 1880. Chester a son age 18 was born in September 1881. Abagail a daughter age 12 was born in September 1887. Semore a son age 8 was born in 1892. E.D. 138, Page 87A, Household 66/66.

JOHNSON, ELI W.: (Tuscarora) Age 46 born in January 1854 in New York. Both of his parents were born in New York. Both of his parents were Tuscarora. Adeline his wife age 45 was born in March 1855 in New York. Both of her parents were born in New York. Both of her parents were Tuscarora. Frank E., a son age 19 was born in June 1880. Martin a son age 6 was born in February 1896. E.D. 138, Page 85B/86A, Household 52/52.

JOHNSON, ELIAS: (Tuscarora) Age 63 born in January 1857 in English Canada (Ontario). Both of his parents were both born in New York. Both of his parents were Tuscarora. Julia his wife age 61 was born September 1838 in New York. Both of her parents were born in New York. Horacio D., a son age 36 was born in February 1864. Stanley P. JOHNSON a grand son age 7 was born in September 1892 in New York. Both of his parents were born in New York. Both of his parents were Tuscarora. E.D. 138, Page 82B, Household 17/17.

JOHNSON, ENOS: (Tuscarora) Age 55 born in September 1844 in New York. Both of his parents were born in New York. Both of his parents were Tuscarora. Jane PATTERSON mother (Of Enos Johnson) age 79 was born in September 1820 in New York. Both of her parents were born in New York. Both of her parents were Tuscarora. E.D. 138, Page 85B, Household 51/51.

JOHNSON, LEVI: (Tuscarora) Age 43 born in October 1856 in New York. Both of his parents were born in New York. Both of his parents were Tuscarora. Lucy his wife age 47 was born in October 1852 in New York. Both of her parents were born in New York. Both of her parents were Tuscarora. E.D. 138, Page 85B, Household 47/47.

JOHNSON, WILLIAM: (Tuscarora) Age 42 born in February 1858 in New York. Both of his parents were born in New York. Both of his parents were Tuscarora. Lucy his wife age 45 born in July 1855 in New York. Both of her parents were born in New York. Both of her parents were Tuscarora. Cora a daughter age 17 was born in March 1883. Betrice a daughter age 10 was born in April 1890. Alberta S., a daughter age ? was born in March 1893. James HANDRELY (He was listed as white) a servant age 38 was born in 1862 in Ireland. E.D. 183, Page 81B, Household 4.

JONES, HORACE: (Seneca) Age 53 born in April 1847 in New York. both of his parents were born in New York. Both of his parents were Seneca. Both of his parents were born in New York. Helen his wife age 46 was born in December 1853 in New York. Both of her parents were Tuscarora. Lucy a daughter age 25 was born in May 1875. Adolphus B., a son age 19 was born in November 1880. Harriet M., a daughter age 16 was born in January 1884. Haracio A., a son age 11 was born in October 1888. Florence L., a daughter age 9 was born in April 1891. E.D. 138, Page 86B, Household 60/60.

MT. PLEASANT, GRANT: (Tuscarora) Age 32 born in October 1868 in New York. Both of his parents were born in New York. Both of his parents were Tuscarora. Minerva his wife age 36 born in June 1863 in New York. Both of her parents were born in New York. Both of her parents were Tuscarora. Almon a son age 9 was born in July 1890. Elton a son age 8 was born in January 1892. Josephine a daughter age 7 was born in October 1895. Hamilton a son age 3 was born in 1897, Clinton a son age 1 was born in 1899. E.D. 138, Page 88B, Household 83/83.

MT. PLEASANT, AMOS: (Tuscarora) Age 26 born in September 1873 in New York. Both of his parents were born in New York. Both of his parents were Tuscarora. Rebecca his wife age 41 was born in April 1859 in New York. Both of her parents were born in New York. Both of her parents were Tuscarora. E.D. 138, Page 89A, Household 86/86.

MT. PLEASANT, SCHERLOTTE: (Tuscarora/Onondaga) Age 70 born in March 1830 in New York. Both of her parents were born in New York. She was listed as a Tuscarora. Her father was a Tuscarora. Her mother was an Onondaga. Lawrence a son age 44 was born in February 1856. Both of his parents were born in New York. Both of his parents were Tuscarora. E.D. 183, Page 85A, Household 41/41.

MT. PLEASANT, RACHAIL: (Tuscarora) Age 46, born in July 1853 in New York. Both of her parents were born in New York. Both of her parents were Tuscarora. E.D. 181B, Page 81B, Household 8/8.

MT. PLEASANT, FRANKLIN: (Tuscarora) Age 44 was born in March 1856 in New York. Both of his parents were born in New York. Both of his parents were Tuscarora. Mary A. SMITH a sister age 53 was born in March 1847 in New York. William Mt. Pleasant a son age 18 was born in August 1881. Frank a son age 16 was born in June 1883. Edison a son age 9 was born in September 1890. Mamie a daughter age 6 was born in October 1893. Spencer SMITH a nephew age 24 was born in October 1875 in New York. Edith SMITH a niece age 20 was born in February 1880 in New York. Everyone in this household was listed as Tuscarora. All of the parents of everyone in this household were born in New York. E.D. 138, Page 87B, Household 71.

PAMBLETON (OR PEMBLETON?) LEVI: (Tuscarora) Age 21 born in October 1878 in New York. Both of his parents were born in New York. Both of his parents were Tuscarora. Emily JACOBS grand mother (Of Levi Pambleton) age 56 was born in November 1843 in New York. Both of her parents were born in New York. Both of her parents were Tuscarora. Daisy MT. PLEASANT a servant age 33 was born in December 1866 in New York. Both of her parents were born in New York. Both of her parents were Tuscarora. E.D. 138, Page 85B, Household 46/46.

PAMBLETON (OR PEMBLETON) SIMEON: (Onondaga/Tuscarora) Age 47, born in July 1852 in New York. Both of his parents were born in New York. He was listed as an Onondaga. His father was a Tuscarora. His mother was an Onondaga. Avis his wife age 48 was born in December in 1851 in New York. Both of her parents were born in New York. Both of her parents were Tuscarora. Louise a daughter age 16 was born in August 1885? E.D. 183, Page 82A, Household 11/11.

PAMBLETON (OR PEMBLETON) JAMES: (Tuscarora) Age 33, born in 1867 in New York. Both of his parents were born in New York. Both of his parents were Tuscarora. E.D. 138, Page 83B, Household 29/29.

PAMBLETON (OR PEMBLETON) SARAH: (Tuscarora) Age 57 born in March 1843 in New York. Both of her parents were born in New York. Both of her parents were Tuscarora. E.D. 138, page 86A, Household 56/56.

PAMBLETON (OR PEMBLETON) MARY: (Tuscarora) Age 64, born in 1836 in New York. Both of her parents were born in New York. Both of her parents were Tuscarora. Dennis a son age 46 was born in 1854 in New York. Both of his parents were born in New York. Both of his parents were Tuscarora. E.D. 138, Page 85A, Household 45/45.

PAMBLETON, ELIZA: (Tuscarora) Age 53 born in April 1847 in New York. Both of her parents were born in New York. Both of her parents were

Tuscarora. Alice? or Avis? a daughter age 17 was born in January 1883 in New York. Her father was born in New York. Both of her parents were Tuscarora. Rosa THOMPSON a niece age 13 was born in June? 1886 in New York. Both of her parents were born in New York. Both of her parents were Tuscarora. E.D. 138, Page 85B, Household 49/49.

PATTERSON, DELIA: (Tuscarora) Age 70 born in August 1829 in New York. Both of her parents were born in New York. Both of her parents were Tuscarora. E.D. 138, Page 88B, Household 81/81.

PATTERSON, GEORGE: (Tuscarora) Age 45 born in New York. Both of his parents were born in New York. Both of his parents were Tuscarora. Betsey his wife age 30 was born in March 1870 in English Canada (Ontario). Both of her parents were born in English Canada. Both of her parents were Tuscarora. Nancy a daughter age 8 was born in 1892. Louise a daughter age 5 was born in 1895. Mina a daughter age 1 was born in 1899. E.D. 138, Page 87A, Household 68/68.

PATTERSON, HOLLAND? (Tuscarora) Age 44 born in March 1856 in New York. The birthplace of his father was unknown. His mother was born in New York. Both of his parents were Tuscarora. A daughter not named age 20 was born in August 1879 in New York, Asa a son age 23 was born in February 1877 in New York. Sadie JOHNSON a grand daughter? or adopted daughter? age 15 was born in September 1884 in New York. Both of her parents were born in New York. Both of her parents were Tuscarora. The mother of the children of Holland Patterson was born in New York. She was listed as a Tuscarora. E.D. 138, Page 84A, Household 35/35.

PATTERSON, ISAAC: (Tuscarora) Age 63 born in March 1837 in New York. Both of his parents were born in New York. Both of his parents were Tuscarora. Elizabeth his wife age 73 was born in March 1827 in New York. Both of her parents were born in New York. She was listed as a Tuscarora. Her father was an Onondaga. Her mother was a Tuscarora. Julia A. CARRIE a neice age 19 was born in March 1881 in English Canada (Ontario). Her father was born in English Canada (Ontario). Her mother was born in New York. Emma CARRIE a neice age 16 was born in July 1883 in English Canada. Susan CARRIE a niece age 2 was born in November 1897 in English Canada. Everyone in this household was listed as Tuscarora. The father of Julia, Emma, and Susan CARRIE was listed as a Canadian Tuscarora. Their mother was listed as a Tuscarora. E.D. 138, Page 84A, Household 33/33.

PATTERSON, JESSE: (Tuscarora) Age 29 born in June 1870 in New York. Both of his parents were born in New York. Both of his parents were Tuscarora. Leah his wife age 29 was born in October 1870 in New York. Both of her parents were born in New York. She was listed as an Onondaga. Her father was a Tuscarora. Her mother was an Onondaga. Edna a daughter age 6 was born in February 1894. Burt a son age 4 was born in December 1895. Herman a son age 2 was born in December 1897. Edna, Burt and Herman PATTERSON were listed as Onondaga. E.D. 138, Page 89A, Household 84/84.

PATTERSON, JOSEPH: (Tuscarora) Age 40 born in September 1859 in New York. Both of his parents were born in New York. Both of his parents were Tuscarora. Mary J., his wife age 30 was born in August 1869 in English Canada (Ontario). Her father was born in English Canada

(Ontario). Her mother was born in Ireland. She was listed as a Mohawk. Her father was a Mohawk. Her mother was listed as a Tuscarora? Other tribal information on the census page indicates that Mary J. Patterson was possibly white? Frank E. Patterson a son (Of Joseph Patterson) age 19 was born in December 1880 in New York. Both of his parents were born in New York. Both of his parents were listed as Tuscarora. E.D. 138, Page 88A, Household 76/76.

PATTERSON, TITUS: (Tuscarora/Onondaga) Age 37, born in October 1862 in New York. Both of his parents were born in New York. He was listed as a Tuscarora. His father was a Tuscarora. His mother was an Onondaga. Julia his wife age 41 was born in May 1859 in New York. Both of her parents were born in New York. She was listed as a Tuscarora. Both of her parents were Tuscarora. Nellie a daughter age 12 was born in April 1888. Harry a son age 6 was born in September 1893. Elizabeth a daughter age 3 was born in January 1897. Wesley a son age 2 was born in May 1898. E.D. 183, Page 82A, Household 14/14.

PATTERSON, WILLIAM: (Tuscarora) Age 72 born in 1828 in New York. Both of his parents were born in New York. Both of his parents were Tuscarora. E.D. 138, Page 87A, Household 65/65.

PATTERSON, WILLIAM: (Tuscarora) Age 60, born in June 1839 in New York. Both of his parents were born in New York. Both of his parents were listed as Tuscarora. Margarette his wife age 57, was born in October 1842 in New York. Both of her parents were born in New York. She was listed as a Tuscarora. Her father was an Onondaga. Her mother was a Tuscarora. William M., a son age 27 was born in January 1873. Rachel age 25 was born in August 1874. E.D. 138, Page 84B, Household 37/37.

PETERS, LEVI: (Tuscarora/Oneida) Age 39 born in April 1861 in New York. His father's birthplace was listed as unknown. His mother was born in New York. He was listed as a Tuscarora. His father was an Oneida. His mother was a Tuscarora. John RASKET? OR RACKET? a boarder was age 53 was born in 1846 in English Canada (Ontario). Both of his parents were born in English Canada. He was listed as a Tuscarora. His father was a white man. His mother was a Tuscarora. He immigrated in 1853 to the United States and was naturalized in 1879. Jacob PATERSON a boarder age 37 was born in Sept in 1862 in New York. Both of his parents were born in New York. He was listed as a Tuscarora. Both of his parents were Tuscarora. E.D. 138, Page 81A, Household 2.

PETERS, MARCUS? (Tuscarora) Age 50 was born in July 1849 in New York. Both of his parents were born in New York. Both of his parents were Tuscarora. Lucy his wife age 46 was born in December 1853 in New York. Both of her parents were born in New York. Both of her parents were Tuscarora. Casper a son age 25 was born in July 1874 in New York. Minnie a daughter age 13 was born in July 1886 in New York. Sally a daughter age 6 was born in May 1894 in New York. Clara MILLER? a grand daughter age 18 was born in May 1882 in New York. Moses MILLER a grand son age 20 was born in 1880 in New York. All were listed as Tuscarora. The parents of Clara and Moses Miller were both born in New York. The parents of everyone in this household were Tuscarora. E.D. 138, Page 83A/83B, Household 23/23.

PETERS, WILBER J.: (Tuscarora) Age 27 born in September 1872 in New York. Both of his parents were born in New York. Both of his parents were Tuscarora. Linnie? his wife age 25 was born in September 1874 in New York. Both of her parents were born in New York. Both of her parents were Tuscarora. E.D. 138, Page 82A, Household 12/12.

PRINTUP, CHARLES: (Onondaga/Tuscarora) Age 36 born in March 1864 in New York. Both of his parents were born in New York. He was listed as an Onondaga. His father was a Tuscarora. His mother was an Onondaga. Leah his wife age 28 was born in April 1872 in New York. both of her parents were born in New York. She was listed as a Tuscarora. Her father was a Onondaga. Her mother was a Tuscarora. Johnathan a son age 9 was born in November 1890. Neillie? or Lillie? a daughter age 8 was born in January 1892. Abraham a son age 6 was born in December 1893. Altia a daughter age 2 was born in June 1897 in New York. E.D. 138, Page 87B, Household 70/70.

PRINTUP, DANIEL: (Tuscarora) Age 59 born in ? 1841 in New York. Both of his parents were born in New York. Both of his parents were Tuscarora. Sarah THOMPSON a housekeeper age 63 was born in 1837 in New York. Both of her parents were born in New York. Both of her parents were Tuscarora. E.D. 138, Page 89A, Household 88/88.

PRINTUP, ELEAZER: (Tuscarora) Age 34 born in June 1865 in New York. Both of his parents were born in New York. Both of his parents were Tuscarora. Nancy his wife age 28 born in June 1871 in English Canada (Ontario). Her father was born in English Canada. Her mother was born in New York. Both of her parents were Tuscarora. Jessie a son age 8 was born in March 1892. Chester a son age 6 was born in July 1893. Harvey a son age 4 was born in August 1895. Elizabeth P., a daughter age 3 was born in March 1897. Eliza J., a daughter age 1 was born in December 1898. Moses PRINTUP a brother age 38 was born in January 1888 in New York. Moses PRINTUP JUN., a brother age 38 was born in November 1861. Alvin PRINTUP a nephew age 12 born in New York. Both of his parents were born in New York. Moses PRINTUP JUN., a nephew age 8 born in June 1891. Eziele PRINTUP a brother age 29 born in January 1871 in New York. Both of his parents were born in New York. Daniel PRINTUP Junior, a brother age 22 was born in May 1878 in New York, Harrison PRINTUP a brother age 32 was born in March 1868 in New York. Everyone in this household was listed as Tuscarora. Both of the parents of everyone in this household was Tuscarora. E.D. 138, Page 88A, Household 77/77.

PRINTUP, LAFAYETTE: (Tuscarora) Age 51 born in 1849 in New York. Both of his parents were born in New York. Both of his parents were Tuscarora. Catharine his wife age 46 was born in May 1854 in New York. Her father was born in English Canada (Ontario). Her mother was born in New York. Both of her parents were Tuscarora. Cevere? or Sever? a son age 19 was born in January 1881. E.D. 138, Page 87B, Household 72/72.

PRINTUP, LYDIA: (Tuscarora) Age 41 born in November 1858 in New York. Both of her parents were born in New York. Both of her parents were Tuscarora. Julia a daughter age 12 was born in May in 1888 in New York. Benjamin PAMBLETON a boarder age 32 was born in 1868 in New York. Both of his parents were born in New York. He was listed as a

Tuscarora. Both of his parents were Tuscarora. E.D. 138, Page 84B, Household 40/40.

PRINTUP, MARY J.: (Tuscarora) Age 46, born in July 1853 in New York. Both of her parents were born in New York. Both of her parents were Tuscarora. E.D. 138, Page 83B, Household 26/26.

RICKARD? (Or RICHARD?) GEORGE: (Tuscarora) Age 42, born in January 1858 in New York. Both of his parents were born in New York. Both of his parents were Tuscarora. Lucy his wife age 37 was born in July 1862 in New York. Both of her parents were born in New York. Both of her parents were Tuscarora. Edger a son age 20 was born in October 1879. Frederick a son age 20 was born in February 1880. Clinton a son age 19 was born in May 1881. Chester a son age 17 was born in January 1883. E.D. 138, Page 83A, Household 21/21.

SMITH, ELIAS: (Tuscarora) Age 60 born in March? 1840 in New York. Both of his parents were born in New York. Both of his parents were Tuscarora. Hasley a son age 18 was born in 1882. Daniel a son age 20 was born in 1880. Both of the parents of the children of Elias Smith were born in New York. Both of their parents were listed as Tuscarora. E.D. 138, Page 89A, Household 85/85.

SMITH, RACHEL: (Tuscarora) Age 71, born in May 1829 in New York. Both of her parents were born in New York. Both of her parents were Tuscarora. Frank WILLIAMS a grand son age 23 was born in May 1877 in New York. Albert WILLIAMS a grand son age 20 was born in July 1879 in New York. Arthur WILLIAMS a grand son age 12 was born in March 1888 in New York. The parents of Rachel Smith's grandson's were both born in New York. Both parents were Tuscarora. E.D. 138, Page 82A, Household 10/10.

SYLVESTER, NOAH: (Penobscot) Age 43, born in March in 1857 in Maine. Both of his parents were born in Maine. He was listed as a Penobscot. Both of his parents were Penobscot. Mary his wife age 43 was born in May in 1851 in New York. Both of her parents were born in New York. Both of her parents were Tuscarora. Ida THOMPSON a servant age 25 was born in 1875 in New York. Both of her parents were born in New York. Both of her parents were Tuscarora. E.D. 138, Page 84A, Household 34/34.

THOMPSON, JOSEPH: (Tuscarora/Onondaga) Age 50, was born in April 1850 in New York. Both of his parents were born in New York. He was listed as a Tuscarora. His father was an Onondaga. His mother was a Tuscarora. Jennie his wife age 48 was born in June 1854 in New York. Both of her parents were born in New York. Both of her parents were Tuscarora. Moses a son age 23 was born in July 1874 in New York. Anna a daughter age 23 was born in July 1876 in New York. Jennie a daughter age 11 was born in August 1888 in New York. Malissa THOMPSON a niece age 20 was born in August 1879 in New York. Both of her parents were born in New York. Both of her parents were Tuscarora. The sex of Malissa Thompson was listed erroneously as a male. Elizabeth PRINTUP an aunt (Of Joseph Thompson) age 66 was born in August 1853 in New York. Both of her parents were born in New York. She was listed as a Tuscarora? Her father was a Mohawk. Her mother was an Onondaga. E.D. 138, Page 84B, Household 38.

218

THOMPSON, LUCINDA?: (Machinaw/Tuscarora) Age 50 born in January 1850 in New York. Both of her parents were born in New York. Both of her parents were Tuscarora. Sally THOMPSON mother (Of Lucinda Thompson) age 73 was born in October 1826 in New York. Her father was born in Michigan. Her mother was born in New York. She was listed as a Tuscarora. Her father was a Machinaw Indian. Her mother was a Tuscarora. Mary Thompson sister (Of Lucinda Thompson) age 35 was born in November 1864 in New York. Both of her parents were born in New York. She was listed as a Tuscarora. Both of her parents were Tuscarora? William CHEW a servant, age 29 was born in February 1871 in New York. Both of his parents were born in New York. He was listed as a Tuscarora. Both of his parents were Tuscarora. E.D. 138, Page 81A, Household 3.

THOMPSON, SUSAN: (Tuscarora) Age 58 born in April 1842 in New York. Both of her parents were born in New York. Both of her parents were Tuscarora. Lenthaniel? a son age 39 was born in September 1860 in New York. Both of his parents were born in New York. Both of his parents were Tuscarora. E.D. 138, Page 86A, Household 53/53.

WILLIAMS, ADAM: (Tuscarora) Age 58 born in July 1841 in New York. Both of his parents were born in New York. Both of his parents were Tuscarora. Catherine J., his wife age 25 was born in December 1874 in English Canada (Ontario). Her father was born in English Canada. Her mother was born in New York. Both of her parents were Tuscarora. Sylvester a son age 6 was born in November 1893. Elma a daughter age two months born in March 1900. E.D. 138, Page 86A, Household 57/57.

WILLIAMS, DANIEL: (Tuscarora/Onondaga) Age 41, born in January 1859? in New York. Both of his parents were born in New York. No tribal origins were given for his parents. Adaline his wife age 39 was born in December 1860 in New York. Both of her parents were born in New York. She was listed as a Tuscarora. Her father was an Onondaga. Her mother was a Tuscarora. Wilson CUSICK a stepson age 19 was born in June 1880 in New York. Both of his parents were born in New York. Both of his parents were Tuscarora. E.D. 138, Page 83B, Household 25/25.

WILLIAMS, LUCY: (Tuscarora) Age 64, born in January 1836 in New York. Both of her parents were born in New York. Both of her parents were Tuscarora. Sampson a son age 39 was born in May 1861 in New York. Both of his parents were born in New York. Both of his parents were Tuscarora. Emma JOHNSON a daughter age 24 was born in February 1876. Foster JOHNSON son-in-law age 34 born in September 1865 in New York. Elias CUSICK a grand son age 16 was born in August 1883 in New York. Both the parents of Emma JOHNSON and Foster JOHNSON were born in New York. Both parents were listed as Tuscarora. E.D. 138, Page 84A, Household 32/32.

WILLIAMS, MAGGY: (Tuscarora) Age 26 born in May 1874 in New York. Both of her parents were born in New York. Both of her parents were Tuscarora. John WILLIAMS her husband age 31 was born in October 1868 in New York. Both of his parents were born in New York. Both of his parents were Tuscarora. Alexander a son age 3 was born in August 1896. Pearl a daughter age three months was born in February 1900. E.D. 138, Page 86B, Household 61/61.

WILLIAMS, THOMAS: (Tuscarora) Age 45 born in ? 1855 in New York. His father was born in English Canada (Ontario). His mother was born in New York. Both of his parents were Tuscarora. Sarah PRINTUP a housekeeper age 45 was born in 1855 in New York. Both of her parents were born in New York. Both of her parents were Tuscarora. E.D. 138, Page 89A, Household 89/89.

WILSON, JACOB: (Onondaga/Tuscarora) Age 55, born in November 1844 in New York. His father was born in Oneida, New York. His mother was born in New York. Jacob Wilson was listed as an Onondaga. His father was a Tuscarora. His mother was an Onondaga. Dennis a son age 17 was born in March 1883 in New York. He was listed as an Oneida? His mother may have been an Oneida?. His parents were listed as Onondaga. Edward a son age 15 was born in March 1885. He was listed as an Onondaga. Both of his parents were Onondaga. Eunice HILL a servant age 25 was born in June 1874 in English Canada (Ontario). Both of her parents were born in English Canada (Ontario). She immigrated in 1899. She was listed as an Onondaga. Both of her parents were Onondaga. Alice HILL a servant age 31 was born in 1863 in English Canada. Both of her parents were born in English Canada. She immigrated in 1899. She was listed as an Onondaga. Both of her parents were listed as Onondaga. E.D. 138, Page 81B, Household 5/5.

SURNAME CROSS INDEX	HEAD OF HOUSEHOLD
CARRIE, Emma	Isaac Patterson
CARRIE, Julia A.	Isaac Patterson
CARRIE, Susan	Isaac Patterson
CHEW, William	Lucinda Thompson
CUSICK, Elias	Lucy Williams
CUSICK, Thomas A.	Helen M. Beaver
CUSICK, Wilson	Daniel Williams
DOCTOR, Lensy?	Elias Bissell
GREEN, Marthy	Thomas Isaac
GREEN, Mary	Thomas Isaac
GREEN, Minnie	Thomas Isaac
HENDRELY, James	William Johnson
HILL, Alice	Wilson Jacobs
HILL, Alice	Jacob Wilson
HILL, Eunice	Wilson Jacobs
HILL, Eunice	Jacob Wilson
JACOBS, Emily	Levi Pambleton
JEMISON, John	Eunice Hill
JOHNSON, Althia	Timothy Henry
JOHNSON, Emma	Lucy Williams
JOHNSON, Foster	Lucy Williams
JOHNSON, Sadie	Holland Patterson
MILLER?, Clara	Marcus Peters
MT. PLEASANT, Daisy	Levi Pambleton
PAMBLETON, Benjamin	Lydia Printup
PAMELTON?, Enoch	David Chew
PATTERSON, Jane	Enos Johnson

TUSCARORA RESERVATION, NIAGRA COUNTY, 1900 CENSUS
CROSS INDEX

PATTERSON, Mabel	Silas Chew
PATTERSON, Mary	Silas Chew
PATTERSON, Myron	David Chew
PETERS, Elizabeth	Eunice Hill
PETERSON, Jacob	Levi Peters
PRINTUP, Elizabeth	Joseph Thompson
PRINTUP, Sarah	Thomas Williams
RACKET, John	Levi Peters
SMITH, Edith	Franklin Mt. Pleasant
SMITH, Mary A.	Franklin Mt. Pleasant
SMITH, Spencer	Franklin Mt. Pleasant
THOMPSON, Ida	Noah Sylvester
THOMPSON, Jerrymiah	Eliza Green
THOMPSON, Rosa	Eliza Pambleton
THOMPSON, Sarah	Daniel Printup
WILLIAMS, Albert	Rachel Smith
WILLIAMS, Althia	Holly Chew
WILLIAMS, Arthur	Rachel Smith
WILLIAMS, Frank	Rachel Smith
WILLIAMS, Lucinda	Timothy Henry

THE SHINNECOCK, MONTAUK & POOSAPATUCK OF SUFFOLK COUNTY LONG ISLAND, NEW YORK, 1900 CENSUS

Suffolk County was created in 1683. It was one of New York's original counties. The county seat is Riverhead. Today it is the home of the reserve of the remaining Montauk's. Many Indian tribes lived in the Long Island area in the 1670's. Among these tribes included the Manhassets, Montauk, Poosapatuck and Shinnecok (Shinnecock). The Montauk lived on the eastern end of the Island. The Manhassets lived on Shelter Island. The Poosapatuck lived on a tract of land on the west side of Forge River at Mastic. The Montauk, Poosapatuck and Shinnecock were members of the Montauk Confederacy. Jacque Cortelyou or Castelayne bought land from the Indians on Long Island and allowed them to remain on a section of it. the West Indian Company in 1645 bought from the Indians all the land extending to what is now Coney Island. Colonel William Smith purchased reserve land in 1691 on the west side of Forge River at Mastic for the Indians. Sources: "Setauket, the First Three Hundred Years," 1655-1955, by Edwin P. Adkins, David Mc Kay Company, 1955, 108 pages. "The Long Island Indians," by Thomas R. Bayles, four (4) pages, available on inter-library loan from the Church of Jesus Christ of Latter-day Saints (Mormon) Family History Library Centers on film number 1036082, Item 11. "Journal of a Voyage to New York," and a Tour in Several American Colonies in 1679-80, by Peter Dankers and Peter Sluyter, (Of Wiewerd in Friesland) translated from the original in Dutch for the Long Island Historical Society by Henry C. Murphy in 1867, pages 6-12, 122, 126, 127, 267. "A Brief Description of New York, Formerly called New-Netherlands," by Daniel Denton, London, England, published by Daniel Denton in 1670, Reprinted by University Microfilms, Inc., 1966, pages 6-12. "History of Long Island," by B. F. Thompson & C. J. Werner, Dodd, New York, New York, 1918, four (4) Volumes.

EUGENICS RECORD OFFICE FILES:

Files of the Eugenics Record Office of Cold Spring Harbor, New York, 1900-1940 have been compiled on 440 reels of microfilm. They represent compiled files of the records at Dight Institute, University of Minnesota in Minneapolis, Minnesota. They contain information about thousands of people in the United States as part of genetics studies. On one microfilm which details data about the Indians of Gay's Head, Martha's Vineyard, Massachusetts, is a pedigree chart clearly showing the families of the Shinnecock Indians of Suffolk County, New York. The charts are not itemized or labeled in any way. They appear on this film only after some random information about the Haskell Institute (Indian school in Kansas). No identifying remarks are attached to the charts as to the ethnic origins of the persons on the charts. From the information on the 1900 United States Census of Suffolk County, New York a researcher can quickly determine that theses charts chronicle the genealogy of the Montauk/Shinnecock Indians of Long Island. Direct and indirect surnames included: Adams, Arch? or Atch, Beaman, Boardman, Brown, Bunn, Burton, Carl, Cloverdale, Coghill, Crippen, Cuffee, Davis, Dawes, Dennis? Eleazer, Hall, Harvey, Horton, Hunter, Kellis, Lee, Lewis, Jackson, Johnson, Jourdon, Marshall, Martine, Minns, Reese, Ryer, Sands, Shippen, Smith, Thompson, Quinn, Waters, alher? Walker Wright and Quinn. A copy of the Eugenics Record Office Files is available on inter-library loan from the Church of Jesus

Christ of Latter-day Saints (Mormon) Family History Library Centers on film numbers 1839870-71, Item 1.

BIOGRAPHICAL REFERENCES

FOWLER FAMILY: David Fowler was a Montauk Indian from Long Island, who worked with the Oneida of New York and Wisconsin. "The Oneida People", by Cara E. Richards published by Indian Tribal Series, Phoenix, 1974, page 42.

WYANDANCH: Wyandanch was a Montauk Chief and grand Sachem of Long Island Indians in the 1650's who made war on the Narragansett. The Montauk population was reduced by war and disease. "The Long Island Indians," by Thomas R. Bayles, four (4) pages, available on microfilm on inter-library loan through the Church of Jesus Christ of Latter-day Saints (Mormon) Family History Library Center on film number 1036082.

1870 UNITED STATES CENSUS OF SUFFOLK COUNTY, NEW YORK

After the enumeration of the town of East Hampton, page 471 a separate paper was attached entitled, "A list of Indians not taxed," compiled by enumerator Jeremiah Parsons Jr., Assistant Marshal. The names on that list included the following people in.

FOWLER, WILLIAM: (Indian) Age 48, Mary age 49, Hanah 23, John 15, Charles 11, George 9, Herbert 5.

PHARAOH, DAVID L: (Indian) Age 33, Maria age 23, Wyandanch? (Male Indian) age 7, Maggie age 4, Samuel age 2, Ebenezer age 5 months.

PHARAOH, ELISHA: (Indian) Age 70.

PHARAOH SYLVESTER: (Indian) Age 65, Jerusha age 40, Ephraim age 24.

PHARAOH, STEPHEN: (Indian) Age 48, Samuel E. age 14.

TOWN OF SETAUKET, SUFFOLK COUNTY, LONG ISLAND: Page 345, Household 522/586.

CUFFY, JEREMIAH: (Indian) 45 residing in the household of Russel? Woodhull.

1900 UNITED STATES FEDERAL CENSUS, SUFFOLK COUNTY, NEW YORK

This census abstract is not in its original order. It has been alphabetized for this book. All of the people in each of the following households were members of the same tribe as the head of that household. Exceptions were noted where individuals were members of another tribe, or race. Everyone in each household was born in New York unless otherwise stated. Everyone in each household has the same surname as the head of that household. If an individual in a household had a different surname than the head of household that surname was highlighted by capital letters. The following names were recorded as they were spelled in the original record. The accuracy of the genealogy information represented in this abstract depends on the information recorded for the creation of the original census. A question mark was placed after the names, ages and dates where the spelling was in doubt. The surname Smith appears to be spelled as Swish on the 1900 census. This census abstract begins with Southampton Township, Enumeration District 785, Page 143/A.

BREWER, CAROLINE: (Shinnecock) She was born in June 1838 in New York. Both of her parents were born in New York. Both of her parents were listed as Shinnecock Indians. Southampton Township, E.D. 785, Page 143, Household 13.

BREWER, MARY: (Shinnecock) Age 81 was born in February 1819 in New York. Both of her parents were born in New York. Both of her parents were listed as Shinnecock. Ella a daughter age 60 was born in May 1840 in New York. Mernerva a daughter age 27 was born in November 1872. John W., a son age 8 was born in March 1892. The parents of everyone in Mary Brewer's household were listed as Shinnecock. Southampton Township, E.D. 785, Page 144A, Household 12/12.

BREWER, MILTON: (Shinnecock) Age 50 was born in August 1849 in New York. Both of his parents were born in New York. Both of his parents were Shinnecock. Golden L., a daughter age 14 was born in April 1886. Hattie a daughter age 12 was born in August 1887. Lottie a daughter age 9 was born in October 1890. Lela? or Leta? a daughter age 7 was born in November 1892. Etta a daughter age 5 was born in December 1894. Both of the parents of the children of Milton Brewer were both listed as Shinnecock. Southampton Township, E.D. 785, Page 143A, Household 4/4.

BUNN, CAROLINE: (Shinnecock) Age 61 was born in June 1838 in New York. Both of her parents were born in New York.. Both of her parents were Shinnecock. Clarence a son age 33 was born in November 1866 in New York. Both of his parents were born in New York. Both of his parents were Shinnecock. Southampton Township, E.D. 785, Page 144A, Household 13/13.

BUNN, CHARLES: (Shinnecock) Age 35 was born in May 1865 in New York. Both of his parents were born in New York. Both of his parents were Shinnecock. Marie his wife age 37 was born in May 1863 in New York. Both of her parents were born in New York. Both of her parents were Shinnecock, David W., a son age 3 was born in September 1896. Dora E., a daughter age 1 was born in January 1899. Annie PARKMAN (She was listed as Black) a boarder age 12 was born in September 1887 in

Virginia. Both of his parents were born in Virginia. Southampton Township, E.D. 785, Page 143A, Household 8/8.

BUNN, GILBERT: (Shinnecock) Age 28 was born in November 1871 in New York. Both of his parents were born in New York. Both of his parents were Shinnecock. Aida his wife age 30 born in January 1870 in New York. Both of her parents were born in New York. Both of her parents were Shinnecock, Aida a daughter age 5 was born in April 1895. Mabel a daughter age 3 was born January 1897. Fanny SWISH mother-in-law age 66 was born in September 1833 in New York. Both of her parents were born in New York. She was listed as a Shinnecock. Both of her parents were listed as Shinnecock. Southampton Township, E.D. 785, Page 144B, Household 16/16.

BUNN, JAMES A.: (Shinnecock) Age 51 was born in June 1848 in New York. Both of his parents were born in New York. Both of his parents were listed as Shinnecock. Fanny M,. his wife age 46 born in December 1853 in New York. Both of her parents were born in New York. Both of her parents were listed as Shinnecock, Nelson a brother (of James A. Bunn) age 68 was born in October 1831 in New York. Southampton Township, E.D. 785, Page 144, Household 19.

BUNN, WARREN: (Shinnecock) Age 58 was born in November 1849 in New York. Both of his parents were born in New York. Both of his parents were Shinnecock. Francis his wife age 52 was born in April 1848 in New York. Both of her parents were born in New York. Both of her parents were Shinnecock. James L., a son age 17 was born in December 1884. Sophia a daughter age 18 was born in October 1886. Seymoure ELEAZOR a son-in-law was born in January 1879 in New York. Both of his parents were born in New York. Both of his parents were Shinnecock. Anna ELEAZOR a daughter age 20 was born in November 1879. Southampton Township, E.D. 785, Page 144A, Household 14.

CUFFREY (OR CUFFEY?) NATHAN J.: (Shinnecock/West Indies Indian) He was born in October in 1853 in New York. His parents were both born in New York. He was listed as a Shinnecock. Marie his wife was born in September 1869 in the West Indies. She was listed as Indian. Both of her parents were born in the West Indies. Marie Cuffrey immigrated in 1882. Shelter Island, E.D. 776, Page 8A, Household 158.

CUFFY, EUGENE: (Shinnecock) Age 30 was born in May 1870 in New York. Both of his parents were born in New York.. Both of his parents were Shinnecock. Ida? his wife age 19 was born in September 1880 in New York. Both of her parents were born in New York. Both of her parents were Shinnecock. Southampton Township, E.D. 785, Page 144A, Household 11/11.

CUFFREY? (OR CUFFEY?) ARON H: (Shinnecock) He was born in January in 1835 in New York. Both of his parents were born in New York. He was listed as a Shinnecock Indian. Mary his wife was born in April 1846 in New York. Both of her parents were born in New York. She was listed as a Shinnecock. Phebe S. ROEN, mother? (Of Aron Cuffrey?) was listed as an Indian. She was born in May 1827 in New York. Both of her parents were born in New York. Shelter Island, E. D. 776, Page 8A, Household 159.

CUFFY, EDWARD W.: (Shinnecock) Age 40 was born in June 1859 in New York. Both of his parents were born in New York. Both of his parents were Shinnecock. Mary T., his wife (She was listed as white) age 36 was born in August 1863 in Massachusetts. Both of her parents were born in Ireland. Southampton Township, E.D. 785, Page 145B, Household 29/29.

CUFFY, EMERSON: (Shinneock) Age 40 was born in November 1859 in New York. Both of his parents were born in New York. Both of his parents were Shinnecock. Minnie his wife age 35 was born in March 1865 in New York. Both of her parents were born in New York. Both of her parents were Shinnecock. Lena C., a daughter age 22 was born in August 1877. George a son age 17 was born in August 1882. Douglass a son age 15 was born in September 1884. Wicham or Micham a son age 14 was born in July 1885. Lawrence a son age 7 was born in June 1892. William a son age 5 was born in June 1894. Southampton Township, E.D. 785, Page 145B, Household 27/27.

CUFFY, JAMES: (Shinnecock) Age 42 was born in October 1857 in New York. Both of his parents were born in New York. Both of his parents were Shinnecock. Annie his wife age 29 was born in September 1870 in New York. Both of her parents were born in New York. Both of her parents were Shinnecok. Southampton Township, E.D. 785, Page 145A, Household 26/26.

CUFFY, JAMES: (Shinnecock) Age 73 was born in July 1826 in New York. Both of his parents were born in New York. Both of his parents were listed as Shinnecock. Roxanna his wife age 58 was born in August 1841 in New York. Both of her parents were born in New York. Both of her parents were listed as Shinnecock. Southampton Township, E.D. 785, Page 144B, Household 20/20.

CUFFY, MARY A.: (Shinnecock) Age 77 was born in January 1823 in New York. Both of her parents were born in New York. Both of her parents were Shinnecock. Mary E. BUNN age 45 a grand daughter was born in March 1855 in New York. Both of her parents were born in New York. Both of her parents were Shinnecock. Mary R. BUNN a grand daughter age 23 was born in November 1876 in New York. Both of her parents were born in New York. Both of her parents were Shinnecock. Southampton Township, E.D. 785, Page 143B, Household 9/9.

CUFFY, WILLIAM: (Shinnecock) Age 73 was born in June 1826 in New York.. Both of his parents were born in New York.. Both of his parents were Shinnecock. Ellen his wife age 60 was born in November 1839 in New York. Both of her parents were born in New York. Both of her parents were Shinnecock, Simon a grand son age 18 was born in October 1881. Both of his parents were born in New York. Both of his parents were Shinnecock. Southampton Township, E.D. 785, Page 144B, Household 22/22.

ELEAZER, CHARLES: (Shinnecock) Age 31 was born in June 1868 in New York. Both of his parents were born in New York Both of his parents were Shinnecock. Edna his wife age 30 was born in December 1869 in New York. Both of her parents were born in New York. Both of her parents were Shinnecock. Southampton Township, E.D. 785, Page 143B, Household 8/8.

ELEAZER, HERBERT S.: (Shinnecock) Age 30 was born in January 1870 in New York. Both of his parents were born in New York. Both of his parents were Shinnecock. Betie D., his wife age 31 was born in April 1869 in New York. Both of her parents were born in New York. Both of her parents were Shinnecock. Anny CUFFY mother-in-law (Of Herbert S. Eleazer) age 65 was born in November 1834 in New York. Both of her parents were born in New York. Both of her parents were listed as Shinnecock. Southampton Township, E.D. 785, Page 144A, Household 15/15.

ELEAZOR, ALFOREZO?: (Shinnecock) Age 68 was born in March 1832 in New York. Both of his parents were born in New York. He was listed as a Shinnecock. Henrietta his wife age 63 born in May 1837 in New York. Both of her parents were born in New York. Both of her parents were Shinnecock. Grace a daughter age 15 was born in July 1884. Ethel a daughter age 14 was born in November 1885. Rowland a son age 11 was born in October 1888. Southampton Township, E.D. 785, Page 145A, Household 23/23.

ELEAZOR, CORNELIUS: (Shinnecock) Age 46 was born in February 1854 in New York. Both of his parents were born in New York. Both of his parents were Shinnecock. Alice his wife age 47 was born in May 1853 in New York. Both of her parents were born in New York. She was listed as a Shinnecock Indian. Both of her parents were born in New York. Howard a son age 16 born in January 1884, Louisa ELEAZOR the mother (Of Cornelius Eleazor) age 75 was born in June 1824 in New York. Both of her parents were born in New York. Both of her parents were Shinnecock. Southampton Township, E.D. 785, Page 145A, Household 25/25.

ELEAZOR, NETTIE: (Shinnecock) Age 42 was born in November 1857 in New York. Both of her parents were born in New York. She was listed as a Shinnecock. Seymoure a son age 21 was born in August 1878. Osser? a son age 14 was born in July 1885. Leroy a son age 12 was born in November 1888?. Paul a son age 9 was born in August 1890. Harriett a daughter age 7 was born in October 1892. An Eleazor son not named age 1 born in November 1898. Harriet CUFFY mother (Of Nettie Eleazor) age 76 was born in May 1824 in New York. Both of her parents were born in New York. Both of her parents were Shinnecock. The father of the children of Nettie Eleazor was born in New York. He was listed as a Shinnecock. Southampton Township, E.D. 785, Page 145A, Household 24/24.

HARVEY, SAMUEL: (Shinnecock) Age 42 was born in May 1858 in New York. His father was born in Virginia. His mother was born in New York. Both of his parents were listed as Shinnecock? Southampton Township, E.D. 785, Page 146B, Household 36/36.

KELLIS (OR KELLY?) MARY E.: (Shinnecock) Age 46 was born in October 1853 in New York. Both of her parents were born in New York. Both of her parents were Shinnecock. Arthur C., a son age 22 was born in July 1877. Oliver a son age 19 was born in February 1881. Elliott a son age 18 was born in January 1882. Charles a son age 12 was born in July 1887. Jesselina a daughter age 10 was born in March 1890. Southampton Township, E.D. 785, Page 146A, Household 32/32.

KELLIS (OR KELLY?) DAVID: (Shinnecock) Age 34 was born in January 1866 in New York. Both of his parents were born in New York. Both of his parents were Shinnecock. Hattie E. his wife age 42 born in June 1857 in New York. both of her parents were born in New York. Both of her parents were born in New York. Both of her parents were Shinnecock, Percy C., a son age 19 was born in February 1881. Isabelle a daughter age 16 was born in April 1884. Estelle a daughter age 16 was born in April 1884. David E., a son age 14 born in April 1886. George a son age 12 was born in December 1887. Southampton Township, E.D. 785, Page 145B, Household 28/28.

KELLY? (OR KELLIS?) JOSHUA: (Shinnecock) Age 56 was born in March 1844 in New York. Both of his parents were born in New York. Both of his parents were Shinnecock. Anna C., his wife? age 55 born in February 1845 in New York. Both of her parents were born in New York. Both of her parents were Shinnecock. Fred a son? age 26 was born in February 1874. Edna a daughter age 6 was born in October 1893. Southampton Township, E.D. 785, Page 143B, Household 10/10.

LEE, JAMES L.: (Shinnecock) Age 35 was born in November 1864 in New York. Both of his parents were born in New York. Both of his parents were Shinnecock. Lillian J., his wife age 28 born in December 1871 in New York. Both of her parents were born in New York. Both of her parents were Shinnecock. James a son age 10 was born in May 1890. Margarett a daughter age 8 was born in January 1892. Mary A., a daughter age 5 was born in August 1894. Lillian a daughter age 2 was born in December 1897. Emma J. LEE mother (Of James L. LEE) age 60 was born in November 1839 in New York. Both of her parents were born in New York. Both of her parents were Shinnecock. Southampton Township, E.D. 785, Page 146A, Household 31/31.

RYER, CHARLES: (Shinnecock) Age 43 was born in December 1856 in New York. Both of his parents were born in New York. Both of his parents were Shinnecock. Belle his wife age 36 born in September 1863 in New York. Both of her parents were Shinnecock. Martha WOOD sister-in-law of Charles RYER was born in March 1867 in New York. She was listed as a Shinnecock. Both of her parents were Shinnecock. Southampton Township, E.D. 785, Page 146A, Household 34/34.

RYER, NANCY: (Shinnecock) Age 76 was born in March 1824 in New York. Both of her parents were born in New York. Both of her parents were Shinnecock. Freelove a son age 41 was born in June 1858 in New York. Both of his parents were born in New York. Both of his parents were Shinnecock. William JOHNSON a son-in-law (He was listed as black) age 53 was born in May 1847 in New York. Both of his parents were born in New York, Augusta JOHNSON (She was listed as an Indian) a daughter age 44 was born in August 1855. Marion THOMAS (She was listed as an Indian) a daughter age 33 was born in May 1867. Vida M. THOMAS a grand daughter age 2 was born in May 1867. A THOMAS grand daughter not yet named age two months was born in April 1900. Both parents of the Thomas grand children of Nancy Ryer were listed as Shinnecock. Southampton Township, E.D. 785, Page 143A, Household 3/3.

SMITH, FREDERICK: (Shinnecock) Age 28 was born in January 1872 in New York. Both of his parents were born in New York. Both of his parents were Shinnecock. Bessie his wife was born in November 1869 in New

York. Both of her parents were born in New York. Both of her parents were listed as Shinnecock. Southampton Township, E.D. 785, Page 144B, Household 18/18.

SMITH, JAMES: (Shinnecock) Age 27 was born in July 1872 in New York. both of his parents were born in New York. Both of his parents were Shinnecock. Nancy his wife (She was listed as black) age 27 was born in Virginia. Both of her parents were born in Virginia. John Jr., a son age 5 was born in December 1894. Mary G., a daughter age 4 was born in November 1895. Both of the children of James Swish or Smith were listed as Shinnecock. Southampton Township, E.D. 785, Page 143A, Household 1/1.

SMITH, JOHN: (Shinnecock) Age 29 was born in April 1871 in New York. Both of his parents were born in New York. Both of his parents were Shinnecock. Huldah his wife age 26 born in November 1873 in New York. Both of her parents were born in New York. Both of her parents were Shinnecock. Lincoln E. a son age three months born in March 1900. Southampton Township, E.D. 785, Page 146A, Household 33/33.

SMITH, SARAH: (Shinnecock) Age 55 was born in September 1844 in New York. Both of her parents were born in New York. Both of her parents were Shinneock. Henrietta THOMPSON a daughter age 44 was born in September 1855. Mary DORRICK a daughter was age 46. Both parents of the daughters of Sarah Swish were born in New York. Both parents were Shinnecock. Southampton Township, E.D. 785, Page 145B, Household 30/30.

SMITH, THOMAS: (Shinnecock) Age 22 was born in September 1877 in New York. Both of his parents were born in New York. Both of her parents were Shinnecock. Charles a brother age 29 was born in November 1870. Herbert a brother age 34 was born in September 1875. Southampton Township, E.D. 785, Page 143A, Household 1/1.

THOMPSON, JOHN H.: (Shinnecock) Age 59 was born in September 1840 in New York. Both of his parents were born in New York. Ellen his wife age 45 was born in October 1854 in New York. Both of her parents were born in New York. Both of her parents were Shinnecock. Augustus a son age 17 was born in May 1883. Lillian E., a daughter age 14 was born in January 1886. Alice a daughter age 9 was born in November 1890. Southampton Township, E.D. 785, Page 143B, Household 6/6.

WATERS, ADELINE: (Shinnecock/Montauk/Poosapatuck) Age 55 was born in June 1844 in New York. Both of her parents were born in New York. She was listed as a Shinnecock. Her father was a Shinecock. Her mother was a Montauk. Alfred DAVIS a son age 28 was born in July 1871. His father was a Poosapatuck. Southampton Township, E.D. 785. Page 143B, Household 5/5.

WILLIAMS, THOMAS: (He was listed of black ancestry) Age 57 was born in September 1842 in Virginia. His father was born in Virginia. His mother was born in New York. Rosie (She was listed as Shinnecock) his wife age 36 was born in August 1863 in New York. Her father was born in Virginia. Her mother was born in New York. Her mother was listed as a Shinnecock. Cornelia a daughter age 17 was born in April 1883. Harry a son age 15 was born in April 1885. Ada a daughter age 12 was born in

May 1888. Gertrude a daughter age 10 was born in August 1889. Agnes a daughter age 8 was born in March 1892. Archie a son age 7 was born in April 1893. Helen a daughter age 5 was born in December 1894. Laura a daughter age 2 was born in May? 1858. Southampton Township, E.D. 785, Page 146B, Household 35/35.

1900 CENSUS SUFFOLK COUNTY, NEW YORK CROSS INDEX	
SURNAME CROSS INDEX	**HEAD OF HOUSEHOLD**
BUNN, Mary E.	Mary A. Cuffy
BUNN, Mary R.	Mary A. Cuffy
CUFFY, Harriet	Nettie Eleazor
DAVIS, Alfred	Adeline Waters
DORRICH, Mary	Sarah Swish?
ELEAZOR, Seymoure	Warren Bunn
JOHNSON, William	Nancy Ryer
ROEN, Phebe	Aron H. Cuffrey?
THOMAS, Marion	Nancy Ryer
THOMAS, Vida M.	Nancy Ryer
THOMPSON, Henrietta	Sarah Swish?
WOOD, Martha	Charles Ryer